Early Praise for *Kotlin and Android Development featuring Jetpack*

Learning a new language and platform at the same time can seem daunting, but this book makes it both fun and easily understandable. The sample apps make complex topics such as view binding and unit testing relatable and easy to understand.

➤ **Markus Neuhoff**
Android/Kotlin Course Author, Pluralsight

Michael does an excellent job explaining Kotlin, from the basics to the most advanced topics. The two example applications are incredibly helpful for both beginners and advanced developers. Coming from a different background in mobile development, having the step-by-step on the basics on how to use Android Studio and following the examples in the book made it easy to focus on the important topic, which is learning Kotlin.

➤ **Pablo Siller**
Mobile Lead, Trek Bicycle

If you're serious about developing Android applications with Kotlin, you've found a thorough and yet an approachable book that will guide you through every step of developing and testing.

➤ **Dr. Venkat Subramaniam**
Founder, Agile Developer, Inc.

A great walkthrough of using Kotlin for Android development. Plenty of code examples and a clear trajectory from beginner to advanced.

➤ **Greg Levenhagen**
Principal Consultant, MS Regional Director, MS AI MVP, Skyline Technologies, Inc.

Whether you're new to or have experience with Kotlin, this book is a valuable resource. With great project-based examples, you'll easily be able to adapt what you learn to your own projects. This is a must-have for any developer's collection.

➤ **Rolando Lopez**
Senior Mobile Applications Developer, Milwaukee Tool

As someone that has no Android-development experience, but a strong software development background, I found this to be a very engaging and informative first step into the world of Android. Highly recommended for anyone looking to get into this world!

➤ **Brandon Martinez**
Senior Service Engineer, Microsoft

Kotlin and Android Development featuring Jetpack

Build Better, Safer Android Apps

Michael Fazio

The Pragmatic Bookshelf
Raleigh, North Carolina

For our complete catalog of hands-on, practical, and Pragmatic content for software developers, please visit *https://pragprog.com.*

The team that produced this book includes:

CEO: Dave Rankin
COO: Janet Furlow
Managing Editor: Tammy Coron
Development Editor: Michael Swaine
Copy Editor: Sakhi MacMillan
Indexing: Potomac Indexing, LLC
Layout: Gilson Graphics
Founders: Andy Hunt and Dave Thomas

For sales, volume licensing, and support, please contact *support@pragprog.com.*

For international rights, please contact *rights@pragprog.com.*

ISBN-13: 978-1-68050-815-4
Book version: P1.0—June 2021

Contents

Part II — Android Baseball League

Part III — Test Your App

Part IV — Appendixes

Acknowledgments

First off, a big thank you to the entire Pragmatic Bookshelf team, and especially three particular people. I want to express a great deal of gratitude to my editor, Michael Swaine, for taking this journey with me, supporting me at each step of the process, and sometimes just giving me the "You're all good, don't worry" that really I needed. This book would never have been a possibility without Brian MacDonald coming up to me at THAT Conference and saying "Hey, do you want to write a book on Kotlin?", then working with me through the entire pre-book process. And finally Brian Hogan, who assured me that PragProg was great (turns out they are) and that I could actually do this book (turns out I could).

My sincere appreciation to my tech reviewers: Joe Vetta, Rolando Lopez, Ben Gavin, Brandon Martinez, and Andrew Petersen. The fact that you all took the time to read through my book and help make it better means so much to me, and I'm eternally grateful for that. Also, thank you to Keno Basedow for finding a number of ways I could improve the book and make it clearer during the beta process.

I've been lucky enough to have support from everyone around me. This includes the whole Skyline crew, who have been great with this crazy side project of mine. Craig and Joe, for tolerating my incessant "OMG KOTLIN" comments the past few years. Rolando, for being as excited as anyone when I found out the book was happening. And all my friends and family who knowingly (or unknowingly) are part of the book in the Android Baseball League.

As I'm definitely no artist, I needed some help with the icons and logos in the book. Many of them are right from Google's Material Design library, which can be found inside Android Studio, but I did grab a number from a few sites. The full list can be found in the source code under images/image-rights.txt, but here's the quick summary: most of the team logos and icons were from www.flaticon.com, made by Freepik, Good Ware, Smashicons, smalllikeart, and

Vitaly Gorbachev. The Skyline logo is from Skyline Technologies, my company when writing this book, and the People's Flag of Milwaukee[1] is used as the Milwaukee Sunrise logo. The scoreboard icon from the ABL app as well as both the dice and coin icons from Penny Drop are from www.materialdesignicons.com.

And finally, to my family, I love you all so much:

Mom and Dad, thank you for always being there for me and doing everything possible to help me succeed. Your constant love and support has made me who I am today and is the example I follow now as a father.

Hazel, you're the coolest kiddo, and I love getting to be your dad. I'm so very proud of you, and hearing you say that you're proud of me for the book means the world to me.

Emily, thank you for holding down things while I've been getting the book done and everything that went with it. There's no way I could have accomplished this without you saying "You do whatever you need to, I've got everything else covered." There's so much more I could say, but I'll just leave it at —you're the best.

---

1. https://milwaukeeflag.com/

Preface

With Kotlin and Jetpack, Android development is now smoother and more enjoyable than ever before. In this book, we're going to dive right into Android development by writing two complete Android apps.

With the first app, Penny Drop, you will create a full game complete with random die rolls, customizable rules, and AI opponents. You'll build lightweight Fragment views with data binding, quickly and safely update data with ViewModel classes, and handle all app navigation in a single location. You'll be guided to use Kotlin with Android-specific Kotlin extensions to efficiently write null-safe code without all the normal boilerplate required for pre-Jetpack + Kotlin apps. You'll see how to persist and retrieve data as full objects with the Room library, then display that data with ViewModels and list records in a RecyclerView.

Next, you'll create the official app for the Android Baseball League. It's a fake league but a real app, where you use what you learn with Penny Drop and build up from there. You'll navigate all over the app via a navigation drawer, including specific locations via Android App Links. You'll handle asynchronous and web service calls with Kotlin coroutines, display that data smoothly with the Paging library, and send notifications to a user's phone from your app.

Ready? Let's build some Android apps!

Introduction

Welcome to modern Android development! I know I've already thrown the phrase "modern" out a few times, but it's accurate. Kotlin makes the entire Android dev experience so much nicer than it was in the past, and then you add in the Jetpack frameworks and concepts? The whole situation gets better and better.

When we first discussed creating this book, I knew I wanted a way to share my love of Kotlin with others but wasn't sure what I wanted for a topic. Android was always the most logical spot because I've worked with Android for years, but I felt like there were already so many Android books out there. How would my book be any different?

Attempting to make the book unique led me to two conclusions: I wanted to focus on the newest approaches/libraries possible, and I wanted to make the apps interesting. The former was handled by squaring in on Jetpack. This is Google's recommended approach for Android dev, and they've done such a good job of introducing better ways to handle standard actions within an Android app. It may not seem as revelatory if you're new to Android development, but as someone who's done this for years, trust me that the Jetpack libraries make your life *so* much easier.

The second piece here is the apps. While there's nothing wrong with starting with a "To-Do List" app, I wanted something more *fun*. Building your first Android app and it's a game? That's way better! I love how Penny Drop is a nice, simple table game, so we can instead focus on everything else we need to do to build the app. Plus, once we get the core game running, we have a bunch of ways to add on additional features while highlighting useful parts of Android development.

Then there's the Android Baseball League. This is in a lot of ways my personal baseball fandom coming out, but it also gives us a sample app that looks like something you'd see in the Play Store. Plus, we end up with a number of ways to pull data into the app from APIs, which is basically a requirement for Android apps nowadays.

Actually, the APIs are probably the best example of my love of baseball. All the data for the Android Baseball League was created and/or generated by me. This includes the teams, players, box scores, all of it. As a developer, two of the things I've wanted to do most in my life were to write a book and create a baseball simulator, and I was able to do both at once. I so enjoy how great Penny Drop works as an app, but the ABL app is the most near and dear to my heart. I first and foremost included ABL because it's an excellent advanced app, but man, was it ever fun to put together.

I love Kotlin, I love Android, and I love having this chance to share both with you. I hope you feel the same way once you've gone though the book and that you can sense my excitement the entire way.

Who Is This Book For

This book is intended both for new developers and anyone experienced with Android and/or Kotlin. I try to explain what's going on for new devs but also give a heads-up when something may be review for Android pros. My intent is that all skill levels can benefit in one way or another from the apps we build.

We tested this out during the review process, where developers of varying skill levels went through the book and all of them said they learned new things. Even the most senior professional Android developer that went through the book sent me multiple messages about all the new things he was learning, so I'm optimistic you'll get a bunch out of this book no matter where you are with Android or Kotlin.

If You're New to Android and/or Kotlin

This may seem overwhelming at first, but as the book goes on, things will make more and more sense. I recommend checking out the source code I'll mention in the next section to see how things fit together. With Android apps, a high-level overview is that your UI (what the user sees) is mostly handled within XML, while the logic is handled with the Kotlin code.

Speaking of Kotlin, you'll find a number of mentions to Java in the book. Now, we are *not* going to be writing any Java code in the book, but we will be interacting with it, as most Android libraries were written in Java. Therefore, our Kotlin setup includes associating with a Java version, and we even use a directory called `java` for our Kotlin code. This is all because both Java and Kotlin compile down to the same byte code, so we can use them interchangeably. Just try to not be thrown off when you see Java mentioned, because it doesn't mean you need to start writing Java code or anything.

How to Read This Book

As I mentioned above, the book is split into two apps: Penny Drop and Android Baseball League. Penny Drop is intended as a introduction to Android, Jetpack, and Kotlin. If you're new to any of those, it'll definitely be worth your time to build the Penny Drop app (plus, it's fun). But even for those of you who know Android well, I bet you'll learn a few things as well in going through the first app.

The ABL app is where things get more advanced. Many of the chapters are effectively part two of ones from Penny Drop. For example, Chapter 5, Persist Game Data with Room, on page 115, is the introduction to using Room, Android's ORM (object-relational mapping) library, which makes for easier database interaction. Then, Chapter 10, Load and Save Data with Coroutines and Room, on page 235, takes those database concepts and adds in API calls and more coroutines. As a result, while building Penny Drop first isn't a requirement, it does make things clearer. I go through things faster with the ABL app, and there's more pre-existing code for you to integrate instead of building everything yourself.

Speaking of which, all the source code for the book can be found at https://media.pragprog.com/titles/mfjetpack/code/mfjetpack-code.zip. I included the end result from each chapter of the book so you always have both a reference and a starting point for the next chapter as needed. Also, with the ABL app, there's code to copy from that ZIP file into your project. The intent here is to get a more full-featured app without you having to write every bit of code but instead letting you focus on the main concepts of the chapter.

The last two main chapters of the book are focused on testing, in particular unit and Android UI testing. Those both use the Penny Drop app as the basis. If you didn't want to build Penny Drop but instead just want to try out the testing pieces, you can always grab code from the ZIP to use as your baseline when getting everything set.

You'll also find three appendixes at the end of the book: one with instructions for installing Android Studio, one with troubleshooting tips for development, and one with all the dependencies used in the book. The key feature of the last appendix is that all the dependency version numbers can be found there. I went that route instead of mentioning them in each chapter to avoid inconsistencies, plus then we have a single spot to check for any dependency.

Finally, a heads-up that while the book was written (mostly) on Windows and the screenshots are all of the Windows version of Android Studio, things will work the same if you're using a Mac. This means you're free to develop on the OS you're most comfortable using.

Development Tips for the Book

Android development, while great, can be a bit tricky. Even getting things set up can be a pain, but I hope Appendix 1, Install Android Studio, on page 367, makes that process smoother. The emulator works really well now, so you don't need a physical device, but it can be nice to see the apps working on an actual phone.

Also, if you're using the emulator, know that it can lose connectivity, making most of the ABL chapters impossible. This in particular can happen when the emulator is running and your computer goes to sleep. Don't be afraid to restart the emulator or ADB server (and even your computer if needed).

Along those lines, when in doubt, uninstall the app. This is especially valuable when working with Room and a database. Any structural DB changes would normally require a migration (a proper change/upgrade to a DB), but since we're still in dev, you can skip it with a reinstallation of the app.

Online Resources

Your first stop for everything book-related should be https://pragprog.com/titles/mfjetpack/kotlin-and-android-development-featuring-jetpack/. Here we have links to the aforementioned source code ZIP as well as the Devtalk forum for errors/typos/suggestions.[1]

For Google resources, the Jetpack home page is a good one, as it covers various things mentioned in this book as well as the latest features/libraries found in Jetpack.[2] Also, the Android Codelabs[3] cover even more content than what we could do in this book. Go there for some extra Android samples and tutorials.

For Kotlin help, the official https://kotlinlang.org/ site has useful language docs as well as https://play.kotlinlang.org/, a sandbox for testing Kotlin code.

Ready to Go?

Come on, it'll be fun! Let's go write ourselves a game (or a baseball app, that one's great too).

1. https://devtalk.com/books/kotlin-and-android-development-featuring-jetpack
2. https://link.mfazio.dev/jetpack
3. https://codelabs.developers.google.com/?cat=android

Part I

Penny Drop

We kick things off with a game called Penny Drop: roll a die, place a coin, repeat—a simple game and a great subject for our introductory app. You learn how to create an app from scratch, including all the pieces that go into it.

You've already developed an Android app before? There's still plenty for you here—Jetpack libraries, Kotlin code all over the place, and at the very least you're left with a playable game.

CHAPTER 1

Initialize the Penny Drop App

Here we are! It's time to build our first app, a game called Penny Drop. If you're new to Android development, don't worry, this chapter covers how to get started with building Android apps in Android Studio using the Kotlin programming language and the Android Jetpack libraries. We'll go through the steps to generate an app from scratch (with an overview of what is generated for us), then create a couple of mostly empty views, and set up the app to navigate between them.

If you've created an Android app before, Penny Drop will be a useful introduction to Jetpack and/or Kotlin. You'll learn, in particular, the Navigation component, how to use a `ViewModel` with `Fragment` classes, and database access with Room. As I mentioned in the previous paragraph, this chapter is focused on generating an app skeleton in Android Studio, creating two `Fragment` classes, and using the Navigation component in conjunction with a bottom navigation bar.

But if you're comfortable with all of that, take a look at the rules of Penny Drop in the next section, then just meet up with us again at Summary and Next Steps, on page 25.

How to Play Penny Drop

All of Part I of this book is focused on the game Penny Drop, so let's make sure everyone's comfortable with the rules. Penny Drop is a tabletop game for two or more players where the players take turns rolling a single *D6* (normal six-sided dice are called *D6s*). The rules are as follows:

- Player rolls a number, then puts a penny (a small coin) into the slot number that they just rolled.
- If the slot is a 6, the penny falls through the board and is out of the game.

- If the slot is already filled, the player takes all the pennies on the board and play passes on to the next player.
- Players must roll at least once, but can then pass their turn to the next person.
- The first player to get rid of all their pennies is the winner.

As you can see, there isn't a ton to this game: roll, put a penny or take pennies, repeat until someone's out. This allows us to focus on the Android components rather than a ton of game logic (though we'll have a bit we need to consider in Chapter 4, Update LiveData with Conditional Game Logic, on page 91). Given those rules, the Game screen of our app will end up looking like this:

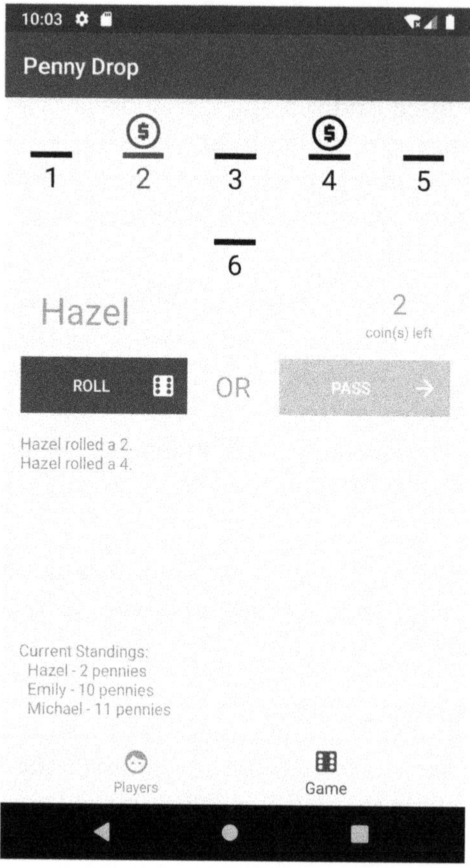

Create the App

It's time to build our app, and we're going to let Android Studio do a bunch of the work for us. Open up Android Studio and you'll be presented with a screen that looks like the image shown on page 5.

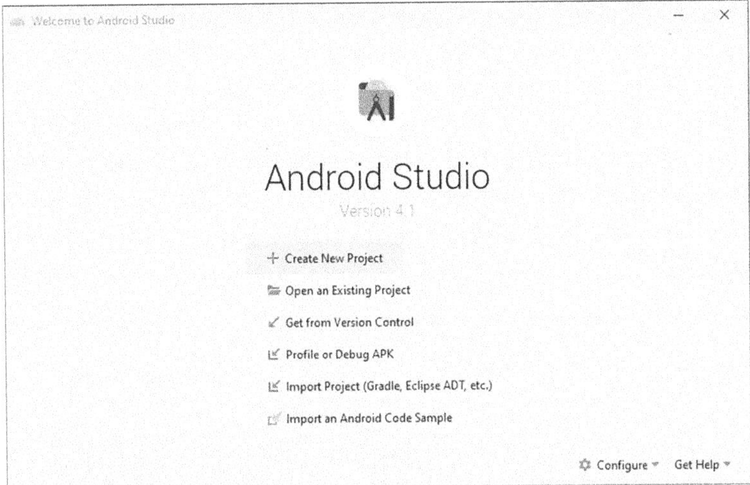

Click the Create New Project link, select the Empty Activity option, and click the Next button.

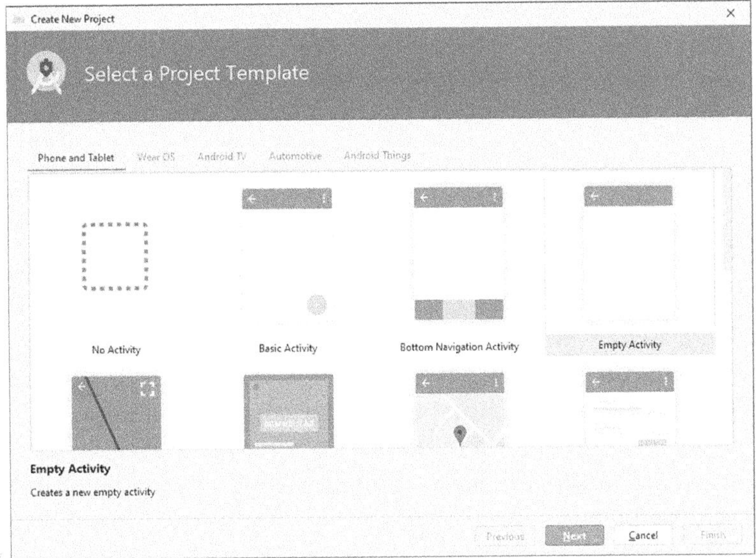

On this next screen, we're going to set some values for our app:

- *Name*: the name of the application we'll see everywhere. For this app, we can use *Penny Drop*.
- *Package name*: this value serves a dual purpose with Android apps. First, it's the unique application ID that will identify your app on a user's device as well as in the Google Play Store. Second, it's the Kotlin package name in our app. This is the primary grouping for all our code, meaning our

app's code files will have a package declaration with this package name. We can then add onto the package name for more specific parts. For example, my app's package name is dev.mfazio.pennydrop, so I'll put my Fragment classes in dev.mfazio.pennydrop.fragments. You can decide however you want to group your files; since packages are organized into folders on your system, you can look at this like putting your code into those different folders. And keep in mind that package names should be all lowercase.

- *Save location*: wherever on your machine you want to save your code.
- *Language*: Kotlin (otherwise you're reading the wrong book!).

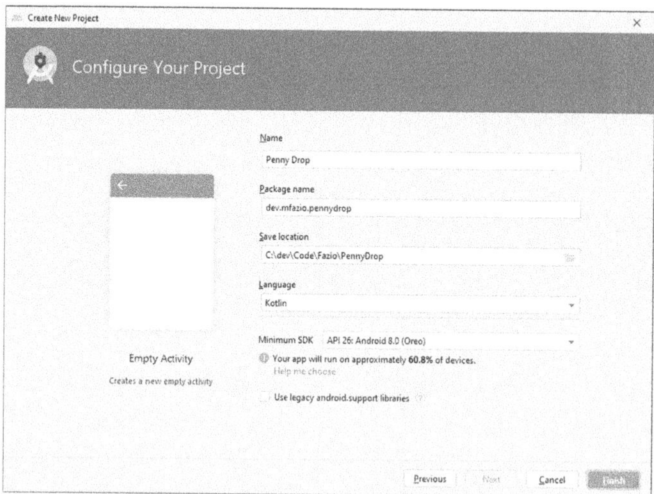

The *Minimum API Level* value determines the lowest operating system (OS) version that can run your app. It can be a bit confusing having API levels, OS codenames, *and* OS version numbers, so for this book, I'm going to stick to at least calling out the API level. API level is a bit more precise, as OS codenames can mean multiple versions, plus the API levels are what we'll use in our configuration files.

Choosing a minimum API level can be tricky, as this can limit which devices are able to get your app. Choose an API level that's too high/new and older devices will be blocked from using the app. Choose an API level that's too low/old and you won't have access to newer Android features. The Help Me Choose link will give you a bit more info, including an estimate on the percentage of users with at least a given API level and also the features included at each API level. That screen will look something like the image shown on page 7.

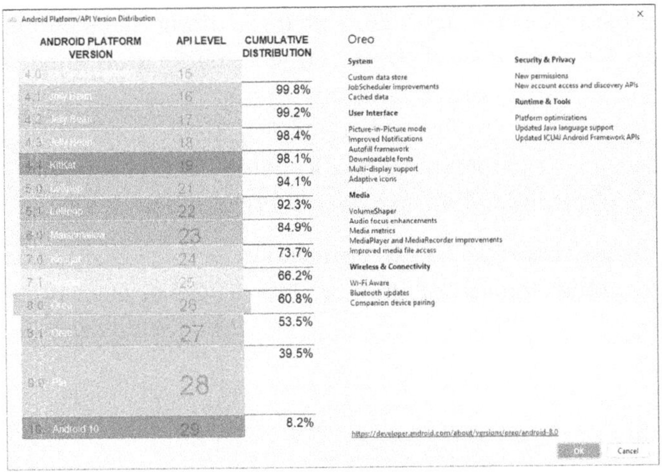

At the time of this writing (late 2020), API Level 26 is over three years old and is likely (though not guaranteed) to be a safe baseline. If you think you can move to a newer version and/or you really need a feature, you can upgrade. Keep in mind, you can always change this value down the road.

The last option in the list is “Use legacy android.support libraries”. We want to leave this unchecked, as we’re better off using the new AndroidX libraries.

AndroidX

For those of you who are familiar with the old Android Support Library, those packages have been moved into AndroidX. If the Android Support Library is new to you, just know it’s a way to have backward compatibility across Android versions (now handled by AndroidX packages). All AndroidX packages are separately maintained and updated, allowing you to bring in any libraries as you wish and also update them individually. This means you only need to pull in what you want and nothing more.

Once all your values are set, click Finish, and Android Studio will start creating your app!

What Did This Do?

Android Studio has generated a number of files for us and has started indexing our codebase. This means it’s getting a list of all the files/symbols in the project so it can quickly give us feedback on whether or not classes exist, dependencies are loaded, or types conflict in multiple files—basically, all the handy features in Android Studio for writing our code.

We have one last piece of setup before we move along—let's configure our app to target Java 8 from the start. Doing so will enable more language features and the ability to use a couple of handy library components. To do this, we go into the app's build.gradle file and add a few items: kotlinOptions.jvmTarget = 1.8 and two settings in a compileOptions block inside the android section, as well as update the Kotlin standard library dependency to use the JDK8 version.

Before making any changes, make sure you're in the build.gradle with (Module: Penny_Drop.app) or something similar after it. Otherwise, none of this will work properly.

Gradle Scripts
build.gradle (Project: Penny_Drop)
build.gradle (Module: Penny_Drop.app)

The inside of that file should look something like this:

```
android {
  // Other options still live up here.
  kotlinOptions {
      jvmTarget = 1.8
  }
}

dependencies {
  implementation fileTree(dir: "libs", include: ["*.jar"])
  implementation "org.jetbrains.kotlin:kotlin-stdlib-jdk8:$kotlin_version"

  // The rest of the dependencies are still in here.
}
```

Once Android Studio is done indexing your project (which could take a few minutes), we can start moving around our new codebase. There isn't much here yet, but we're able to run the app in its current state. Android Studio will build the code, generate an APK (Android Package, effectively an .exe for Android), and deploy it to the device/emulator. Once it does that, the app will look something like the first image shown on page 9.

See? I wasn't joking when I said there wasn't much here yet, but we'll be adding to it soon enough. First, let's cover what's been created for us by Android Studio, as shown in the second image on page 9.

AndroidManifest.xml

The manifest file contains info about your application, including the app name, package name, the launcher icon, the default theme, and any Activity classes in the app. In here, we can also use <intent-filter> tags to tell the app how to handle certain actions on the device. *Intents* are descriptions of an

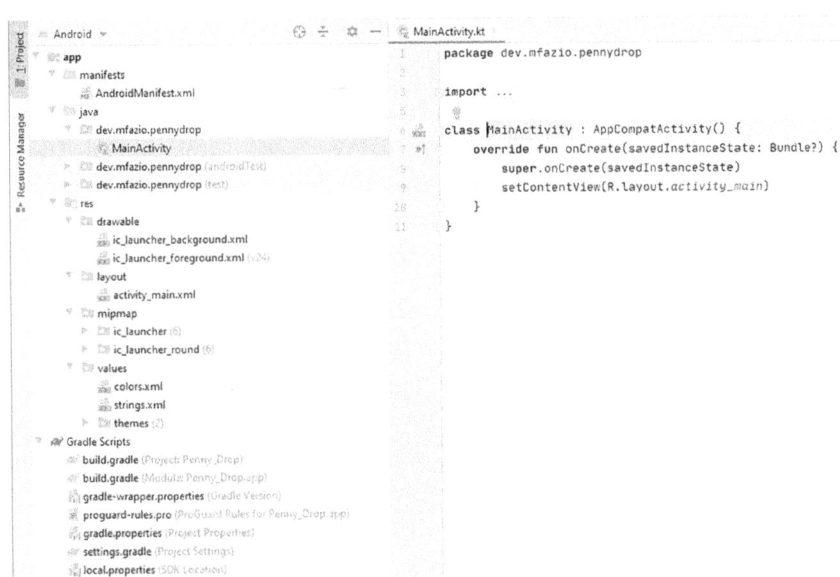

action to be performed and (optionally) associated data. We'll cover what an Activity is momentarily.

At a minimum, we need to have two tags in our default Activity to tell the device which activity to launch by default:

```
<activity android:name=".MainActivity">
  <intent-filter>
      <action android:name="android.intent.action.MAIN" />
      <category android:name="android.intent.category.LAUNCHER" />
  </intent-filter>
</activity>
```

MainActivity

This is the main entry point for our app and the primary screen we see currently. Activity classes are the core components in an Android application. Each Activity also has an associated layout file, generally with an inverted name as compared to the Activity name. For example, MainActivity becomes activity_main.xml. We'll talk about these layout files in just a second.

drawable Files

Drawables in Android are the images you use in your app. We'll be adding more later, but for now there are two *vector* files with info about your launcher image (the image you see in your app drawer on a device). A vector image in Android is like an SVG (Scalable Vector Graphics) where the image is drawn out by listing path coordinates rather than having a static image. This allows the image to be scaled to different sizes without any issues. We'll be updating the image later, but it can stay as is for now.

Now, if we have standard static images (JPGs, PNGs, and so on), they will generally go in subfolders within the drawable folder. With drawable files, we'll generally have multiple versions of the same file at different resolutions, marked by a size value: mdpi, hdpi, xhdpi, xxhdpi, and xxxhdpi.

These images correspond to different *dots per inch (DPI)* values, which are ways of representing the ratio between resolution and display size of a device. If DPI values are higher, this means the pixels on the device are smaller. This could be due to a higher resolution screen or a smaller device, since we have more pixels per inch of screen space. If two devices are the same resolution but have different screen sizes, the device that's smaller would have a higher DPI. Along those same lines, if two devices are the same size but with different resolutions, the higher resolution device would have the higher DPI value.

Rather than having to worry about all these different resolutions, most of the images we'll be using in the two apps will be vector images since they can scale to any size with a single XML file. But if you do need images, they should have all these different resolutions. By uploading an AAB (Android App Bundle) to the Play Store, the extra image resolutions will be removed when the user downloads the app.

Layout Files

Layout files are XML files that handle the UI for your application. Everything in a layout file will live in a hierarchy with View and ViewGroup objects. In our case, the activity_main.xml layout file contains a single ViewGroup (ConstraintLayout) and a single View component (TextView). We'll be adding a bit more to this soon and a great deal more as we move along in this book.

Mipmap Files

Now, these look similar to the drawable files I mentioned earlier, and they are, but the difference here is that all the mipmap files are included when a user downloads the app. The reason is that sometimes we want images to be available that are a different resolution than the phone's DPI. In our case, we have launcher images in here which could require a higher resolution image for a user's home screen (for example) than what would usually be included.

Take care to only include images in here that require higher resolution images than what the phone would usually need, like launcher icons. Every set of images included here will increase your app size.

Adaptive Icons

I've thrown out this term enough, so it's probably time I actually discuss it. *Adaptive icons* were added in API level 26 and allow a device to display a launcher icon in a number of shapes. Plus, it gives the system the ability to add animations to icons (due to having separate foreground and background layers). The ic_launcher_*.xml files we saw earlier in drawable define the background and foreground for the adaptive icon. We then add <adaptive-icon> XML files to app\src\main\res\mipmap-anydpi-v26, which are used for any DPI devices (since the vector files are drawn rather than scaled images).

More about Adaptive icons can be found at https://link.mfazio.dev/adaptive-icons.

Values Files

A common practice with Android development is to use resources within an app instead of static or hardcoded values. This includes strings, colors, themes, fonts, and even animations. A few reasons for this practice are that it allows you to define a particular value in one spot and use it in multiple locations, it makes some values more readable (for example, *alert_red* over *#bc121d*), and with strings, it allows for easier translations.

You can define multiple values-* directories (for example, values-es for Spanish) that hold values for different languages. If you're going to be working with translations, Android Studio has a built-in Translations Editor that can make this process quicker: https://link.mfazio.dev/translations.

Gradle Scripts

Gradle is the default build tool for Android applications. Gradle scripts are used to set dependencies for the app (we'll be in here whenever we add a new Jetpack component), configure the Kotlin version you're using, and specify which SDK versions you're using for your app. It uses the values and check boxes we set when creating our app to populate the scripts, but we can tweak anything as we wish. Right now, what's in there is good, but we'll be back to add dependencies and update some settings later on.

What Else Do We Need?

Android Studio added a bunch of files for us to help us get started on the app, but there are a few more things we'd like to add before we try hooking everything up. Here's what we still need:

- Fragment classes that we're using for our views.
- A menu to tell the bottom nav which options to display.
- A navigation graph to tell the MainActivity which view to display.
- Images for the bottom navigation.
- Updates to MainActivity to bring everything together.

Fragment Classes

While the MainActivity is going to be the entry point for our app, we're actually only going to be using that single Activity for our app. For any experienced Android developers used to large, heavy Activity classes doing everything, this may seem odd.

However, having one Activity and swapping out Fragment views inside of it is more efficient and now the recommended approach from Google. Plus, as we'll see in the next chapter, this makes sharing data between views much smoother.

For now, we're going to create two Fragment classes: PickPlayersFragment and GameFragment. These Fragment classes will eventually be used to set up the players for a game and then play the game. For now, we'll create both Fragment classes but not add proper content until Chapter 2, Build Views with Fragments, on page 27.

Before you create the Fragment classes, it'd be helpful to add a new fragments package just to organize things a bit better. Right-click your main package in the Project view (mine is dev.mfazio.pennydrop, for example) and choose *New > Package*. It'll want the full package name, so just include your main package with "fragments" at the end. In my case, this is dev.mfazio.pennydrop.fragments.

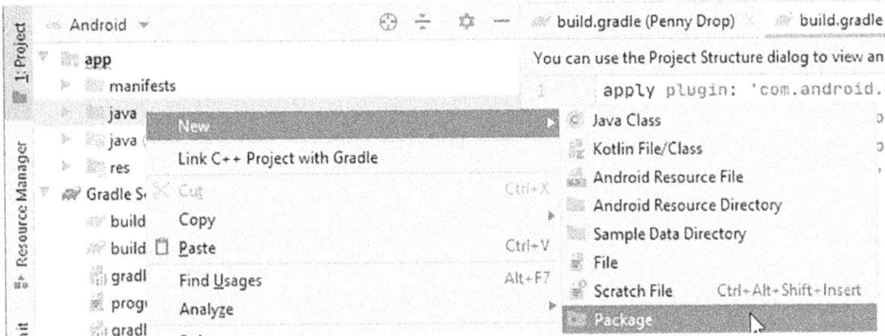

Once that's done, we can create the actual Fragment classes.

PickPlayersFragment

For both Fragment classes, we're going to let Android Studio do the work for us, then we can clean things up afterward. Right-click your fragments package name in the Project view (in my case, under app/java/dev.mfazio.pennydrop.fragments) and select *New > Fragment > Fragment (Blank)*. Enter the fragment name PickPlayersFragment and leave the fragment layout name as fragment_pick_players. Ensure the source language is Kotlin, then click Finish.

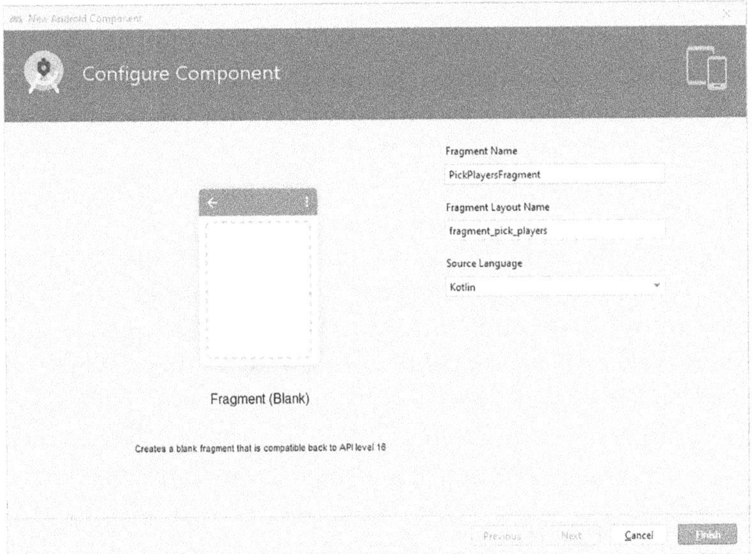

Once Android Studio is done, you'll have the new PickPlayersFragment class as well as the fragment_pick_players.xml layout file. Open fragment_pick_players.xml so we can make the <TextView> here say Pick Players Fragment.

While you could use the Design view for layout editing, I'm going to be referencing the Code view whenever we work with layout files. This view displays the XML behind each layout and gives us more exact control over the values used in a layout. Once you're more comfortable with what goes into a layout file, feel free to use that Design tab. To switch which view you're using, click the Code button in the top right of your editor:

Once you're in the Code view, update the android:text= attribute on the <TextView> to be "Pick Players Fragment":

```
<?xml version="1.0" encoding="utf-8"?>
<FrameLayout xmlns:android="http://schemas.android.com/apk/res/android"
  xmlns:tools="http://schemas.android.com/tools"
  android:layout_width="match_parent"
  android:layout_height="match_parent"
  tools:context=".fragments.PickPlayersFragment">

  <TextView
    android:layout_width="match_parent"
    android:layout_height="match_parent"
    android:text="Pick Players Fragment" />

</FrameLayout>
```

I must let you know that putting text directly into a layout file is actually a bad practice. But since this is just a placeholder until we've got real content, it's fine for now.

GameFragment

We're going to do the same thing here as we did with the PickPlayersFragment. Right-click, create a new blank Fragment, and let Android Studio finish up. We're going to use a shortcut to get to the layout file quickly: hold down Ctrl / Cmd and click fragment_game inside onCreateView(...). This will take you to the fragment_game.xml file. You can use this same shortcut to jump into any classes, files, or even resources in your app. Inside a layout XML? You can click string resources to see where they are. It's a handy way to quickly move around your application.

Update the <TextView> the same we did with PickPlayersFragment, but with "Game Fragment" for the text value. Now that both Fragment classes are created, we can create navigation.xml and a navigation graph with both Fragment classes included.

Build the App's Navigation

These two files will tell the app what to display: the navigation.xml <menu> file will tell the bottom nav which Fragment should be selected in the nav, while the nav_graph.xml <navigation> file will handle which Fragment is displayed.

navigation.xml

For our menu, we can let Android Studio take care of creating the file and folder structure. Right-click res and choose *New > Android Resource File*. In this dialog, enter the filename navigation.xml and a Resource type as Menu. Source set should be main, and the directory name should be menu. Click OK once everything is set to create the file.

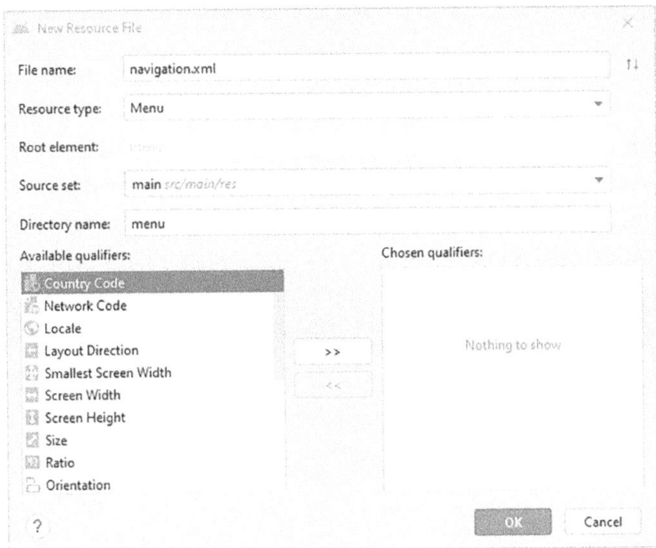

Once the file's created, open it up, switch to the Code tab (again, located in the top right of the editor window), and add in two <item> tags: One for PickPlayersFragment and one for GameFragment. Each <item> will have an ID and title:

```
<menu xmlns:android="http://schemas.android.com/apk/res/android">
    <item
        android:id="@+id/pickPlayersFragment"
        android:title="Players" />
    <item
        android:id="@+id/gameFragment"
        android:title="Game" />
</menu>
```

These will work, but we could use two changes: make the android:title= values string resources and add some images for each option. Android Studio should already be highlighting both android:title= values, telling you “;Hardcoded string ‘Players’, should use @string resource.” We already addressed why you want to do this in Values Files, on page 11, and Android Studio makes the change for us: put your cursor on one of the highlight strings, then press Alt-Enter to get an Extract Resource dialog. The default values are likely fine, so click the OK button and move on. Once both android:title= values are pointing to string resources, head to your strings.xml file to see what was done:

```
<resources>
    <string name="app_name">Penny Drop</string>

    <!-- TODO: Remove or change this placeholder text -->
    <string name="hello_blank_fragment">Hello blank fragment</string>
➤   <string name="players">Players</string>
➤   <string name="game">Game</string>
</resources>
```

Both values are now set up properly, so delete the hello_blank_fragment entry, then we can move on to the images. Android Studio comes with a number of images we can use, so we're going to start there for our PickPlayersFragment image. All the icons are licensed under the Apache License Version 2.0, which will likely work for your app (though you'll want to make sure). Right-click the res/drawable folder and choose *New > Vector Asset*. This will show you the Configure Vector Asset screen. In here, we'll choose Clip Art as the Asset Type. Then double-click the Android icon next to Clip Art:

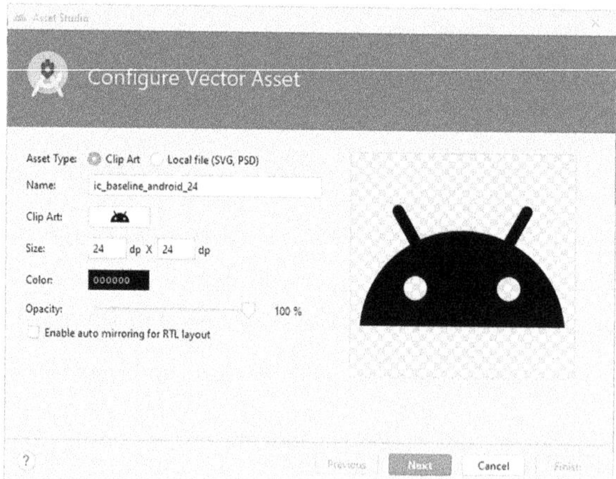

The Select Icon screen that's displayed contains all the available images for us to use (again, we can always import our own as well). You can use the search bar with the magnifying glass (located in the upper-left corner) to search for icons or use the categories located on the left.

I recommend going with Face for PickPlayersFragment, though you can choose whatever icon you wish (not like I can stop you). Once you've selected your icon, click OK to head back to the Configure Vector Asset screen. Once there, hit Next and then Finish. You'll see a new file under res/drawable called ic_baseline_face_24.xml (just rolls off the tongue, doesn't it?). If you open the file up, you'll see that it's another vector asset like we saw with the generated launcher images. This means the icon can scale as we wish and we only need a single version for all devices. Also, I'll explain the 24dp piece in just a bit, so don't worry about that yet.

Quite a few icons are already in Android Studio, yet somehow there aren't dice images (which we could really use for a dice-rolling game). That means we need to go elsewhere to find an image. We can find images online in number of places, but I'm going to use one from https://materialdesignicons.com/. We can grab a wonderful *D6* icon at https://materialdesignicons.com/icon/dice-6. The site supports downloading vector drawables, so this will be quick to bring into the app. Save the XML file and rename it as you wish—I'm going with mdi_dice_6_black_24dp.xml since the mdi prefix helps remind me it's from the Material Design Icons website. Finally, move the file into your drawable directory (you can drag and drop the file on the directory in Android Studio).

Once that image is ready, we can head back into navigation.xml and add in our images. We're going to add an android:icon= attribute to each <item> with the resource syntax you may have seen with the strings earlier: *@drawable/[filename]*.

```
<?xml version="1.0" encoding="utf-8"?>
<menu xmlns:android="http://schemas.android.com/apk/res/android">
    <item
        android:id="@+id/pickPlayersFragment"
        android:icon="@drawable/ic_baseline_face_24"
        android:title="@string/players" />
    <item
        android:id="@+id/gameFragment"
        android:icon="@drawable/mdi_dice_6_black_24dp"
        android:title="@string/game" />
</menu>
```

Now the navigation.xml file is all set and we can move on to our navigation graph.

Navigation and nav_graph.xml

Before we jump into the nav_graph.xml file, let's add our dependencies to the app's build.gradle file. This is the file that has (Module:app) after the filename in the project view (left side of Android Studio by default). The reason there are two Gradle files in the project is that we have one top-level file for all modules in our project and another for the app module. In our case, we only have the single module, so the project-level file is less useful, but it's still handy for us for build variables.

In fact, let's add a quick variable to our top-level build.gradle called nav_version. Adding this variable allows us to have a single place to change the version for all navigation-related dependencies rather than having to deal with each individual dependency declaration.

While we're only adding two dependencies here, it's a good practice to learn for when we have more to deal with in the future. Heads up that I'll be going with variables for all dependencies throughout the book. If you need to find the dependency versions used or want more info about each dependency, please see Appendix 3, Gradle Dependencies, on page 395.

The variable is added under the buildscript section of the top-level build.gradle file, inside an ext block:

```
buildscript {
  ext {
    kotlin_version = '1.4.30'
    nav_version = '2.3.3'
  }
  //Rest of the buildscript block
}
```

Then we can add the two dependencies in the app's build.gradle file:

```
dependencies {
  implementation fileTree(dir: 'libs', include: ['*.jar'])

  //Other dependencies

  implementation "androidx.navigation:navigation-fragment-ktx:$nav_version"
  implementation "androidx.navigation:navigation-ui-ktx:$nav_version"

  //Other dependencies
}
```

Now that we've got the proper dependencies added (make sure to run the Gradle sync; there should be a banner that pops up with Sync Now), we can move on to adding in the navigation graph. The navigation graph will tell the Navigation component where to start and all the places users can go in the app. We can configure multiple *destinations* for an app as well as the start destination. Destinations are locations a user can go in an app; in our case, it's the Fragment classes we created earlier. We'll see a bit more navigation in Chapter 7, Customize an App with Settings and Themes, on page 169, then see more-advanced navigation with the Android Baseball League app in Chapter 9, Navigate via Navigation Drawer, on page 215. For now, we just need to create the <navigation> file, add our two fragments, and we'll be ready to head back to MainActivity to put this all together.

Add nav_graph.xml by right-clicking res and once again choosing *New > Android Resource File*. This time, name the file nav_graph and choose Navigation as the Resource type. Click OK and again switch to the Text tab to see a pretty empty <navigation> XML tag. In fact, it may be underlined with red denoting an error. We're going to fix that soon (it's mad it's not being used yet), so don't worry about it for now. We want to add a few things to this file: two <fragment> tags and an app:startDestination= attribute. Each <fragment> will have an ID, name, and label, while the app:startDestination= will point to the GameFragment.

```
<?xml version="1.0" encoding="utf-8"?>
<navigation xmlns:android="http://schemas.android.com/apk/res/android"
  xmlns:app="http://schemas.android.com/apk/res-auto"
  xmlns:tools="http://schemas.android.com/tools"
  android:id="@+id/nav_graph"
  app:startDestination="@id/gameFragment">
  <fragment
    android:id="@+id/pickPlayersFragment"
    android:name="dev.mfazio.pennydrop.fragments.PickPlayersFragment"
    android:label="fragment_pick_players" />

  <fragment
    android:id="@+id/gameFragment"
    android:name="dev.mfazio.pennydrop.fragments.GameFragment"
    android:label="fragment_game" />
</navigation>
```

The main items of note here: the fragment names match the fully qualified class names (including packages), the android:label= matches with the name of the layout file for the Fragment, and the IDs here match the IDs in navigation.xml. The last piece may be less obvious than the first two, but it's exceedingly useful. By using the same IDs in both navigation.xml and nav_graph.xml, the Navigation component will be able to automatically switch what's being displayed for you without any need for extra configuration. We'll get a better idea what this means once we're done with our MainActivity.

Also, a heads-up that the *@+id/* syntax is us *adding* a new ID to the app. We need to do this when first adding an item in a layout. Then, once we go to use that ID, we can use the *@id/* syntax that we see with app:startDestination=*@id/gameFragment*.

With that done, we can head over and add everything we need to activity_main.xml.

Update activity_main.xml

So far, we've created a number of supporting items, but if we run the app now, we still have our Hello World! text and that's it. This is because we haven't actually added anything to the layout file for MainActivity. layout_main.xml will only have two views: a container <fragment> for the different views we created a bit ago and the bottom navigation we were setting up previously. So let's start with the bottom nav since the alignment for the <fragment> depends on it, but first, I want to cover the <ConstraintLayout> that will surround both views.

What is a ConstraintLayout?

I mentioned in Layout Files, on page 11, that layouts are made up of ViewGroup and View classes, and the ConstraintLayout is the main ViewGroup we'll be using throughout the book. It's an improved version of the existing RelativeLayout where all views are aligned based on each other or their parent. This avoids having level after level of nested views in your layout XML, as is common with many Android applications. Plus, while we're going to be editing our layouts via the XML text view, building UIs with a ConstraintLayout works nicely in Android Studio's Layout Editor.

The key with ConstraintLayout is that every view inside the ConstraintLayout needs to have at least one vertical and one horizontal constraint on it relative to something else in the layout. This allows the OS to handle where things should go on each device, meaning your UI will show up the same way on multiple screen sizes and resolutions without worrying about pixel counts.

Note that adding constraints in a <ConstraintLayout> requires the app namespace. You can either type in *appNs* and let Android Studio autocomplete it for you or manually add the namespace:

```
<androidx.constraintlayout.widget.ConstraintLayout
  xmlns:android="http://schemas.android.com/apk/res/android"
  xmlns:app="http://schemas.android.com/apk/res-auto"
  ...>
```

Add the BottomNavigationView

The bottom nav, which uses the <com.google.android.material.bottomnavigation.BottomNavigationView> tag, is added to the bottom of our view. As we're using a <ConstraintLayout>, it doesn't matter to the app where in the layout file we put the <BottomNavigationView> tag. However, I do recommend adding it as the last element in the <ConstraintLayout> to make things easier to read.

Here, the constraints are simple: left, right, and bottom are all going to match up with the parent <ConstraintLayout>. This means the bottom nav is aligned with the bottom and side edges of the layout. The last piece is the android:layout_height=*"wrap_content"*, which automatically sizes a view based on what's inside of it. The three constraints and *wrap_content* value together put the bottom nav where you'd expect it, on the bottom of the view.

One other attribute is required on a view, android:layout_width=. Usually, this would have a value like *wrap_content* or *match_parent* (which makes the view as wide as its parent), but since we have the constraints telling the view to match the ends to its parent, we can just set an android:layout_width=*"0dp"*. That turns the responsibility of sizing the view over to the <ConstraintLayout>. Note that we can actually use the *match_parent* value for the width and exclude both the left/right constraints, but I wanted to highlight adding constraints in a straightforward example.

Also, I want to mention that left and right attribute values in Android should generally use start and end instead. In most cases, you won't see a difference, but this allows for better support if your app is ever translated to a language where things are read right to left.

Before we move on to the last couple of attributes for our bottom nav, I want to point out what *0dp* actually means. While you can use *wrap_content* or *match_parent*, sometimes we need to actually set partial height values. This can be done with a numeric value and dp, which refers to a certain number of *density-independent pixels*. This is a measurement that allows you to have similar layouts on devices with varying resolutions.

Proper Units of Measure

With Android apps, we're not going to use px for sizing, since screen sizes and resolutions can differ. Instead, we use dp and sp.

- dp: density-independent pixels—use with layouts (instead of px).
- sp: scale-independent pixels—like dp, but also considers a user's font scaling. Use with text sizing.

More info: https://link.mfazio.dev/dimension.

We've got two more attributes to add, a background for the bottom nav and the associated menu. We'll quickly set a default background for the bottom nav, which is nothing too exciting. But the next piece is much more exciting. Remember navigation.xml we created earlier? We're going to add that in as the bottom nav's menu, meaning the items we set in the <menu> XML will be used here. Let's take a look at the full <BottomNavigationView> XML:

```
<com.google.android.material.bottomnavigation.BottomNavigationView
 android:id="@+id/bottom_nav"
 android:layout_width="0dp"
 android:layout_height="wrap_content"
 android:background="?android:attr/windowBackground"
 app:layout_constraintBottom_toBottomOf="parent"
 app:layout_constraintEnd_toEndOf="parent"
 app:layout_constraintStart_toStartOf="parent"
 app:menu="@menu/navigation" />
```

Notice how navigation.xml is referenced here? That's because it's a resource, so we bring in the file the same as we would for a <drawable> or <string> resource. The syntax for the background is an attribute reference, meaning a value that may be changed elsewhere, usually in a theme. We'll talk about this more in Chapter 7, Customize an App with Settings and Themes, on page 169.

Also, the android:background= value may look weird here. The *?attr* is a reference to an attribute specified somewhere in the app, with *?android/attr* referring to a built-in Android attribute. In this case, we're referencing a built-in background we can use for the bottom nav. Otherwise, we're ready to move on to the container <fragment>.

Add the Main Container

This is the last piece of the app we're handling in this chapter and will be the last bit we'll need to do with navigation until Chapter 6, Build a List with RecyclerView, on page 151. This <FragmentContainerView> will hold the views of all the different Fragment classes we use in the app.

We can start on the <FragmentContainerView> with constraints, similar to what we saw with the bottom nav. The top, start, and end constraints are all going to be relative to the parent view, while the bottom is going to be associated with the top of the bottom nav bar. This causes the container to take up all the available space inside the <ConstraintLayout> other than where the bottom nav resides:

```
<androidx.fragment.app.FragmentContainerView
  android:id="@+id/containerFragment"
  app:layout_constraintBottom_toTopOf="@id/bottom_nav"
  app:layout_constraintEnd_toEndOf="parent"
  app:layout_constraintStart_toStartOf="parent"
  app:layout_constraintTop_toTopOf="parent" />
```

We reference views in Android layout files by their ID, as seen here with the *@id/bottom_nav*. Remember, if you want to assign an ID for a view or view group, you set android:id= to *@+id/[viewID]*, and we only need to do this when declaring our views or view groups for the first time.

We've already defined contraints for the top, bottom, start, and end of the <FragmentContainerView>, which means we know how large that view will be. As a result, we can do something like we did with the bottom nav and set both our layout_width= and layout_height= to *0dp*.

```
<androidx.fragment.app.FragmentContainerView
  android:id="@+id/containerFragment"
  android:layout_width="0dp"
  android:layout_height="0dp"
  app:layout_constraintBottom_toTopOf="@id/bottom_nav"
  app:layout_constraintEnd_toEndOf="parent"
  app:layout_constraintStart_toStartOf="parent"
  app:layout_constraintTop_toTopOf="parent"/>
```

Now, we're on to the navigation pieces of our <FragmentContainerView>. We need to tell the <FragmentContainerView> that it'll be a navigation-specific fragment included in androidx.navigation: NavHostFragment. This is a special Fragment that also helps with NavController interaction for us, so we only need to send in the NavController we're using (this will be clearer when we finish up MainActivity).

From there, we can add in the <app:navGraph> that we created earlier (nav_graph.xml) and mark this fragment as the default navigation host with app:defaultNavHost=*"true"*.

```
<androidx.fragment.app.FragmentContainerView
  android:id="@+id/containerFragment"
  android:name="androidx.navigation.fragment.NavHostFragment"
  android:layout_width="0dp"
  android:layout_height="0dp"
```

```
    app:defaultNavHost="true"
    app:layout_constraintBottom_toTopOf="@id/bottom_nav"
    app:layout_constraintEnd_toEndOf="parent"
    app:layout_constraintStart_toStartOf="parent"
    app:layout_constraintTop_toTopOf="parent"
    app:navGraph="@navigation/nav_graph" />
```

The Completed activity_main.xml

Here's what we've got for the MainActivity layout: a single <ConstraintLayout> with a holder for the different Fragment views that we display plus the bottom nav.

```
<androidx.constraintlayout.widget.ConstraintLayout
  xmlns:android="http://schemas.android.com/apk/res/android"
  xmlns:app="http://schemas.android.com/apk/res-auto"
  android:id="@+id/container"
  android:layout_width="match_parent"
  android:layout_height="match_parent">

  <androidx.fragment.app.FragmentContainerView
      android:id="@+id/containerFragment"
      android:name="androidx.navigation.fragment.NavHostFragment"
      android:layout_width="0dp"
      android:layout_height="0dp"
      app:defaultNavHost="true"
      app:layout_constraintBottom_toTopOf="@id/bottom_nav"
      app:layout_constraintEnd_toEndOf="parent"
      app:layout_constraintStart_toStartOf="parent"
      app:layout_constraintTop_toTopOf="parent"
      app:navGraph="@navigation/nav_graph" />

  <com.google.android.material.bottomnavigation.BottomNavigationView
      android:id="@+id/bottom_nav"
      android:layout_width="0dp"
      android:layout_height="wrap_content"
      android:background="?android:attr/windowBackground"
      app:layout_constraintBottom_toBottomOf="parent"
      app:layout_constraintStart_toStartOf="parent"
      app:layout_constraintEnd_toEndOf="parent"
      app:menu="@menu/navigation" />

</androidx.constraintlayout.widget.ConstraintLayout>
```

Now that the layouts are all completed, there's one thing left to do: let's connect everything in MainActivity and run the app.

Complete MainActivity

Right now, all our MainActivity has is the onCreate(), which calls the onCreate() method on AppCompatActivity and associate activity_main.xml with MainActivity via the setContentView() method. We've created the primary <FragmentContainerView> and the bottom nav, which means we need to connect both of those to the MainActivity. I would start some brand-new sections explaining everything that goes into this, but it's not necessary. We just need to get the NavController from this Activity and initialize the bottom nav with it. Doing so takes three lines of code:

```
val navHostFragment = supportFragmentManager
  .findFragmentById(R.id.containerFragment) as NavHostFragment

this.navController = navHostFragment.navController

findViewById<BottomNavigationView>(R.id.bottom_nav)
  .setupWithNavController(this.navController)
```

The first two lines grab the <FragmentContainerView> an initialized NavController with the container view it'll be using to display the other views, while the third tells the bottom nav to use that NavController. Other than adding the declaration for this.navController, our MainActivity is done. Here's the full class:

```
class MainActivity : AppCompatActivity() {

  private lateinit var navController: NavController

  override fun onCreate(savedInstanceState: Bundle?) {
    super.onCreate(savedInstanceState)
    setContentView(R.layout.activity_main)

    val navHostFragment = supportFragmentManager
      .findFragmentById(R.id.containerFragment) as NavHostFragment

    this.navController = navHostFragment.navController

    findViewById<BottomNavigationView>(R.id.bottom_nav)
      .setupWithNavController(this.navController)
  }
}
```

After all the work we've done, if we run our app now, we get something that looks like the image shown on page 26.

While it's still not much to look at, we now have a working BottomNavigationView pulling in the correct fragments with the names and images we configured, without us having to do anything besides give the proper IDs. When developing with Fragment classes before Jetpack, this kind of navigation would have been handled manually. Let's take one more look at everything we've done so far.

Summary and Next Steps

As a review (or for those of you who just skipped the last twenty-five or so pages), here's what we just did:

- Created a new app called *Penny Drop*.
- Created two Fragment classes: PickPlayersFragment and GameFragment.

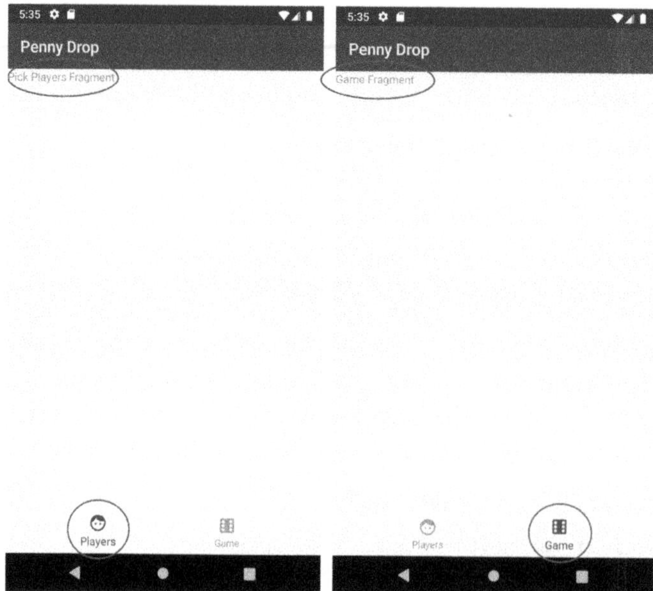

- Created a <menu> called navigation.xml with our two Fragments as items.
- Added two images as Vector Assets.
- Created a navigation graph called nav_graph.xml and included both Fragment classes as destinations.
- Added a container <FragmentContainerView> and BottomNavigationView to activity_main.xml.
- Connected everything in MainActivity.

The foundation for our app is complete. We can use the bottom nav to move around the app, and adding more options just takes a Fragment plus a few XML items. Until we start adding theming, the MainActivity is complete. And we have a couple of Fragments just waiting to be completed, which is our next stop. We know we can get to both Fragment classes, so now we're going to make them useful.

CHAPTER 2

Build Views with Fragments

In the last chapter, we got ourselves a working app with a base navigation setup. Plus we created the skeletons of two views, PickPlayersFragment and GameFragment. We'll build out both Fragment classes in this chapter, starting with PickPlayersFragment to teach you the concepts. Once that Fragment is ready, we'll go through a similar process with GameFragment but in quicker fashion. At the end of the chapter, PickPlayersFragment and GameFragment will look something like this:

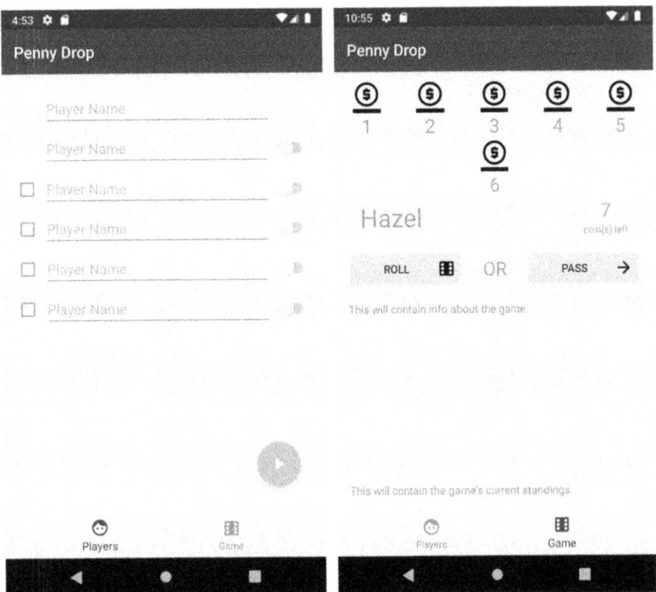

We're going to start in fragment_pick_players.xml with the <ConstraintLayout> that'll be the core of our view, then add in the *floating action button (FAB)* that'll eventually start our game.

Build a Fragment (Pick Players)

Throughout this book, we're going to be using <ConstraintLayout> view groups as the main containers for most of our screens. We could handle things a few ways, but <ConstrainLayout> is a great way to get things right where you want them on each screen while still allowing for the flexibilty needed for multiple device types. In fragment_pick_players.xml, we can replace the entire existing <FrameLayout> tag with this new <ConstraintLayout>. The XML will then look like this:

```
<?xml version="1.0" encoding="utf-8"?>
<androidx.constraintlayout.widget.ConstraintLayout
    xmlns:android="http://schemas.android.com/apk/res/android"
    xmlns:app="http://schemas.android.com/apk/res-auto"
    xmlns:tools="http://schemas.android.com/tools"
    android:layout_width="match_parent"
    android:layout_height="match_parent"
    android:layout_margin="16dp"
    tools:context=".fragments.PickPlayersFragment">

    <!-- Content will eventually go in here. -->

</androidx.constraintlayout.widget.ConstraintLayout>
```

If Android Studio is complaining that the xmlns:app= attribute isn't being used, that's OK. It won't be used until we start adding constraints to the views inside this <ConstraintLayout>.

Once you've added the empty <ConstraintLayout>, we can move on to the FAB.

Change the Navigation Graph's Start Destination

We're going to be spending the first part of this chapter in the PickPlayersFragment, and you'll likely be starting and restarting your app multiple times. To avoid having to click over from the GameFragment every time you start the app, go into nav_graph.xml and change app:startDestination= to *@id/pickPlayersFragment*. We can switch this back later on, but it'll save you a bit of development frustration.

Add the FAB

A floating action button is a circular button that executes the primary function of your current view. In our case, it's the Play button, which will start the game of Penny Drop using the players we've set in this view. Thankfully, adding a FAB takes minimal work. The only unique pieces we'll be setting are a drawable (the Play button you saw before) and a drawable *tint*, which sets a color for the image. The XML code will look like this:

```
<com.google.android.material.floatingactionbutton.FloatingActionButton
  android:id="@+id/buttonPlayGame"
  android:layout_width="wrap_content"
  android:layout_height="wrap_content"
  android:layout_margin="16dp"
  android:contentDescription="@string/play_button"
  android:src="@drawable/ic_baseline_play_arrow_24"
  app:layout_constraintBottom_toBottomOf="parent"
  app:layout_constraintEnd_toEndOf="parent"
  app:tint="@android:color/white" />
```

Code Completion in Android Studio

Android Studio offers code completion throughout the application, including in XML files. This means you can type in part of an XML tag or attribute name and it'll tell you what's available. This is really handy when looking for longer attribute names, like the image android:src= value in the FAB.

Most of this will look familiar based on what we did last chapter: the FAB should only be as large as needed and will be locked into the bottom-right corner of the parent view. We're adding a *16dp* margin to push the FAB away from the side and bottom a little. We also have a text description of the FAB for accessibility (make sure to define the string resource).

Finally, we've got the drawable attributes I mentioned before. We haven't actually created the *@drawable/ic_baseline_play_arrow_24* image yet, so do that in the same fashion as the bottom nav images last chapter: right click app/res/drawable and choose New > Vector Asset. In there, search for the play-arrow clip art, keep the default values, click Next, then Finish.

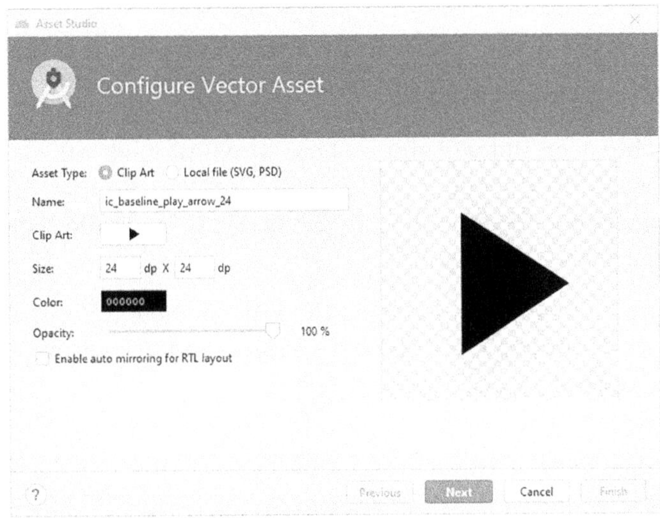

The app:tint= attribute gives the entered drawable a color, usually different than the normal one. We're going to want the Play button to be white, and even though the image itself is black (it even says so in the filename), we can just *tint* the image to something else.

Please note that the tint attribute is using the app namespace and *not* the android namespace. This is due to how the Design Support Library handles FABs, and if we use android:tint=, we may not get the color change we expect.

Also, see how the white color on the FAB is prefixed with "android:? That's because we're referencing the built-in colors that come with the Android Framework. We can also use custom color values, which are kept inside the res/values/colors.xml resource file. For example, the res/values/colors.xml could look like this:

```
<resources>
  <color name="colorPrimary">#6200EE</color>
  <color name="colorPrimaryDark">#3700B3</color>
  <color name="colorAccent">#03DAC5</color>
  <color name="plainGray">#CCC</color>
</resources>
```

With that set of colors defined, we could make that same FAB's icon the app's primary color by doing this:

```
<com.google.android.material.floatingactionbutton.FloatingActionButton
  android:id="@+id/buttonPlayGame"
  android:layout_width="wrap_content"
  android:layout_height="wrap_content"
  android:layout_margin="16dp"
  android:contentDescription="@string/play_button"
  android:src="@drawable/ic_baseline_play_arrow_24"
  app:layout_constraintBottom_toBottomOf="parent"
  app:layout_constraintEnd_toEndOf="parent"
  app:tint="@color/colorPrimary" />
```

For now, a white icon tint will suit us best. The FAB itself will also automatically be colored with the value set for colorAccent. We can now quickly check the app; if you run your app after adding the FAB, it should look something like the image shown on page 31.

Right now, we just care about getting the FAB to show up, not do anything. We'll take care of binding the FAB next chapter, and for now we can move on to the player rows.

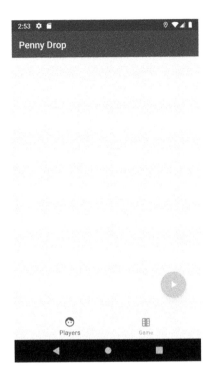

Add Player Rows Without Repeating Yourself (Too Much)

In the image on page 27, we saw multiple rows for players that will be in the game. We're required to have at least two players for a game, so we excluded the check box to say whether or not a player is playing in that game for the first two players. All but the first player had a toggle to say whether or not this player was human or an AI player, plus everyone had some kind of name. The AI players had a spinner to choose which AI you wanted, but we're also using that identifier as their name. The main point here is that all six of the rows were basically the same, just with a bit of conditional logic based on where they were in the list and what type of player they'll be.

If we were in some Kotlin code and wanted to do the same thing six times with minor differences, we'd create a function with a couple of parameters to handle those differences. While this may seem less straightforward in a layout XML, we thankfully have the <include> tag available to do something very similar. We create a base layout file to be used by each item, then we can use <include> within fragment_pick_players to add the rows. We'll start out with creating the layout file called player_list_item.xml.

Build Player List Items

Each player item will include the same three components that I mentioned earlier: a <CheckBox> saying if they're in the game, a name field (or AI spinner), and a human/AI toggle (a <SwitchCompat>). We're going to hold off on the AI spinner for now and just focus on human players.

Please note that we're using <SwitchCompat> rather than <Switch> in this player list item layout. This is because <SwitchCompat> will look consistent between Android versions, while <Switch> may look different on older devices. It's a nice safeguard to make sure your users are getting the visual experience you expect.

Create a new file called player_list_item.xml under res/layout by right-clicking the layout folder and selecting New > Layout resource file. Set the name as player_list_item and the Root element as androidx.constraintlayout.widget.ConstraintLayout (you can also type in *Constraint* and let it search for you). Everything else in this dialog can be left as is.

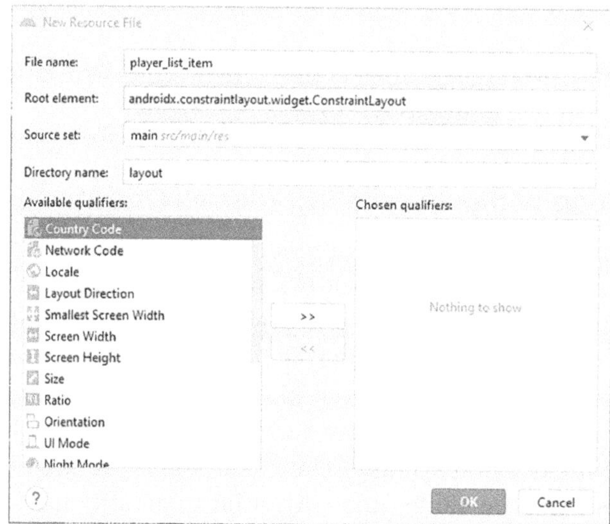

Click Finish, open up player_list_item.xml, and switch to editor's Code view. You can do this by pressing the icon with four lines in the upper right of our editor window.

```
<?xml version="1.0" encoding="utf-8"?>
<androidx.constraintlayout.widget.ConstraintLayout
    xmlns:android="http://schemas.android.com/apk/res/android"
    android:layout_width="match_parent"
    android:layout_height="wrap_content">

</androidx.constraintlayout.widget.ConstraintLayout>
```

Android Studio has given us an empty <ConstraintLayout> to work with, so we can start adding our views once we go through what we're planning to do.

We want to add in the three components I mentioned earlier. The <CheckBox> will be aligned to the start of its parent view while the switch is aligned to the end. The <EditText> (a text field where you can enter data) in the middle will be controlling the rest of the alignment. We'll use the *0dp* trick we saw earlier to allow the <EditText> to fill up all remaining space, since its start and end will be against the <CheckBox> and <SwitchCompat>, respectively.

The vertical alignment is the neat part here; both the <CheckBox> and <SwitchCompat> will match their top and bottom to the <EditText>, which in conjunction with an android:layout_height= of *wrap_content*, centers the outside views with the <EditText> while maintaining their height. The <EditText> will be aligned to the top of the parent view, which ends up aligning the entire row.

For reference, the same thing happens with horizontal constraints. If we use *wrap_content* on a view with start and end constraints, it'll be centered between those two constraint points.

One last bit of usability for the <EditText>: we're going to add android:hint= and android:inputType= attributes. The hint adds text to the <EditText> to let the user know what should go into that field. The hint text is then hidden once they start typing, too, so it doesn't get in the way. The input type helps to let keyboards know what type of data should go into this field and at times constrain what can be entered.

For example, an android:inputType= of *number* will cause the user's keyboard to show a number pad and restrict non-numeric characters from being entered. Also, certain input types will work with autofill to suggest relevant values. In our case, we're going to use *textPersonName*, which is like a standard text field but with spell-checking off, and sometimes name suggestions from a user's contacts. Given all that, the code inside player_list_item.xml will end up looking like this:

```
<androidx.constraintlayout.widget.ConstraintLayout
  xmlns:android="http://schemas.android.com/apk/res/android"
  xmlns:app="http://schemas.android.com/apk/res-auto"
  android:layout_width="match_parent"
  android:layout_height="wrap_content">

  <CheckBox
    android:id="@+id/checkbox_player_active"
    android:layout_width="wrap_content"
    android:layout_height="wrap_content"
    app:layout_constraintBottom_toBottomOf="@id/edit_text_player_name"
```

```
    app:layout_constraintStart_toStartOf="parent"
    app:layout_constraintTop_toTopOf="@id/edit_text_player_name" />

  <EditText
    android:id="@+id/edit_text_player_name"
    android:layout_width="0dp"
    android:layout_height="wrap_content"
    android:layout_margin="5dp"
    android:hint="@string/player_name"
    android:inputType="textPersonName"
    app:layout_constraintEnd_toStartOf="@id/switch_player_type"
    app:layout_constraintStart_toEndOf="@id/checkbox_player_active"
    app:layout_constraintTop_toTopOf="parent" />

  <androidx.appcompat.widget.SwitchCompat
    android:id="@+id/switch_player_type"
    android:layout_width="wrap_content"
    android:layout_height="wrap_content"
    app:layout_constraintBottom_toBottomOf="@id/edit_text_player_name"
    app:layout_constraintEnd_toEndOf="parent"
    app:layout_constraintTop_toTopOf="@id/edit_text_player_name" />
</androidx.constraintlayout.widget.ConstraintLayout>
```

You're going to need to define the @string/player_name string resource just as we did back in Build the App's Navigation, on page 15. Put your cursor on the (likely red) @string/player_name attribute value, hit Alt-Enter, and choose "Create string value resource 'player_name'". Set the Resource value to Player Name and click OK. With that done, we can start including the player rows.

Include Player Rows in the Fragment

Back in fragment_pick_players.xml, we've got a <ConstraintLayout> and our lonely FAB. Now we can add in our player rows with minimal configuration. Each player row will be added to the Fragment via the <include> tag, which takes in a layout= resource plus our standard android:id=.

```
<include
  android:id="@+id/mainPlayer"
  layout="@layout/player_list_item" />
```

Note that we're skipping the android:layout_width=, and android:layout_height= attributes. This is because the player row layout is handling the sizing for us. We could always overwrite these values from fragment_pick_players.xml if we wanted, too.

We could add as many players to our view as we see fit, but six feels like a reasonable number—we get a larger group on the app without having the number of players we're managing become unwieldy. Now, for our list of six players, we could give each one constraints, aligning each item to the last via app:layout_constraintTop_toBottomOf=, but let's take a simpler approach here. All six items will be added into a <LinearLayout>, one of the basic ViewGroup types in Android. <LinearLayout> groups multiple View components into a row, either horizontal or vertical. If we include each player row in the <LinearLayout> and set the android:orientation= to *vertical*, it'll take care of aligning everything for us. We just need to set the proper constraints to the <LinearLayout>. The entire <LinearLayout> will look like this:

```
<LinearLayout
  android:layout_width="match_parent"
  android:layout_height="wrap_content"
  android:orientation="vertical"
  app:layout_constraintEnd_toEndOf="parent"
  app:layout_constraintStart_toStartOf="parent"
  app:layout_constraintTop_toTopOf="parent">

  <include
    android:id="@+id/mainPlayer"
    layout="@layout/player_list_item"/>

  <include
    android:id="@+id/player2"
    layout="@layout/player_list_item"/>

  <include
    android:id="@+id/player3"
    layout="@layout/player_list_item" />

  <include
    android:id="@+id/player4"
    layout="@layout/player_list_item" />

  <include
    android:id="@+id/player5"
    layout="@layout/player_list_item" />

  <include
    android:id="@+id/player6"
    layout="@layout/player_list_item" />
</LinearLayout>
```

We have to repeat ourselves a bit with the layout= attribute, but it's certainly less code to deal with than we could have had otherwise. Now that we've got our six player rows added, the app looks like the image shown on page 36.

There we go! Everything shows up and both the <CheckBox> and <SwitchCompat> can be toggled. Sure, they don't do anything yet, but at least everything's showing up.

Actually, everything showing up is a problem. Remember how I said we're requiring two players in the game and how one of them has to be a human?

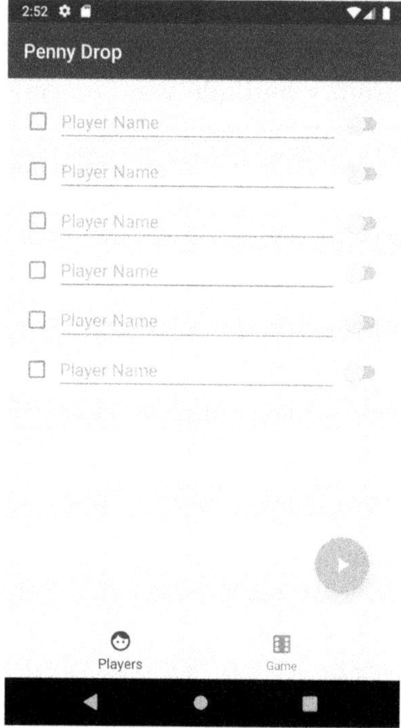

We shouldn't be showing the <CheckBox> for the first two players, nor should the <SwitchCompat> be there for that top user. We're reusing the same layout for each item, so how are we going to send in those parameters?

This is the time for us to start using Jetpack's Data Binding library. The Data Binding library will allow us to assign values and use variables within our XML. We're going to be doing a whole lot with this library throughout the book, but step one will be turning on data binding and adding some conditional logic to the player rows.

Add Data Binding to the App

Here, we're going to turn on data binding for our app and add some configuration for each player item. In my opinion, data binding is one of the best and most useful parts of Jetpack. It allows us to take explicit property binding out of our Activity and Fragment classes and put it into the layout XML. We can then use these bindings to set values, hide/show views, and even create forms like the Players form here in PickPlayersFragment. We'll be able to send the variables from fragment_pick_players.xml into each instance of player_list_item.xml and use those variables to conditionally display pieces of the list items. But first, we need to turn the feature on for our project.

Enable Data Binding

This will be a two-step process in the app's build.gradle file: add the Kotlin kapt plugin and add the dataBinding flag. kapt is the Kotlin-specific annotation processing plugin, which allows us to use (among other things) data binding in the app.

```
apply plugin: 'com.android.application'

apply plugin: 'kotlin-android'

➤ apply plugin: 'kotlin-kapt'

android {
➤    buildFeatures {
➤      dataBinding = true
➤    }
  «Rest of the android block is down here.»
}
// Dependencies live down here
```

With both those changes made and following a Gradle sync, we can move on to layout_pick_players.xml, where we'll wrap our <ConstraintLayout> in a generic <layout> tag.

Add a Generic layout Tag to fragment_pick_players.xml

To use data binding in a view component, we need to wrap the entire view in a generic <layout> tag. This tag won't change the look and feel of the view, but it will cause a class to be generated to allow bindings to occur. We move the xmlns:*= declarations to that generic <layout> tag and fill in our main view like normal:

```
<?xml version="1.0" encoding="utf-8"?>
<layout xmlns:android="http://schemas.android.com/apk/res/android"
    xmlns:app="http://schemas.android.com/apk/res-auto"
    xmlns:tools="http://schemas.android.com/tools">

    <androidx.constraintlayout.widget.ConstraintLayout
        android:layout_width="match_parent"
        android:layout_height="match_parent"
        android:layout_margin="16dp">

        <!-- All the inner views stay the same -->

    </androidx.constraintlayout.widget.ConstraintLayout>
</layout>
```

If we run the app after this change, it'll look exactly the same as it did before. But we can now update the PickPlayersFragment to use the FragmentPickPlayersBinding class that was generated for us, start adding binding statements to our views, and reference one or more <variable> tags in a layout. We'll start by making the changes to PickPlayersFragment, add some <variable> tags over in player_list_item.xml, then finally come back to layout_pick_players.xml to send in the values.

Update PickPlayersFragment

Right now, the onCreateView() inside PickPlayersFragment should look something like this:

```
override fun onCreateView(
    inflater: LayoutInflater, container: ViewGroup?,
    savedInstanceState: Bundle?
): View? {
    // Inflate the layout for this fragment
    return inflater.inflate(
      R.layout.fragment_pick_players,
      container,
      false
    )
}
```

We now need to change some things up to use data binding for the view, including how we inflate the view.

Use Data Binding in PickPlayersFragment

We've already turned on data binding for PickPlayersFragment when we added the generic <layout> inside fragment_pick_players.xml, so now we just have to use it inside our code. We're going to use the generated FragmentPickPlayersBinding class to inflate our view with the additional binding components.

```
override fun onCreateView(
  inflater: LayoutInflater, container: ViewGroup?,
  savedInstanceState: Bundle?
): View? {
  val binding =
    FragmentPickPlayersBinding.inflate(inflater, container, false)

  return binding.root
}
```

Once our view is inflated with the FragmentPickPlayersBinding class, we can directly access components via ID instead of having to call findViewById(). As you'll see soon, this is a much better approach than the "old" way of handling things.

We'll do a lot more with the binding object once we get to our ViewModel classes. Also, we're going to stick with the two-line version of onCreateView() even though we could turn this into a single-expression method. This is because we're going to be binding components in there soon.

Now, if we weren't using the Data Binding library, the inside of onCreateView() would look more like the upcoming code block. We'd spend time in here looking up different views by ID, then setting their properties like this:

```
val view = inflater.inflate(
  R.layout.fragment_pick_players,
  container,
  false
)
with(view?.findViewById<View>(R.id.mainPlayer)) {
    this?.findViewById<CheckBox>(R.id.checkbox_player_active)?.let {
        it.isVisible = false
        it.isChecked = true
    }
}
return view
```

Wait, What Was That Code Block?

Even though we're not using that code block, it could use some explanation, as it probably looks crazy to anyone just starting out with Kotlin. The high-level idea here is that we grab the row that we want, then from there get the <CheckBox> inside. Once we have the <CheckBox>, we can set a couple of properties. This is actually the same thing we're going to do in a bit in our XML view.

The first block is a with() block, which takes whatever is in the parentheses and converts that to the keyword this. with() is one of the many *scope functions* in Kotlin, where we execute a block of code using the context of a given object. I chose with() here to illustrate its use, plus it made logical sense to me to look at the function as "With the mainPlayer view, find the active player checklist." You could use other scope functions here instead if you prefer.

In the case of this example, we have an expression that uses the main view of the Fragment and searches for another view with the ID mainPlayer. The result of that search is passed into the with block. The last item of note on this line is the ?, which is the *null-safe operator*.

This causes the code to only run the subsequent expression(s) if the preceding expression is not null. In this case, if view is null, we never try to call findViewById(), and so we avoid the NullPointerException. This is similar to calling if (view != null) { ... } around this line, but with less code.

Inside the with block, we're doing something similar. If the result was null, we skip the second look up by ID. If not, then we attempt to find the CheckBox with the ID checkbox_player_active. We then do one more null-safe check, but we use the let() function this time. let() is another scope function (like with()) that is especially useful for situations like this one, as we can use ? to only execute the block if the expression coming into let() is not null. Once inside the let() block, we can refer to the CheckBox with the implicit variable it. Kotlin automatically creates it for us inside any block where we haven't explicitly named the parameters coming in. For example, we could give the CheckBox view a name and use this code instead:

```
this?.findViewById<CheckBox>(R.id.checkbox_player_active)?.let { checkBox ->
  checkBox.isVisible = false
  checkBox.isChecked = true
}
```

Hopefully this block is clearer to you, as the Kotlin-specific syntax will definitely be useful down the road. But as far as the PickPlayersFragment is concerned, we're going to stick with the data-binding approach.

Update the Pick Players Layout

Now that our layout file has a generic <layout> tag and we've changed our PickPlayersFragment to use FragmentPickPlayersBinding, we can add in a <data> block with one or more <variable> tags. The <data> tag gives us a place to import classes or declare variables, while the <variable> tag lets us list those variables for use within our views.

In this case, we're going to start with hiding the <CheckBox> and <SwitchCompat> views for a couple of rows, then leaving them in for the rest. For the first player, we know our game must have at least two players and one of them has to be a human player. So we can hide both the <CheckBox> and <SwitchCompat> on the first row. The second player must also be included (meaning the <CheckBox> is hidden again), but we want to leave the <SwitchCompat> in case someone wants to play against a single AI player.

We can update the attributes in player_list_item.xml, then send the values in from fragment_pick_players.xml once that's done. Keep in mind that there's nothing more we have to do right now inside PickPlayersFragment to get these pages to work (though we'll be making changes there later). Let's start with the <data> and <variable> tags inside player_list_item.xml, then we can set the values for each view.

Add data and variable Tags Inside player_list_item.xml

Just as we did in fragment_pick_players.xml, we're going to add a generic <layout> tag around our existing <ConstraintLayout> to allow for data binding. Once we add that <layout> tag, we can add a <data> tag along with two <variable> tags: checkoutHidden and switchHidden. Both variables are Boolean types, which we'll declare within the <variable> tags.

```
<layout xmlns:android="http://schemas.android.com/apk/res/android"
xmlns:app="http://schemas.android.com/apk/res-auto">

  <data>
      <variable
          name="checkboxHidden"
          type="Boolean" />

      <variable
          name="switchHidden"
          type="Boolean" />
  </data>
  <!-- The rest of our view lives down here. -->
</layout>
```

That's all we have to do to configure the variables, so we can start using them in our view. First stop, the <Checkbox> tag.

Conditionally Display the CheckBox for a Player

Now, we want to conditionally set the visibility= and checked= attributes for our <CheckBox>. We do that by using the special data-binding syntax, which looks something like this:

```
android:checked="@{checkboxHidden}"
```

By putting the variable inside the brackets with an @ in front, the Data Binding library knows that this is a *data-binding expression* and it will use the variables we declared in the <data> section. So whatever value is set to checkboxHidden is used to set a default value for android:checked=.

I say "default value" here because it's only the value that's used when the view is created, rather than updating every time the android:checked= value changes. This is important because if the value of checkboxHidden would change when clicking a <CheckBox>, it would also hide our <CheckBox> at the same time. We *are* going to work with binding in this fashion, called *two-way binding*, in a little while but not quite yet. Now, we need to change the android:visibility= based on what's in checkboxHidden.

It may seem odd that I started with android:checked= when the focus here is hiding the <CheckBox>, but I wanted to show a simpler example first where we just assign a variable before getting any more complicated. The Data Binding library allows us to do quite a bit inside a binding expression, as the library's expression language contains a ton of operators/keywords, from mathematical symbols to logical comparisons to method calls.

In our case, we're going to add a ternary operator ([conditional] ? [if true] : [else]) to change the android:visibility= based on the value inside checkboxHidden. For the android:visibility= attribute, we're going to switch between two states: *VISIBLE* and *INVISIBLE*. A third state, *GONE*, is also available, but that completely removes the view from its parent. In our case, this would cause the Player Name text field to expand to the left side of the view instead of staying the same size as the other rows. The end result for android:visibility= will look like this:

```
android:visibility="@{checkboxHidden ? View.INVISIBLE : View.VISIBLE}"
```

We need to prepend both visibility states with View since they're actually constant int values on that class. The slight issue with that is the fact our view doesn't know about the View class, but we can quickly fix that inside our <data> section. Add an <import> tag with the type= attribute containing the (fully-qualified) name of the class you want to include. In our case, it's android.view.View.

```
<data>
➤   <import type="android.view.View" />

    <variable
        name="checkboxHidden"
        type="Boolean" />

    <variable
        name="switchHidden"
        type="Boolean" />
</data>
```

Now our <CheckBox> is ready to go, at least inside player_list_item.xml. The <SwitchCompat> is going to be the same idea but using switchHidden instead:

```
android:visibility="@{switchHidden ? View.INVISIBLE : View.VISIBLE}"
```

Kotlin Has No Concept of a Ternary Statement

I know, we appeared to have just used them with android:visibility=, but that was the data-binding expression language rather than true Kotlin code. Instead of using ternary statements, we'll use if...else expressions in our Kotlin code. Since if..else blocks are *expressions* in Kotlin (meaning they return a value), they can be assigned to values or directly returned from methods. We'll look at this more in Chapter 4, Update LiveData with Conditional Game Logic, on page 91.

We're done with player_list_item.xml, so let's move back to pick_players_fragment.xml.

Assign Values to Variables

Back in pick_players_fragment.xml, we're able to assign values to the two variables in each item. By referencing the app namespace, we can assign the variables as we would any other attributes. This means we have access to both app:checkboxHidden= and app:switchHidden= and can use the same binding expressions we saw earlier to set these values:

```
<include
  android:id="@+id/mainPlayer"
  layout="@layout/player_list_item"
  app:checkboxHidden="@{true}"
  app:switchHidden="@{true}" />
```

By setting the values here, only the mainPlayer player item will hide the <CheckBox> and <SwitchCompat> and the rest will remain as is. Remember that we also want to hide the <CheckBox> for player two in the same manner. Taking both sets of changes will turn the <LinearLayout> into this:

```
<LinearLayout
  android:layout_width="match_parent"
  android:layout_height="wrap_content"
  android:orientation="vertical"
  app:layout_constraintEnd_toEndOf="parent"
  app:layout_constraintStart_toStartOf="parent"
  app:layout_constraintTop_toTopOf="parent">
➤   <include
➤       android:id="@+id/mainPlayer"
➤       layout="@layout/player_list_item"
➤       app:checkboxHidden="@{true}"
➤       app:switchHidden="@{true}" />
➤   <include
➤       android:id="@+id/player2"
➤       layout="@layout/player_list_item"
➤       app:checkboxHidden="@{true}" />
    <include
        android:id="@+id/player3"
        layout="@layout/player_list_item" />
    <include
        android:id="@+id/player4"
        layout="@layout/player_list_item" />
    <include
        android:id="@+id/player5"
        layout="@layout/player_list_item" />
    <include
        android:id="@+id/player6"
        layout="@layout/player_list_item" />
</LinearLayout>
```

With those values being sent in, our Pick Players screen now looks like this:

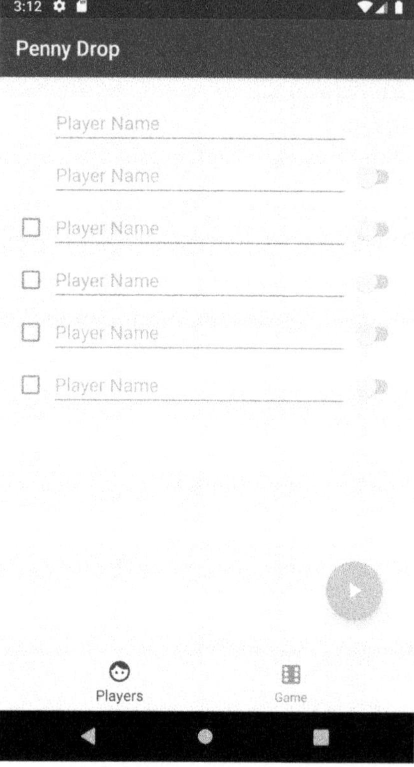

The Pick Players form is finally taking shape! The screen is looking more and more like it will in the end, and with data binding enabled, it'll be smoother to add additional logic here. The next step for this screen will be keeping track of what's been entered for each user and having that available for setting up a game. The best way to handle this will be introducing a new concept called a ViewModel, which is a class that stores data for a given view and alerts the view if that data changes. But before we worry about ViewModel classes, we're going to build out the other main fragment of the app, GameFragment.

Build Another Fragment (Game)

We created GameFragment last chapter, but it still looks pretty sad, especially compared to the PickPlayersFragment. By the time we wrap up this chapter, we'll have a screen that looks like the image shown on page 45.

The rest of this chapter will be spent in GameFragment, so I recommend going to navigation/nav_graph.xml and setting app:startDestination= to *@id/gameFragment*. Then, we'll start by enabling data binding for GameFragment.

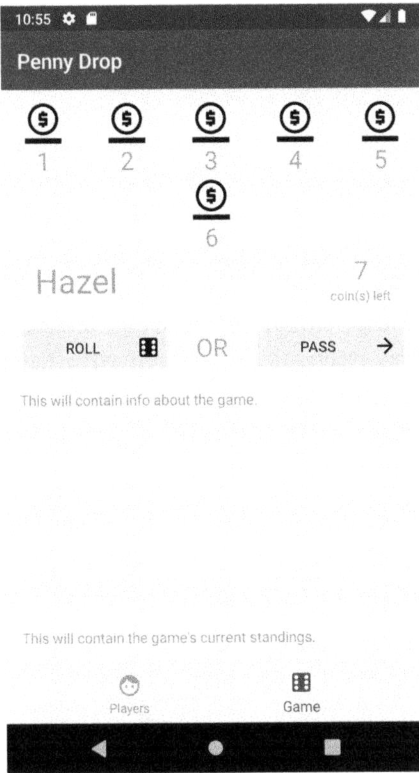

Enable Data Binding for GameFragment

As we're just turning on data binding in GameFragment right now, all we need to do in fragment_game.xml is add that generic <layout> tag plus an empty <ConstraintLayout>. While the <ConstraintLayout> isn't critical for data binding, we're going to be using it soon, so might as well add it now. Our bare-bones view's XML will look like this:

```
<?xml version="1.0" encoding="utf-8"?>
<layout xmlns:android="http://schemas.android.com/apk/res/android"
    xmlns:app="http://schemas.android.com/apk/res-auto"
    xmlns:tools="http://schemas.android.com/tools">

    <androidx.constraintlayout.widget.ConstraintLayout
        android:layout_width="match_parent"
        android:layout_height="match_parent"
        android:animateLayoutChanges="true"
        tools:context="dev.mfazio.pennydrop.fragments.GameFragment">

    </androidx.constraintlayout.widget.ConstraintLayout>
</layout>
```

It's not exciting, and the view doesn't even display the name of the Fragment anymore, but that's OK, it's only temporary. Plus, by getting this part set up, we can complete most of the GameFragment class.

The items of note here are the android:animateLayoutChanges= and tools:context= attributes. Adding android:animateLayoutChanges= attribute gives us animations when things change in our view. In particular, this will add a little animation when a penny is added or removed from a slot. As far as tools:context= goes, nothing in the tools= namespace affects the app when it's run. Instead, it tells Android Studio something. In this case, we're letting Android Studio know that the main <ConstraintLayout> is associated with GameFragment. Adding this attribute doesn't do too much, but it does help with theming and where to put onClick() functions if we add one via XML. tools:context= is totally optional, so it's up to you if you want to add it.

The next step is to inflate this view within the GameFragment class. As we saw with PickPlayersFragment, we're switching onCreateView() to use FragmentGameBinding. We can add some bindings in a bit, but for now, let's just turn things on:

```
class GameFragment : Fragment() {
  override fun onCreateView(
      inflater: LayoutInflater, container: ViewGroup?,
      savedInstanceState: Bundle?
  ): View? {
      val binding =
        FragmentGameBinding.inflate(inflater, container, false)

      return binding.root
  }
}
```

That's all we need to do in here for now, so we can head back over to fragment_game.xml to start building our view.

Start the GameFragment UI

We're going to build the UI in chunks, starting with the player info, then buttons, then the game info, and finally the slots (as they're the most complex part of this screen.)

Add Player Info

First, we can add three <TextView> tags: the current player's name, how many coins they have left, and a coin(s) left label. For the time being, we're going to add some placeholder text in the first two fields so the app has something to use. We're also going to be adding the tools:text= attribute to give the Preview window in Android Studio some text. Like tools:context=, this doesn't change the actual app, just when we're creating it here in the IDE. Here is an example of the Preview window with tools= attributes set:

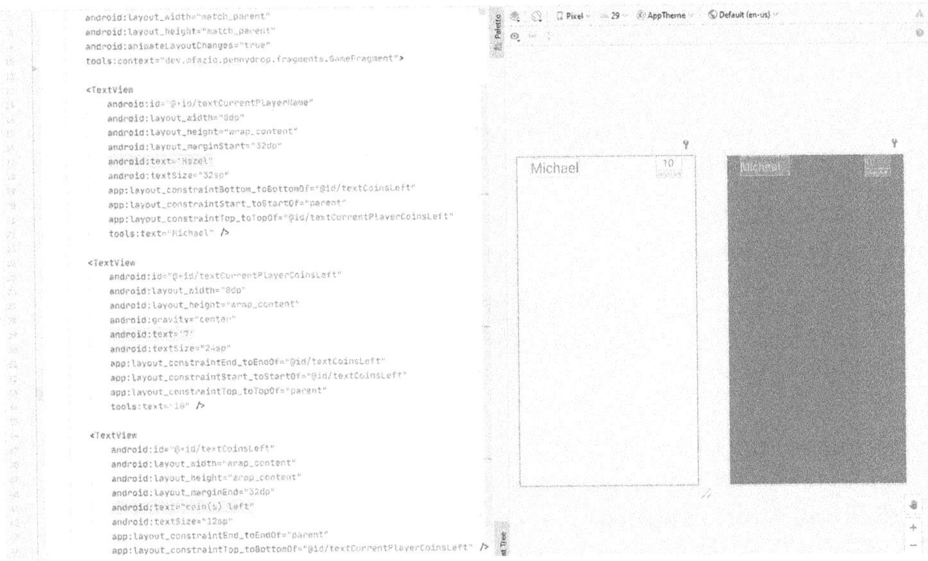

For the sake of clarity, here are the three <TextView> tags from that screenshot:

```
<TextView
  android:id="@+id/textCurrentPlayerName"
  android:layout_width="0dp"
  android:layout_height="wrap_content"
  android:layout_marginStart="32dp"
  android:text="Hazel"
  android:textSize="32sp"
  app:layout_constraintBottom_toBottomOf="@id/textCoinsLeft"
  app:layout_constraintStart_toStartOf="parent"
  app:layout_constraintTop_toTopOf="@id/textCurrentPlayerCoinsLeft"
  tools:text="Michael" />

<TextView
  android:id="@+id/textCurrentPlayerCoinsLeft"
  android:layout_width="0dp"
  android:layout_height="wrap_content"
  android:gravity="center"
  android:text="7"
  android:textSize="24sp"
  app:layout_constraintEnd_toEndOf="@id/textCoinsLeft"
  app:layout_constraintStart_toStartOf="@id/textCoinsLeft"
  app:layout_constraintTop_toBottomOf="@id/coinSlot6"
  tools:text="10" />

<TextView
  android:id="@+id/textCoinsLeft"
  android:layout_width="wrap_content"
```

```
android:layout_height="wrap_content"
android:layout_marginEnd="32dp"
android:text="coin(s) left"
android:textSize="12sp"
app:layout_constraintEnd_toEndOf="parent"
app:layout_constraintTop_toBottomOf="@id/textCurrentPlayerCoinsLeft" />
```

The only interesting new piece is the android:gravity=*center* attribute, which centers the "coin(s) left" text in the <TextView>.

If we could run the app now, it would look similar to the preview we saw previously. Here's how the top of the app looks:

However, we can't run the app as written since *coinSlot6* doesn't currently exist. If you do want to see the app run (which isn't a bad idea), change the attribute like this: app:layout_constraintTop_toTopOf=*parent*. Just make sure you set the attribute back once the slots exist. Either way, the next step is to add the Roll and Pass buttons to the screen.

Add Roll and Pass Buttons

These two buttons are eventually going to be the main components for playing the game, but for now we're just worried about showing them on the screen. Both buttons have a drawable image on them, but we only have one of those images currently in our project. As we did before, right-click your res/drawable directory and choose New > Vector Asset. In here, we'll pick the arrow-forward clip art and add it to our project.

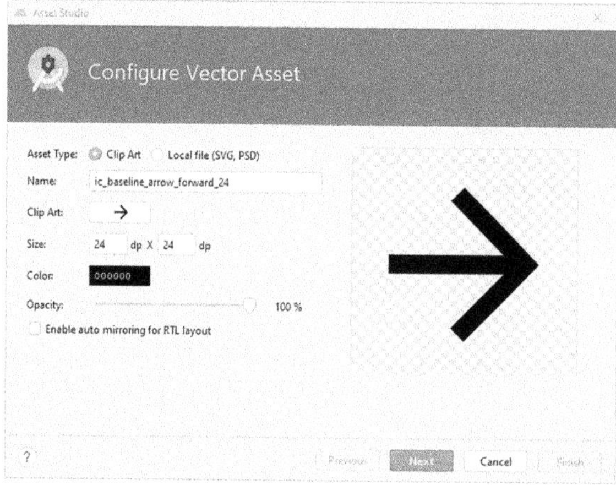

Before we get to the code itself, we should add some string resource values to res/values/strings.xml. As we saw last chapter, this is the place where we want to keep all text values. We're adding three new values, representing the button text and the OR between the buttons.

```
<resources>
  <!-- Existing string resources live up here. -->

  <string name="roll">Roll</string>
  <string name="or">OR</string>
  <string name="pass">Pass</string>
</resources>
```

With the string resources in place, we can add the buttons and OR text to our view.

```
<LinearLayout
  android:id="@+id/layoutButtons"
  android:layout_width="0dp"
  android:layout_height="wrap_content"
  android:layout_margin="16dp"
  android:orientation="horizontal"
  app:layout_constraintEnd_toEndOf="parent"
  app:layout_constraintStart_toStartOf="parent"
  app:layout_constraintTop_toBottomOf="@id/textCoinsLeft">

  <Button
    android:layout_width="0dp"
    android:layout_height="wrap_content"
    android:layout_weight="3"
    android:drawableEnd="@drawable/mdi_dice_6_black_24dp"
    android:padding="10dp"
    android:text="@string/roll" />

  <TextView
    android:layout_width="wrap_content"
    android:layout_height="match_parent"
    android:layout_weight="1"
    android:gravity="center"
    android:text="@string/or"
    android:textSize="24sp" />

  <Button
    android:layout_width="0dp"
    android:layout_height="wrap_content"
    android:layout_weight="3"
    android:drawableEnd="@drawable/ic_baseline_arrow_forward_24"
    android:padding="10dp"
    android:text="@string/pass" />
</LinearLayout>
```

The new items here are the android:orientation= attribute on the <LinearLayout> tag (which tells you which way the layout is directed, *horizontal* or *vertical*), the android:drawableEnd= attributes (which add an image to the right side of a button), and the android:layout_weight= attributes. android:layout_weight= gives a relative size ratio to each component, distributing the item accordingly.

In our case, this means we have seven "sections" in the <LinearLayout>, with each button getting three of those "sections." In practice, this means both buttons are the same size and the OR in the middle gets the leftover space from the buttons.

With that addition, the GameFragment now looks like this:

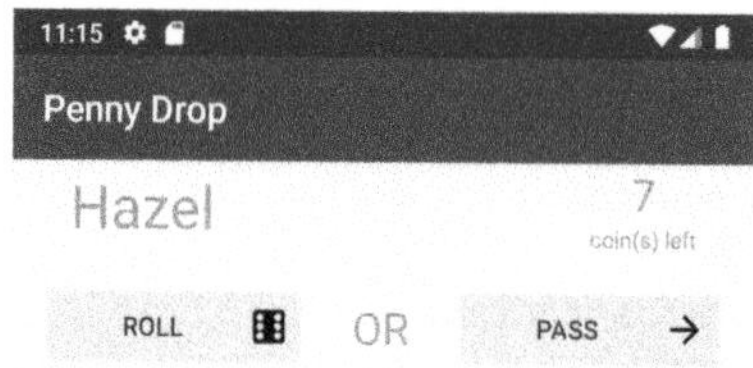

Add Game Information Boxes

We want to have two information boxes on the Game screen: one for the current turn and another for the current standings.

```
<TextView
  android:id="@+id/textCurrentTurnInfo"
  android:layout_width="0dp"
  android:layout_height="0dp"
  android:layout_margin="16dp"
  android:scrollbars="vertical"
  android:text="This will contain info about the game."
  app:layout_constraintBottom_toTopOf="@id/textCurrentStandingsInfo"
  app:layout_constraintEnd_toEndOf="parent"
  app:layout_constraintStart_toStartOf="parent"
  app:layout_constraintTop_toBottomOf="@id/layoutButtons"
  tools:text="Michael rolled a 4.\nMichael rolled a 6!" />

<TextView
  android:id="@+id/textCurrentStandingsInfo"
  android:layout_width="0dp"
  android:layout_height="wrap_content"
  android:layout_marginStart="16dp"
  android:layout_marginEnd="16dp"
  android:layout_marginBottom="16dp"
  android:text="This will contain the game's current standings."
  app:layout_constraintBottom_toBottomOf="parent"
  app:layout_constraintEnd_toEndOf="parent"
  app:layout_constraintStart_toStartOf="parent"
```

```
app:layout_constraintTop_toBottomOf="@id/textCurrentTurnInfo"
tools:text="Current Scores:\t\nHazel: 4 coins\n\tMichael: 7 coins" />
```

The two interesting pieces here are the textCurrentTurnInfo <TextView> that has no apparent width or height and the android:scrollbars= attribute. The lack of an explicit width and height with textCurrentTurnInfo is another example of letting the <ConstraintLayout> handle component sizing—in this case the turn info box will fill the parent and also any space between the buttons and the standings box.

The android:scrollbars= attribute, unsurprisingly, adds vertical scroll bars to our text box. Since it's possible for the info box to be larger than the space available, we want to allow users to scroll through all the text. However, the XML attribute only displays the scroll bars if the box is able to scroll. To enable that functionality, we need to set the movementMethod property on the <TextView>. This can be done inside GameFragment as part of the binding initialization. In there, we add an apply() block, then assign textCurrentTurnInfo.movementMethod to a new ScrollingMovementMethod instance in there. Yes, we can reference components by their ID due to the Data Binding library, which is really handy. The code looks like this:

```
FragmentGameBinding.inflate(inflater, container, false).apply {
  textCurrentTurnInfo.movementMethod = ScrollingMovementMethod()
}
```

With those changes in place, the UI is coming along. It now looks like the image shown on page 52.

Again, the filler android:text= value will go away later, but it's handy to have something on the screen when we run the app. The tools:text= value will remain and show up in the Preview window. Now we can move on to the most interesting part of this page, at least from a UI perspective.

Include Six Coin Slots

The penny slots for our game will show which slots are filled and which are open, plus the sixth always-open slot. As you can probably guess, we can use the <include> tag for all six slots. Add in a bit of conditional logic, as we did with the player list items earlier in the chapter, and we can save ourselves a lot of code.

The plan here is to create the layout resource file for a slot, layout_coin_slot.xml, then <include> it six times in fragment_game.xml with a few parameters. Once we're done getting those created, we'll take a look at the entire fragment_game.xml as it stands, along with how the screen looks.

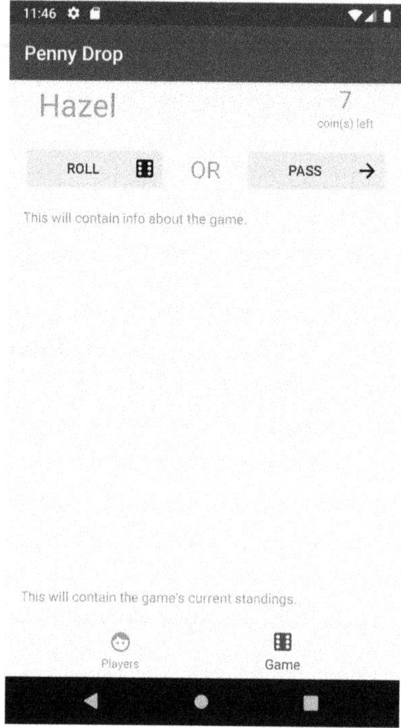

Create the Coin Slot Layout XML

layout_coin_slot.xml will be under res/layout; right-click, choose New > Layout Resource File, and give it a ConstraintLayout root element. This layout file will contain a coin <ImageView>, a <TextView> for the slot number, and a generic <View> which gives the slot a bit of shape.

Get the Coin Drawable

Android Studio doesn't include a good drawable we can use for a coin, so we're going to head back to https://materialdesignicons.com/ to get one, in particular https://materialdesignicons.com/icon/currency-usd-circle-outline. I went with this icon because I love the look of it in the game, but feel free to grab a different one if you wish. Save the icon to res/drawable/mdi_coin_black_24dp.xml to follow the same convention as our *D6* icon last chapter (update the name if you chose a different image). Once the image is ready, we can get to building the XML.

You should know the drill by now: generic <layout> tag containing a <ConstraintLayout>, then our view components inside there. Plus, we're going to include a <variable>, slotNum, to use with the <TextView>. The layout file will look like this:

```
<?xml version="1.0" encoding="utf-8"?>
<layout xmlns:android="http://schemas.android.com/apk/res/android"
    xmlns:app="http://schemas.android.com/apk/res-auto"
    xmlns:tools="http://schemas.android.com/tools">

    <data>
      <variable
          name="slotNum"
          type="int" />
    </data>

    <androidx.constraintlayout.widget.ConstraintLayout
        android:id="@+id/constraintLayoutCoinSlot"
        android:layout_width="wrap_content"
        android:layout_height="wrap_content">

        <ImageView
            android:id="@+id/coinImageCoinSlot"
            android:layout_width="wrap_content"
            android:layout_height="wrap_content"
            android:contentDescription="@string/coin_icon"
            android:minWidth="36dp"
            android:minHeight="36dp"
            android:src="@drawable/mdi_coin_black_24dp"
            app:layout_constraintEnd_toEndOf="parent"
            app:layout_constraintStart_toStartOf="parent"
            app:layout_constraintTop_toTopOf="parent" />

        <View
            android:id="@+id/bottomViewCoinSlot"
            android:layout_width="0dp"
            android:layout_height="5dp"
            android:background="@android:color/black"
            app:layout_constraintEnd_toEndOf="@id/coinImageCoinSlot"
            app:layout_constraintStart_toStartOf="@id/coinImageCoinSlot"
            app:layout_constraintTop_toBottomOf="@id/coinImageCoinSlot" />

        <TextView
            android:id="@+id/slotNumberCoinSlot"
            android:layout_width="wrap_content"
            android:layout_height="wrap_content"
            android:text='@{slotNum + ""}'
            android:textSize="24sp"
            app:layout_constraintEnd_toEndOf="@id/coinImageCoinSlot"
            app:layout_constraintStart_toStartOf="@id/coinImageCoinSlot"
            app:layout_constraintTop_toBottomOf="@id/bottomViewCoinSlot"
            tools:text="3" />

    </androidx.constraintlayout.widget.ConstraintLayout>
</layout>
```

Again, I hope most of this looks familiar enough by now. The pieces to call out are:

- All <ImageView> tags should have an android:contentDescription= attribute for accessibility, in particular screen readers. Make sure you create the @string/coin_icon entry inside strings.xml.
- We're using tools:text= again to fill in a value within Android Studio.
- In case you missed it last chapter, we're using dp for view sizing and sp for text sizing. Both values are scaled for the user's device, helping us a ton with different device sizes/resolutions/and so on.

Wait, What's with the Last Text Value?

Yes, it looks weird, but it's not a typo. It's the binding-expression syntax we saw before, but we're concatenating our slotNum variable (which is an int) to an empty string (which makes the result a string). We're doing this because android:text= is expecting a string. If we give it an int, it instead tries to use that value to look up a *string resource* value from strings.xml. That leads to a rather unhelpful error (if you don't know what you're looking for):

```
2020-07-12 14:50:38.797 18112-18112/? E/AndroidRuntime: FATAL EXCEPTION: main
    Process: dev.mfazio.pennydrop, PID: 18112
    android.content.res.Resources$NotFoundException: String resource ID #0x1
        at android.content.res.Resources.getText(Resources.java:348)
        at android.widget.TextView.setText(TextView.java:5831)
        at dev.mfazio.pennydrop.databinding.LayoutCoinSlotBindingImpl.executeBindings(LayoutCoinSlotBindingImpl.java:184)
        at androidx.databinding.ViewDataBinding.executeBindingsInternal(ViewDataBinding.java:473)
```

We could send slotNum into layout_coin_slot.xml as a string, but since the slot is a number, I feel this is the better route to go. How you approach this part is up to you; just know you need to give android:text= a string value or a string resource value (for example, android:text=*"@string/or"*).

Now that the layout_coin_slot.xml file is ready, we can add the slots to fragment_game.xml.

Add Coin Slots to GameFragment

At the top of the <ConstraintLayout> inside fragment_game.xml, we're going to use a <LinearLayout> with five <include> tags representing our slots. Each slot will reference the layout_coin_slot layout file we created earlier and have an app:slotNum= property with the slot number being sent in. The code will look something like this:

```
<LinearLayout
  android:id="@+id/layoutCoinSlots"
  android:layout_width="0dp"
  android:layout_height="wrap_content"
```

```
    android:layout_marginTop="10dp"
    android:layout_marginBottom="5dp"
    android:baselineAligned="false"
    android:gravity="center"
    android:orientation="horizontal"
    app:layout_constraintEnd_toEndOf="parent"
    app:layout_constraintStart_toStartOf="parent"
    app:layout_constraintTop_toTopOf="parent">

    <include
        android:id="@+id/coinSlot1"
        layout="@layout/layout_coin_slot"
        android:layout_width="0dp"
        android:layout_height="wrap_content"
        android:layout_weight="1"
        app:slotNum="@{1}" />

    <!-- The other four slots live down here -->
    <!-- They only differ by ID and slotNum values -->
</LinearLayout>
```

A couple items of note: as we saw with PickPlayersFragment, the value for app:slotNum= needs to be an int inside a binding expression rather than just *"1"*. The latter value will cause the compiler to say that app:slotNum= doesn't exist. Also, we're using android:baselineAligned=*"false"* for the sake of performance. With this attribute set to false, rendering the <LinearLayout> will be faster since there are fewer alignment calculations being done.

The sixth coin slot is included after the <LinearLayout> and has a couple of differences, but otherwise it's the same as the other five slots:

```
<include
  android:id="@+id/coinSlot6"
  layout="@layout/layout_coin_slot"
  android:layout_width="wrap_content"
  android:layout_height="wrap_content"
  app:layout_constraintEnd_toEndOf="parent"
  app:layout_constraintStart_toStartOf="parent"
  app:layout_constraintTop_toBottomOf="@id/layoutCoinSlots"
  app:slotNum="@{6}" />
```

Last piece before we run the app: if you changed it previously, update the textCurrentPlayerCoinsLeft <TextView> to have its top constraint point to the sixth coin slot:

```
<TextView
  android:id="@+id/textCurrentPlayerCoinsLeft"
  ...
  app:layout_constraintTop_toBottomOf="@id/coinSlot6"
  />
```

And with that, version one of the GameFragment is ready to go! Let's take a look:

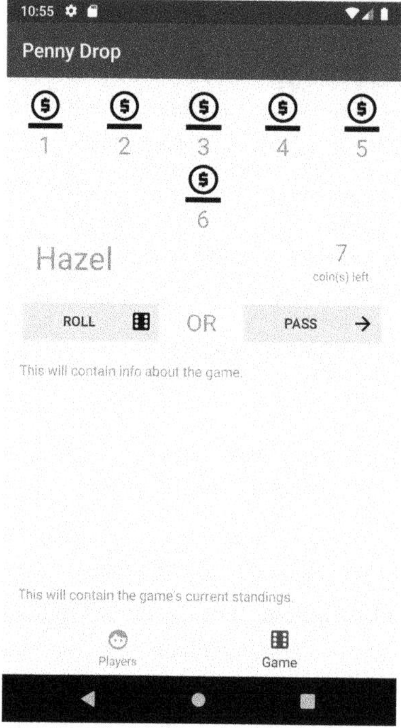

Summary and Next Steps

Not bad! The coins aren't able to be toggled yet and the buttons aren't functional, but we're in a good spot. While we could spend a bit more time in here adding extra properties, I think it's time to move on to the proper approach: using a ViewModel with LiveData to update the views as needed. Having ViewModel classes will let us bind data from code in our Fragment classes in a life-cycle aware way. Head over to the next chapter to find out what that means!

CHAPTER 3

Bind Data with ViewModels

In the previous chapter, we created two views: PickPlayersFragment and GameFragment. While they look nice right now, they don't do much yet. We still need to bring both screens to life, which we can do with data binding and ViewModel classes. We're going to create ViewModel classes for both views and get things connected up so we can then move on to the game logic.

Create a ViewModel (Pick Players)

View models as a concept aren't an exclusively Android-focused idea; plenty of other languages/frameworks/platforms have the concept of a view model in one way or another. In a general sense, a view model holds UI-related data for a given view. This way, the UI can focus on what to display while the view model handles how you get that data.

With Jetpack, ViewModel is a specific class we can use to handle UI data for view components, in our case the Fragment classes. A ViewModel may also contain LiveData, which will automatically send updates to a UI controller whenever the data changes. Since ViewModel classes are *life-cycle aware*, they only send LiveData over when a given Fragment (or Activity) is currently active. This avoids potential errors and unnecessary data updates, making your app faster and more stable.

We're going to create a new ViewModel called PickPlayersViewModel, bind it to our PickPlayersFragment, and create some NewPlayer objects as LiveData for use in setting up the game. But first, as we did with the Navigation component, we need to add two dependencies before we can use the library.

Add the ViewModel and LiveData Dependencies

To use ViewModel classes and LiveData objects, we need to add their dependencies to the project. Both are contained in the androidx.lifecycle package, which means we only need a single variable called lc_version (*lc* for life-cycle) to the project-level build.gradle file

```
buildscript {
  kotlin_version = '1.4.30'
  gradle_version = '4.1.2'

  app_compat_version = '1.2.0'
  constraint_layout_version = '2.0.4'
  core_version = '1.3.2'
➤ lc_version = '2.3.0'
  nav_version = '2.3.3'
}
```

After that, we can add the two dependencies to our app's build.gradle file:

```
dependencies {
  implementation fileTree(dir: 'libs', include: ['*.jar'])
  implementation "org.jetbrains.kotlin:kotlin-stdlib-jdk8:$kotlin_version"
  implementation "androidx.appcompat:appcompat:$app_compat_version"
  implementation
    "androidx.constraintlayout:constraintlayout:$constraint_layout_version"
  implementation "androidx.core:core-ktx:$core_version"
➤ implementation "androidx.lifecycle:lifecycle-livedata-ktx:$lc_version"
➤ implementation "androidx.lifecycle:lifecycle-viewmodel-ktx:$lc_version"
  implementation "androidx.navigation:navigation-fragment-ktx:$nav_version"
  implementation "androidx.navigation:navigation-ui-ktx:$nav_version"

  «Other dependencies»
}
```

Sync your project to pick up the new dependencies. You should get a banner on the top of the editor saying you need to sync, but if that doesn't appear, you can start a sync via the Gradle tool window on the right of the IDE. Here, we can see all the Gradle tasks that are available for our project, but right now, we just care about syncing things.

To do that, right-click the top Penny Drop entry and choose Reload Gradle Project:

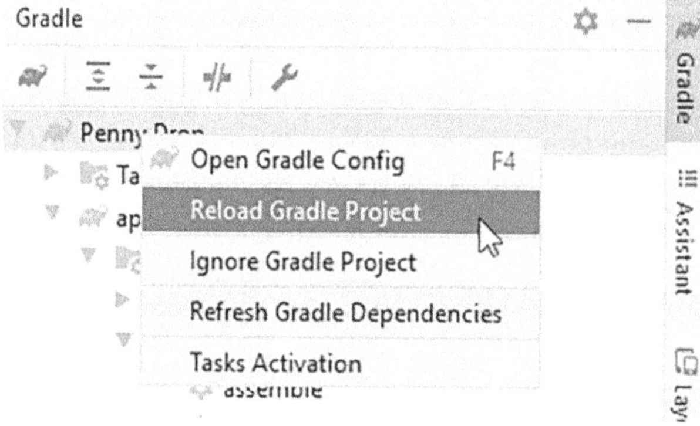

With things synced, we can move on to adding the NewPlayer and PickPlayersViewModel classes. We'll start with NewPlayer since we'll be using it in PickPlayersViewModel.

Add NewPlayer data class

The NewPlayer data class will hold the info about each of the players we want to add into our game. The class will match up with what's in each of the player items in the view. This means we're going to have a name, some attributes about the user (Human vs. AI, can be removed/toggled), and a bit of handling for AI players. We'll come back to the AI part later, so we can skip the AI handling for now.

Notice that I said a couple of times that we're creating a data class. In Kotlin, a data class is a specific type of class that is intended to hold data and has some extra functionality added by the compiler. This includes equals()/hashcode() functions, a human-readable toString(), and a copy() function. While we're not using the latter function here, it's very useful when you want a new version of an object with minimal changes. With data class types, we need to have at least one parameter in our constructor, and all parameters must be marked val or var.

Just to make sure we're clear, val makes a parameter/object a value, meaning it's *immutable* and the assignment cannot be changed. Conversely, an object with var is a variable, meaning we can reassign it.

With NewPlayer, we want the player's name to be a var so that a user can change that name from the front end. All other parameters can be marked with val. This may seem odd when dealing with the CheckBox and SwitchCompat for a player, but we're going to do something slightly different with those two fields. We're going to instead use an ObservableBoolean class to handle any changes, as normal variables don't work properly with two-way binding, which we'll cover in a bit.

Let's create our class—right-click the main package (in my case, dev.mfazio.pennydrop) and select New > Kotlin File/Class. There, we can set the name as types.NewPlayer and set a Kind of *Class*. By putting the types part on the filename, Android Studio will put NewPlayer in the types package. If it doesn't end up in the types package automatically, you may have created a Kotlin File rather than Class. Again, packages are ways we can organize our code to make things easier to understand. Once we get this class and PickPlayersViewModel created, we can do a bit of organizing of our existing classes. But for now, let's fill in our data class. The entire NewPlayer.kt will look like this:

```
package dev.mfazio.pennydrop.types

import androidx.databinding.ObservableBoolean

data class NewPlayer(
  var playerName: String = "",
  val isHuman: ObservableBoolean = ObservableBoolean(true),
  val canBeRemoved: Boolean = true,
  val canBeToggled: Boolean = true,
  var isIncluded: ObservableBoolean = ObservableBoolean(!canBeRemoved)
)
```

I want to call out a couple of things before we move on. Notice that we can set default values for each of our parameters; this means we can create an instance of NewPlayer without worrying about setting every value (since most new players are going to be set up the same way).

Also, for people used to Java, this syntax might look odd. Normally, classes need to have curly brackets { ... } around constructors and functions, but not in Kotlin. If the class doesn't have any functions in it, we can just declare the class name plus the parameters we need and call it good. This is a common trend with Kotlin: you only write the code needed to understand what's going on and no more. It allows us to skip a lot of the boilerplate code we see in other languages.

Finally, in Kotlin constructors, we can use other parameters in the constructor as long as they are earlier in the order and will have been initialized first. In our case, we're defaulting isIncluded to true if a user can't be removed from the game, otherwise they default to false.

With NewPlayer created, we can move on to PickPlayersViewModel and its list of NewPlayer objects.

Add PickPlayersViewModel

We're not going to be doing too much in PickPlayersViewModel right now, as we only need a single List of NewPlayer, wrapped inside a LiveData instance (in our case, MutableLiveData). Let's create the class, then we can add in the NewPlayer objects. We're going to have some fun with the initialization process.

As we did with NewPlayer, we can add PickPlayersViewModel to our project by right-clicking the main package and selecting New > Kotlin File/Class. There, we can set the name as viewmodels.PickPlayersViewModel and a Kind of *Class*. This will put the class inside the new viewmodels package. Inside the code, we're going to make our class inherit from ViewModel. The class declaration will look like this:

```
class PickPlayersViewModel : ViewModel() {
  //We'll be adding this code in a bit.
}
```

That code block is an example of inheritance in Kotlin: PickPlayersViewModel is now a child class of ViewModel. Since the ViewModel class has a constructor, we need to tell the compiler how we want to initialize the parent class when creating our child class, which we do via the *constructor invocation* syntax. This is why the ViewModel class is referenced like a function. That syntax tells the compiler that we're invoking the default constructor of ViewModel when we create an instance of PickPlayersViewModel. On the plus side, if you forget this part, Android Studio will yell at you to fix it.

Add NewPlayer Instances to PickPlayersViewModel

We're going to declare the List of NewPlayer instances in PickPlayersViewModel, then add the possible players to that List. We can do this ahead of time since we know we have six player spots and whether or not they're in the game is controlled by the isIncluded property.

Let's look first at the LiveData declaration, then we can deal with the players themselves.

```
val players = MutableLiveData<List<NewPlayer>>()
```

This creates players as a public value of type MutableLiveData which itself holds a List of NewPlayer. Notice that we don't have to explicitly set the type for players since we can see the type in the assignment. This is a useful convention to avoid adding extra, redundant code in our app.

Now we can move on to creating the players (or player slots, however you want to think about them). To do this, we're going to use Kotlin's apply() scope function (we first used scope functions in Wait, What Was That Code Block?, on page 39). apply() takes the object that it was called upon and runs a code block with the original object implicitly declared as this. You can assign values to the object, then apply() returns the original object with the modifications made.

In our case, we're going to do something like this:

```
val players = MutableLiveData<List<NewPlayer>>().apply {
    this.value = listOf() // This will be some players
}
```

Collection Helper Functions

Kotlin has a number of built-in helper functions on the Collection class. listOf(), setOf(), and mapOf() are all useful functions to quickly create a Collection. You can either enter some values inside the parentheses or leave it empty for an empty collection.

The apply() function is a handy way to create an object and assign some variables all at once. We're going to be using apply() again in just a minute with our NewPlayer instances, but first, let's look at a neat Kotlin trick.

We're going to be creating six NewPlayer instances where the first two players cannot be removed from the game since we need a minimum of two players to have a game. Also, the first player cannot be toggled to an AI player since someone has to be playing the game. A quick way to create a certain number of items is as follows: we create an IntRange, then map() each item to a new instance of our class. We don't need to use the current index in map(); we just want to have a number of items in a list equal to the length of the IntRange. The code for creating the six NewPlayer instances looks like this:

```
(1..6).map {
  NewPlayer()
}
```

This will give us the List of NewPlayer instances that we want, so now we just need to add in the conditional logic. canBeRemoved is true for all but the first two players, and canBeToggled is true for all but player one. We can add a couple of greater-than statements to set both fields:

```
(1..6).map {
  NewPlayer(
➤   canBeRemoved = it > 2,
➤   canBeToggled = it > 1
  )
```

Notice that we only need to set the parameters that we want and every other parameter uses its default value. Plus, due to the order of our parameters, isIncluded gets a value based on canBeRemoved.

As is always the case in software development, we could have handled this logic a number of ways. I like the succinct (1..6) syntax for creating a list of items, and hopefully this was a clear example of how you can use apply() in your code. Let's take one last look at the entire PickPlayersViewModel:

```
import androidx.lifecycle.MutableLiveData
import androidx.lifecycle.ViewModel
import dev.mfazio.pennydrop.types.NewPlayer
```

```
class PickPlayersViewModel : ViewModel() {
  val players = MutableLiveData<List<NewPlayer>>().apply {
    this.value = (1..6).map {
      NewPlayer(
        canBeRemoved = it > 2,
        canBeToggled = it > 1
      )
    }
  }
}
```

With both NewPlayer and PickPlayersViewModel complete, we can head back over to PickPlayersFragment and our layout files to start using the new ViewModel for data binding.

Bind ViewModel to a Fragment (Pick Players)

Now it's time for us to really get into the Data Binding library. So far, we've done a bunch of setup (sorry, there's a bit more coming) and some static binding with isVisible and isChecked, but using dynamic variables is where data binding really shines. The ability to set up complex objects in our code, then bind them to the UI with minimal work is why I'm recommending data binding so emphatically. Working though this next section will set us up for later chapters where we're displaying data from a database or web services. But first, we need to finish up a few more things to get this all working.

Update PickPlayersFragment to Use PickPlayersViewModel

To use the PickPlayersViewModel we just created, we're going to need to do a few things:

1. Add a <variable> called viewModel to fragment_pick_players of type PickPlayersViewModel.
2. Declare a value of type PickPlayersViewModel via the by activityViewModels() syntax.
3. Bind that instance to the viewModel variable on FragmentPickPlayersBinding.

Once those steps are complete, we can start using viewModel in our layout file to reference the NewPlayer instances we created last section. Now, off to fragment_pick_players!

Add a viewModel Variable to the Layout File

Inside fragment_pick_players, we're going to be adding a new <data> with a vm <variable> inside. This is like what we did inside player_list_item.xml in Add data and variable Tags Inside player_list_item.xml, on page 40. That means your <data> tag will look like this:

```
<data>
  <variable
      name="vm"
      type="dev.mfazio.pennydrop.viewmodels.PickPlayersViewModel" />
</data>
```

As long as you make sure your package name matches what you're using for your app (mine is dev.mfazio.pennydrop, yours may be different), the <data> is set. You should go through and delete the app:checkboxHidden= and app:switchHidden= attributes on your player rows since those variables don't exist anymore. We're not going to assign viewModel to the player rows until after we finish with the rest of our setup, but we'll be back to that part soon enough. Now that viewModel exists in our layout, we can reference it within PickPlayersFragment. This means we can assign the PickPlayersViewModel to its layout once we have an instance. To get that instance of PickPlayersViewModel, we'll use the slick by activityViewModels() syntax.

Get an Instance of PickPlayersViewModel

As we've discussed, ViewModel classes are useful for handling data and sending that data to a UI component in a life-cycle aware way. Another advantage of a ViewModel class is that we can also use it to store data outside of the life cycle of a Fragment class by associating the ViewModel with the parent Activity. These two concepts are related: ViewModel classes won't send data to a UI component when that UI component isn't active, but it also means the data stored in the ViewModel won't necessarily disappear when the UI component using that ViewModel is destroyed. Instead of having to reload the list of players each time the PickPlayersFragment is created, it just uses the data that we already set up inside the PickPlayersViewModel (which is tied to MainActivity).

Note that this isn't the same as persistence, meaning the data will be destroyed if the app is *closed*. But if we switch to the Game view, for example, the Android OS could destroy the PickPlayersFragment since it's not currently active. If that happens, we'd normally lose our data, but not if it's stored in a ViewModel bound to MainActivity.

At one point, this next part was three pages of explaining how to get an instance of PickPlayersViewModel from our Activity along with a few supporting concepts from Kotlin. Instead, we're left with this code block to declare and retrieve the object:

```
private val pickPlayersViewModel
  by activityViewModels<PickPlayersViewModel>()
```

This only works if we're using JDK 1.8 and above (which we set in Chapter 1). Normally, we would also need to add the fragment-ktx library as well, but since we're already including the navigation-fragment-ktx library, the former was added as a transitive dependency of the latter. Simply put, navigation-fragment-ktx uses fragment-ktx, so we automatically get everything from the fragment-ktx library.

In addition to taking less effort, any Fragment tied to a given Activity will get the same instance of the ViewModel without us needing to do any extra work, which helps with sharing data between Fragment classes.

Now that we have our PickPlayersViewModel instance associated with MainActivity, we can move on to binding data to the UI.

Bind PickPlayersViewModel

Currently, we're just inflating our layout via the FragmentPickPlayersBinding class since that enabled data binding in our layout files. But we can also use this binding class to assign variables, in particular the pickPlayersViewModel variable we just retrieved.

To do this, we're going to use the apply() scope function we saw earlier:

```
private val pickPlayersViewModel
  by activityViewModels<PickPlayersViewModel>()

override fun onCreateView(
  inflater: LayoutInflater, container: ViewGroup?,
  savedInstanceState: Bundle?
): View? {
  val binding = FragmentPickPlayersBinding
    .inflate(inflater, container, false)
➤   .apply {
➤     this.vm = pickPlayersViewModel
➤   }

  return binding.root
```

What we've done here is assign pickPlayersViewModel to the vm <variable> within fragment_pick_players. That means the PickPlayersViewModel instance can be used in our layout, including grabbing individual players from the ViewModel and assigning them to player items.

No View/Lifecycle/Activity References in ViewModel Classes

A ViewModel must never reference a view, Lifecycle, or any class that may hold a reference to the activity context. Doing so breaks the life-cycle separation between ViewModel classes and other life-cycle owners. If you do need the Application context for some reason, you can use AndroidViewModel instead.

Bind NewPlayer to Player Slots

Each <include> tag in fragment_pick_players references a possible player for our game, which we can connect to each of the NewPlayer instances in PickPlayersViewModel. The player list items will then use canBeRemoved and canBeToggled from the NewPlayer to handle the proper display of each item. Even better, though, is that we can set up the three pieces of each item (name, isIncluded, and isHuman) to link back to the NewPlayer instance in our PickPlayersViewModel. That will give us the proper settings for each player without any additional work.

Add app:player Attributes

The first step needed is to replace the existing <variable> tags in player_list_item.xml with a new <variable> called player. We're going to bind each NewPlayer instance from PickPlayersViewModel to the list items, which can then be accessed inside player_list_item.xml.

```
<data>
  <variable
      name="player"
      type="dev.mfazio.pennydrop.types.NewPlayer" />
</data>
```

Again, make sure you update the package name for the NewPlayer type declaration to whatever you're using, then we can move back to fragment_pick_players to set a value for player.

Inside fragment_pick_players, each of our <include> tags will have an added attribute called app:player=. The name of the attribute matches the name of our <variable> in the tag's layout, in this case the player <variable> we set up previously. We can then use a collection syntax (for example, viewModel.players[0]) to get each individual player. Each of the <include> tags will look something like this:

```
<include
  android:id="@+id/player3"
  layout="@layout/player_list_item"
  app:player="@{vm.players[2]}" />
```

The app:player= attribute doesn't exist normally on an <include> or any type of Layout, but declaring the <variable> inside the <include> creates that attribute for us. This is one of the ways to add custom attributes, along with *binding adapters*, which we'll see in Create Binding Adapters, on page 88. Now that we've assigned players to each player item, we can bind values from NewPlayer.

Use NewPlayer in player_list_item.xml

We've prepped everything we need to use a NewPlayer in a player list item, so now we can update the android:visibility= attributes that were referring to the old variables. All we need to do is change the referenced variable in the conditional section of the ternary expressions.

```
android:visibility="@{player.canBeRemoved ? View.VISIBLE : View.INVISIBLE}"
```

We'll do the same with player.canBeToggled in the <SwitchCompat> farther down our layout. Once both of these conditionals are updated, we'll be back at the same spot as we were before with our bindings, but we'll be accessing the actual NewPlayer objects instead of the true and false values from earlier. In fact, go ahead and run your app right now. It'll look the same as before, but you know it's now set up in a much more flexible manner.

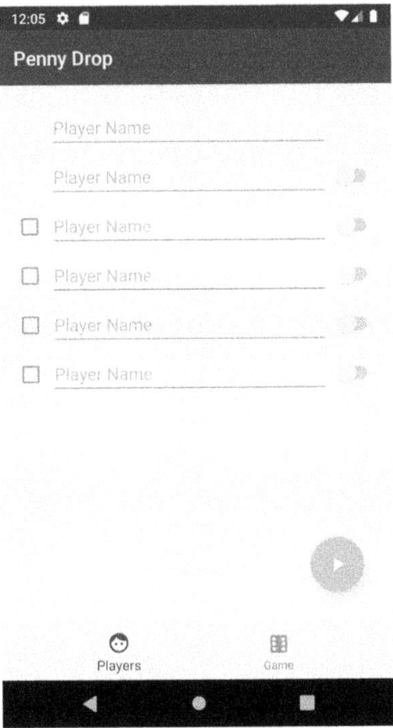

Now that our visibilities are configured correctly, we can start expanding the functionality of this form. First item up is the name field.

Binding a Player's Name with Two-Way Binding

We've seen a few examples of data binding so far in this chapter, but all of them are working in the same way: we set up a value either in a higher-level layout or in our code with a ViewModel, then send a value to a view as an attribute. If we were to do something similar with a name, we could generate a name for each player to be displayed in each item. But if we change those names on the front end, the back-end values would never change accordingly. In practice, this is useless since we lose any changes a user would make. Instead, we need to take advantage of *two-way binding* in our layout. This means we still send in values from our ViewModel, but changes on the UI side will be sent back to the ViewModel to be saved. For example, if we default the first player's name to Player 1, but the user goes and changes that name to Rolando, with two-way binding we would store the value Rolando in the NewPlayer instance inside PickPlayersViewModel.

If we were going to use one-way binding with the player name <EditText>, we would write something like this:

```
android:text="@{player.playerName}"
```

But if we wanted to change that to a two-way binding expression, we would add an = sign to the same expression:

```
android:text="@={player.playerName}"
```

Now the name value we set on the front end will be sent to PickPlayersViewModel for use when starting our game. Along the same lines, we need to make some updates for the CheckBox and SwitchCompat on each player item. In both cases, we're already updating the visibility, but now we need to send the control's status back to the ViewModel with the android:checked= property.

```
<CheckBox
  android:id="@+id/checkbox_player_active"
  android:layout_width="wrap_content"
  android:layout_height="wrap_content"
  android:checked="@={player.isIncluded}"
  android:visibility=
    "@{player.canBeRemoved ? View.VISIBLE : View.INVISIBLE}"
  app:layout_constraintBottom_toBottomOf="@id/edit_text_player_name"
  app:layout_constraintStart_toStartOf="parent"
  app:layout_constraintTop_toTopOf="@id/edit_text_player_name" />

<androidx.appcompat.widget.SwitchCompat
  android:id="@+id/switch_player_type"
```

```
  android:layout_width="wrap_content"
  android:layout_height="wrap_content"
  android:checked="@={player.isHuman}"
  android:visibility=
    "@{player.canBeToggled ? View.VISIBLE : View.INVISIBLE}"
  app:layout_constraintBottom_toBottomOf="@id/edit_text_player_name"
  app:layout_constraintEnd_toEndOf="parent"
  app:layout_constraintTop_toTopOf="@id/edit_text_player_name" />
```

Both controls use a two-way binding syntax on android:checked= to send back their current status. We can then use those values when starting the game. Now, that's all we need for UI changes to be sent back to PickPlayersViewModel at the moment. If you want to verify the data in the back end, I've got a few ideas over in Appendix 2, Troubleshooting Your App, on page 381. But this isn't required to build this screen, so we can continue with the AI spinner.

Add AI Spinner to Player List Items

Given that we're making a game here, it'd be helpful to have a way for people to play against computer-controlled players. To do that, we're going to create some AI players, then give users the ability to choose which of those AI players they're facing. In this part, we're only going to worry about giving the AI players names, and we'll leave the actual logic for Chapter 4, Update LiveData with Conditional Game Logic, on page 91. We're going to create an AI class with a number of possible AI players, then update the player items to include these AI players. Whether a user is shown a name text field for a player or the AI Spinner will depend on the state of the SwitchCompat on that player item. Before we get to the UI, let's create the AI class.

Create the AI Class

Our AI will be another data class, this time living in the game package. For the time being, it'll only contain one property, name, a toString() method that returns that name, and a companion object with a List of AI called basicAI. In here, we'll declare eight AI players to be used in the Spinner. The code looks like this:

```
package dev.mfazio.pennydrop.game

data class AI(val name: String) {

  override fun toString() = name

  companion object {
    @JvmStatic
    val basicAI = listOf(
      AI("TwoFace"),
      AI("No Go Noah"),
      AI("Bail Out Beulah"),
```

```
            AI("Fearful Fred"),
            AI("Even Steven"),
            AI("Riverboat Ron"),
            AI("Sammy Sixes"),
            AI("Random Rachael")
        )
    }
}
```

This class doesn't have too much, but a few things may be new for you. The companion object syntax denotes an object that is associated with a given class. There's only one instance of this object per class (meaning it's a *singleton*) and functions/values/variables in here can be accessed in a similar way to how we would reference static types. In this case, we can get basicAI elsewhere by referencing AI.basicAI.

Since the new toString() function is just going to return the name value on the AI instance, we can use *expression syntax* to directly assign name to toString(). That is equivalent to this:

```
override fun toString(): String {
  return name
}
```

The last piece that may look weird is the @JvmStatic annotation on basicAI. Adding this annotation tells the compiler to create an additional static get() method for basicAI. This will allow us to reference basicAI in a static way within a player list item, which we'll see in a bit. Since this is all we need in the AI class currently, we're going to add the Spinner list inside player_list_item.xml.

Add AI Spinner in player_list_item.xml

I keep mentioning the <Spinner> tag, which is what we sometimes call a "drop-down list" or "select" in HTML. A <Spinner> contains some number of items and allows the user to select one of those items. Our AI <Spinner> is going to live in the same spot as the name <EditText>, and we'll toggle which one we're displaying using the <SwitchCompat> associated with the player item. As a result, the constraints for the <Spinner> will match up with the <EditText> on all four sides. We'll also need another android:visibility= attribute on both the <EditText> and <Spinner> based on the player's value for isHuman.

Finally, once we get the conditional logic completed, we can handle the AI items themselves. Normally, we'd need to create some kind of SpinnerAdapter to include our items, but we're going to take a different approach thanks to the Data Binding library. The android:entries= attribute will allow us to bind an object as the list of items in the <Spinner>.

In our case, we could use AI.basicAI or AI.getBasicAI()() for that android:entries= attribute. The reason there are two options is because the former value is the Kotlin property while the latter is a getter method that's generated for use with Java. Now, we normally want to go with the Kotlin approaches all over, but if you use AI.basicAI, Android Studio will complain (even though it works). Instead, you can avoid the error by using the Java getter syntax in our binding.

No matter the approach you take with the list of AI objects, we need to update NewPlayer to include a new Int variable—selectedAIPosition.

```
data class NewPlayer(
  var playerName: String = "",
  val isHuman: ObservableBoolean = ObservableBoolean(true),
  val canBeRemoved: Boolean = true,
  val canBeToggled: Boolean = true,
  var isIncluded: ObservableBoolean = ObservableBoolean(!canBeRemoved),
➤ var selectedAIPosition: Int = -1
)
```

This will track the index of the selected AI (retrieved from AI.basicAI or AI.getBasicAI()). In our XML, we'll use the android:selectedItemPosition= attribute with selectedAIPosition. All these pieces together will look like this in the layout file:

```
<Spinner
  android:id="@+id/spinner_ai_name"
  android:layout_width="0dp"
  android:layout_height="wrap_content"
  android:entries="@{AI.getBasicAI()}"
  android:selectedItemPosition="@={player.selectedAIPosition}"
  android:visibility="@{player.isHuman ? View.INVISIBLE : View.VISIBLE}"
  app:layout_constraintBottom_toBottomOf="@id/edit_text_player_name"
  app:layout_constraintEnd_toStartOf="@id/switch_player_type"
  app:layout_constraintStart_toEndOf="@id/checkbox_player_active"
  app:layout_constraintTop_toTopOf="@id/edit_text_player_name" />
```

We established that we can use AI.basicAI or AI.getBasicAI() to get our list of AI options, but we haven't established *why* they're available yet. It's because we added the @JvmStatic annotation in the AI class. Without that, the Data Binding library wouldn't have been able to figure out how to send in the data. To use AI.basicAI or AI.getBasicAI(), we also need to import the AI type inside our <data> block:

```
<data>

  <import type="android.view.View" />
➤ <import type="dev.mfazio.pennydrop.game.AI" />

  <variable
      name="player"
      type="dev.mfazio.pennydrop.types.NewPlayer" />
</data>
```

Also of note is that android:selectedItemPosition= is a two-way binding expression to our new selectedAIPosition property on NewPlayer. Otherwise, this item is similar to the <EditText> we created earlier. Speaking of that <EditText>, don't forget to include the android:visibility= attribute there:

```
<EditText
  android:id="@+id/edit_text_player_name"
  android:layout_width="0dp"
  android:layout_height="wrap_content"
  android:layout_margin="5dp"
  android:hint="@string/player_name"
  android:inputType="textPersonName"
  android:text="@={player.playerName}"
  android:visibility="@{player.isHuman ? View.VISIBLE : View.INVISIBLE}"
  app:layout_constraintEnd_toStartOf="@id/switch_player_type"
  app:layout_constraintStart_toEndOf="@id/checkbox_player_active"
  app:layout_constraintTop_toTopOf="parent" />
```

Since we're now getting an AI from the front end (or at least the index for one), we can get the currently selected AI object via a new function called selectedAI(). This function will return null either if the isHuman is true or the AI at the given index can't be found.

```
data class NewPlayer(
    var playerName: String = "",
    var isIncluded: ObservableBoolean = ObservableBoolean(false),
    val isHuman: ObservableBoolean = ObservableBoolean(true),
    val canBeRemoved: Boolean = true,
    val canBeToggled: Boolean = true,
    var selectedAIPosition: Int = -1
) {

  fun selectedAI() = if (!isHuman.get()) {
    AI.basicAI.getOrNull(selectedAIPosition)
  } else {
    null
  }
}
```

Now the form works as we need it to for the game, but we could make this a bit prettier and user friendly. Let's go ahead and add a couple of nice-looking UI features: disabling excluded players and iconography for the <SwitchCompat>. Both changes will give the app a more polished feel.

Customize the Player List Items

Again, the Pick Players screen is currently functional as is, but once you get some real users on the app, there's bound to be some confusion. Nothing is telling users what happens when you check or uncheck the check box for a player or what that switch at the end means. Disabling unchecked items gives users an indication what they're doing when they check the box since they've seen forms like this before.

For the <SwitchCompat> tag, we can change the on/off states from just being a generic-looking switch to human and AI icons. This way people will be able to quickly tell what's going on with each control without the need for a bunch of text on the screen. First up is the <CheckBox> and the android:enabled= attribute.

Allow the Items to Be Enabled and Disabled

We want to disable any players that aren't included in the game as determined by the check box in each row. This serves two purposes: it tells the user what that check box does and avoids setting up players that aren't going to be used. To disable views in a player list item, we will use the android:enabled= attribute which will reference player.isIncluded. The <EditText>, <Spinner>, and <SwitchCompat> tags will all contain android:enabled="@{*player.isIncluded*}". Doing this will disable those views based on the status of the <CheckBox>, which will look like this after we enter info for a few players:

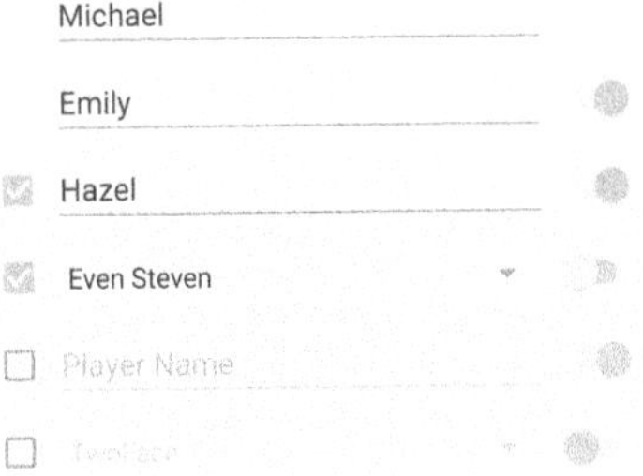

Having those views disabled makes it much clearer to the user that the players are not included in the game. However, it's a bit hard to tell the difference between a player that's switched to AI versus one that's been disabled. Plus, I still don't think people can tell at first glance what's going on with that latter <SwitchCompat> tag. We need to get some icons onto that switch and get away from a gray option (which will mean *disabled* rather than *AI*).

Add Some Color to the Player Type Switch

The last improvement for the Pick Players Screen is the player type <SwitchCompat>. Having it change between a person's face and a robot will tell users a great deal more than a switch that goes between pink and gray. We're going to add a new icon (the robot), a new drawable background, and a dynamic color file that changes the color of the <SwitchCompat> based on its state.

Add the Android Icon

Adding our Robot icon will work the same way as the other built-in icons in the last chapter: right-click res/drawable and choose New Vector Asset. In there, pick the android clip art, then Next and Finish back on the Asset Studio screen. This will create a new Robot-head icon (belonging to the unnamed Android mascot, unofficially known as Bugdroid) to use with the <SwitchCompat>. Once he's ready to go, we can create our drawable background with this new icon and our existing Face icon.

Add the drawable Background

Here, we'll add a new resource XML file to the res/drawable folder called ai_toggle_bg. Once created, it will contain an empty <selector> tag. In here, we can add two <item> tags: one for the Face icon, one for the Android icon. Both <item> tags will have two attributes: android:drawable= and android:state_checked=. The <android:drawable> attribute will point to each item's icon. For android:state_checked=, the face item will have an attribute of *"true"* while the android item will be *"false"*. These attributes tell the app which icon to use when the <SwitchCompat> is in each state.

```
<?xml version="1.0" encoding="utf-8"?>
<selector
  xmlns:android="http://schemas.android.com/apk/res/android">

  <item
    android:drawable="@drawable/ic_baseline_face_24"
    android:state_checked="true" />

  <item
    android:drawable="@drawable/ic_baseline_android_24"
    android:state_checked="false" />
</selector>
```

We can use this drawable background by adding a single attribute to our <SwitchCompat>: android:thumb=*"@drawable/ai_toggle_bg"*:

```
<androidx.appcompat.widget.SwitchCompat
  android:id="@+id/switch_player_type"
  android:layout_width="wrap_content"
  android:layout_height="wrap_content"
  android:checked="@={player.isHuman}"
  android:enabled="@{player.isIncluded}"
  android:visibility=
    "@{player.canBeToggled ? View.VISIBLE : View.INVISIBLE}"
  android:thumb="@drawable/ai_toggle_bg"
  app:layout_constraintBottom_toBottomOf=
    "@id/edit_text_player_name"
  app:layout_constraintEnd_toEndOf="parent"
  app:layout_constraintTop_toTopOf="@id/edit_text_player_name" />
```

Adding the android:thumb= attribute changes the "thumb" (the small ball on the switch) to one of the two icons, depending on the state of the <SwitchCompat>.

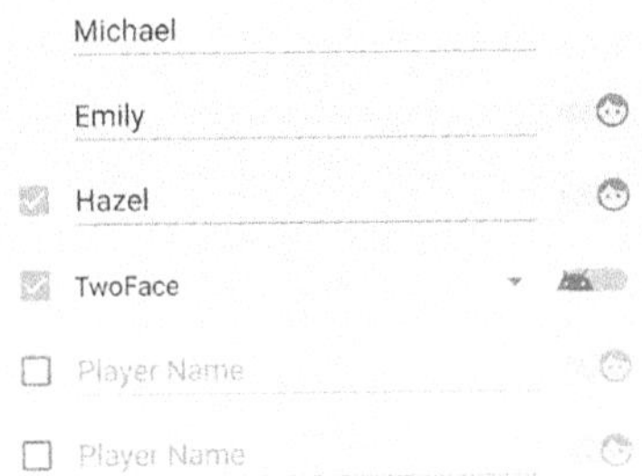

Now, having the icons does make things clearer, but the black-and-white nature of the icons leaves a bit to be desired here. Adding some color to each icon will make the <SwitchCompat> really pop on the screen and make the change clearer for users.

Add Color to the Switch

Adding color to the <SwitchCompat> is a similar process to adding the icons: we need a new resource XML file (this time under res/color), we add entries for different <SwitchCompat> states, then we add it as an attribute on the <SwitchCompat>.

If res/color doesn't exist, create a new Resource Directory of type Color by right-clicking the res folder and choosing New > Android Resource Directory.

Adding a new resource file will look like this:

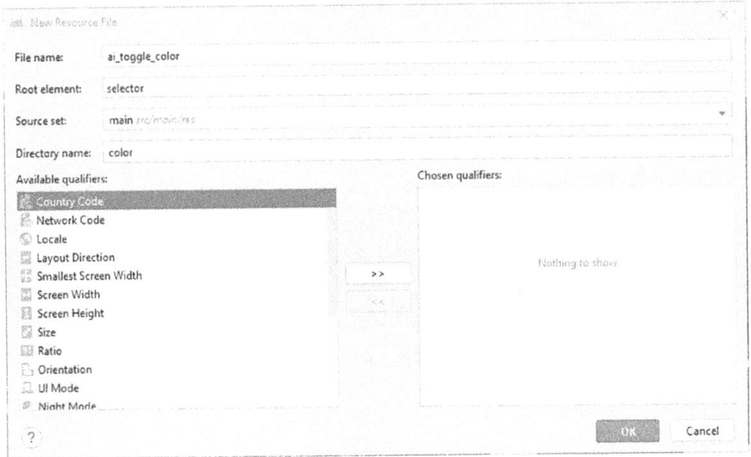

Your new resource XML file, ai_toggle_color, is called a *color state list resource.* Color state list resource files have a single <selector> tag containing one or more <item> tags. In our case, we have three <item> tags.

All three entries will be based on states of the <SwitchCompat>: a dark gray for when the <SwitchCompat> isn't enabled (since the next two colors will override the default color) and two items for the android:state_checked= options, similarly to before:

```
<?xml version="1.0" encoding="utf-8"?>
<selector xmlns:android="http://schemas.android.com/apk/res/android">
    <item
      android:color="@android:color/darker_gray"
      android:state_enabled="false" />
    <item
      android:color="@android:color/holo_blue_bright"
      android:state_checked="true" />
    <item
      android:color="@android:color/holo_green_light"
      android:state_checked="false" />
</selector>
```

Just keep in mind that order matters in this file: if we put the darker gray <item> at the end of the list, it would never fire since the other two colors will take precedence. Now, to add the colors to the <SwitchCompat> tag, we add two attributes: android:thumbTint= and android:trackTint=. Both attributes will have the color file as their value; we're using two attributes since android:thumbTint= changes the color of the "ball" on the <SwitchCompat> tag, while android:trackTint= changes the color of the track the thumb moves along. With those additions, the <SwitchCompat> tag looks like this:

```
<androidx.appcompat.widget.SwitchCompat
  android:id="@+id/switch_player_type"
  android:layout_width="wrap_content"
  android:layout_height="wrap_content"
  android:checked="@={player.isHuman}"
  android:enabled="@{player.isIncluded}"
  android:visibility=
    "@{player.canBeToggled ? View.VISIBLE : View.INVISIBLE}"
  android:thumb="@drawable/ai_toggle_bg"
  android:thumbTint="@color/ai_toggle_color"
  android:trackTint="@color/ai_toggle_color"
  app:layout_constraintBottom_toBottomOf=
    "@id/edit_text_player_name"
  app:layout_constraintEnd_toEndOf="parent"
  app:layout_constraintTop_toTopOf="@id/edit_text_player_name" />
```

And now our app finally looks like this:

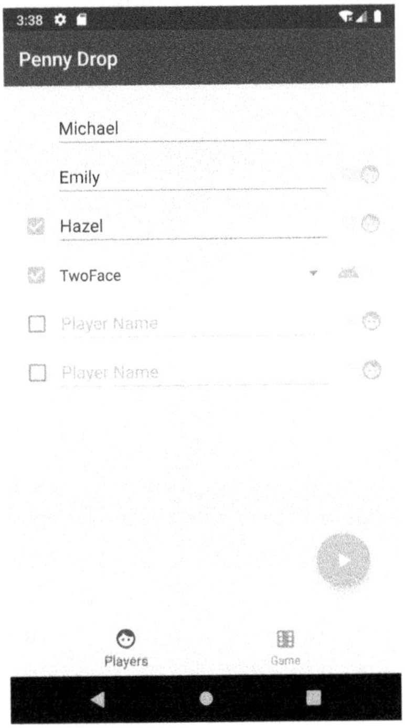

Ah, isn't that lovely? The app has a bit more personality, and it should be easier for our users to understand what's happening when they're setting up a game. We're at the point where we can send the players from the Pick Players screen into the Game screen and start a real game. We can do that once we create GameViewModel and send it the list of players.

Create Another ViewModel (Game)

This class will look similar to PickPlayersViewModel on a high level, but there's going to be a lot more going on here since this will handle the connection between the Game view and the GameHandler we'll be building in Chapter 4, Update LiveData with Conditional Game Logic, on page 91.

We're going to start with an empty GameViewModel class, and we can add the pieces in later on. It'll look like this:

```
package dev.mfazio.pennydrop.viewmodels

import androidx.lifecycle.ViewModel

class GameViewModel: ViewModel() {
  //Logic will go in here.
}
```

Once GameViewModel is available, we can add a List<Player> to hold everyone we added in the Pick Players view. We'll need a little setup before we can do that, though.

Add Players to the Game

To get the players into a game, we're going to need to do a few things: we need a Player class, we need the List<Player> that I mentioned a bit ago, and finally, we need a way to get players from the Pick Players view into GameViewModel. Let's walk through each of these steps now.

Create the Player Class

It may seem silly that we're going to create an entirely separate class, Player, when NewPlayer already exists. Why didn't I just make the Player class in the first place?

The reason for the two classes is that they serve two different purposes. The NewPlayer class is intended to figure out who's in the game and who they are (human vs. AI, what's their name or which AI), while Player will be for tracking the player's status in a game (currently rolling, pennies left, and so on). While we could have created a single large Player class with all these fields, going with the two separate classes is a better separation of concerns.

With that being said, the Player class will contain five properties: the player's name, whether or not they're human, the selected AI, whether or not they're currently rolling, and how many pennies they currently have.

All of the properties will have a default value, but only selectedAI can be null. Also, we're going to keep pennies and isRolling outside of the constructor since neither is likely to be set to something other than its default value upon initialization.

Finally, we want to add a function called addPennies() to the Player class. While it may seem overkill now, we'll have a situation later where we get an instance of a Player?, and trying to add to a property of a nullable type is a pain.

The full Player class code looks like this:

```
package dev.mfazio.pennydrop.types

import dev.mfazio.pennydrop.game.AI

data class Player(
    val playerName: String = "",
    val isHuman: Boolean = true,
    val selectedAI: AI? = null
) {
```

```
    var pennies: Int = defaultPennyCount

    fun addPennies(count: Int = 1) {
      pennies += count
    }

    var isRolling: Boolean = false

    companion object {
        const val defaultPennyCount = 10
    }
}
```

Note how we're using the defaultPennyCount value here inside our companion object like we would use a static read-only or constant value in Java.

To get our List<Player>, we need a way to convert a NewPlayer into a Player. The best spot to do this is a new function inside the NewPlayer class. This function will get the player's name (or name of the AI, if applicable), then map a few more values from NewPlayer:

```
fun toPlayer() = Player(
  if (this.isHuman.get()) {
    this.playerName
  } else {
     (this.selectedAI()?.name ?: "AI")
  },
  this.isHuman.get(),
  this.selectedAI()
)
```

With the Player class ready, we can move on to the GameViewModel and its List<Player>. We'll be both adding the property and getting the data from the Pick Players view.

Add Players to GameViewModel

Adding the players variable is the quick part, though it does use a new function, emptyList(). This function (unsurprisingly) gives us an empty instance of whatever type of List we're expecting. We could have just used listOf() here, but emptyList() is *slightly* more efficient and makes it clearer that we wanted an empty list and didn't just forget to populate a listOf() call. Plus, it's good for you to know that it exists.

Also, to plan ahead, we can create a new function inside GameViewModel called startGame(), which brings in the List<Player> and gets a game set up.

```
import androidx.lifecycle.MutableLiveData
import androidx.lifecycle.ViewModel
import dev.mfazio.pennydrop.types.Player
```

```
class GameViewModel : ViewModel() {
    private var players: List<Player> = emptyList()

    fun startGame(playersForNewGame: List<Player>) {
        this.players = playersForNewGame
        // More logic will be added here later.
    }
}
```

With that added, we can head into PickPlayersFragment to get the data sent over. Thankfully, using a ViewModel class makes this process much simpler. Inside PickPlayersFragment, we can bring in an instance of GameViewModel (just as we did with PickPlayersViewModel) and transfer over the players when someone clicks the Play button. We do this by mapping each NewPlayer to a Player via the toPlayer() function we created.

Note that since players is actually LiveData, we need to use pickPlayersViewModel.players.value to get out the List<NewPlayer>. Also, all value calls return a nullable instance of whatever it contains, so we need to have a fallback in case it's null, which will be an empty listOf(). In our case, it'll never be null, but we still need to handle the scenario.

Once we have the List<NewPlayer>, we want to filter each NewPlayer instance to make sure isIncluded is true, then convert each NewPlayer to a Player instance via the toPlayer() function. That conversion is done inside a map block, which creates a new List from another List after performing some kind of transformation on each element. Please note that the original list is never modified during this process but instead you're given a new List with all new items.

The last piece of the Play button functionality is to switch over to the GameFragment. Luckily, this is a single line call to grab the current NavController then navigate to the GameFragment via ID.

```
class PickPlayersFragment : Fragment() {
  private val pickPlayersViewModel
    by activityViewModels<PickPlayersViewModel>()
➤ private val gameViewModel by activityViewModels<GameViewModel>()

  override fun onCreateView(
    inflater: LayoutInflater, container: ViewGroup?,
    savedInstanceState: Bundle?
  ): View? {
    val binding = FragmentPickPlayersBinding
      .inflate(inflater, container, false)
      .apply {
        this.vm = pickPlayersViewModel

➤       this.buttonPlayGame.setOnClickListener {
➤         gameViewModel.startGame(
```

```
                pickPlayersViewModel.players.value
                ?.filter { newPlayer ->
                  newPlayer.isIncluded.get()
                }?.map { newPlayer ->
                  newPlayer.toPlayer()
                } ?: emptyList()
              )

              findNavController().navigate(R.id.gameFragment)
            }
          }

        return binding.root
      }
    }
```

With those changes, we now have gone from displaying info about the current players to sending them into the GameViewModel. If you want to confirm this, you can either set a breakpoint inside the GameViewModel startGame() function or add a Toast.makeText() call in there (both approaches are covered in Appendix 2, Troubleshooting Your App, on page 381). Now that we have players in the GameViewModel, we can work on getting things displayed on the screen from the ViewModel.

Add LiveData to GameViewModel

We've got a bunch of LiveData values to add here, which we'll then bind to components in layout_game.xml.

The values are as follows:

- slots: the six Slot objects with their current status.
- currentPlayer: the player that's currently rolling.
- canRoll: whether or not the current player can roll.
- canPass: whether or not the current player can pass (remember, players must roll at least once).
- currentTurnText: the info text on the bottom of the screen.
- currentStandingsText: the text of scores in the current game.

We'll look at the GameViewModel with all these LiveData objects in just a second, but we need to create the Slot class first.

```
package dev.mfazio.pennydrop.types

data class Slot(
    val number: Int,
```

```
    val canBeFilled: Boolean = true,
    var isFilled: Boolean = false,
    var lastRolled: Boolean = false
)
```

Whew, now that we're done with all that work, we can add all eight LiveData values to the GameViewModel. Most of the LiveData will just be holding Boolean flags (with their starting values), while the slots variable is the one particularly interesting part. Here, we're going to do something similar to what we did in Add NewPlayer Instances to PickPlayersViewModel, on page 61, with the (1..6).map { } block. This will create six Slot instances with their given slot number and the flag of canBeFilled, which is true for all but the last slot. Finally, we'll set the current player to the first player in the game, mark them as rolling, and set canRoll to true.

```
class GameViewModel : ViewModel() {
  private var players: List<Player> = emptyList()

  val slots =
      MutableLiveData(
          (1..6).map { slotNum -> Slot(slotNum, slotNum != 6) }
      )

  val currentPlayer = MutableLiveData<Player?>()

  val canRoll = MutableLiveData(false)
  val canPass = MutableLiveData(false)

  val currentTurnText = MutableLiveData("")
  val currentStandingsText = MutableLiveData("")

  fun startGame(playersForNewGame: List<Player>) {
      this.players = playersForNewGame
      this.currentPlayer.value =
        this.players.firstOrNull().apply {
          this?.isRolling = true
        }
      this.canRoll.value = true
  }
}
```

With all those LiveData values set up, we can head over and get everything bound together.

Bind ViewModel to a Fragment (Game)

We did most of the UI work here last chapter in Build Another Fragment (Game), on page 44, so there's less to worry about now. The first thing we need is to add a <variable> for GameViewModel called vm.

```
<layout xmlns:android="http://schemas.android.com/apk/res/android"
  xmlns:app="http://schemas.android.com/apk/res-auto"
  xmlns:tools="http://schemas.android.com/tools">

  <data>
    <variable
        name="vm"
        type="dev.mfazio.pennydrop.viewmodels.GameViewModel" />
  </data>

  <androidx.constraintlayout.widget.ConstraintLayout
      android:layout_width="match_parent"
      android:layout_height="match_parent"
      android:animateLayoutChanges="true"
      tools:context=".GameFragment">
    <!-- Previously created views are in here. -->
  </androidx.constraintlayout.widget.ConstraintLayout>
</layout>
```

Now that the vm <variable> exists in our layout, we can go back and complete the binding inside GameFragment. This will look similar to what we did in Bind PickPlayersViewModel, on page 65. We need to get an instance of GameViewModel, then apply() the GameViewModel binding.

While we're here, we'll also set a lifecycleOwner, which ensures our LiveData will update properly. We can send in the viewLifecycleOwner value that comes from the Fragment class. This tells the LiveData inside GameViewModel to follow the same life cycle (creation/disposal/and so on) as the entered life-cycle owner. In our case, that's the GameFragment.

Finally, the textCurrentTurnInfo.movementMethod assignment is still in here, too.

```
class GameFragment : Fragment() {
  private val gameViewModel by activityViewModels<GameViewModel>()

  override fun onCreateView(
    inflater: LayoutInflater, container: ViewGroup?,
    savedInstanceState: Bundle?
  ): View? {
    val binding = FragmentGameBinding
      .inflate(inflater, container, false)
      .apply {
          vm = gameViewModel

          textCurrentTurnInfo.movementMethod = ScrollingMovementMethod()

          lifecycleOwner = viewLifecycleOwner
      }

    return binding.root
  }
}
```

With the GameViewModel now bound to GameFragment, we can get all the bindings in place inside the layout. We're going to update the slots at the end since that requires updates in multiple files. Let's get everything done in here first before we move anywhere else.

Update fragment_game.xml Bindings

We're going to work our way down the layout (skipping the Slot views), updating each of the views to use the GameViewModel. First stop is the textCurrentPlayerName <TextView>. Here, we're going to use the name of the current player from the ViewModel by referencing vm.currentPlayer.playerName. In case we don't have a value for currentPlayer (like before a game's been started), we're also going to add a fallback string resource value called na (with the value N/A). The binding syntax (remember, this isn't Kotlin code, it's the syntax language) will look like this:

```
android:text='@{vm.currentPlayer.playerName ?? @string/na}'
```

Interestingly enough, if vm.currentPlayer is null, this expression is still fine. We don't have to include any additional checks; it'll just fall back to the @string/na string resource value.

The text for the textCurrentPlayerCoinsLeft <TextView> will be similar, though make sure to turn it into a String, as an Int will try to reference a string resource rather than the actual Int value.

```
android:text='@{vm.currentPlayer.pennies + ""}'
```

No binding is needed for textCoinsLeft; just make sure to create a string resource for the coin(s) left text, then use that instead of a hardcoded String.

```
android:text='@string/coins_left'
```

Skipping to the end of the layout file, the textCurrentTurnInfo box will have this binding:

```
android:text="@{vm.currentTurnText}"
```

and the textCurrentStandingsInfo will have this binding:

```
android:text="@{vm.currentStandingsText}"
```

With all those bindings done, our screen looks a bit more put together than it did before, as shown in the image on page 85.

The last piece here that we want to handle is the Roll and Pass buttons. I'm calling those out on their own since we have a few changes to make for each one.

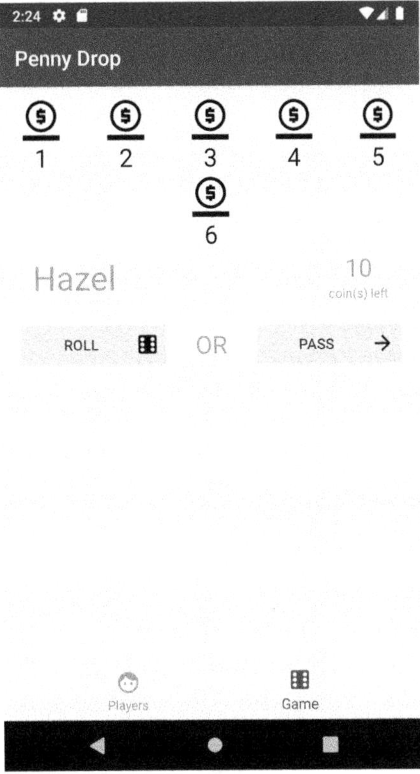

Update Button Bindings

Each button requires similar changes: we want to change the text and image colors to white, set whether or not the button is enabled, and set up conditional background color logic. We also need to add click handlers to each button.

Making things white will be straightforward enough, as we just need to add two attributes: `android:textColor=` and `android:drawableTint=` to each button. Both of those will have the value *@android:color/white*. The `android:enabled=` attribute will use the values from `vm.canRoll` or `vm.canPass`, depending on which button we're working with.

The background logic will be similar, as we're going to also use those `Slot` properties. However, here we'll be using a ternary statement to decide if the button is gray or a specific app color from `res/values/colors.xml`. The following code block is for the Roll button, but both buttons will be basically the same. The only real differences are which `Slot` property to use and that the Pass button is using `colorAccent` (instead of `colorPrimary`) for the background.

```
<Button
  android:layout_width="0dp"
  android:layout_height="wrap_content"
  android:layout_weight="3"
  android:background=
    "@{vm.canRoll ? @color/colorPrimary : @color/plainGray}"
  android:drawableEnd="@drawable/mdi_dice_6_black_24dp"
  android:drawableTint="@android:color/white"
  android:enabled="@{vm.canRoll}"
  android:onClick="@{() -> vm.roll()}"
  android:padding="10dp"
  android:text="@string/roll"
  android:textColor="@android:color/white" />
```

You'll need to add the @color/plainGray entry to res/values/colors.xml. I'm using #CCC, but you're free to use whatever you think will look good.

The last piece with the buttons is to add the roll() and pass() functions to GameViewModel. You probably saw in the code block for the Roll <Button> the android:onClick="@{() -> vm.roll()}" attribute. This is a listener binding, which means an expression that runs when an event occurs.

Inside a listener binding, we can add whatever we like, including references to other <variable> references in the binding. But as that's not necessary right now, we're left with a minimal expression.

Since the roll() and pass() functions don't yet exist, Android Studio is probably displaying an error right now, so let's create those quickly.

Both functions inside will be empty to start since we're going to add in the functionality during More GameViewModel Functions: roll() and pass(), on page 103:

```
fun roll() {
  // Implementing later
}

fun pass() {
  // Implementing later
}
```

The next step will be getting all the penny slots updated to use the data from the GameViewModel. We can even set up some test values in there to confirm things are working once all the bindings are complete.

Update Slot Bindings

Each of our slot <include> tags will change from something like app:slotNum=*"@{1}"* to app:slot=*"@{vm.slots[0]}"*. The full <include> tags will now look like this:

```
<include
  android:id="@+id/coinSlot1"
  layout="@layout/layout_coin_slot"
  android:layout_width="0dp"
  android:layout_height="wrap_content"
  android:layout_weight="1"
  app:slot="@{vm.slots[0]}" />
```

Then, in layout_coin_slot.xml, we can replace the slotNum <variable> with slot. This <variable> will reference our Slot class.

```
<data>
➤  <variable
➤      name="slot"
➤      type="dev.mfazio.pennydrop.types.Slot" />
</data>
```

With the new <variable> in place, we can start updating each item in layout_coin_slot.xml. We're going to go in reverse order since the slotNumberCoinSlot <TextView> is the quickest change. Here, we just need to update android:text= to use slot.number instead of slotNum and set the text color. We want all pieces of a slot to be our app's primary color (from res/values/colors.xml) if that was the slot last rolled by the player. Otherwise, everything should be black.

```
android:text='@{slot.number + ""}'
android:textColor=
  "@{slot.lastRolled ? @color/colorPrimary : @android:color/black}"
```

Next up is the bottomViewCoinSlot <View> and its android:background= property. We do effectively the same thing as we did with the slot text:

```
android:background=
  "@{slot.lastRolled ? @color/colorPrimary : @android:color/black}"
```

Now we can move back to the coinImageCoinSlot <ImageView>. This is basically set, but we don't currently have a way to dynamically show and hide the coin. In our Slot class, we have the canBeFilled and isFilled variables that can control this, so now we need to use them in our layout.

We could add a ternary statement for the android:visibility= attribute like we did with the colors, but this feels like a good time to introduce *binding adapters*.

Create Binding Adapters

Binding adapters allow you to effectively create new attributes on a layout view. Create a new package called binding and then a new file inside there called BindingAdapters. This shouldn't be a class, since we're just going to have stand-alone *package-level functions* in here. These are functions that aren't associated with a particular class but instead just live as part of a package. We can bring these into other classes by importing dev.mfazio.pennydrop.binding (or your equivalent package name).

Back to the binding adapters: these functions will bring in a View object and a property, then do something with those values. It's possible to avoid having custom logic in the binding adapter, but each of our functions will include custom logic, as we've got conditionals to consider.

For this block, we're going to create a new binding adapter function called bindIsHidden(), which will create a new app:isHidden= attribute on all views. Note that the name of the new attribute comes from the @BindingAdapter annotation associated with the function. The logic is similar to what we did before in the ternary statement:

```
import android.view.View
import androidx.databinding.BindingAdapter

@BindingAdapter("isHidden")
fun bindIsHidden(view: View, isInvisible: Boolean) {
    view.visibility = if (isInvisible) View.INVISIBLE else View.VISIBLE
}
```

Now we can head back to our coinImageCoinSlot <ImageView> to add this new attribute. We'll also set the color of the coin using the android:tint= attribute.

```
android:tint="@{slot.lastRolled ? @color/colorPrimary : @android:color/black}"
```

```
app:isHidden="@{!slot.canBeFilled || !slot.isFilled}"
```

With all the binding for our layout_coin_slot.xml layout completed, this is a great time to run the app and check things out. But since we're not doing anything with the Slot classes yet, the page won't look too interesting. So we're going to set up test data.

Inside the Slot, make two updates: isFilled should now default to true for even numbers, and lastRolled will be true for slots 2 and 5.

```
data class Slot(
    val number: Int,
    val canBeFilled: Boolean = true,
    var isFilled: Boolean = number % 2 == 0,
    var lastRolled: Boolean = number % 3 == 2
)
```

With these hardcoded values in place, we can see everything working in the app:

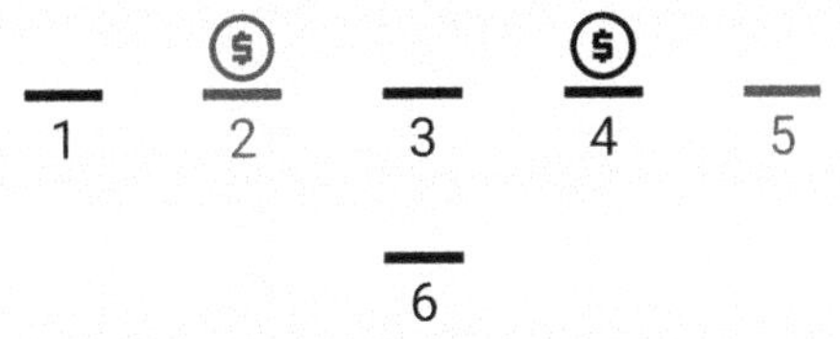

Before we move on, go back to the Slot class and remove the test values we put in there. In the next chapter, we're going to get the game logic working, so we won't need them. Better to revert things before we forget!

```
data class Slot(
    val number: Int,
    val canBeFilled: Boolean = true,
    var isFilled: Boolean = false,
    var lastRolled: Boolean = false
)
```

Summary and Next Steps

Believe it or not, the core UI is effectively complete for Penny Drop. We can enter the game's players, send them into the game, and display all the information needed. But we don't yet have any game logic built in. That's what we're doing next chapter, building out all the guts of Penny Drop. It's going to be a lot of Kotlin code and only a little bit of math—let's get to it!

CHAPTER 4

Update LiveData with Conditional Game Logic

Let's recap what we've done so far:

- Created our Penny Drop Android app and configured the Navigation component.
- Built both PickPlayersFragment and GameFragment with associated ViewModel classes and layout files.
- Set up data binding in both screens.

We're at the point where we have an app, and it *looks* like a game, but we need to get our game logic in place. To do that, we'll build a separate GameHandler class that will handle the game actions and leave the GameViewModel to take care of game state and UI interaction.

By doing this, the GameViewModel handles everything for the UI and where the game is at a given moment. The GameHandler class, on the other hand, will consist of stateless functions that take care of rolling and passing, then return a result to GameViewModel. This allows us to have most of the game logic isolated but also keep any Android-specific components out of GameHandler.

Once we're done with this chapter, we'll have a full, working game. Using the UI components we set up previously, we'll be able to handle real user interactions plus all the rules for Penny Drop.

Create GameHandler

As I mentioned earlier, GameHandler is where all our game logic is going to live. In this way, we greatly simplify what needs to be done within the GameViewModel and avoid causing too much bloat in that class. Given that GameHandler has no state of its own, we can define it as a Kotlin *object declaration* rather than a class. Similar to companion objects we saw in Create the AI Class, on page 69, object declarations are singleton instances. They look very similar to classes but instead use the object keyword, as you'll see.

In our case, GameHandler will be an object declaration with only functions (as it will not be holding any state) that we can use to run our game. Create that object (under the game package) with some empty functions:

```
package dev.mfazio.pennydrop.game

object GameHandler {

  fun roll(
    players: List<Player>,
    currentPlayer: Player,
    slots: List<Slot>
  ): TurnResult { }

  fun pass(
    players: List<Player>,
    currentPlayer: Player
  ): TurnResult { }

  private fun rollDie(sides: Int = 6) { ... }

  private fun nextPlayer(
    players: List<Player>,
    currentPlayer: Player
  ): Player { }
}
```

You can see the methods we'll be implementing in this section, which will then be (mostly) called by the GameViewModel. I say "mostly" because the GameHandler can always call its own methods as well, which we'll see near the end of the chapter.

Also, most of the functions return a TurnResult? object, which contains game statuses/information. We use this class to send that info back to the GameViewModel.

Let's create a new data class called TurnResult. This class will have everything the GameViewModel needs to know and no more. We can first get TurnResult out there, then worry about implementing the functions in GameHandler.

Create the TurnResult data class

The TurnResult class contains everything the GameViewModel needs to know after a turn (or for the start of the game). We'll look at how GameViewModel uses these values later on in this chapter, but let's look at the TurnResult code first:

```
package dev.mfazio.pennydrop.game

import dev.mfazio.pennydrop.types.Player

data class TurnResult(
    val lastRoll: Int? = null,
    val coinChangeCount: Int? = null,
    val previousPlayer: Player? = null,
    val currentPlayer: Player? = null,
    val playerChanged: Boolean = false,
    val turnEnd: TurnEnd? = null,
    val canRoll: Boolean = false,
    val canPass: Boolean = false,
    val clearSlots: Boolean = false,
    val isGameOver: Boolean = false
)

enum class TurnEnd { Pass, Bust, Win }
```

Not too much to consider here, but let's talk more about data class and enum class. We already used the data class designation for classes in Add NewPlayer data class, on page 59, but I want to call out two of the automatically generated functions that are included on every data class.

- copy(), which uses a given object as a base, then changes whichever values you send into the function:

  ```
  // filledSlot will have the same values as rolledSlot,
  //  but isFilled and lastRolled will be true
  val filledSlot = rolledSlot.copy(isFilled = true, lastRolled = true)
  ```

- componentN() functions, which allow for destructuring declarations (where properties can be split into multiple variables). For example, we can take the filledSlot object and split it into two separate values. The order is based on the order the properties are declared in the Slot class.

  ```
  val (slotNum, slotCanBeFilled) = filledSlot
  ```

Before we move on, let's dig into this last piece a bit more. As I mentioned, destructuring objects means we split an object into some number of variables. We already saw one example, but my favorite use case for destructuring declarations is when you're dealing with a loop and a Map.

If we take a Map<String, Int> where the String is a player's name and Int is their score, we traditionally would have to do something like this to print out the scores:

```
playerScores.forEach {entry ->
  println("${entry.key} - ${entry.value} pennies.")
}
```

Instead, we can split our entry into two variables, name and score, making this same block look much better:

```
playerScores.forEach {(name, score) ->
  println("$name - $score pennies.")
}
```

We're left with cleaner, more readable code and minimal overhead. We can destructure any objects that implement componentN() functions, including (but not limited to) data class, List, and Map objects. With data class covered, let's quickly check out what's going on with the TurnEnd enum class.

Create TurnEnd enum class

An enum class holds one or more constant values. In our case, TurnEnd contains the three ways a turn can be over: a user passes, a user busts (and takes the pennies on the board), and a user wins. The reason we're using TurnEnd instead of an Int or String value is because enum class objects are typed. This means instead of having turnEnd be an unclear Int value like 1 or a mistake-prone String like "pass", we use TurnEnd.Pass. It makes your code more readable and less prone to errors. The TurnEnd enum class will look like this:

```
enum class TurnEnd { Pass, Bust, Win }
```

With TurnResult ready, we can get back to implementing the GameHandler class.

Handle User Rolls

Quick reminder: rolling in Penny Drop consists of the current player taking a single *D6* (a six-sided die) and putting a penny in the slot that they roll. If that slot is taken, they bust and take *all* the coins currently on the board, then play passes to the next player. If they roll a six, they drop the penny into the open six slot which is kept in the reservoir. With a physical version of the game, the reservoir would be under the main board, but here we just remove the penny and optionally keep track of the number of pennies in the reservoir.

Our roll() function will do something similar: we'll roll the *D6*, grab the corresponding Slot, then send back a TurnResult based on what happened. We use the let() function on rollDie(), not as a null check (as we have previously) but rather as a way to have lastRoll be available to us for use in our next few lines of code. It's completely valid to do the same thing with a standard assignment like val lastRoll = rollDie(), but I like the let { ... } syntax. Again, it's personal preference for you and your team.

We end this section by grabbing the selected Slot and using that to generate the TurnResult. If the slot is null here, we use the *null-coalescing* or *Elvis operator* (?:) to fall back to a default TurnResult object.

The Elvis operator (named for the legendary musician and his legendary hair) is added after an expression, and if that expression is null, the expression on the right side of the Elvis operator is then executed.

The full code (minus the TurnResult generation) looks like this:

```
fun roll(players: List<Player>,
         currentPlayer: Player,
         slots: List<Slot>): TurnResult =
  rollDie().let { lastRoll ->
    slots.getOrNull(lastRoll - 1)?.let { slot ->
      // TurnResult is created here
    } ?: TurnResult(isGameOver = true)
  }
```

For reference, our rollDie() function takes in a number of sides and gives us a random number from 1 until our entered number of sides (plus one, which I'll explain in a minute). If we haven't entered a value for sides, the function uses the *default value* of 6.

```
private fun rollDie(sides: Int = 6) = Random.nextInt(1, sides + 1)
```

I want to call out something in particular with the function declaration of nextInt():

```
Random.nextInt(from: Int, until: Int) { ... }
```

This function will give us a random number starting with the value of from and up to (but not including) the value for until. The fact that the upper bound is non-inclusive is why rollDie() has the second value of sides + 1 instead of just sides. I'm mentioning this not only because it'll help with Random.nextInt() (and the other functions on the Random class) but because when you're dealing with ranges, until is a keyword there (as opposed to the parameters where until is a variable).

We used an IntRange when generating our Slot objects in the GameViewModel, a technique we first saw in Add NewPlayer Instances to PickPlayersViewModel, on page 61.

```
val slots =
  MutableLiveData(
    (1..6).map { slotNum -> Slot(slotNum, slotNum != 6) }
  )
```

We could have instead started with 0 and counted up to 6, but not actually include 6:

```
val slots =
  MutableLiveData(
    (0 until 6).map { ind -> Slot(ind + 1, ind != 5) }
  )
```

As both examples work, I would *highly* recommend going with the first approach here. Having until is definitely useful in other situations, though, which is why I mentioned it.

Before we move on, I want to also cover the slots logic from earlier. For reference, it's this block in particular:

```
slots.getOrNull(lastRoll - 1)?.let { slot ->
  // TurnResult is created here
} ?: TurnResult(isGameOver = true)
```

We're grabbing the rolled slot using the getOrNull() function, which either returns the slot at the given index or null. We then use the Elvis operator to only continue on if we have an actual slot. Given that we control how rollDie() works and what's in the List<Slot>, we'd probably be safe with just using get() or indexing (for example, slots[lastRoll - 1]). We're in control of what's going on—that means there's no way that call can fail, right?

Far too many devs have said something like this, only to have their app crash. To make sure that doesn't happen to us, let's use the safe approach by adding the null-safe ?.let() block. Now we can move on to the logic inside there.

As I mentioned at the beginning of this section, there are two primary outcomes for a roll: a player rolls the number of an empty slot (including 6) or they roll an already-filled slot. If they roll an empty slot, they put a penny in that slot (unless they roll a six, which goes into the reservoir), and we see if they won the game. As tempting as it is to use Kotlin's awesome when block here, we only have two sets of two choices, so a standard if...else will suffice. Don't worry, we'll discuss when statements later in this chapter when dealing with the game text.

The inside block that goes with our previous roll() code will be structured like this:

```
if (slot.isFilled) {
  // Player busts, play continues to next player
} else {
  if (!currentPlayer.penniesLeft(true)) {
      // Player wins
  } else {
      // Game continues
  }
}
```

While we still have blocks of code to complete here, we should first add penniesLeft() to our Player class.

Add a Helper Method to Player Class

The penniesLeft() function is straightforward, as it checks if a user's penny count is greater than zero. But notice the true flag in our call? That's a flag called subtractPenny, which tells our method to take one away from a user's penny count when checking if they have any pennies left. This is done because we're checking the future state for a user, meaning how many pennies they'll have *after* taking the current roll into consideration. The Player class will now look like this:

```
data class Player(
  var playerName: String = "",
  var isHuman: Boolean = true,
  var selectedAI: AI? = null
) {
  var pennies: Int = defaultPennyCount

  fun addPennies(count: Int = 1) {
    pennies += count
  }

  var isRolling: Boolean = false

  fun penniesLeft(subtractPenny: Boolean = false) =
      (pennies - (if(subtractPenny) 1 else 0)) > 0

  companion object {
      const val defaultPennyCount = 10
  }
}
```

Let's jump back to the GameHandler class. We'll go through the implementation details of roll() in a bit, but first, I want to highlight what's coming out of the nested let() blocks in that method.

Returning an if...else?

Yes, the inside block of roll() is an if...else block without a return statement. Yet, the TurnResult objects we create are returned successfully. How can this be? It's because of two language features in Kotlin. The inside of a lambda function, like inside a let(), will return the last value in the block. This includes values/variables and any expressions. Please note that normal functions can't do this, only expression blocks.

Speaking of which, the reason the if..else block can be returned is that they're actually *expressions* in Kotlin. This means they return a value themselves instead of just causing side effects like in other languages. We no longer have to declare an empty variable outside an if...else only to assign it inside, but instead can have immutable values assigned directly from the if...else block. This is also part of the reason the ternary operator ([condition] ? [if true] : [if false]) doesn't exist in Kotlin; if...else blocks can handle the same syntax without the need for two conventions. Using them also avoids nested ternary statements that can be extremely difficult to understand.

If you look at the penniesLeft() function we added, it's using if...else in a similar way. Instead of having to add an extra value like extraPennies or whatever we'd want to call it to remove the extra penny, we can just inline the if...else statement. You probably get the point by now, so let's move on to the code inside the if...else blocks.

Let's start with the block when the rolled Slot is already filled, since there's only one thing that happens here, the creation of a TurnResult object. To get the number of coins going to the player, we can see how many slots are already filled and assign that to coinChangeCount. We also get the next player in the list via the nextPlayer() function (which we'll look at in a second) and get things ready for a new turn. The code looks like this:

```
if (slot.isFilled) {
  TurnResult(
    lastRoll,
    coinChangeCount = slots.count { it.isFilled },
    clearSlots = true,
    turnEnd = TurnEnd.Bust,
    previousPlayer = currentPlayer,
    currentPlayer = nextPlayer(players, currentPlayer),
    playerChanged = true,
    canRoll = true,
    canPass = false
  )
}
```

While we don't need to have the parameters explicitly listed out here, it makes this call much clearer. Otherwise, we'd be looking at a whole bunch of Boolean values trying to remember which is which. This is another personal-preference situation, but I think the labels make the code more readable.

Grab the Next Player

We saw the nextPlayer() function call in the TurnResult class, so let's dig into that now.

We're doing three things in this method:

- Get the index of the current player in the list of players.
- Figure out the next player's index (which may wrap around).
- Return the next player.

```
private fun nextPlayer(
  players: List<Player>,
  currentPlayer: Player): Player? {
    val currentIndex = players.indexOf(currentPlayer)
    val nextIndex = (currentIndex + 1) % players.size

    return players[nextIndex]
}
```

indexOf() will give us the position of our current player (from zero to the number of players in the game minus one), which we can then use to find the next player in turn order. In most cases, we take the current index, add one (to move to the next player), and we're ready. However, if we reach the end of the player list, we want to swing back around to the beginning of the list. That's why I included the second half the expression: % players.size.

The % operator is the *modulo* or *remainder* operator, which divides the left-hand value by the right-hand value but returns the left-over amount (the remainder) rather than the actual result. This means our index can never be higher than the number of players in the game and will wrap back around to zero if the index is higher than the limit.

For example, if we have five players in our game, player four is playing and their turn ends, player five would be up. As a result, currentIndex is 3 (since indexes start at 0), players.size is 5, and nextIndex is 4:

```
val nextIndex = (3 + 1) % 5 // 4 % 5 == 4
```

The % operator doesn't do much here, but if player five's turn ends and we need to swing back to player one, things could be trickier. currentIndex is 4 and adding one to that would put the index outside of the bounds of players (since indexes are going from 0 to 4). Adding % makes nextIndex 0 since there's no remainder when dividing five by five.

```
val nextIndex = (4 + 1) % 5 // 5 % 5 == 0
```

One last item of note is that the % operator is equivalent to the .rem() function, meaning the following code is equivalent to what we did before:

```
val nextIndex = (currentIndex + 1).rem(players.size)
```

You can use either the function or operator interchangeably, and even overload an operator by overloading its associated function. This is outside the scope of this book, but more info can be found at https://link.mfazio.dev/operator-overloading.

We're now set if the player rolls a slot number that already has a penny, so we can move to open slots.

Handle an Open Slot

If the current Player rolls an open slot number (including the 6), the logic will differ a bit. We use the penniesLeft() function we saw earlier to see if the current player has won, but otherwise both of these TurnResult instances are straightforward.

```
} else {
  if (!currentPlayer.penniesLeft(true)) {
    TurnResult(
      lastRoll,
      currentPlayer = currentPlayer,
      coinChangeCount = -1,
      isGameOver = true,
      turnEnd = TurnEnd.Win,
      canRoll = false,
      canPass = false
    )
  } else {
    TurnResult(
      lastRoll,
      currentPlayer = currentPlayer,
      canRoll = true,
      canPass = true,
      coinChangeCount = -1
    )
  }
}
```

With those changes in place, we're set on logic for when players roll on their turn. Now, we can move on to when players pass their turn.

Handle Users Passing

We've addressed the possibilities when a user rolls in Penny Drop. Now we can address the scenario where the current player has rolled at least once on their turn, decides "Nah, I'm good," and passes to the next player.

Since we don't have to handle a roll result, less will be going on when a user passes. Here's the entire function:

```
fun pass(players: List<Player>, currentPlayer: Player) =
  TurnResult(
      previousPlayer = currentPlayer,
      currentPlayer = nextPlayer(players, currentPlayer),
      playerChanged = true,
      turnEnd = TurnEnd.Pass,
      canRoll = true,
      canPass = false
  )
```

Looks similar enough to roll(), right? We're still returning a TurnResult, plus marking the next player as able to roll but not pass (since it's the first roll of their turn), and we're grabbing the next player in the game. We also include the previousPlayer so the UI can update the text view properly with a message like "Michael passed. They currently have 7 pennies."

With that, the GameHandler is mostly ready and we can start updating the UI.

Start a Game

In Penny Drop, two primary pieces are tracked: the players and the slots. We added both of these to GameViewModel last chapter, so all we need to do is initialize them when starting a game. Since we have the players for the game, we can grab the first player in the list and set them as the currentPlayer. We're also going to initialize two other variables, canRoll (true) and canPass (false). Finally, we're going to clear out the Slots, set the currentTextValue to "The game has begun!", and generate the standings for the game.

```
fun startGame(playersForNewGame: List<Player>) {
  this.players = playersForNewGame
  this.currentPlayer.value = this.players.firstOrNull().apply {
      this?.isRolling = true
  }

  canRoll.value = true
  canPass.value = false

  slots.value?.clear()
  slots.notifyChange()
```

```
    currentTurnText.value = "The game has begun!\n"
    currentStandingsText.value = generateCurrentStandings(this.players)
}
```

We'll cover the generateCurrentStandings() function in a bit, but I want to talk about the slots section first, as there may be some confusion as to what's going on. We'll take a quick look at both lines and what each part means.

As slots is a MutableLiveData object, we need to call .value to get the actual List<Slot>. Also, every value that comes out of a LiveData object will be nullable, which is why the next clear() call uses the null-safe syntax we first saw back in Wait, What Was That Code Block?, on page 39.

As far as the clear() function, it's actually an *extension function* added to the List type inside of Slot.kt. This is the same file where the Slot class lives, but the extension function is defined *outside* of the Slot class itself. Since it's an extension on Slot and not part of the Slot class itself, we can put the code anywhere that makes sense. I chose the Slot class since it's an extension on that class and will make the code easier to find. The code looks like this:

```
// Slot.kt
package dev.mfazio.pennydrop.types

data class Slot(
  val number: Int,
  val canBeFilled: Boolean = true,
  var isFilled: Boolean = false,
  var lastRolled: Boolean = false
)

//START_HIGHTLIGHT
fun List<Slot>.clear() = this.forEach { slot ->
  slot.isFilled = false
  slot.lastRolled = false
}
```

The other slots-related callout is the slots.notifyChange() function. If we update the .value of a LiveData object, it'll automatically send an event to all listeners with the update. But if we update something *inside* of .value, nothing happens.

To give a specific example, if we call slots.value = listOf<Slot>(), the UI would be updated automatically (and we'd lose our slots on the screen). However, if we do something like slots.value?.clear() as we did in startGame(), the UI update event isn't sent. So we need to force that update to occur. I'm using .notifyChange(), which is a quick extension function to fire off a LiveData event:

```
private fun <T> MutableLiveData<List<T>>.notifyChange() {
  this.value = this.value
}
```

I've added this function at the end of GameViewModel, and yes, it's kind of a hack. But given the nature of LiveData, it's what we have to do if we just want to change properties on a class—especially when the LiveData contains a List.

Now, going back to the generateCurrentStandings() function. This function brings in a List<Player>, sorts it by the player's current penny count, then use joinToString() to bring everything together. If you read Appendix 2, Troubleshooting Your App, on page 381, you saw an example of this function in use. If not, the quick version is that it takes in a Collection of some kind and generates a String using each item. We also can send in values for how to separate each item plus both prefix and postfix values. In our case, we want to separate each item by a newline character (\n) and append a header to the list. Usually that header will be Current Standings, but for the sake of reuse, we make it configurable.

```
private fun generateCurrentStandings(
  players: List<Player>,
  headerText: String = "Current Standings:"
) =
  players.sortedBy { it.pennies }.joinToString(
    separator = "\n",
    prefix = "$headerText\n"
  ) {
    "\t${it.playerName} - ${it.pennies} pennies"
  }
```

More GameViewModel Functions: roll() and pass()

I've pushed it off long enough; let's finally look at what's happening with all those TurnResult objects we've been creating. We're adding or updating three functions in the GameViewModel: roll(), pass(), and updateFromGameHandler(result: TurnResult). The latter method will be called in the first two functions to set our LiveData values accordingly.

We'll get to the updateFromGameHandler() piece in a minute, but first I want to address the roll() and pass() functions, as both have similar implementations to each other. Both functions will get the current player (the first with isRolling as true), make sure the resulting Player? object is not null, check if the requested move is valid, then call the GameHandler. The response from the GameHandler function will then be sent into the updateFromGameHandler() function. In addition, the roll() function will get the game's current slots and send those along to the GameHandler. The code for both functions looks like this:

```
fun roll() {
  slots.value?.let { currentSlots ->
    // Comparing against true saves us a null check
```

```
    val currentPlayer = players.firstOrNull { it.isRolling }
    if (currentPlayer != null && canRoll.value == true) {
      updateFromGameHandler(
          GameHandler.roll(players, currentPlayer, currentSlots)
      )
    }
  }
}

fun pass() {
  val currentPlayer = players.firstOrNull { it.isRolling }
  if (currentPlayer != null && canPass.value == true) {
    updateFromGameHandler(GameHandler.pass(players, currentPlayer))
  }
}
```

By now, a lot of this syntax should look familiar. But the use of .value may look odd. With slots.value, we're using a null-safe call to let() since we're getting the (nullable) value out of a LiveData object. This is the reason for the slightly strange conditional statements in each function, too. We can't just use canRoll.value and canPass.value on their own since they're technically not Boolean objects but rather Boolean? objects. Luckily, instead of having to do a null check then check the Boolean value, we can compare against true. By doing this, a value of false or null will both fail and we skip going to the GameHandler. It's a handy shortcut that gets us the exact functionality we want.

With both actions in place, we can get to the core piece of GameViewModel: the updateFromGameHandler() function.

Update the UI

We're finally here! Once the UI can display what happened in the GameHandler, then we'll have a fully working game. Let's get a quick overview of what's going to happen in here: we'll add/remove the current player's pennies, mark the proper player as rolling, update the slots, generate turn and standings text, change canRoll/canPass flags, and finally handle game-over scenarios if applicable.

```
private fun updateFromGameHandler(result: TurnResult) {
  if (result.currentPlayer != null) {
    currentPlayer.value?.addPennies(result.coinChangeCount ?: 0)
    currentPlayer.value = result.currentPlayer
    this.players.forEach { player ->
        player.isRolling = result.currentPlayer == player
    }
  }
```

```
  if (result.lastRoll != null) {
    slots.value?.let { currentSlots ->
        updateSlots(result, currentSlots, result.lastRoll)
    }
  }

  currentTurnText.value = generateTurnText(result)
  currentStandingsText.value = generateCurrentStandings(this.players)

  canRoll.value = result.canRoll
  canPass.value = result.canPass

  if (!result.isGameOver && result.currentPlayer?.isHuman == false) {
    canRoll.value = false
    canPass.value = false
  }
}
```

As we saw in the last chapter, we're getting both the player's name and their current coin count from the currentPlayer, so we can just update the MutableLiveData<Player> value from the TurnResult. Most of the other pieces should make sense, but updateSlots() and generateTurnText() have more going on. We'll start off with updateSlots(), which brings in the TurnResult plus the current state of the Slots and the last roll to update everything we need from a UI perspective.

```
private fun updateSlots(
    result: TurnResult,
    currentSlots: List<Slot>,
    lastRoll: Int
) {
  if (result.clearSlots) {
    currentSlots.clear()
  }

  currentSlots.firstOrNull { it.lastRolled }?.apply { lastRolled = false }

  currentSlots.getOrNull(lastRoll - 1)?.also { slot ->
      if (!result.clearSlots && slot.canBeFilled) slot.isFilled = true

      slot.lastRolled = true
  }

  slots.notifyChange()
}
```

We saw currentSlots.clear() and slots.notifyChange() earlier in the chapter, but we can chat about a couple of other pieces. firstOrNull() and getOrNull() here are similar to each other. We're grabbing an item from our List<Slot>, either the first item to return true for a given expression (firstOrNull()) or via an index we send in (getOrNull()). If either search fails, we get back null and the attached blocks are skipped (due to the ?.apply() and ?.also() calls).

Speaking of which, let's talk about the .also { ... } function, which at first glance probably looks similar to .let { ... }. Turns out they *are* similar. The only real difference is that .let returns a value from its subsequent block whereas .also { ... } returns this, which is the object .also { ... } was called on. Since we're not using the returned value here, we could use either function, but it was a good opportunity to bring up the also() function.

With the code in updateSlots(), our slots will reflect the changes coming from the GameHandler. Now we can move on to the TextView holding the informational text for the current turn.

Create Turn Summary Text

We added the large <TextView> near the bottom of the Game screen in the previous chapter to give users info about the current turn, how a turn ends, and a summary of scores when a game ends. Right now, when a turn starts, that area says nothing. And once a turn ends, that area then says...nothing. Yes, that value's still empty from the previous chapter and is, well, useless. Let's fix that!

We already have this block of code inside updateFromGameHandler():

```
//result is a TurnResult object
currentTurnText.value = generateTurnText(result)
```

As a result, we have two main additions:

- A clearText variable, which tells us if we should clear the <TextView>.
- A new generateTurnText() method.

Step one should be done about...now (seriously, go ahead and quickly add the variable under the currentStandingsText declaration). Step two, however, gets a bit more complex. We're going to be displaying different messages based on what's happening with a given turn.

Let's address everything in the function *except* the new text, then deal with the messages. The function has three primary pieces: clear out the existing text if the previous event was the end of a turn, flag if the next set of text should be on a cleared view, and display the next set of text.

```
private fun generateTurnText(result: TurnResult): String {
  if (clearText) currentTurnText.value = ""
  clearText = result.turnEnd != null

  val currentText = currentTurnText.value ?: ""
  val currentPlayerName = result.currentPlayer?.playerName ?: "???"
```

```
  return when {
      //TurnResult-based logic and text
  }
}
```

Nothing earth-shattering here, so we'll move on to the when statement.

Handle Multiple Conditionals with when Statements

For the uninitiated, a when is similar to switch statements in Java, C#, and other languages. when blocks are a list of conditional expressions that return a Boolean and then some action that's executed if the conditional is true. Each conditional line is executed in order, and if none of them result in a true value, an else expression is run.

```
when {
  result.isGameOver -> //Game's over, let's get a summary
  result.turnEnd == TurnEnd.Bust -> //Player busted, got some pennies
  result.turnEnd == TurnEnd.Pass -> //Player passed.
  result.lastRoll != null -> //Roll text
  else -> ""
}
```

Note that the when block isn't *quite* complete; I excluded the actual text logic so we can focus on the conditionals. Keep in mind that instead of the comments I have in my example, you would have some expression to be run.

A couple of quick notes about when blocks:

- You can include a variable with the when call to have each line reference the same object:

  ```
  val slotIsFilled = when(rollResult) {
    in 1..5 -> true
    6 -> false
    else -> throw IllegalArgumentException("That's not a D6.")
  }
  ```

- If you want to run multiple lines of code for a given condition, you can always add braces around any of the expressions:

  ```
  val slotIsFilled = when(rollResult) {
    in 1..5 -> true
    6 -> false
    else -> {
        val message = "That's not a D6."
        throw IllegalArgumentException(message)
    }
  }
  ```

- If you're using Kotlin 1.3 and above (which you should be), you can also add an inline variable to your when function:

```
val slotIsFilled = when(val rollResult = rollDie()) {
  in 1..5 -> true
  6 -> false
  else -> {
      val message = "That's not a D6."
      throw IllegalArgumentException(message)
  }
}
```

Feel free to use whichever text you want for all of the conditions other than result.isGameOver. Most of the conditional expressions in our when will look like the following block:

```
result.lastRoll != null ->
  "$currentText\n$currentPlayerName rolled a ${result.lastRoll}."
```

We're using *string interpolation* to include variables in our text with a $ symbol and curly braces. We use whatever was already in the text box as the beginning (inside currentText), then add on our new line of information. Here, we're adding something like "Michael rolled a 4." to the info box, depending on the variables sent in.

However, the result.isGameOver text has more to it:

```
result.isGameOver ->
  """
  |Game Over!
  |$currentPlayerName is the winner!
  |
  |${generateCurrentStandings(this.players, "Final Scores:\n")}
  }}
  """.trimMargin()
```

The triple-quote syntax is a *raw string*, which allows us to put in text without any escaping or need for newline characters. As you can see, we can still interpolate variables, but we don't need to be throwing in a ton of newline characters (\n) to display our lines.

The other weird part here is the pipe (|) character, which is a *margin prefix*. This character denotes where the beginning of the line will be rather than the first column in the code. We can customize the margin prefix character by sending something else into the trimMargin() function, just in case you want to include a | character in your String. Having the margin prefix in place keeps our output looking like this:

```
Game Over!
Hazel is the winner!

Final Scores:
    Hazel - 0 pennies.
    Emily - 3 pennies.
    Michael - 12 pennies.
```

Without the margin prefix, we'd get this:

```
        Game Over!
            Hazel is the winner!

            Final Scores:
              Hazel - 0 pennies.
Emily - 3 pennies.
Michael - 12 pennies.
```

Believe it or not, the GameViewModel is ready to go, and we can start with Penny Drop! But before we run off to play, let's address one more cool feature. Remember in Chapter 2 how we added the toggle for a human vs. AI player? We've been ignoring that piece and the isHuman flag so far, but no more. Let's get some "intelligent" computer players in our game.

Handle AI Turns with Coroutines and First-Class Functions

We're going to add the ability for the app to run one (or more) of the players in the game and give users the option to have Penny Drop be a single-(human-)player game. When the AI is playing, we're going to disable both the Roll and Pass buttons and have the app start rolling/passing on its own. A handy way to trigger this is from the updateFromGameHandler() function once everything else is updated. Add a call to playAITurn() near the end of that function:

```
if (!result.isGameOver && result.currentPlayer?.isHuman == false) {
  canRoll.value = false
  canPass.value = false
  playAITurn()
}
```

We're only going to have a player be run by the app if we're sure it's *not* human. We're using the same approach we did earlier with our LiveData, where we compare against false as result.currentPlayer?.isHuman is a Boolean? rather than a Boolean.

The playAITurn() function in the GameViewModel is our first example of Kotlin *coroutines*. However, I don't want to get into them too much here since there's too much to discuss in one section. If you want to see more, we're going to use them again in Chapter 5, Persist Game Data with Room, on page 115, and especially in Chapter 10, Load and Save Data with Coroutines and Room, on page 235. For the sake of this example, just know there's an existing viewModelScope due to us including the lifecycle-livedata-ktx library. We launch the coroutine in here, which then allows us to make asynchronous calls without freezing up the UI for the user. In this case, we're delaying for a second between AI moves to make it feel more like a real person is playing the game. Again, we'll cover coroutines more in-depth later on, but this was a perfect opportunity to include them.

We launch our coroutine, wait for a second (1000 milliseconds), then call GameHandler.playAITurn() (which we'll create shortly). The approach here is similar to both roll() and pass(), but with a slight difference. We're calling GameHandler.playAITurn(), then using a null-safe let() call to handle scenarios where we get back null rather than a TurnResult instance. This can happen if we try to play an AI turn with a player that's missing a valid selectedAI property.

```
private fun playAITurn() {
  viewModelScope.launch {
    delay(1000)
    slots.value?.let { currentSlots ->
      val currentPlayer = players.firstOrNull { it.isRolling }

      if(currentPlayer != null && !currentPlayer.isHuman) {
        GameHandler.playAITurn(
          players,
          currentPlayer,
          currentSlots,
          canPass.value == true
        )?.let { result ->
          updateFromGameHandler(result)
        }
      }
    }
  }
}
```

Once the turn's done and the UI is updated, the check from the beginning of this section will be run again to see if we execute playAITurn() again. Most of the AI logic lives in GameHandler, so let's head over there to get this working.

Inside GameHandler, we need to add the playAITurn() function. In there, we need to *safely* grab the current player's selectedAI property, meaning we must add in some kind of null check. Once we have a valid AI instance, we figure out if that AI will roll or pass based on the currently filled slots.

```
fun playAITurn(
  players: List<Player>,
  currentPlayer: Player,
  slots: List<Slot>,
  canPass: Boolean = false
): TurnResult? =
  currentPlayer.selectedAI?.let { ai ->
    if (!canPass || ai.rollAgain(slots)) {
      roll(players, currentPlayer, slots)
    } else {
      pass(players, currentPlayer)
    }
  }
```

For reference, ai.rollAgain(slots) is a function on each AI instance. We update the AI to include a rollAgain property in the following format:

```
data class AI(
  val name: String,
➤ val rollAgain: (slots: List<Slot>) -> Boolean
) {
```

This means rollAgain refers to a function that brings in a List<Slot> as a parameter and returns a Boolean value. Specifically, we've got a function for each AI that makes some kind of calculation based on the current Slot values and returns whether or not that AI player wants to roll. Functions in Kotlin are *first-class*, meaning they can be used like any other variables. This allows us to send an implementation for the rollAgain() function when we initialize an AI object.

For example, the AI player Fearful Fred will only roll again if there are two or fewer slots filled (unless it's the first roll of his turn and he doesn't have a choice). We can generate this AI player like this (other AI implementations can be found in the code from the PragProg site[1]):

```
AI("Fearful Fred") { slots -> slots.fullSlots() <= 2 }
```

Notice that instead of putting the function as the second parameter inside the AI constructor, we can instead just include it inside brackets *after* the constructor. This is the case with all types where the last (or only) parameter is a function.

Now, when our playAITurn() function sends the current game's slots into the rollAgain() method for Fearful Fred, it'll run the entered expression to see if they want to roll or not. We could get as complicated as we want with the roll/don't-roll logic, but this works fine for our purposes. We call the .fullSlots() extension

1. https://pragprog.com/titles/mfjetpack/kotlin-and-android-development-featuring-jetpack

function and see if that value is 2 or less. The fullSlots() function, which lives inside Slot.kt but *outside* the Slot class, looks like this:

```
fun List<Slot>.fullSlots(): Int =
  this.count { it.canBeFilled && it.isFilled }
```

Now that playAITurn() in GameHandler is ready, this game is good to go. Humans can take their turns, AI "players" are ready, and we can play our game without issue.

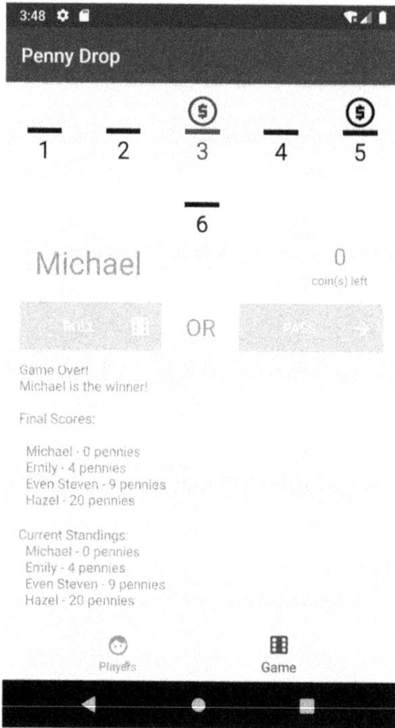

Summary and Next Steps

We accomplished a lot in this chapter! We implemented all the game logic for Penny Drop plus connected the GameHandler to the UI. Plus, since the game logic is isolated in the GameHandler, our GameFragment and GameViewModel classes didn't expand as much as they could have. That being said, keeping the state inside the GameViewModel class makes later code changes easier, as you'll see next chapter.

Also, most of what we did in this chapter isn't even Android-specific but rather illustrates how Kotlin can be used to write clearer code. Taking advantage of various language features like scope functions (.let {...} and .apply { ... }), destructuring declarations, and when expressions can make your code more readable and maintainable. This goes for other Android apps as well as any non-Android Kotlin applications.

Now, the game works beautifully, but there's one small issue: you can't resume games if you close the app. Oh, and it doesn't save the players from previous games. Or track any kind of stats. Actually, it doesn't keep track of anything...

We could use some persistence in our app, and thankfully Jetpack has a great option for us: Room. Room is a wrapper over SQLite that makes database interaction *much* nicer. Next chapter, we'll get into Room, set up our database, and start saving our games of Penny Drop.

CHAPTER 5

Persist Game Data with Room

So far in this book, we've built a fine Penny Drop app. You've learned about Android views, navigation, ViewModel classes, and how they all fit together. The last main piece we need to add is some kind of persistence so our game keeps track of what players have done.

Database interaction with SQLite in Android apps has traditionally been...unpleasant. It took a great deal of work to create a database, there was no query validation, and you had to manually convert data from a Cursor class into your Java or Kotlin objects. Thankfully, a core piece of Jetpack is the introduction of Room, a persistance library created on top of SQLite. You're able to do all the things you could before with on-device databases, just much more smoothly.

In this chapter, you'll learn how to create a SQLite database via Room, how to add tables via Entity classes, and how to connect your database to your Fragment views via ViewModel classes. But before we do all that, we need to add the Room library to our app.

Add Room to the App

This process should look familiar by now. We add a new value under the ext block in the project-level build.gradle file:

```
ext {
  kotlin_version = '1.4.30'
  gradle_version = '4.1.2'

  app_compat_version = '1.2.0'
  constraint_layout_version = '2.0.4'
  core_version = '1.3.2'
  lc_version = '2.3.0'
  nav_version = '2.3.3'
  room_version = '2.3.0-beta01'
}
```

We then add the library artifacts inside the dependencies in the app's build.gradle file. We need to add three different dependencies to do what we want: one for the Room runtime, one for Kotlin extensions and coroutines support in Room, and one for annotation processing:

```
dependencies {
  // Other dependencies still live up here.
➤   implementation "androidx.room:room-ktx:$room_version"
➤   implementation "androidx.room:room-runtime:$room_version"
➤
➤   kapt "androidx.room:room-compiler:$room_version"
}
```

With those added, sync your project and we can add the PennyDropDatabase to the app.

Add a RoomDatabase Class

The PennyDropDatabase is at the core of everything we're doing with Room. This is where we can define our database tables (via Entity classes), set up versioning, and even include some initialization logic. However, our database interactions won't be done directly against the PennyDropDatabase but rather via the PennyDropDao class (which we'll create in a bit).

Create a new class inside the data package called PennyDropDatabase; remember that you can include the package name when creating a class in Android Studio. Once this is created, mark the class as abstract right away and make RoomDatabase its parent class. The last piece is to add the @Database annotation, which tells Room this class is a RoomDatabase and will hold the database configuration. The empty class looks like this:

```
package dev.mfazio.pennydrop.data

import androidx.room.RoomDatabase

@Database(
  // We'll add the Entity classes in a bit.
  entities = [],
  version = 1,
  exportSchema = false
)
abstract class PennyDropDatabase: RoomDatabase() {
  // Adding this next.
}
```

The PennyDropDatabase class is going to end up looking a bit odd. We only have a single abstract function called pennyDropDao(), which returns an instance of the yet-to-be-created PennyDropDao class, and a companion object. The companion object will have a single PennyDropDatabase? variable called Instance and a function called getDatabase(). The getDatabase() function will take in two parameters—the curent Android Context object and a CoroutineScope, used for inserting data into the database upon initialization. The pre-implementation class looks like this:

```
@Database(
  entities = [],
  version = 1,
  exportSchema = false
)
abstract class PennyDropDatabase : RoomDatabase() {
  abstract fun pennyDropDao(): PennyDropDao

  companion object {
    @Volatile
    private var instance: PennyDropDatabase? = null

    fun getDatabase(
      context: Context,
      scope: CoroutineScope
    ): PennyDropDatabase {
      // We'll implement this in a minute.
    }
  }
}
```

Before we move on, I want to call out the @Volatile annotation. This tells the JVM to make assignments to the instance variable visible to all threads. This will help us avoid any inconsistencies across processes in our app, which is especially useful since coroutines can be processed on different threads.

The getDatabase() function is going to serve two purposes. It will always return the current instance of the database, but if the database instance has not yet been created, this function can handle that as well. We'll attempt to return the current instance first, but if it's null, then we'll build the database inside of a synchronized() block. This block ensures that we only create a single instance of our PennyDropDatabase even if there are multiple calls to getDatabase().

getDatabase() uses Room.databaseBuilder() to create the database, which we'll then assign to instance. All we need to send in is the context parameter, the Class object from PennyDropDatabase, and a name for the database (we'll use PennyDrop-Database).

To send in a class reference, we need to use the *class/member reference operator*, which is denoted by ::. Meaning, to get a KClass (Kotlin class) reference for PennyDropDatabase, we use PennyDropDatabase::class.

Now, the catch here is that we're sending in the Java class from PennyDropDatabase rather than the Kotlin class. This is because the Room.databaseBuilder() function was written with Java and therefore expects a Java class. To get the Java version of our class, we can use PennyDropDatabase::class.java. The interoperability between Java and Kotlin makes things tricky sometimes, but thankfully, situations like this are easy enough. The initial getDatabase() function looks like this:

```
fun getDatabase(
  context: Context,
  scope: CoroutineScope
): PennyDropDatabase =
  this.instance ?: synchronized(this) {
    val instance = Room.databaseBuilder(
      context,
      PennyDropDatabase::class.java,
      "PennyDropDatabase"
    ).build()

    this.instance = instance

    instance //This is returned from the synchronized block.
  }
```

With that, we have almost everything we need for the PennyDropDatabase. Your editor should be complaining because we've yet to create the PennyDropDao class, and we still need to create Entity classes, but the main parts of this class are ready. We can start by creating the PennyDropDao class, then move on to the Entity classes that will be mapped to database tables.

Create a DAO Class

As I mentioned before, we're not going to be calling the PennyDropDatabase directly to get our data but will instead send everything through a DAO, or *data access object*. We mark an interface or abstract class as a DAO via the @Dao annotation. Most of the work with PennyDropDao will be handled by the Room library, leaving us to only worry about custom actions as needed. A majority of the functions in the DAO will be abstract with a particular annotation to give the function a purpose. If we need more control over what a function does, we can still write full SQL queries as well. In our case, we only need a single @Query function, with the other functions either using the @Insert or @Update annotations. The PennyDropDao abstract class with a couple of functions looks like this:

```
@Dao
abstract class PennyDropDao {
  @Query("SELECT * FROM players WHERE playerName = :playerName")
  abstract fun getPlayer(playerName: String): Player?
```

```
  @Insert
  abstract suspend fun insertGame(game: Game): Long

  @Insert
  abstract suspend fun insertPlayer(player: Player): Long

  @Insert
  abstract suspend fun insertPlayers(players: List<Player>): List<Long>

  @Update
  abstract suspend fun updateGame(game: Game)
}
```

As you can see, standard actions like inserting and updating of records can be done via the included annotations as seen in this block, while queries or any kind of custom action are written inside the @Query annotation. This includes running SELECT and UPDATE statements against the DB.

In particular, notice the use of the playerName *named bind parameter* in the query. Room allows us to send parameters in an @Query function which will then be used in the statement sent to our DB.

Also of note here is the suspend modifier. This means the function can be started/stopped at any point and requires the function be called either in another suspend function or from a coroutine. We'll see more about how this works in Access the Database from a ViewModel, on page 133.

Our PennyDropDatabase should be much happier now that PennyDropDao exists, but now PennyDropDao is angry because Game doesn't exist. Also, if you tried to remove the Game-related calls and run the app, Room wouldn't like trying to insert Player objects since Player isn't yet an entity. It's time to add some Entity classes to the app.

Add Entity Classes

Entity classes are the tables in our Room database. By adding the @Entity annotation and a bit of configuration, we can convert a normal data class into a Room Entity. In case you're wondering, we'll be putting all the new classes in the data package.

We're going to start with the Game that was used in the PennyDropDao class. This class will hold all the required information about a given game of Penny Drop but none of the player info. If we're thinking about the real-life game, this represents the holder where the pennies are placed.

The Game class will contain a bunch of info: game start/end times, the game state, filled slots, the previous roll value, the turn text, and whether or not players can roll and pass. It will also have a gameId value, which will be the primary key in the database. Finally, we need to annotate the class with the @Entity annotation, which includes the name of the associated database table.

```
@Entity(tableName = "games")
data class Game(
  @PrimaryKey(autoGenerate = true) var gameId: Long = 0,
  val gameState: GameState = GameState.Started,
  val startTime: OffsetDateTime? = OffsetDateTime.now(),
  val endTime: OffsetDateTime? = null,
  val filledSlots: List<Int> = emptyList(),
  val lastRoll: Int? = null,
  val currentTurnText: String? = null,
  val canRoll: Boolean = false,
  val canPass: Boolean = false
)
```

Very little of this class is Room-specific, other than the @Entity and @PrimaryKey annotations. By adding the autoGenerate property to a @PrimaryKey annotation, we let Room calculate the next gameId value for us rather than having to do so manually.

I do want to mention that I chose the OffsetDateTime type here for the dates so that we have the full picture of when a game is played, including the time zone. Now, this admittedly doesn't *really* matter in our case, but it's good practice to make sure you have all the info you need for a datetime.

We do need to quickly create the GameState enum class in the data package:

```
package dev.mfazio.pennydrop.data

enum class GameState {
  Started,
  Finished,
  Cancelled,
  Unknown
}
```

Past that, we're done with this class, so we can move on to converting the Player class into an @Entity.

Make the Player Class an Entity

We created the Player data class back in Create the Player Class, on page 78, so now we just need to change a few things to get it ready to be a database table. We can safely leave it in the types package, though.

As we did with the Game class, we need to annotate this class with the @Entity annotation and add an @PrimaryKey variable. We're also going to make the isHuman and selectedAI properties immutable, as well as tell Room to ignore pennies and isRolling when working with the database table. Here's the end result of those changes:

```
@Entity(tableName = "players")
data class Player(
  @PrimaryKey(autoGenerate = true) var playerId: Long = 0,
  val playerName: String = "",
  val isHuman: Boolean = true,
  val selectedAI: AI? = null
) {
  @Ignore
  var pennies: Int = defaultPennyCount

  fun addPennies(count: Int = 1) {
    pennies += count
  }

  @Ignore
  var isRolling: Boolean = false

  @Ignore
  var gamePlayerNumber: Int = -1

  fun penniesLeft(subtractPenny: Boolean = false): Boolean =
    (pennies - (if(subtractPenny) 1 else 0)) > 0

  companion object {
    const val defaultPennyCount = 10
  }
}
```

Putting @Ignore on the two status fields probably looks odd to you. The reason for this change is that we're shifting ownership of the player's current status in a game from the Player to a new, not-yet-created class called GameStatus. The logic behind this is that it allows the Player class to represent a person (or AI) itself rather than a player in a game and how they're doing in that game. With the way we're setting up the database, a Player can be in multiple games and we're tracking how they did in each game separately.

Given all that, we're still keeping pennies and isRolling as helper variables on a Player. As you'll see later on, when we get a player's status out of the database, we can then assign their current penny count and rolling state to the Player object. This allows us to have a better separation of data in the database while still keeping things logical in our code. I mean "logical" in the sense that we're still getting penny counts and rolling statuses from the player, instead of the front end having to also worry about statuses.

By the way, we *will* be removing the addPennies() function later on, but I want to wait to do that until after we change how updateFromGameHandler() works. Otherwise, your app won't build, and that's annoying.

In the meantime, let's get our GameStatus class added.

Create the GameStatus Entity

As discussed, GameStatus is a database table and Entity that's responsible for holding the user's current (or final) state in a given game. Based on the gameId and playerId, we'll have which number player they are in the game (to preserve turn order), whether or not they're rolling, and how many pennies they have.

This will be similar to the first two Entity classes, but we're going to add the concept of foreign keys to ensure the connection between a GameStatus and both the given Game and Player.

Each foreign key will have a parent and child column, which represents the column name in the other table and the column name here in the game_statuses table, respectively. We can add the list of ForeignKey objects inside the @Entity annotation via the foreignKeys property.

```
@Entity(
  tableName = "game_statuses",
  primaryKeys = ["gameId", "playerId"],
  foreignKeys = [
    ForeignKey(
      entity = Game::class,
      parentColumns = ["gameId"],
      childColumns = ["gameId"]
    ),
    ForeignKey(
      entity = Player::class,
      parentColumns = ["playerId"],
      childColumns = ["playerId"]
    )
  ]
)
data class GameStatus(
  val gameId: Long,
  val playerId: Long,
  val gamePlayerNumber: Int,
  val isRolling: Boolean = false,
  val pennies: Int = Player.defaultPennyCount
)
```

As you can see, the GameStatus class connects the current game and players to each other and to the player's state in a game. Given that, we can reuse this class to retrieve games with the players included via the GameWithPlayers class.

GameWithPlayers will include a Game object and a List<Player>, plus a couple of annotations to help us out. The Game property will have the @Embedded annotation on it since it's the parent Entity, while players has the @Relation annotation.

The @Relation annotation will contain three properties: parentColumn, entityColumn, and associateBy. parentColumn and entityColumn are String values representing the primary key of the parent (Game) and entity (Player) tables. The interesting property here is associateBy, as this takes in a Junction instance. Junction objects bring in a reference to a class that connects two tables together.

Since GameStatus already has a connection between games and players, we can just use that as our Junction class instead of creating a new one. The whole GameWithPlayers class looks like this:

```
data class GameWithPlayers(
  @Embedded val game: Game,
  @Relation(
    parentColumn = "gameId",
    entityColumn = "playerId",
    associateBy = Junction(GameStatus::class)
  )
  val players: List<Player>
)
```

One last change I want to make is to add an index to the playerId value/column on GameStatus:

```
data class GameStatus(
  val gameId: Long,
➤ @ColumnInfo(index = true) val playerId: Long,
  val gamePlayerNumber: Int,
  val isRolling: Boolean = false,
  val pennies: Int = Player.defaultPennyCount
)
```

Adding this in helps speed up searches when using GameStatus as a Junction.

While GameWithPlayers isn't an Entity itself, we'll be using it later to bring in the current game plus all the players in that game in a single query. Otherwise, all our Entity classes are now created, which means we can add them to the entities array in the @Database annotation on PennyDropDatabase.

Add Entities to PennyDropDatabase

When adding Entity classes to a @Database annotation, we're actually adding the KClass values for each Entity class. Note that KClass objects are Kotlin classes as opposed to the Java Class objects we've used elsewhere.

```
@Database(
  entities = [Game::class, Player::class, GameStatus::class],
  version = 1,
  exportSchema = false
)
```

Also, while we're in the PennyDropDatabase and the Player Entity class is ready, we can go ahead and add some players into the database. While we don't yet know who's going to be playing the game, we do know the AI players that are available. We're going to turn them into Player objects and save them to the database on initialization.

Add Data During Database Creation

The RoomDatabase.Builder class, which we're using in our PennyDropDatabase, allows you to add one or more Callback instances. The Callback class contains three functions: onCreate(), onOpen(), and onDestructiveMigration(). These functions all bring in a SupportSQLiteDatabase object and allow you to interact with your database at different times.

In our case, we want to add the AI players when we initially create the database, so we're going to override the onCreate() on a Callback object, then add that to the Room.databaseBuilder() call. Inside the method, we'll call the PennyDropDao function insertPlayers(), which will bring in AI players via the AI.basicAI value. But first, we'll need to convert each AI object to a Player. The function to do that, which lives in the AI class, looks like this:

```
fun toPlayer() = Player(
  playerName = name,
  isHuman = false,
  selectedAI = this
)
```

The last note before getting to the onCreate() function is that all modification actions on a database must be done on a non-UI thread. Luckily, this just means we need to make the call inside of a coroutine block.

The assignment of instance in the getDatabase() function will now look like this:

```
val instance = Room.databaseBuilder(
  context,
  PennyDropDatabase::class.java,
  "PennyDropDatabase"
).addCallback(object : RoomDatabase.Callback() {
  override fun onCreate(db: SupportSQLiteDatabase) {
    super.onCreate(db)
    scope.launch {
      Instance?.pennyDropDao()?.insertPlayers(
        AI.basicAI.map(AI::toPlayer)
      )
    }
  }
}).build()
```

Now, when the app first starts up, we'll have all the AI players in the database inside the players table. Or we would if the database knew how to handle AI objects. If you try to run the app right now, the build will fail with an error like:

> Query method parameters should either be a type that can be converted into a database column or a List / Array that contains such type. You can consider adding a Type Adapter for this.

While it doesn't call it out explicitly, the database doesn't know how to convert the AI into a proper SQLite data type. In fact, Room can't handle saving *any* full objects. Instead, we need to give the database a way to convert to and from an object, in this case an AI object.

All of these conversions happen in a Converters.kt file under the data package. Here, we can build a number of functions with the @TypeConverter annotation, then tell the PennyDropDatabase to use them. While we're in there building the AI converter, we also should build converters for the OffsetDateTime, GameState, and List<Int> properties on the Game class.

Add Converters to the Database

Inside the data package, add a new class called Converters. This class will contain eight functions corresponding to four sets of conversions: OffsetDateTime to/from String, GameState to/from Int, List<Int> to/from String, and AI to Int.

The OffsetDateTime converter functions, used with the startTime and endTime properties inside the Game class, translate OffsetDateTime objects to and from a formatted string using a DateTimeFormatter object. You're welcome to use any logical date/time format here; I'm using DateTimeFormatter.ISO_OFFSET_DATE_TIME since it has all the information we need and is a standardized format. For reference, date/time text in this format will look like 2014-01-24T15:45:05.023Z.

```
private val formatter = DateTimeFormatter.ISO_OFFSET_DATE_TIME

@TypeConverter
fun toOffsetDateTime(value: String?) = value?.let {
  formatter.parse(it, OffsetDateTime::from)
}

@TypeConverter
fun fromOffsetDateTime(date: OffsetDateTime?) = date?.format(formatter)
```

Note that both functions handle scenarios where the entered values are null. We're going to do the same thing with all the converter functions to avoid any conversion issues due to incoming data being null (for example, an ongoing game with a null endDate property).

Next up is the GameState to Int conversion. For this, we're going to use the ordinal property included on all enum classes. This property is the Int value for a given enum value, which we can save to the database.

Converting a GameState object to an Int is the simpler half of the conversion since we're just using the ordinal value of either the entered GameState or GameState.Unknown as a fallback. The conversion back from an Int to GameState object is a bit more complicated, as we want to check if the entered Int value matches the ordinal value of a GameState entry. If not, we once again fall back to GameState.Unknown.

```
@TypeConverter
fun fromGameStateToInt(gameState: GameState?) =
  (gameState ?: GameState.Unknown).ordinal

@TypeConverter
fun fromIntToGameState(gameStateInt: Int?) =
  GameState.values().let { gameStateValues ->
    if (gameStateInt != null &&
      gameStateValues.any { it.ordinal == gameStateInt }
    ) {
      GameState.values()[gameStateInt]
    } else GameState.Unknown
  }
```

In case you're wondering, I used the GameState.values().let block to avoid having to create multiple copies of the Array returned from GameState.values()(). It isn't a big deal here since we only have a few entries in that enum class, but it's something good to think about for other scenarios.

After those is the List<Int> conversion, used for filled slots in the Game class. You may have noticed earlier that I used a List<Int> instead of a List<Slot> for filledSlots. I did that to avoid dealing with all the other properties on the Slot class when retrieving data from the DB. Instead, we just get out a list of the filled slots (if any), then update the isFilled property. As a result, our conversion code is much cleaner: we split the String into Int values, filter out any null or empty values, then map each String to an Int.

The conversion back is similar, as we join the values inside the List<Int> with commas.

```
import android.text.TextUtils

«Other converters are still up here»

@TypeConverter
fun toIntList(value: String?) = value?.split(",")?.let {
  it
    .filter { numberString -> !TextUtils.isEmpty(numberString) }
    .map { numberString -> numberString.toInt() }
} ?: emptyList()

@TypeConverter
fun fromListOfIntToString(numbers: List<Int>?) =
  numbers?.joinToString(",") ?: ""
```

The last piece is saving AI objects to the DB. To do this, instead of saving the entire AI instance, we're just going to save an ID. That means we need to add an aiId property to the AI class, meaning the constructor will now look like this:

```
  data class AI(
➤   val aiId: Long = 0,
    val name: String,
    val rollAgain: (slots: List<Slot>) -> Boolean
)
```

We also need to update the AI instances inside basicAI to include an ID, like this:

```
AI(
➤ 1,
  "Fearful Fred"
) { slots -> slots.fullSlots() <= 2 }
```

Once the ID is in place, the converter functions are simple:

```
@TypeConverter
fun toAI(aiId: Long?) = AI.basicAI.firstOrNull { it.aiId == aiId }

@TypeConverter
fun fromAiToId(ai: AI?) = ai?.aiId
```

Also, since we added aiId to the AI class, we should also include it in the Player conversion method we created earlier:

```
fun toPlayer() = Player(
➤   playerId = aiId,
➤   playerName = name,
➤   isHuman = false,
➤   selectedAI = this
➤ )
```

Also, the NewPlayer.toPlayer() function needs to be updated to handle playerId. We can used named arguments to avoid hard-coding 0 and make the function clearer:

```
fun toPlayer() = Player(
  playerName =
    if (this.isHuman.get()) this.playerName
    else (this.selectedAI()?.name ?: "AI"),
  isHuman = this.isHuman.get(),
  selectedAI = this.selectedAI()
)
```

The last piece with the Converters class is to tell the PennyDropDatabase to use it. All we need to do is add the @TypeConverters annotation:

```
@Database(
  entities = [Game::class, Player::class, GameStatus::class],
  version = 1,
  exportSchema = false
)
➤ @TypeConverters(Converters::class)
abstract class PennyDropDatabase : RoomDatabase()
```

The app is now in a spot where we can start it up and the database will be initialized with the AI players. Of course, we aren't using the values from the database yet, but the foundation is in place. The next step is to create a *repository* class, then start calling those functions from GameViewModel.

Create a Repository Class

First off, a repository isn't a specific Room-related class but rather a recommended Jetpack convention. The advantage of using a repository is that the ViewModel classes have a single location for all data access, no matter the source of that data. This means that if we were to have web service calls along with our database calls, the front-end components would go to the same place for both and not even care about which was which. Having a repository separates out how you get data with how you use the data.

In our case, having a repository is admittedly overkill since we only have a single data source and, as you'll see, the functions in our repository will just be pass-throughs to PennyDropDao functions. Still, it's good practice to have the repository in place once you move on to more complicated apps, like the Android Baseball League app.

To start, create the PennyDropRepository class in the data package and send in an instance of PennyDropDao as a private value.

```
class PennyDropRepository(private val pennyDropDao: PennyDropDao) { ... }
```

The PennyDropRepository class will have four functions to start: getCurrentGameWithPlayers(), getCurrentGameStatuses(), startGame(), and updateGame(). This highlights another advantage of a repository: we can limit the functions that are shown to the rest of the app while allowing the DAO to have extra internal functionality. While in most cases we could just make those functions protected, this would restrict us from using them in other DB-related activity, such as during RoomDatabase initialization.

As I mentioned before, each of these functions will be calling the corresponding function in PennyDropDao. Also, the latter two functions will be marked with the suspend keyword, as they're modifying the database. The entire PennyDropRepository looks like this:

```
class PennyDropRepository(private val pennyDropDao: PennyDropDao) {

  fun getCurrentGameWithPlayers() =
    pennyDropDao.getCurrentGameWithPlayers()

  fun getCurrentGameStatuses() =
    pennyDropDao.getCurrentGameStatuses()

  suspend fun startGame(players: List<Player>) =
    pennyDropDao.startGame(players)

  suspend fun updateGameAndStatuses(
    game: Game,
    statuses: List<GameStatus>
  ) = pennyDropDao.updateGameAndStatuses(game, statuses)
}
```

The PennyDropRepository is now complete, but unfortunately none of the DAO functions currently exist. Let's head back over to PennyDropDao and add them in.

Add PennyDropDao Functions

We've got four functions to add, and we're going to go in order. First up, getCurrentGameWithPlayers(). This function is similar to what we saw earlier (in particular, the getPlayer() function) but it also includes the @Transaction annotation. This annotation tells Room that the function you're calling references multiple tables and the data should be retrieved in a single atomic operation. In our case, we're getting data from both the games and players tables.

```
@Transaction
@Query("SELECT *  FROM games ORDER BY startTime DESC LIMIT 1")
abstract fun getCurrentGameWithPlayers(): LiveData<GameWithPlayers>
```

While the query only mentions the games table, we're pulling in data from both tables due to the @Relation annotation and the @Junction on the GameStatus class. That tells Room to get the associated Player records for the Game without having to write out that piece of the SQL query.

The next function is getCurrentGameStatuses(). Unfortunately, there isn't an easy way with Room to grab a game, the players, *and* the statuses for each player in a single query and map the results to an object. So we need to pull in the GameStatus objects separately. This @Query will get the latest GameStatus instance by performing a subquery on the games table. We get the most recent open game, then sort the statuses by the gamePlayerNumber property (to ensure players are in the right play order). Note that this will also be an @Transaction since we're referencing multiple tables.

```
@Transaction
@Query(
  """
  SELECT * FROM game_statuses
  WHERE gameId = (
    SELECT gameId FROM games
    WHERE endTime IS NULL
    ORDER BY startTime DESC
    LIMIT 1)
  ORDER BY gamePlayerNumber
  """
)
abstract fun getCurrentGameStatuses(): LiveData<List<GameStatus>>
```

As you can see, the @Query annotation gives us a lot of flexibilty in retreiving data from the database. But sometimes an @Query still isn't enough and we need to call multiple functions in a single @Transaction. For that scenario, we can instead create an open function and implement the function ourselves rather than letting Room do that for us. The ability to have fully implemented functions in our DAO is the reason PennyDropDao is an abstract class rather than an interface (as is commonly seen in the Room documentation).

In the case of startGame(), we're going to bring in a List<Player>, close up any existing games, create a new Game, get or insert the entered Player objects from/into the database, then add new GameStatus entries for each player before returning the newly created game's ID. To do all this, we'll call other functions inside PennyDropDao to do the work for us. We already created insertGame() and insertPlayer() when first building PennyDropDao, so we just need two additional new functions.

The first function is called closeOpenGames(), which goes through the database and sets the current time as the endTime and state of Cancelled for any still-open games. We previously saw named bind parameters in Create a DAO Class, on page 118, but here they're more interesting.

We can't send in complex types by default, but since we previously created type converters for both types, this works just fine.

```
@Query("""
  UPDATE games
  SET endTime = :endDate, gameState = :gameState
  WHERE endTime IS NULL""")
abstract suspend fun closeOpenGames(
  endDate: OffsetDateTime = OffsetDateTime.now(),
  gameState: GameState = GameState.Cancelled
)
```

Note the use of default values for each property. We can include parameters we have no intention of overwriting purely to be able to include them as parameters in a query, yet still keep the flexibility to overwrite if needed for any reason.

Also, since this function is modifying the database, it needs to be a transaction. But instead of having to add the @Transaction annotation, Room automatically wraps all modifying actions as a transaction. This includes functions with an @Insert, @Update, or @Delete annotation.

The other function we still need is insertGameStatuses(), which just requires the @Insert annotation.

```
@Insert
abstract suspend fun insertGameStatuses(gameStatuses: List<GameStatus>)
```

This highlights another nice Room feature: we can send in a List<GameStatus> and all GameStatus records are entered into the database instead of manually having to insert them one by one.

Now that all the functions we're using are created, we can get back to startGame() itself. Note that even though we have the implementation for startGame() in here, it still has to be marked as open since it has the @Transaction annotation.

The function code looks like this:

```
@Transaction
open suspend fun startGame(players: List<Player>): Long {
  this.closeOpenGames()

  val gameId = this.insertGame(
    Game(
      gameState = GameState.Started,
      currentTurnText = "The game has begun!\n",
      canRoll = true
    )
  )

  val playerIds = players.map { player ->
    getPlayer(player.playerName)?.playerId ?: insertPlayer(player)
  }

  this.insertGameStatuses(
    playerIds.mapIndexed { index, playerId ->
      GameStatus(
        gameId,
        playerId,
        index,
        index == 0
      )
    }
  )

  return gameId
}
```

The one piece I want to call out here is how we're getting the playerIds value. We check the database for a player and either use that to get the playerId or, if the player's not found, we create the player and then send back its player ID. Since insertPlayer() returns a Long, we get back the database ID right away without having to do a secondary lookup. Plus, the Elvis operator allows us to keep everything in one expression instead of having to include extra conditional logic.

We have one remaining function to cover in the PennyDropDao, which is the updateGameAndStatuses() function. This function does exactly what you'd expect: it updates the DB versions of the entered Game and GameStatus objects, all wrapped in a single @Transaction. updateGame() already exists, but we need to create updateGameStatuses() quickly:

```
@Update
abstract suspend fun updateGameStatuses(gameStatuses: List<GameStatus>)
```

From there, updateGameAndStatuses() is calling those two functions, wrapped in a @Transaction:

```
@Transaction
open suspend fun updateGameAndStatuses(
  game: Game,
  statuses: List<GameStatus>
) {
  this.updateGame(game)
  this.updateGameStatuses(statuses)
}
```

The last part of the PennyDropRepository I want to cover is adding the ability to have a singleton instance of the repository for use anywhere. This is optional, but it'll be useful to avoid creating multiple instances of PennyDropRepository for different views.

The idea is the same as with PennyDropDatabase: we get the existing instance variable unless it's null, then we create a new instance and return that. We're also going to take advantage of the synchronized() block to avoid having multiple simultaneous attempts at creating the PennyDropRepository. All of this will live inside PennyDropRepository in its companion object:

```
companion object {
  @Volatile
  private var instance: PennyDropRepository? = null

  fun getInstance(pennyDropDao: PennyDropDao) =
    this.instance ?: synchronized(this) {
      instance ?: PennyDropRepository(pennyDropDao).also {
          instance = it
      }
    }
}
```

With that, the PennyDropRepository and PennyDropDao classes are now all set. We have all the logic we need to persist our game data in a local database. The remaining piece is to pull that data back out of the database and use it inside GameViewModel.

Access the Database from a ViewModel

As before, the GameViewModel will be the data source for the GameFragment view. But now, instead of holding onto values within GameViewModel, they'll be coming from PennyDropDatabase via the PennyDropRepository. We still have LiveData for the UI as we did previously, but GameViewModel is no longer handling setting those values directly.

The first thing we need to do is get an instance of PennyDropRepository. To do this, we need to get instances of both PennyDropDatabase and PennyDropDao. But that presents a problem: getting the PennyDropDatabase instance requires access to a Context object. Normally, ViewModel classes shouldn't access any type of Context object, as it can cause memory leaks due to life-cycle discrepancies (that is, an Activity or Fragment is disposed before the ViewModel, leaving an invalid context reference in the ViewModel). However, when we require a Context object, we can use the AndroidViewModel class instead of ViewModel as the parent class. This allows us to have a reference to an Application object, which is a Context subclass.

```
class GameViewModel(application: Application) :
  AndroidViewModel(application) {
  «The GameViewModel code is going in here.»
}
```

Now that we have a Context object available, we can get the PennyDropDatabase instance, which in turns lets us retrieve a PennyDropRepository instance. We'll add the PennyDropRepository declaration, called repository, under the clearText variable without any initialization. Instead, we assign the value inside an init block. This block runs when a class is instantiated and allows us to initialize values separately from their declaration while maintaining immutability.

```
class GameViewModel(application: Application) :
  AndroidViewModel(application) {

  private var players: List<Player> = emptyList()

  val slots =
      MutableLiveData(
          (1..6).map { slotNum -> Slot(slotNum, slotNum != 6) }
      )

  val currentPlayer = MutableLiveData<Player?>()

  val canRoll = MutableLiveData(true)
  val canPass = MutableLiveData(false)

  val currentTurnText = MutableLiveData("")
  val currentStandingsText = MutableLiveData("")

  private var clearText = false

➤ private val repository: PennyDropRepository
➤
➤ init {
➤   val database =
➤     PennyDropDatabase.getDatabase(application, viewModelScope)
➤
➤   this.repository =
➤     PennyDropRepository.getInstance(database.pennyDropDao())
➤ }

  «Rest of GameViewModel»
}
```

I like splitting up the assignment of this.repository here into multiple pieces to illustrate the components that are going into the repository, but we could just as easily join this all into a single expression:

```
this.repository =
  PennyDropDatabase
    .getDatabase(application, viewModelScope)
    .pennyDropDao()
    .let { dao ->
      PennyDropRepository.getInstance(dao)
    }
```

I would generally write my code this second way when not in an educational setting, but it's up to you. Remember that both approaches are functionally equivalent, so focus on what feels more readable to you.

In case you're wondering, the viewModelScope CoroutineScope we're sending in here is available because of the lifecycle-viewmodel-ktx dependency we added at the beginning of the chapter.

Start a Game

With the PennyDropRepository available in GameViewModel, we can start interacting with the database. The logical first step here is to give ourselves a way to get data into the database, which we do inside the startGame() function. Since we're changing up how we access game info in GameViewModel, the startGame() function will look significantly smaller.

```
suspend fun startGame(playersForNewGame: List<Player>) {
  repository.startGame(playersForNewGame)
}
```

All our previous initialization is gone since we're handling it inside PennyDropDao.startGame() and we're adding the suspend keyword to the function. The suspend keyword is added since the functions we're calling also have it (as they're eventually modifying data in the database). Now, the change to a suspend function requires us to change how we're calling startGame() over in PickPlayersFragment as well.

Thankfully, it's not a particularly large change, as we just wrap the contents of this.buttonPlayGame.setOnClickListener() in a coroutine launch block. We can access the launch() function from viewLifecycleOwner.lifecycleScope, a coroutine scope tied to the life cycle of the LifecycleOwner (in this case, this is the GameFragment> itself). All this means is that if the Fragment is disposed for any reason, the coroutine call will be cancelled automatically. The updated code looks like this:

```
this.buttonPlayGame.setOnClickListener {
  viewLifecycleOwner.lifecycleScope.launch {
    gameViewModel.startGame(
      pickPlayersViewModel.players.value
        ?.filter { newPlayer ->
            newPlayer.isIncluded.get()
        }?.map { newPlayer ->
            newPlayer.toPlayer()
        } ?: emptyList()
    )

    findNavController().navigate(R.id.gameFragment)
  }
}
```

With that code added, starting a game will now insert a game into the local database rather than saving game information inside the GameViewModel. We're not retrieving anything yet, but we can still run the app and insert a game or two. Once we have data in the database, we can use Android Studio's Database Inspector to see what's in there.

View Data with the Database Inspector

Since we haven't yet hooked up the data from the database to our view, we need a different way to view what's in the database. Luckily, starting with Android Studio 4.1, there's now the Database Inspector built into our IDE. By opening up the Database Inspector in the bottom of Android Studio and selecting the current device with Penny Drop, we can see what's in PennyDropDatabase.

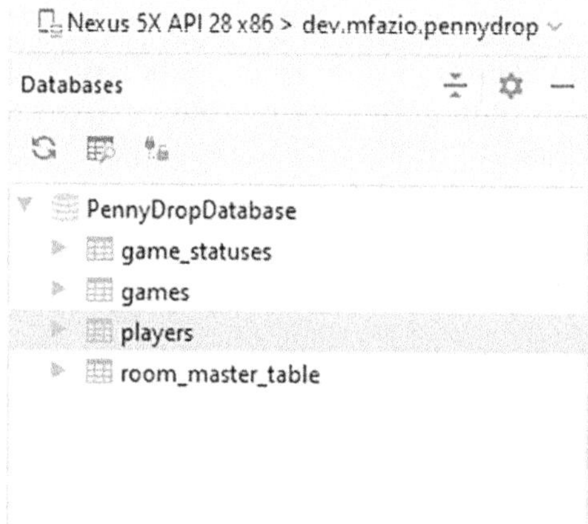

If you double-click a table name, say players, you'll be presented with the data in the table, as shown in the image on page 137.

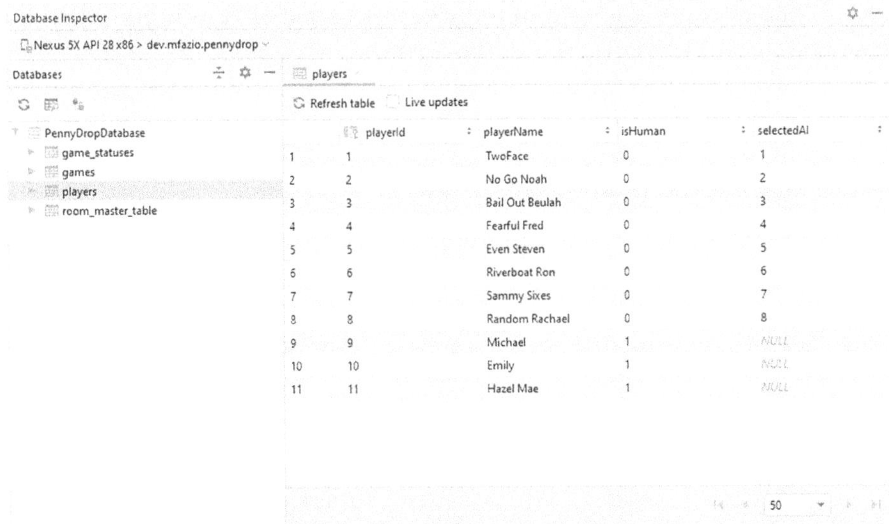

This is a wonderfully useful tool for checking out what's going on in your database. If the default query isn't sufficient, you're also able to run custom queries on the database. This way you can not only see the data in your database but can test out queries you want to add to a DAO without having to constantly recompile and redeploy your app to make sure they work.

Another great feature here is the ability to edit data in the database via the Database Inspector and have it update in real time. Since we'll be using Room to listen to database changes via LiveData objects, we can change database values directly and see how they'll look in the app.

For example, if I change the name Hazel to Hazel Mae while in a game, my app will update the player name and standings on the Game screen to the new name. Note that the game summary text won't change since we're saving the text values rather than generating them based on database values.

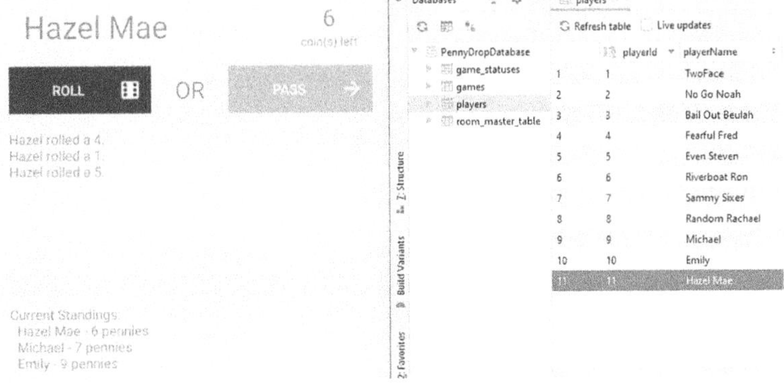

Now, we can see that the local database has game data, but your app isn't displaying anything from the database yet, so why don't we fix that? Head back over to GameViewModel so we can get your view connected to PennyDropDatabase.

Get the Current Game of Penny Drop

Right now, GameViewModel has a number of MutableLiveData objects declared at the top of the class. We're going to take this:

```
class GameViewModel(application: Application) :
  AndroidViewModel(application) {

  private var players: List<Player> = emptyList()

  val slots =
    MutableLiveData(
      (1..6).map { slotNum -> Slot(slotNum, slotNum != 6) }
    )

  val currentPlayer = MutableLiveData<Player?>()

  val canRoll = MutableLiveData(true)
  val canPass = MutableLiveData(false)

  val currentTurnText = MutableLiveData("")
  val currentStandingsText = MutableLiveData("")

  private var clearText = false

  «Rest of GameViewModel»
}
```

And turn it into this:

```
class GameViewModel(application: Application) :
  AndroidViewModel(application) {

  private var clearText = false

  private val repository: PennyDropRepository

  val currentGame = MediatorLiveData<GameWithPlayers>()

  val currentGameStatuses: LiveData<List<GameStatus>>
  val currentPlayer: LiveData<Player>
  val currentStandingsText: LiveData<String>

  val slots: LiveData<List<Slot>>

  val canRoll: LiveData<Boolean>
  val canPass: LiveData<Boolean>

  «Rest of GameViewModel»
}
```

Go ahead and swap out those values and variables now. The new ones should live after the class declaration (as shown in both examples) and above the init block. Don't worry about the "Property must be initialized or be abstract" errors; we're going to create them inside the init block in just a minute.

The main piece that should jump out to you (other than the errors) is the introduction of MediatorLiveData. MediatorLiveData values are objects that observe LiveData objects (including other MediatorLiveData objects) and handle OnChanged() events.

For example, the currentGame value will watch LiveData objects from both the getCurrentGameStatuses() and getCurrentGameWithPlayers() repository functions. As the complete picture of a current game needs the game info, the players playing, and the game statuses, we want the currentGame value to reflect changes to all of those. The code to do so, which lives inside the init block, looks like this:

```
this.currentGameStatuses = this.repository.getCurrentGameStatuses()

this.currentGame.addSource(
  this.repository.getCurrentGameWithPlayers()
) { gameWithPlayers ->
  updateCurrentGame(gameWithPlayers, this.currentGameStatuses.value)
}

this.currentGame.addSource(this.currentGameStatuses) { gameStatuses ->
    updateCurrentGame(this.currentGame.value, gameStatuses)
}
```

The MediatorLiveData was initialized when we declared currentGame, so here we're just adding the two sources. This means anytime data changes in the database and triggers an update of the exposed LiveData, one (or both) of the associated source functions will be run.

If you look closely, you can see that the two sources are both doing effectively the same thing, just with different values coming in. The reason updateCurrentGame() is in here is so we can have a single piece of logic for both scenarios. That function brings in both the GameWithPlayers and List<GameStatus> values and combines them via a new updateStatuses() function on GameWithPlayers. The updateCurrentGame() function look like this:

```
private fun updateCurrentGame(
  gameWithPlayers: GameWithPlayers?,
  gameStatuses: List<GameStatus>?
) {
  this.currentGame.value = gameWithPlayers?.updateStatuses(gameStatuses)
}
```

The updateStatuses() function takes in the statuses and maps each GameStatus to the correct Player. This is why we left the pennies and isRolling variables on the Player class but excluded them from the database. We can keep the data separate in the database but combine them in our code so referencing the values in the view layout file is kept the same. Plus, it makes more sense in code to have the status values on the Player class.

We grab each Player, find their GameStatus, and then assign the status variables. We have a couple of null checks in here, too: if the gameStatuses value is null, the GameWithPlayers is unchanged. Similarly, if we can't find a proper GameStatus, we return an unchanged Player object.

```
fun updateStatuses(gameStatuses: List<GameStatus>?) =
  if (gameStatuses != null) {
    this.copy(
      players = players.map { player ->
        gameStatuses
          .firstOrNull { it.playerId == player.playerId }
          ?.let { gameStatus ->
            player.apply {
              pennies = gameStatus.pennies
              isRolling = gameStatus.isRolling
              gamePlayerNumber = gameStatus.gamePlayerNumber
            }
          } ?: player
      }.sortedBy { it.gamePlayerNumber }
    )
  } else this
```

A particular item of note here is the this.copy() call wrapping the block. This is done since we want to create a new instance of GameWithPlayers with an update List<Player> rather than change the existing object (which we couldn't anyway since it's a val). In the end, this function returns a GameWithPlayers, possibly with changes, and the UI will update accordingly after we make a few changes there. Before we get to the UI, we're going to set up the rest of the LiveData objects in the init block inside GameViewModel.

Get the Current Player and Slots

We already have the currentGame set up, which means to get the current player, we just need to find the one who's currently rolling. While we could have added this piece to updateCurrentGame(), I'm separating out the call for two reasons. One, I don't love having side effects in functions like that (since the focus is on the currentGame value), and two, this is a great showcase for the Transformations class.

The Transformations class has a few functions on it which allow you to bring in a LiveData parameter and execute a function on it, returning a brand-new LiveData object. In our case, we're going to use Transformations.map() to take the currentGame and get out the currently rolling player.

```
this.currentPlayer =
  Transformations.map(this.currentGame) { gameWithPlayers ->
    gameWithPlayers?.players?.firstOrNull { it.isRolling }
  }
```

By the way, if this feels similar to the MediatorLiveData work we did before, that's because it is. Under the covers, Transformations.map() and Transformations.switchMap() are both using MediatorLiveData objects to transform the entered LiveData objects.

Now, instead of manually setting a value for currentPlayer, we can update the database, which will then update the UI via our LiveData object. Plus, the UI data binding code for the current player doesn't even have to change, but we still get persisted data when the app is closed and resumed later.

Similarly, currentStandingsText is now also using Transformations.map() on currentGame with some help from generateCurrentStandings():

```
this.currentStandingsText =
  Transformations.map(this.currentGame) { gameWithPlayers ->
    gameWithPlayers?.players?.let { players ->
      this.generateCurrentStandings(players)
    }
  }
```

We're going to do the same thing with the Slots value, but here we're going to use a new function from the Slot class called mapFromGame() to handle the conversion logic. First, the Transformations.map() function looks like this:

```
this.slots =
  Transformations.map(this.currentGame) { gameWithPlayers ->
    Slot.mapFromGame(gameWithPlayers?.game)
  }
```

Then, inside the companion object of Slot, the mapFromGame() function looks like this:

```
fun mapFromGame(game: Game?) =
  (1..6).map { slotNum ->
    Slot(
      number = slotNum,
      canBeFilled = slotNum != 6,
      isFilled = game?.filledSlots?.contains(slotNum) ?: false,
      lastRolled = game?.lastRoll == slotNum
    )
  }
```

This is similar to the updateSlots() function we were using before, combined with the Slot initialization logic we used to have here in GameViewModel. An extra advantage of this approach as opposed to the previous one in updateSlots(), other than the whole persistence aspect, is that we no longer need to call slots.notifyChange(). That function can be removed completely since any updates to the currentGame will be reflected and handled automatically without any extra hacks.

We now have wired up the currentGame and have used that as the source for other fields, but we've yet to handle the button logic. Next up are the canPass and canRoll values, which use both the currentGame and currentPlayer LiveData values.

Handle canRoll and canPass

Here, to determine which buttons should be shown, we need to use both the currentGame and currentPlayer values. As a reminder, we only enable the Pass button after a user's rolled once, and we disable both buttons for any AI players. We could go with another MediatorLiveData object and add both currentGame and currentPlayer as sources since we're using both values. But it makes more sense to set up a single Transformation.map() call for each value with currentPlayer as the source since currentPlayer comes from currentGame. This will cause the function to be run whenever either the currentPlayer or currentGame are updated. Please note that this doesn't mean that we got a new player, just that the currentPlayer value was updated due to a change in the currentGame LiveData. As a result, the assignments of canRoll and canPass look like this:

```
this.canRoll = Transformations.map(this.currentPlayer) { player ->
  player?.isHuman == true && currentGame.value?.game?.canRoll == true
}

this.canPass = Transformations.map(this.currentPlayer) { player ->
  player?.isHuman == true && currentGame.value?.game?.canPass == true
}
```

With that, all of our LiveData values are initialized and the init block is finally complete. Next up is changing our roll() and pass() functions to work with the new values. Thankfully, neither of these functions will have to change dramatically.

Update roll() and pass() Functions

Our current versions of roll() and pass() are similar; we get the current player, check if the move (rolling or passing) is valid, call the corresponding GameHandler function, and send the result into updateFromGameHandler(). roll() has an extra piece at the beginning to get the current state of the slots, too. Notice that we already did most of the work in these functions earlier, so instead of getting all those values again from scratch, we just need to add in a bunch of null checks.

Both functions are now going to follow the same format: create a handful of new variables for all the data we need, make sure each one is not null, validate the action you want to take (canRoll or canPass), and then call the GameHandler piece. The roll() function looks like this:

```
fun roll() {
  val game = this.currentGame.value?.game
  val players = this.currentGame.value?.players
  val currentPlayer = this.currentPlayer.value
  val slots = this.slots.value

  if (game != null && players != null && currentPlayer != null &&
      slots != null && game.canRoll
  ) {
    updateFromGameHandler(
      GameHandler.roll(players, currentPlayer, slots)
    )
  }
}
```

To be honest, I don't love the long line of null checks in this method. I thought about adding an extension function called something like allNotNull() and throwing it on the List class:

```
fun <T> List<T?>.allNotNull() = this.all { it != null }
```

Adding the extension function would allow us to check all the variables in this fashion:

```
listOf(game, players, currentPlayer, slots).allNotNull()
```

However, there's a problem with this. Moving the null checks to an extension method breaks Kotlin's ability to *smart cast*. In the first block of code, explicitly checking a variable (like game) for null causes the compiler to automatically cast that variable to its not-null counterpart.

For example, inside the if() block, the game is now a Game object instead of a Game? object. Also, game is seen as not null in the rest of the if() conditional expression, meaning game.canRoll returns a Boolean rather than a Boolean? object. If we use something like allNotNull(), we lose that smart casting and have to effectively check for null again or use the *!!* operator to assert that all the variables are not null.

The !! operator is the "not-null assertion operator" and is described in the official Kotlin docs as being "for NPE-lovers." NPE in this case means NullPointerException, as we're effectively ignoring Kotlin's attempts to safely check variables for null and removing one of the best features of the language. Hopefully it's clear that we shouldn't be using this operator unless it's *absolutely necessary*. Slightly shrinking down a conditional? That doesn't seem absolutely necessary to me, so I'm going with the chain of null checks instead.

The pass() function looks the same; the only difference is that we don't need the current slots.

```
fun pass() {
  val game = this.currentGame.value?.game
  val players = this.currentGame.value?.players
  val currentPlayer = this.currentPlayer.value

  if (game != null && players != null &&
    currentPlayer != null && game.canPass
  ) {
    updateFromGameHandler(
      GameHandler.pass(players, currentPlayer)
    )
  }
}
```

Both functions are done and ready to be used by the UI without any changes in fragment_game.xml. Next up are the modifications in the updateFromGameHandler() function that we're calling in these two functions. The outcome of updateFromGameHandler() is basically the same as before, but we need to make some changes to work with the database.

Modify the updateFromGameHandler Function

The previous version of this function had four sections: update the players, update the slots, modify game-related variables (currentTurnText, canRoll, and canPass), then kick off an AI turn if applicable. Now, we have three sections: update the Game, update all applicable GameStatus objects, and kick off the AI turn. Our end result is largely the same, but we're once again coming at it from a different angle.

The first step is to get a game value, which is a copied value based on currentGame. We check for null via a let block, then use the currentGameWithPlayers value inside there along with the copy() function. Inside the copy function, we're updating most of currentGameWithPlayers with the TurnResult object coming into updateFromGameHandler().

While this process will look familiar enough given what we've done before, the interesting part of this assignment comes if currentGame.value is null for any reason. If that's the case, we're using the Elvis operator and adding a return statement to the right side of that operator. This is a completely valid approach in Kotlin and saves us from both taking time to get statuses we're not going to use and an extra null check when calling the database. The game assignment block looks like this:

```
val game = currentGame.value?.let { currentGameWithPlayers ->
  currentGameWithPlayers.game.copy(
    gameState =
      if (result.isGameOver) GameState.Finished else GameState.Started,
    lastRoll = result.lastRoll,
    filledSlots =
      updateFilledSlots(result, currentGameWithPlayers.game.filledSlots),
    currentTurnText = generateTurnText(result),
    canPass = result.canPass,
    canRoll = result.canRoll,
    endTime = if (result.isGameOver) OffsetDateTime.now() else null
  )
} ?: return
```

We already have almost everything used in this function in place, save for the updateFilledSlots() function, which replaces updateSlots(). This new function maps to a single when block that checks if we need to clear slots or if a slot has been newly filled. If we need to clear out the slots, the filledSlots value on currentGame becomes an empty List<Int>. If we just rolled something other than a six, we add the rolled slot to the filledSlots list, meaning, we literally say filledSlots + result.lastRoll, which creates a new List<Int> for us to send out of this function. If neither of those conditions are true, we return the filledSlots as is. The function in its entirety looks like this:

```
private fun updateFilledSlots(
  result: TurnResult,
  filledSlots: List<Int>
) = when {
  result.clearSlots -> emptyList()
  result.lastRoll != null && result.lastRoll != 6 ->
      filledSlots + result.lastRoll
  else -> filledSlots
}
```

With the game value set, we can move on to statuses. This will take a similar approach, but since we're dealing with a List<GameStatus>, we use map rather than let for the null check. The inside of the map block is going to be a single when() statement which compares the player IDs of the current GameStatus and Player objects on the TurnResult object.

If the GameStatus matches the previous player, we mark them as no longer rolling and add the pennies to their total. If we have the current player's GameStatus, we say that they're now rolling (even if they already were marked as rolling) and remove any pennies from the player if the player didn't change last roll. If we're not looking at the GameStatus of either of these players, then we just return the existing GameStatus untouched. Finally, if currentGameStatuses is null, we return an empty List.

```
val statuses = currentGameStatuses.value?.map { status ->
  when (status.playerId) {
    result.previousPlayer?.playerId -> {
      status.copy(
        isRolling = false,
        pennies = status.pennies + (result.coinChangeCount ?: 0)
      )
    }
    result.currentPlayer?.playerId -> {
      status.copy(
        isRolling = !result.isGameOver,
        pennies = status.pennies +
          if (!result.playerChanged) {
            result.coinChangeCount ?: 0
          } else 0
      )
    }
    else -> status
  }
} ?: emptyList()
```

Now that we have updated versions of both our game and statuses objects, we can send them along to the PennyDropRepository. Since we're modifying the database and calling a suspend function, we have to wrap the call in a viewModelScope.launch block.

```
viewModelScope.launch {
  repository.updateGameAndStatuses(game, statuses)
}
```

We saw this same launch block last chapter with the playAITurn() function. There, we included it due to the delay() function rather than any database transactions, but it's used in the same fashion. That means instead of having two separate coroutines running in two different launch blocks, we can instead call them both in the same one. As a result, we can move the launch block out of playAITurn() and add the call to repository.updateGameAndStatuses() inside there:

```
viewModelScope.launch {
  repository.updateGameAndStatuses(game, statuses)
  if (result.currentPlayer?.isHuman == false) {
    playAITurn()
  }
}
```

We do have to change playAITurn() to be a suspend function with this approach, in addition to the changes required to handle our state coming from the database.

First, we're going to change playAITurn() and mark this function with the suspend keyword. The rest of the function is similar to what we did inside roll() and pass() with a bunch of null checks and calls to the GameHandler. The biggest difference as compared to those two functions is that GameHandler.playAITurn() can return null, so we need to account for that in our function. The code looks like this:

```
private suspend fun playAITurn() {
  delay(1000)
  val game = currentGame.value?.game
  val players = currentGame.value?.players
  val currentPlayer = currentPlayer.value
  val slots = slots.value

  if (game != null && players != null &&
      currentPlayer != null && slots != null
  ) {
    GameHandler
      .playAITurn(players, currentPlayer, slots, game.canPass)
      ?.let { result ->
        updateFromGameHandler(result)
      }
  }
}
```

With the playAITurn() function in place, this would be a good time to go back and remove the addPennies() function from the Player class before we forget. Then we can complete the last piece of GameViewModel: the generateTurnText() function.

Update GenerateTurnText()

Thankfully, most of this method will stay the same. The assignment of the currentText value will now be a single statement since we're no longer assigning a value to currentTurnText LiveData in here. Also, since generating game over text is now more complicated, we're better off creating a separate function called generateGameOverText(). This leaves us with the following function code, excluding other turn scenarios. I'm leaving those out since there's nothing new there. If you want to see the full code, check out the source code found on the PragProg site. The rest of the function is here:

```
private fun generateTurnText(result: TurnResult): String {
  val currentText =
    if (clearText) "" else currentGame.value?.game?.currentTurnText ?: ""

  clearText = result.turnEnd != null

  val currentPlayerName = result.currentPlayer?.playerName ?: "???"

  return when {
      result.isGameOver -> generateGameOverText()
      // Other scenarios are here
  }
}
```

The new generateGameOverText() function will end up printing out the same style String as it did before, but it will take a bit more work to get there. The issue is that we're generating the turn text before the database has been updated, so our final text will be slightly off for the winner. As a result, we need to make sure everything accurately reflects the end-of-game state, then we can generate the text.

We get the List<GameStatus>, then update the List<Player> from the currentGame with those statuses. After that, we get the winning player (and set their pennies to 0 since we know they're out) then get the "Game Over!" raw string. If we don't have players or a winningPlayer, we just return "N/A". Here's the entire function:

```
private fun generateGameOverText(): String {
  val statuses = this.currentGameStatuses.value
  val players = this.currentGame.value?.players?.map { player ->
    player.apply {
      this.pennies = statuses
        ?.firstOrNull { it.playerId == playerId }
        ?.pennies
      ?: Player.defaultPennyCount
    }
  }

  val winningPlayer = players
    ?.firstOrNull { !it.penniesLeft() || it.isRolling }
    ?.apply { this.pennies = 0 }

  if (players == null || winningPlayer == null) return "N/A"
```

```
    return """Game Over!
            |${winningPlayer.playerName} is the winner!
            |
            |${generateCurrentStandings(players, "Final Scores:\n")}
            """.trimMargin()
}
```

That was the last piece we needed to update in GameViewModel, so we're free to move elsewhere. The final part is making all our updates inside fragment_game.xml. And by "all," I mean the one change that's required.

Update the UI Data Binding

By starting with LiveData in GameViewModel and fragment_game.xml, switching from holding state in GameViewModel to, instead, the PennyDropDatabase requires minimal rework. In fact, if we had started with a Game object in GameViewModel instead of separating out the currentTurnText, nothing would have had to change in here. That's the way you want to design your View/ViewModel relationship: the View shouldn't care about *how* you're getting your data, just that it has the data it needs.

In this case, I intentionally waited on the Game since it didn't add any value last chapter. With saving data in the database, however, a single Game object made more sense. It allows us to have a historical record of the games that were played previously plus hold the state of the currently played game. A little bit of rework is an acceptable trade-off for not overcomplicating our architecture.

As I alluded to in the previous paragraph, we just need to update how fragment_game.xml is getting game text, which is from the currentGame LiveData value. The *@+id/textCurrentTurnInfo* <TextView> at the bottom of the layout now has the android:text= attribute with a value of *"@{vm.currentGame.game.currentTurnText}"*.

Summary and Next Steps

With those data binding changes, we can finally run our app! As shown in the image on page 150.

OK, so this isn't as exciting as it feels like it should be. Since the app doesn't work much differently than it did previously, we won't see much of a difference while playing. We changed how things are handled in the back end, but the UI is basically the same. However, we can now close our app and pick right up where we left off, plus we have a stored record of all the games we've played.

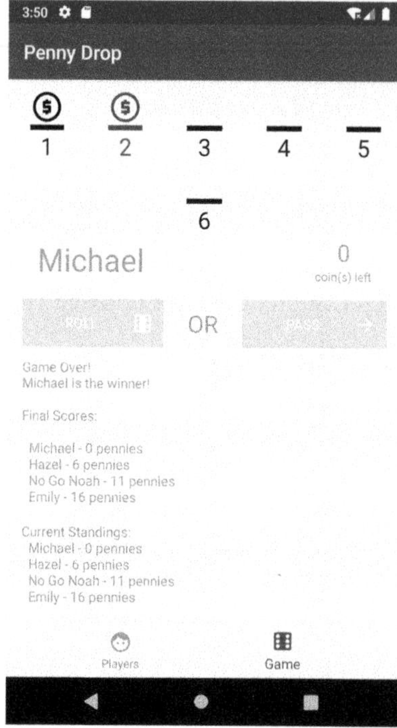

The next chapter is going to take advantage of that record of previously played games to show users some player rankings. We're going to display the win and games played counts for each player, sorted by the player with the most wins all-time. This will all be done in a new tab tied to a new fragment, taking advantage of Android's RecyclerView component. This view component displays a list of items and can handle large numbers of entries, which in our case are retrieved from the database. We'll even have the ability to style each list item as we wish with conditional logic based on the player being displayed.

CHAPTER 6

Build a List with RecyclerView

We're finally in the home stretch with our Penny Drop app. The app is complete in the game sense, as you can play games against people or AI players plus come back to a game at a later time. But we can still add a few more items of value.

First up, we're going to add rankings into the app. We're going to add a new RankingsFragment containing a RecyclerView list. A RecyclerView is a way to display a list of items in Android efficiently, as there are a number of behind-the-scenes optimizations being done by the view. Items users can't yet see are bound ahead of time to ensure smooth scrolling, plus new list items are created automatically and proactively. We're even able to inform the RecyclerView of how to determine if a list item has changed, avoiding a full list refresh when only a single item has been updated.

In addition to the RecyclerView, a couple of other supporting classes will be added to populate the list. Some of these we've seen before: a new ViewModel class, the Room @Relation annotation, and an additional data class to hold the data for each item. In addition, we're creating an *adapter* class that handles the data for a RecyclerView along with the binding for each list item via a component called a ViewHolder. For reference, ViewHolder classes are responsible for handling how to bind data between an item and a row in a RecyclerView list.

At the end of the chapter, we're going to have a rankings tab that looks something like the image shown on page 152.

Now would be a good time to play some extra games of Penny Drop. The more games that are played, the more interesting our rankings list will be. Play some games with new players and/or include a bunch of the AI players. Do whatever you'd like that'll get some extra data for us to use. Once you're done with that, we'll move on to getting a RecyclerView into our app.

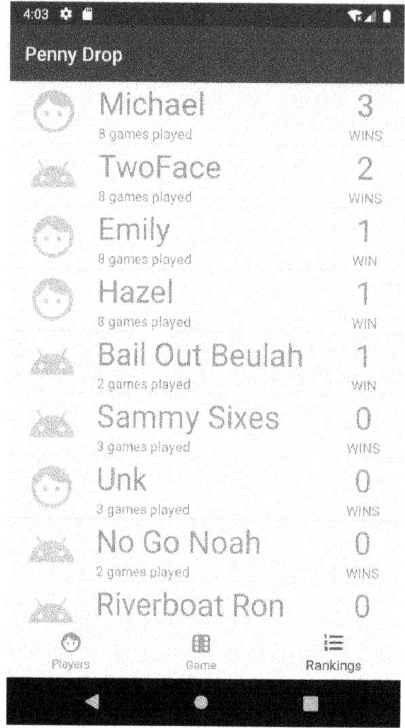

Add the RecyclerView

Our first stop is the new RankingsFragment class and the RecyclerView component inside. We *could* add the new Fragment class just as we did before, with right-clicking the fragments package and choosing New > Fragment > Fragment (Blank). Take note that one of the options in that menu is Fragment (List); that would do a lot of the needed work for us.

But I said "could" generate the Fragment class for a reason. I want to create each piece by hand the first time so it's clear what all goes into setting up a RecyclerView. Plus, Android Studio adds a bunch of code we don't need, so let's save ourselves the trouble of having to delete all of that stuff we don't need. Go ahead and add a new class to the fragments package called RankingsFragment and a file called fragment_rankings.xml to res > layout. These are the main two pieces that would be added had we generated a new Fragment class.

The RankingsFragment class doesn't need much right now. The class should inherit from Fragment, and we need to load the view layout inside onCreateView().

```
class RankingsFragment : Fragment() {

  override fun onCreateView(
    inflater: LayoutInflater,
    container: ViewGroup?,
    savedInstanceState: Bundle?
  ): View? {
    val view =
      inflater.inflate(R.layout.fragment_rankings, container, false)

    return view
  }
}
```

Before we add the <RecyclerView> to the layout file, we need to include the library and dependency variable in our build.gradle files.

```
ext {
  // Other dependencies still here
  nav_version = '2.3.3'
➤ recycler_view_version = '1.1.0'
  room_version = '2.3.0-beta01'
}

dependencies {
  «Other dependencies»
  implementation "androidx.navigation:navigation-ui-ktx:$nav_version"
➤ implementation
➤   "androidx.recyclerview:recyclerview:$recycler_view_version"
  implementation "androidx.room:room-ktx:$room_version"
  «Other dependencies»
}
```

The fragment_rankings.xml file is similarly brief compared to RankingsFragment, as it just contains the <RecyclerView>. The only attribute of note here is app:layoutManager=, which tells the <RecyclerView> how to display the content. Since we're going to have a basic list, we can use the existing LinearLayoutManager that's part of the RecyclerView library. The entire fragment_rankings.xml file looks like this:

```
<?xml version="1.0" encoding="utf-8"?>
<androidx.recyclerview.widget.RecyclerView
  xmlns:android="http://schemas.android.com/apk/res/android"
  xmlns:app="http://schemas.android.com/apk/res-auto"
  xmlns:tools="http://schemas.android.com/tools"
  android:id="@+id/rankings_list"
  android:name="dev.mfazio.pennydrop.fragments.RankingsFragment"
  android:layout_width="match_parent"
  android:layout_height="match_parent"
  app:layoutManager="LinearLayoutManager"
  tools:context=".fragments.RankingsFragment" />
```

With those two files in place, we can now add the RankingsFragment to the bottom nav. The one bit of prep that's needed is to add a new icon for that bottom nav item. Add this like you did with the previous two bottom nav entries: right-click res > drawable and select New > Vector Asset. I picked the format list numbered image, but you're free to choose whichever image makes sense to you. Once that's added to the project, open menu/navigation.xml and add a new <item>:

```
<?xml version="1.0" encoding="utf-8"?>
<menu xmlns:android="http://schemas.android.com/apk/res/android">
  <item
    android:id="@+id/pickPlayersFragment"
    android:icon="@drawable/ic_baseline_face_24"
    android:title="@string/players" />
  <item
    android:id="@+id/gameFragment"
    android:icon="@drawable/mdi_dice_6_black_24dp"
    android:title="@string/game" />
➤ <item
➤   android:id="@+id/rankingsFragment"
➤   android:icon="@drawable/ic_baseline_format_list_numbered_24"
➤   android:title="@string/rankings" />
</menu>
```

After adding the new *@string/rankings* value ("Rankings"), open navigation/nav_graph.xml and add the new <fragment> entry in there:

```
<?xml version="1.0" encoding="utf-8"?>
<navigation xmlns:android="http://schemas.android.com/apk/res/android"
  xmlns:app="http://schemas.android.com/apk/res-auto"
  android:id="@+id/nav_graph"
  app:startDestination="@id/rankingsFragment">
  <fragment
    android:id="@+id/pickPlayersFragment"
    android:name="dev.mfazio.pennydrop.fragments.PickPlayersFragment"
    android:label="fragment_pick_players" />

  <fragment
    android:id="@+id/gameFragment"
    android:name="dev.mfazio.pennydrop.fragments.GameFragment"
    android:label="fragment_game" />

➤ <fragment
➤   android:id="@+id/rankingsFragment"
➤   android:name="dev.mfazio.pennydrop.fragments.RankingsFragment"
➤   android:label="fragment_rankings" />
</navigation>
```

You may have noticed that I changed my app:startDestination= value to the new *@id/rankingsFragment*. I'm doing this temporarily since this entire chapter will be spent inside that view (unless you want to play some more games to get additional data). We're actually now in a state where we can safely run the app, though it won't display any data at this point. But we can at least verify that navigation is working.

If your app's navigation is good, then let's get some data in there. We're going to start by building the layout file representing how each list item will be displayed, then use that layout inside a new ListAdapter class.

Build the List Item Layout

The end goal for this section is to get PlayerSummaryAdapter ready for use, but the class and layout files I mentioned before should be completed first. That class, PlayerSummary, is a basic data class used to hold the win and games played totals for each user. We'll use this class to determine what to display in each line item. The code for the class looks like this:

```
package dev.mfazio.pennydrop.types

data class PlayerSummary(
  val id: Long,
  val name: String,
  val gamesPlayed: Int = 0,
  val wins: Int = 0,
  val isHuman: Boolean = true
)
```

Not much else to say here, so we can move on to where we'll use instances of the PlayerSummary class, a new layout file called player_summary_list_item.xml.

This layout file will look familiar to past ones, especially the player_list_item.xml layout file we saw back in Add Player Rows Without Repeating Yourself (Too Much), on page 31. We have a generic <layout> tag wrapping the entire view, a <data> tag with a <variable> (the playerSummary variable), and then the main <ConstraintLayout> with all the views. Yes, that generic <layout> tag means we can use data binding for each row of our rankings list, which simplifies the code we need. Everything outside the <ConstraintLayout> looks like this:

```
<layout xmlns:android="http://schemas.android.com/apk/res/android"
  xmlns:app="http://schemas.android.com/apk/res-auto"
  xmlns:tools="http://schemas.android.com/tools">
```

```
<data>

    <variable
        name="playerSummary"
        type="dev.mfazio.pennydrop.types.PlayerSummary" />
</data>

«ConstraintLayout is down here.»
</layout>
```

As a reminder from the beginning of the chapter, rows are going to look like this:

The main <ConstraintLayout> has a height (*wrap_content*) and width (*match_parent*), an <ImageView>, plus four <TextView> components. Much of this will be the same as we've seen in previous chapters, but there are a couple of interesting parts to call out. Let's start with the <ImageView>.

We're reusing the Face and Android icons from Add the drawable Background, on page 74, but instead of creating a new drawable XML file like we did with the human/AI <SwitchCompat>, we're going to create a couple of new functions inside BindingAdapters.kt.

Add BindingAdapters

We need two new @BindingAdapter functions: bindPlayerSummaryAvatarSrc() and bindPlayerSummaryAvatarTint(). Both functions do similar things: set an attribute of the <ImageView> based on whether or not the listed player is human. While we could have combined the two function into one, each function is modifying a different property, so I feel like they make more sense separated out.

bindPlayerSummaryAvatarSrc() calls the setImageResource() function on imageView and assigns it a value from R.drawable, like this:

```
@BindingAdapter("playerSummaryAvatarSrc")
fun bindPlayerSummaryAvatarSrc(imageView: ImageView, isHuman: Boolean) {
  imageView.setImageResource(
    if (isHuman) {
      R.drawable.ic_baseline_face_24
    } else {
      R.drawable.ic_baseline_android_24
    }
  )
}
```

It's not the most exciting function, but it does save us from having some long conditional statements in our layout file. If you'd prefer to do that instead, go ahead. Functionally, they're the same—I just like working with Kotlin code rather than long ternary statements in my layout files. If you do want to go that route, it'd look like this (and when formatted correctly in XML, wouldn't fit on this page):

```
@{playerSummary.isHuman ?
  @drawable/ic_baseline_face_24 :
  @drawable/ic_baseline_android_24}
```

The bindPlayerSummaryAvatarTint() binding adapter is similar, but instead of calling setImageResource(), we use setImageTintList(). This function may look strange, but it's equivalent to using the android:tint= attribute. Also, since we're using Kotlin, the "setter" method can be accessed like a property, meaning we can instead assign a value to imageView.imageTintList.

Another part that's weird here is that we're working with a ColorStateList object rather than just a Color. This is the code equivalent to what we did with the ai_toggle_color.xml file before, where we had a list of colors and their associated state values. But since we're just worried about using one color, we can save ourselves some trouble here.

Inside the androidx.databinding.adapters.Converters package, we can use a function called convertColorToColorStateList(). It's a bit overkill since the body of this function is just ColorStateList.valueOf(color), but I like the readabilty this function offers.

Getting the Color object takes more work than just retrieving the Int as we did before, so we're going to use the Context object on our ImageView to do the conversion. Using a similar conditional block on isHuman, we can grab the resource value for the color we want, then call imageView.context.getColor() to handle the conversion from the color resource ID to a color ID value. The entire @BindingAdapter function looks like this:

```
@BindingAdapter("playerSummaryAvatarTint")
fun bindPlayerSummaryAvatarTint(imageView: ImageView, isHuman: Boolean) {
  imageView.imageTintList = convertColorToColorStateList(
    imageView.context.getColor(
      if (isHuman) {
        android.R.color.holo_blue_bright
      } else {
        android.R.color.holo_green_light
      }
    )
  )
}
```

With both functions ready, we can use them in our <ImageView> XML. This looks like many views we've created already but with a couple of extra attributes specifically for working with the image. android:adjustViewBounds=*"true"* allows the OS to resize the icon to fit the allowed area. Without this, we'd end up with a rather small Face or Android image on the left of each row. The android:scaleType=*"fitCenter"* also works to resize and grow the icon for each row. This tells the OS to actually do the resizing we allowed with android:adjustViewBounds=. The entire <ImageView> with all its attributes looks like this:

```
<ImageView
  android:id="@+id/playerTypeImage"
  android:layout_width="wrap_content"
  android:layout_height="0dp"
  android:layout_marginStart="16dp"
  android:adjustViewBounds="true"
  android:contentDescription="@string/player_type_image"
  android:padding="5dp"
  android:scaleType="fitCenter"
  app:layout_constraintBottom_toBottomOf="parent"
  app:layout_constraintStart_toStartOf="parent"
  app:layout_constraintTop_toTopOf="parent"
  app:playerSummaryAvatarSrc="@{playerSummary.isHuman}"
  app:playerSummaryAvatarTint="@{playerSummary.isHuman}" />
```

As we saw with the app:isHidden= attribute previously, our binding adapters are added to the app namespace and reference the view to which they're added. Make sure to add in the *@string/player_type_image* string resource, and the image is ready to go.

Add TextViews to the List Item

Each row has four separate <TextView> components: the player's name, how many games they've played, their win total, and the word WIN or WINS, depending on the number of wins. We can look at these all at once since there's very little new in them, but with a couple of callouts first.

If you remember, having numeric values as text in data binding expressions caused issues. We could always append an empty string in each of the binding expressions or we could instead add a new value to PlayerSummary. The choice is yours, but I like the extra value approach, so I added winsString, which calls toString() on the wins value. It's not that interesting, but it cleans up the layout file a touch. gamesPlayed would have the same issue, but we're already appending that to a String for the "games played" part of the UI.

The last noteworthy piece is the "win" or "wins" text. While we could add in code to manually switch between the values or just use "win(s)", this feels like a perfect time to introduce the concept of *quantity strings* or *plurals* in Android. Similar to string resources, plurals give you String values via a resource name rather than hard-coding in a text value, helping with translations.

But plurals differ from string resources in that you're adding multiple <item> tags to a <plurals> entry, each <item> representing a different quantity= value. These values are *zero*, *one*, *two*, *few*, *many*, and the fallback *other*.

Note that not all languages will support all of these values. English, for example, only uses *one* and *other*. For more details on all you can do with quantity strings, the docs can be found at https://link.mfazio.dev/plurals.

In our case, we're going to have two quantities: *one* (with a value of "win") and *other* ("wins"). The entire res/values/plurals.xml file looks like this:

```
<?xml version="1.0" encoding="utf-8"?>
<resources>
  <plurals name="wins">
    <item quantity="one">win</item>
    <item quantity="other">wins</item>
  </plurals>
</resources>
```

We can then use the values in our XML via data binding. We reference plurals in the same manner as string resources, but also send in the number used to determine the quantity. That leads to a statement like android:text="*@{@plurals/wins(playerSummary.wins)}*".

One last useful attribute with the Win/Wins text: we want that text to be all uppercase, which we can do via the android:textAllCaps= attribute. This helps avoid having separate string resource values for a given word with either normal case or all uppercase.

Here's the rest of the <ConstraintLayout>, the aforementioned four <TextView> components:

```
<TextView
  android:id="@+id/playerName"
  android:layout_width="wrap_content"
  android:layout_height="wrap_content"
  android:layout_marginStart="16dp"
  android:text="@{playerSummary.name}"
  android:textSize="32sp"
  app:layout_constraintBottom_toTopOf="@id/playerGamesPlayed"
  app:layout_constraintStart_toEndOf="@id/playerTypeImage"
  app:layout_constraintTop_toTopOf="parent"
  tools:text="Michael" />
```

```
<TextView
  android:id="@+id/playerGamesPlayed"
  android:layout_width="wrap_content"
  android:layout_height="wrap_content"
  android:text='@{playerSummary.gamesPlayed + " " + @string/games_played}'
  app:layout_constraintBottom_toBottomOf="parent"
  app:layout_constraintStart_toStartOf="@id/playerName"
  app:layout_constraintTop_toBottomOf="@id/playerName"
  tools:text="23 games played" />

<TextView
  android:id="@+id/playerGamesWon"
  android:layout_width="48dp"
  android:layout_height="wrap_content"
  android:layout_marginEnd="16dp"
  android:text='@{playerSummary.winsString}'
  android:textAlignment="center"
  android:textSize="32sp"
  app:layout_constraintEnd_toEndOf="parent"
  app:layout_constraintStart_toStartOf="@id/textWins"
  app:layout_constraintTop_toTopOf="parent"
  tools:text="10" />

<TextView
  android:id="@+id/textWins"
  android:layout_width="48dp"
  android:layout_height="wrap_content"
  android:layout_marginEnd="16dp"
  android:text="@{@plurals/wins(playerSummary.wins)}"
  android:textAlignment="center"
  android:textAllCaps="true"
  app:layout_constraintBottom_toBottomOf="parent"
  app:layout_constraintEnd_toEndOf="parent"
  tools:text="wins"/>
```

Now that the list item layout is complete, we can start building our PlayerSummaryAdapter class.

Create a Custom ListAdapter

The PlayerSummaryAdapter class is responsible for managing all the PlayerSummary items in our list and handling how they're displayed. We use a custom RecyclerView.ViewHolder inner class (meaning it lives inside PlayerSummaryAdapter) to bind a PlayerSummary item to the layout, then the RecyclerView library handles the rest. All we need to do in PlayerSummaryAdapter is tell the RecyclerView what to do when creating and binding a new ViewHolder plus how to tell the difference between PlayerSummary items in the list.

After creating PlayerSummaryAdapter in the adapters package, first up is the PlayerSummaryViewHolder inner class. The PlayerSummaryAdapter class both contains and depends on this class, so we'll create it first then wrap PlayerSummaryAdapter around it. The PlayerSummaryViewHolder class inherits from RecyclerView.ViewHolder and has a single function, bind(), which takes in a PlayerSummary object.

The bind() function doesn't do much other than assign binding.playerSummary to the item value. The binding value is an instance of PlayerSummaryListItemBinding, which was generated by the Data Binding library when we added the generic <layout> tag to the player_summary_list_item.xml file. The item value, then, is the PlayerSummary object coming into the method. Once that assignment is complete, bind() then ensures bindings are executed so the data shows up properly with the executePendingBindings() function.

```
inner class PlayerSummaryViewHolder(
  private val binding: PlayerSummaryListItemBinding
) :
  RecyclerView.ViewHolder(binding.root) {

  fun bind(item: PlayerSummary) {
    binding.apply {
      playerSummary = item
      executePendingBindings()
    }
  }
}
```

The PlayerSummaryAdapter class around this inner class inherits from ListAdapter, which takes two type parameters and a DiffUtil.ItemCallback instance. The type parameters are the type of item in the list (PlayerSummary) and the type of ViewHolder for those items (PlayerSummaryAdapter.PlayerSummaryViewHolder). The callback piece is a new private class at the end of the file called (uncreatively) PlayerSummaryDiffCallback. That class looks like this:

```
private class PlayerSummaryDiffCallback :
  DiffUtil.ItemCallback<PlayerSummary>() {

  override fun areItemsTheSame(
    oldItem: PlayerSummary,
    newItem: PlayerSummary
  ): Boolean = oldItem.id == newItem.id

  override fun areContentsTheSame(
    oldItem: PlayerSummary,
    newItem: PlayerSummary
  ): Boolean = oldItem == newItem
}
```

With both PlayerSummaryDiffCallback and PlayerSummaryViewHolder ready, we can get PlayerSummaryAdapter created. This class, which inherits from ListAdapter, will also contain a few overridden functions that we'll create in a bit. The class declaration plus the other class and function from before together look like this:

```
class PlayerSummaryAdapter :
  ListAdapter<PlayerSummary, PlayerSummaryAdapter.PlayerSummaryViewHolder>(
    PlayerSummaryDiffCallback()
  ) {

    //Overridden functions will go here in a bit.

  inner class PlayerSummaryViewHolder(
    private val binding: PlayerSummaryListItemBinding
  ) :
    RecyclerView.ViewHolder(binding.root) {

    fun bind(item: PlayerSummary) {
      binding.apply {
        playerSummary = item
        executePendingBindings()
      }
    }
  }
}

private class PlayerSummaryDiffCallback :
  DiffUtil.ItemCallback<PlayerSummary>() {

  override fun areItemsTheSame(
    oldItem: PlayerSummary,
    newItem: PlayerSummary
  ): Boolean =
    oldItem.id == newItem.id

  override fun areContentsTheSame(
    oldItem: PlayerSummary,
    newItem: PlayerSummary
  ): Boolean =
    oldItem == newItem
}
```

An error should be there with the PlayerSummaryAdapter as written since we've yet to implement the two abstract functions from ListAdapter: onCreateViewHolder() and onBindViewHolder(). Both functions are effectively one step, so we can get them done pretty quickly.

onCreateViewHolder() needs to know how to build instances of PlayerSummaryViewHolder. That means we're inflating our layout using the DataBindingUtil class as we have done a few times in this book, sending that into a new PlayerSummaryViewHolder instance, and returning that from the function.

```
override fun onCreateViewHolder(
  parent: ViewGroup,
  viewType: Int
```

```
): PlayerSummaryViewHolder =
  PlayerSummaryViewHolder(
    DataBindingUtil.inflate(
      LayoutInflater.from(parent.context),
      R.layout.player_summary_list_item,
      parent,
      false
    )
  )
```

onBindViewHolder() is even more straightforward, as it uses a PlayerSummaryViewHolder instance from onCreateViewHolder(), then sends a PlayerSummary item into the bind() function. We use the getItem() function from the ListAdapter class to get the correct PlayerSummary based on where we are in the list. This is a major advantage of inheriting from the ListAdapter class—it does almost all the work for us as far as handling the items and retrieving the correct one.

```
override fun onBindViewHolder(
  viewHolder: PlayerSummaryViewHolder,
  position: Int
) {
  viewHolder.bind(getItem(position))
}
```

The PlayerSummaryAdapter is now ready for use, so we can head over to the RankingsFragment class to get everything connected.

Connect Adapter to RecyclerView

Here, we're expanding on what we set up earlier with RankingsFragment. Inside the onCreateView() function, we instantiate a PlayerSummaryAdapter object, then assign that to the RecyclerView. Retrieving that RecyclerView object turns out to be easier than previous times we've gotten view components because the entire view we inflated earlier is a <RecyclerView>. As a result, we can convert the view value into a RecyclerView instance, then assign the adapter property. We're also going to add an ItemDecoration to the RecyclerView, which adds light gray lines between each row.

```
override fun onCreateView(
  inflater: LayoutInflater,
  container: ViewGroup?,
  savedInstanceState: Bundle?
): View? {
  val view =
    inflater.inflate(R.layout.fragment_rankings, container, false)
➤ val playerSummaryAdapter = PlayerSummaryAdapter()
➤
➤ if (view is RecyclerView) {
```

```
      with(view) {
        adapter = playerSummaryAdapter

        addItemDecoration(
          DividerItemDecoration(
            context,
            LinearLayoutManager.VERTICAL
          )
        )
      }
    }

    return view
  }
```

This is another great example of smart casting in Kotlin that we first saw in Update roll() and pass() Functions, on page 142. Since we checked that view is an instance of RecyclerView, view is treated in that entire block as a RecyclerView instance without having to create a new value.

Also, we normally would have assigned a value to the layoutManager property on RecyclerView like this:

```
layoutManager = LinearLayoutManager(context)
```

However, it wasn't required since we already handled setting a LayoutManager in the <RecyclerView> tag inside fragment_rankings.xml.

The RecyclerView is now complete and has an assigned adapter to handle all its data. The last piece we need to cover here is how to get that data from the database into the PlayerSummaryAdapter. To do that, we're going to create RankingsViewModel and *observe* a LiveData value from there.

Load Data into RecyclerView from Database

The RankingsViewModel class is similar to GameViewModel in that we're getting an instance of PennyDropRepository, then getting LiveData back. We use the Transformations class to turn Player and GameStatus objects into PlayerSummary objects. Then, once that's done, we observe() the playerSummaries LiveData value from RankingsViewModel inside RankingsFragment and update PlayerSummaryAdapter with the new data. Let's go through and get each piece created.

Create RankingsViewModel

As I mentioned, this will look similar to GameViewModel in how we get an instance of PennyDropRepository. The entire RankingsViewModel class will look like this, minus the Transformations.map() logic (which we'll cover soon).

```
class RankingsViewModel(application: Application) :
  AndroidViewModel(application) {

  private val repository: PennyDropRepository

  val playerSummaries: LiveData<List<PlayerSummary>>

  init {
    this.repository = PennyDropDatabase
      .getDatabase(application, viewModelScope)
      .pennyDropDao()
      .let { dao ->
        PennyDropRepository.getInstance(dao)
      }

    playerSummaries = Transformations.map(
      this.repository.getCompletedGameStatusesWithPlayers()
    ) { statusesWithPlayers ->
      // We'll fill this in next.
    }
  }
}
```

Before we move on, we need to add a getCompletedGameStatusesWithPlayers() function in both PennyDropRepository and PennyDropDao. Plus, we want a new class, GameStatusWithPlayer, that'll be returned from those functions. The GameStatusWithPlayer is similar to GameWithPlayers but with GameStatus and Player objects instead of Game and a List<Player>:

```
data class GameStatusWithPlayer(
  @Embedded val gameStatus: GameStatus,
  @Relation(
    parentColumn = "playerId",
    entityColumn = "playerId"
  )
  val player: Player
)
```

The repository function is once again just a passthrough to the DAO function, which is a query where we get all GameStatus objects that are part of Finished games. We do this by using a subquery on the games table:

```
@Transaction
@Query(
  """
  SELECT * FROM game_statuses gs
  WHERE gs.gameId IN (
      SELECT gameId FROM games
      WHERE gameState = :finishedGameState
  )
  """
)
```

```
abstract fun getCompletedGameStatusesWithPlayers(
  finishedGameState: GameState = GameState.Finished
): LiveData<List<GameStatusWithPlayer>>
```

It's awkward having a parameter in this function for a value that won't change, but I feel the query is more readable this way as opposed to having something like WHERE gameState = 1. This parameter being set is also why I use the term *completed* in the function name, despite the fact that you could technically send in whichever state you want. By giving it a specific name like that, hopefully the purpose of the function is clear and future devs aren't using it improperly.

In Clauses Are Limited to 999 Items

Due to a limitation with SQLite, we're required to have fewer than 1000 items in any IN list. If you have more, the app will crash. In many cases, this isn't an issue, but it can certainly pop up, so be aware when you're writing your queries.

With the functions added to PennyDropRepository and PennyDropDao, we can head back to add in the Transformations.map() logic.

Inside this block, we take a List<GameStatusWithPlayer> (the statusesWithPlayers value) and convert that into a List<PlayerSummary>. We do this by grouping the GameStatusWithPlayer by the associated player, then mapping each Player/List<GameStatus> pair to new PlayerSummary objects. The gamesPlayed property is the number of GameStatus objects associated with the player, while the wins property gets the number of games where the player's pennies value is 0.

```
statusesWithPlayers
  .groupBy { it.player }
  .map { (player, statuses) ->
    PlayerSummary(
      player.playerId,
      player.playerName,
      statuses.count(),
      statuses.count { it.gameStatus.pennies == 0 },
      player.isHuman
    )
  }
```

The last piece here is to get the PlayerSummary objects in the right order. First and foremost, we want to sort the players by their wins with the most wins at the top and least wins at the bottom. This would just be a matter of adding a call to .sortedByDescending { it.wins } to the end of the previous statement.

But the rankings list would look better if we not only sorted by wins but also by games played. We can see who's won the most, but in the case of a tie, we then order players by who's played the most. Unfortunately, sortedByDescending() doesn't work with multiple criteria, at least not without a bunch of extra code.

Instead, we can use the sortedWith() function and send in a Comparator object to handle the properties. The compareBy() function, which lives in the kotlin.comparisons package, can bring in multiple selectors to use in the comparison. These selectors look similar to the function body with sortedByDescending() and have the added bonus of being able to prepend a minus sign to sort on a value in descending fashion. The final version of the statusesWithPlayers mapping looks like this:

```
statusesWithPlayers
  .groupBy { it.player }
  .map { (player, statuses) ->
    PlayerSummary(
      player.playerId,
      player.playerName,
      statuses.count(),
      statuses.count { it.gameStatus.pennies == 0 },
      player.isHuman
    )
  }
  .sortedWith(compareBy({ -it.wins }, { -it.gamesPlayed }))
```

The RankingsViewModel is now ready to be used, so let's head over to RankingsFragment to get things set up.

Observe Data in RankingsFragment

We can add RankingsViewModel to this class just as we did in the other two Fragment classes, with the activityViewModels() function:

```
private val viewModel by activityViewModels<RankingsViewModel>()
```

Then, inside onCreateView() after we set up the RecyclerView, we're going to observe the playerSummaries LiveData value for changes. When something changes, we'll then call playerSummaryAdapter.submitList() to update the adapter's data, which will then update the RecyclerView. The code to do this looks like this:

```
viewModel.playerSummaries.observe(viewLifecycleOwner) { summaries ->
  playerSummaryAdapter.submitList(summaries)
}
```

We send in the viewLifecycleOwner value to let the Observer know when it should stop observing the data. This means when the RankingsViewModel is disposed, we should also stop observing the playerSummaries value. With that complete, any updates in the database will now be pushed out to the rankings RecyclerView automatically.

Test the Data Updates

Now it's the fun part: run the app and check out the rankings. If you played enough games earlier to get some data in there, you should see a rankings screen that looks like this:

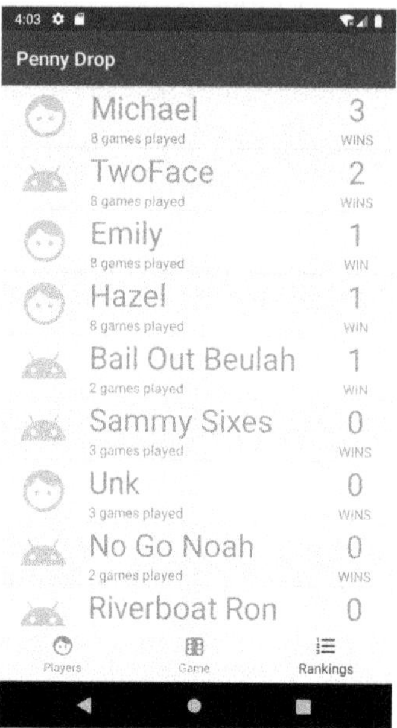

Another good test is to play an additional game of Penny Drop, then flip over to the Rankings view when you're done. Not only should the rankings update, but you should see a nice little animation when the latest game is added to the rankings. Pretty cool, right?

Summary and Next Steps

This chapter was all about displaying lists in your app with a RecyclerView. We got one set up, connected all the required pieces like the PlayerSummaryAdapter, and even saw a slick way of bringing data in from the database. Any time you want to display lists in an Android app, you're going to follow a similar process. Of course, things can get more complicated, as we'll see in Chapter 11, Display Data with Paging, on page 259, but the core components and ideas stay the same.

Next up is for us to do a few things to give users the ability to make the app their own. We're going to add in user-selectable settings and themes to the app by taking advantage of the SettingsFragment class. Users will have the ability to change the number of pennies in their game of Penny Drop, how quickly the AI plays, and even how their app looks.

CHAPTER 7

Customize an App with Settings and Themes

The Penny Drop app is almost finished! Once we're done here with our changes, all the functionality we're covering in this book for Penny Drop will be complete. We'll add some testing later on in Chapter 14, Unit Test Your App with JUnit, on page 329, and Chapter 15, Test Your App's UI with Espresso, on page 351, but this is it for user-facing changes.

What are those changes, you ask? We'll create a `SettingsFragment` with five options, then handle all of those options throughout our app. These settings include pairs of both gameplay and look-and-feel changes. We'll also have some credits about the app since we need to give the https://materialdesignicons.com credit for their awesome work, after all. The five items in our Settings page (as you'll see in an upcoming screenshot) are as follows:

- Starting Penny Count: sets the number of pennies for each player at the start of a game. Goes from 1 to 20.
- Fast AI: changes the AI delay speed from one second to one-tenth of a second (1000 -> 100 milliseconds).
- App Theme: lets users choose from one of the preset themes. We'll see how to do this later in the chapter.
- Theme Mode: users can choose if they always want the app to have a light theme, a dark theme, or use the system's current theme.
- About Penny Drop: takes users to a new `AboutFragment` to give some info about the app and icons used in it.

We'll be going through each preference in order throughout this chapter, seeing how to use the saved values and covering all the other changes required to handle setting changes. Once we're done, the Settings page will look like this:

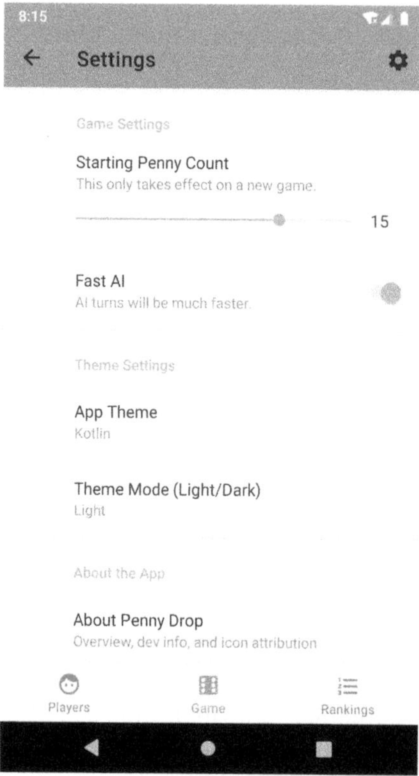

Let's start things out by adding the SettingsFragment class to the app.

Add a New SettingsFragment

Right off the bat, I want to apologize and clarify the terms we're using in this chapter. The class we're creating is called SettingsFragment, which inherits from the AndroidX Preference library's class PreferenceFragmentCompat. The SettingsFragment handles a number of Preference objects and <Preference> tags.

Then why are we calling this "Settings" instead of "Preferences"? The main reason is because the official Android Developers docs refer to the concept as Settings: https://link.mfazio.dev/settings. I know it may be confusing building out Settings with a number of Preference items, but I'm following the conventions established by the Android team. Another reason is the PreferenceFragment class already exists in the Preference library, so naming our class something different avoids any potential conflicts and headaches.

Also, when you click the Settings link in most apps, it uses the label Settings, not Preferences, so we're at least consistent that way. Still, my apologies for any confusion this causes for you.

Hopefully we're all on the same page now and can start building our SettingsFragment class. As I mentioned before, this inherits from the PreferenceFragmentCompat class. Yes, there's one more bit of weirdness with getting this class set up, but there's a good reason to use PreferenceFragmentCompat rather than PreferenceFragment (and it's not just that the latter was deprecated in API level 28).

PreferenceFragment inherits from the old android.app.Fragment class rather than the current androidx.fragment.app.Fragment class. Instead of changing the parent class of PreferenceFragment and breaking any app that isn't using AndroidX libraries, the Android team created a new class and deprecated the old one.

Speaking of AndroidX, we need to include the Preference library dependency in our app. Let's add another ext variable (called preference_version, referencing the latest version of the Preference library) in the project's build.gradle file, then add the preference-ktx dependency to the app's build.gradle:

```
dependencies {
  «Other dependencies»

  implementation "androidx.navigation:navigation-ui-ktx:$nav_version"
  implementation "androidx.preference:preference-ktx:$preference_version"
  implementation
    "androidx.recyclerview:recyclerview:$recycler_view_version"

  «Other dependencies»
}
```

Once you've synced your project, add a new class to the fragments package called SettingsFragment. As I mentioned, this class will inherit from PreferenceFragmentCompat, which is an abstract class with one abstract function: onCreatePreferences(). This function brings in the savedInstanceState of the function and a rootKey String value that we send along to the setPreferencesFromResource() function.

With those parts in place, your class should look like this:

```
package dev.mfazio.pennydrop.fragments

class SettingsFragment : PreferenceFragmentCompat() {
  override fun onCreatePreferences(
    savedInstanceState: Bundle?,
    rootKey: String?) {
    // We'll be filling this in next.
  }
}
```

This is the only function we'll be implementing in this class, which means we're leaving onCreateView() alone. In all our other Fragment classes, we overrode that function to set our layout and handle any binding that needed to be done. However, the PreferenceFragmentCompat class takes care of all of that for us. We don't even need to create a layout file, as it'll be done for us. What we *do* need is some way to tell the SettingsFragment which preferences to display.

We have two options here: XML or code. To keep things more consistent with how we've handled views elsewhere in this app, we're going to go with XML here via an XML resource file. If you want to see how to add preferences via code, check out Chapter 12, Personalize the Android Baseball League App, on page 283.

Add the Preferences Resource File

Unlike layout files, a preferences resource file is a generic XML file inside the res/xml folder. You can call this file whatever you like; I'm going with preferences.xml. This file will look a lot like a normal layout file but without any of the height/weight/constraints that we've used before, as the library will take care of all of that for us.

Go ahead and add preferences.xml (or whatever you'd like to call it) inside res/xml (you may need to add the xml directory), then open up the file. On a high level, this file will have a <PreferenceScreen> tag at the top level with our normal xmlns:android= and xmlns:app= namespace attributes. Then, in our case, we have multiple PreferenceCategory tags, each with one android:title= attribute and one or more <Preference> tags inside. The preferences.xml file, including the <PreferenceScreen> tag with the <PreferenceCategory> tags, will look like this:

```
<?xml version="1.0" encoding="utf-8"?>
<PreferenceScreen
  xmlns:android="http://schemas.android.com/apk/res/android"
  xmlns:app="http://schemas.android.com/apk/res-auto">

  <PreferenceCategory android:title="Game Settings">
    <!-- This will contain the Penny Count and Fast AI preferences -->
  </PreferenceCategory>

  <PreferenceCategory android:title="Theme Settings">
    <!-- This will contain the Theme and Light/Dark Mode preferences -->
  </PreferenceCategory>

  <PreferenceCategory android:title="About the App">
    <!-- This will contain an "About the App" link -->
  </PreferenceCategory>

</PreferenceScreen>
```

With the preferences.xml file created, we can tell the SettingsFragment to use that file to generate our view:

```
override fun onCreatePreferences(
  savedInstanceState: Bundle?,
  rootKey: String?
) {
  setPreferencesFromResource(R.xml.preferences, rootKey)
}
```

Now that the SettingsFragment is created and has the XML in place, we can add it to the app's navigation.

Add Settings Page to Navigation

I want to clarify something right away—when I say we're adding the page to the app's navigation, I'm referring to the navigation graph rather than the bottom navigation component. This means we need a new <fragment> entry in nav_graph.xml:

```
<fragment
  android:id="@+id/settingsFragment"
  android:name="dev.mfazio.pennydrop.fragments.SettingsFragment"
  android:label="@string/settings" />
```

Instead of the bottom nav, settings are accessed via a gear icon in the app's nav bar. To do this, we add a new icon and a new file called options.xml in the res/menu resource directory. The gear Vector Asset is called Settings; add that to the project, then include it in the new <item> inside the new options.xml file:

```
<?xml version="1.0" encoding="utf-8"?>
<menu xmlns:android="http://schemas.android.com/apk/res/android">
  <item
    android:id="@+id/settingsFragment"
    android:icon="@drawable/ic_baseline_settings_24"
    android:title="@string/settings"
    app:showAsAction="ifRoom" />
</menu>
```

A heads up that the app:showAsAction=*ifRoom* attribute means that we'll display the Settings icon as long as there's room in the app bar, and if not, it goes into an overflow (three dots) menu in the top right. The Settings icon should always display for us, but when you add multiple icons to the App Bar, this setting becomes more important.

With the new file ready (don't forget your string resource), we need to tell the MainActivity to use this file.

We do that by overriding the onCreateOptionsMenu() function and inflating the options.xml file.

```
override fun onCreateOptionsMenu(menu: Menu?): Boolean {
  super.onCreateOptionsMenu(menu)

  menuInflater.inflate(R.menu.options, menu)

  return true
}
```

The last piece in MainActivity is to tell the app what to do when someone clicks the Settings gear. Since we only have a single item to choose from, it simplifies the logic for us. We need to check to make sure the navController is ready to navigate us to a different view, and if so, use the onNavDestinationSelected() function that lives on the MenuItem class. If that function call doesn't work (returns false), we fall back to the parent class function.

```
override fun onOptionsItemSelected(item: MenuItem): Boolean =
  if (this::navController.isInitialized) {
    item.onNavDestinationSelected(this.navController) ||
      super.onOptionsItemSelected(item)
  } else false
```

Note that we check if navController is ready by checking the isInitialize property on the *property reference* for navController rather than the property itself. It's a small difference in syntax but makes a big difference in functionality.

Now our app will display the Settings icon, and if we click that link, we're taken to our Settings screen with the empty categories:

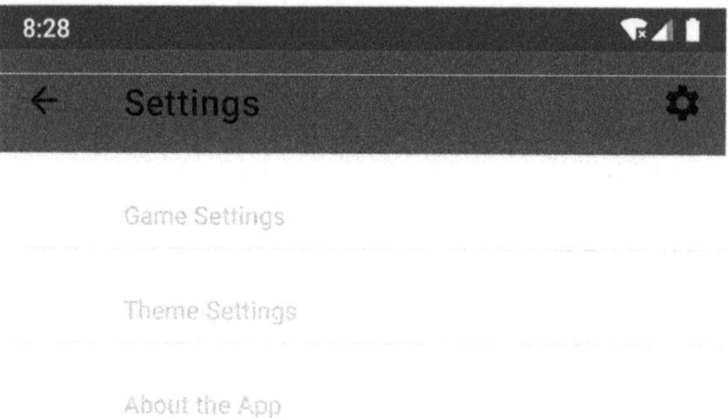

We can get to our Settings page, so now it's time to get some actual preferences in there. First up is the Game Settings section, which is a good introduction into how Preference values work.

Add Game Settings Preferences

These two preferences are your standard examples of how to handle a Preference in an app. We change the value in the SettingsFragment and use it somewhere else in the app. The library takes care of saving the value and giving us a mechanism to retrieve it, meaning there's very little manual work we need to do.

The Starting Penny Count setting is a <SeekBarPreference>, meaning users get a slider representing numbers to choose a value. All of our preferences have key, summary, and title attributes, plus most have a defaultValue attribute as well. With the seek bar, we can additionally set minimum and maximum values and the app:showSeekBarValue= attribute so the number they select shows up at the end of the bar. The XML for the <SeekBarPreference> looks like this:

```
<SeekBarPreference
  android:defaultValue="10"
  android:key="pennyCount"
  android:max="20"
  android:summary="@string/starting_penny_count_new_game"
  android:title="@string/starting_penny_count"
  app:min="1"
  app:showSeekBarValue="true" />
```

Outside of creating a couple of string resources, this is good to go. I do want to call out how the minimum value attribute is in the app namespace instead of android. I honestly don't know why that was the approach taken with these attributes, but as long as you know where to set it, it's not a big deal.

The Fast AI setting is the simpler of the two preferences, with just the basic key, summary, and title attributes. We set these three attributes on a <SwitchPreferenceCompat> tag. Again, we're using the Compat version here, in this case because this ensures things show up properly on older devices. It's pretty much guaranteed to not make a difference with our current app since the minimum API level is 26, but if you're writing an app later on for older devices, using <SwitchPreferenceCompat> will make sure the switch is displayed consistently between OS versions. Here's the code for this preference:

```
<SwitchPreferenceCompat
  android:key="fastAI"
  android:summary="@string/fast_ai_summary"
  android:title="@string/fast_ai" />
```

We can now run the app to see our new Preferences, as shown in the image on page 176.

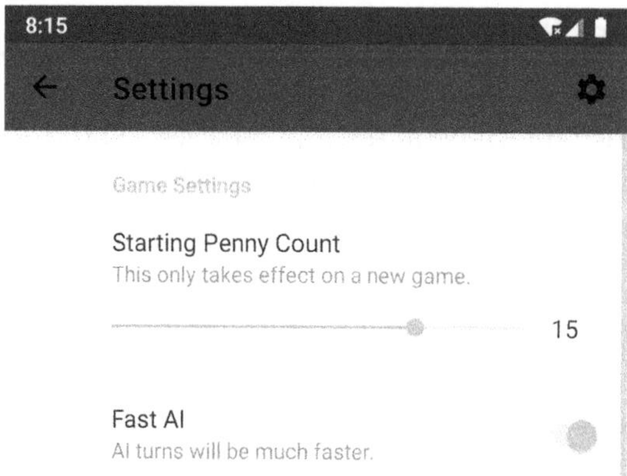

Those preference values can be changed as we wish right now, but they obviously don't do anything yet. Next up is for us to grab preferences out of the PreferenceManager class and use them in our app.

Use Saved Preferences

In addition to all the UI work that's taken care of for us with the PreferenceFragmentCompat class, value changes are also saved and updated automatically. To retrieve those values, we need to get a SharedPreferences instance from the PreferenceManager class. Inside GameViewModel we're going to do just that, assigning the result to a new prefs value:

```
private val prefs =
  PreferenceManager.getDefaultSharedPreferences(application)
```

Use the Fast AI Preference

We can now use prefs to get the preference values as needed. It's out of order for how we set things up in SettingsFragment, but let's start with the Fast AI setting since it's a one-line change.

Down in the playAITurn() function, we currently have a 1000 millisecond delay() function call to simulate a normal player taking time to consider their options. Now, we're going to change that to 100 milliseconds, but only if the Fast AI toggle is flipped to true. We can check the value by calling the getBoolean() function on the prefs value we created and sending in the key value from our <SwitchPreferenceCompat> element. That means the playAITurn() function looks something like this:

```
private suspend fun playAITurn() {
  delay(if (prefs.getBoolean("fastAI", false)) 100 else 1000)

  // Rest of the function is still down here
}
```

That second parameter on getBoolean() is a default value for when the fastAI setting doesn't have a value. Once the user goes to the settings page and flips that setting on, we'll see the AI move a lot faster. Feel free to test this out yourself now to make sure you got everything right. I'd show a screenshot, but speeding up the AI's turns doesn't translate well to a book.

Use the Starting Penny Count Preference

The other setting in this section, pennyCount, is also set inside the GameViewModel. In the startGame() function, we're now going to send in the pennyCount value (with a default value of Player.defaultPennyCount to the PennyDropRepository.startGame() function:

```
suspend fun startGame(playersForNewGame: List<Player>) {
  repository.startGame(
    playersForNewGame,
    prefs?.getInt("pennyCount", Player.defaultPennyCount)
  )
}
```

As your IDE is probably telling you now, this requires a few downstream changes as well. PennyDropRepository.startGame() now looks like this:

```
suspend fun startGame(players: List<Player>, pennyCount: Int? = null) =
  pennyDropDao.startGame(players, pennyCount)
```

In PennyDropDao, the startGame() function now has pennyCount as a parameter, then where we insert GameStatus objects is updated to look like this:

```
this.insertGameStatuses(
  playerIds.mapIndexed { index, playerId ->
    GameStatus(
      gameId,
      playerId,
      index,
      index == 0,
      pennyCount ?: Player.defaultPennyCount
    )
  }
)
```

The likely question here is "Why not get the pennyCount value inside PennyDropDao instead of sending it through all the layers?" The reason is the PreferenceManager.getDefaultSharedPreferences function needs a reference to a Context object. In the docs, it says "[The getDefaultSharedPreferences() function] works from anywhere in your application,"[1] but that's only true if you're able to get a Context object

1. https://link.mfazio.dev/use-saved-values

in said location. Even though we created the PennyDropDatabase with a Context object and get PennyDropDao from there, we don't have access to that object anymore in this class.

While we could save a Context value inside PennyDropDao in some fashion, we don't want Android application context references being saved in random places. The GameViewModel already has access to a Context object (via the application value), so this is the best spot to access our preferences.

Now is a great time to run your app, change both Game Settings, and start a new game. You'll see the starting penny count that you set reflected on the Game screen, and having an AI player will show the change due to the Fast AI toggle.

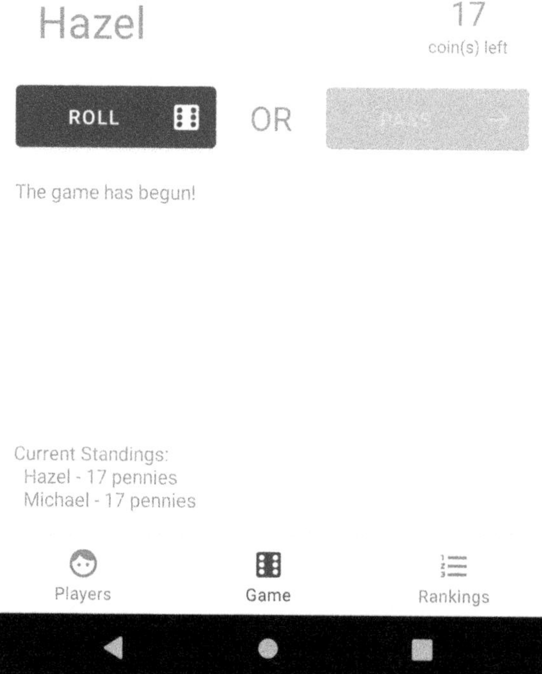

With those in place and you now knowing how to get preference values, we can move on to the Theme Settings. We need to get a few themes created, then we can go ahead and switch between them in our app. Once that's ready, we'll also look at how to swap between light and dark modes.

Add Themes

We are going to add some new themes for users to select from, but before we start on that, I'm recommending we add a new library. The Material Design

Components (MDC) library gives us an easier way to handle Material Design styling in our app.

In particular, I'm having us add this library due to the Material Theming support it offers. Material Theming gives us extra color attributes like colorSurface, which the docs note as setting the "surfaces of components, such as cards, sheets, and menus."

In our case, we're using it to set the background color of our App Bar when we're in a dark theme (the primary color is used in a light theme). Adding the MDC library and changing our parent theme to *Theme.MaterialComponents.DayNight* gives us access to the extra color attributes plus some look-and-feel changes (like rounded buttons).

Add this just like normal, pointing to the latest MDC version, and include a material_version ext variable.

```
dependencies {
  //Still have the other dependencies up here
➤ implementation "com.google.android.material:material:$material_version"
}
```

Themes are added in the res/values/styles.xml file. Right now, you likely just have a single theme called AppTheme which inherits from *Theme.AppCompat.Light.DarkActionBar.* We're changing this to the previously mentioned *Theme.MaterialComponents.DayNight* value, which not only offers the MDC additions I noted but sets us up for handling changes between light and dark modes.

The rest of our themes are going to inherit from AppTheme, allowing us to effectively have default values in other themes, set by the base theme. In practice, we're only worried about *colorSurface*, and that's only a concern for us with dark theming, but this is a technique you can use elsewhere to great effect.

I've created five additional themes in my version of styles.xml, all of which look similar to the theme I'll show in a second. If you want to see all of them, make sure to the check out the chapter-7/app-code folder in the code. This style is based on the Kotlin logo and branding:

```
<style name="Kotlin" parent="AppTheme">
  <item name="colorPrimary">@color/kotlinBlue</item>
  <item name="colorPrimaryDark">@color/kotlinPurple</item>
  <item name="colorAccent">@color/kotlinOrange</item>
</style>
```

As you can see, some new color resource values are defined in this theme, so we need to add those to res/values/colors.xml:

```
<color name="kotlinBlue">#178dd7</color>
<color name="kotlinOrange">#f98908</color>
<color name="kotlinPink">#c359bc</color>
<color name="kotlinPurple">#806fe3</color>
```

Feel free to add any themes you like in this same manner. If you want to test out your app quickly with a new theme, open up your AndroidManifest.xml and change the value of android:theme= inside the <application> tag to something like this:

```
<application
  android:allowBackup="true"
  android:icon="@mipmap/ic_launcher"
  android:label="@string/app_name"
  android:roundIcon="@mipmap/ic_launcher_round"
  android:supportsRtl="true"
  android:theme="@style/AppTheme">
  ...
</application>
```

With the new themes added to styles.xml (and colors.xml as needed), we can move on to giving users a way to quickly switch between themes as they wish.

Change Themes

Back inside preferences.xml, let's add a new <DropDownPreference> to the Theme Settings category. In addition to the normal attributes we've set previously, we have three more we're using here.

Add Additional Preference Attributes

app:useSimpleSummaryProvider= handles updating the summary text whenever we change the value of our preference, which we can use both here and once we get to the night mode support. The other two attributes are android:entries= and android:entryValues=, which give us a way to populate our drop-down list. Both of these values live inside res/values/arrays.xml (which you probably need to create). Before we add those values, here's the full <DropDownPreference>:

```
<DropDownPreference
  android:defaultValue="AppTheme"
  android:entries="@array/themes"
  android:entryValues="@array/theme_values"
  android:key="theme"
  android:title="@string/app_theme"
  app:useSimpleSummaryProvider="true" />
```

Now, let's go add those entry strings.

Add Entries and Entry Values

The arrays.xml resource file contains some number of <array> tags with one or more items inside. In our case, we're creating multiple <string-array> sets called themes and theme_values. These tags will contain multiple child <item> tags with all our labels or values. In case you're wondering what each array represents, we're using *themes* as the label for the drop down, while *theme_values* is the actual value we get from the SharedPreferences object. My arrays.xml file currently looks like this (yours may differ depending on your themes):

```
<?xml version="1.0" encoding="utf-8"?>
<resources>
  <string-array name="themes">
    <item>Default</item>
    <item>Kotlin</item>
    <item>Crew</item>
    <item>FTD</item>
    <item>GPG</item>
    <item>HMF</item>
  </string-array>
  <string-array name="theme_values">
    <item>AppTheme</item>
    <item>Kotlin</item>
    <item>Crew</item>
    <item>FTD</item>
    <item>GPG</item>
    <item>Hazel</item>
  </string-array>
</resources>
```

With those in place and our <DropDownPreference> tag referencing both arrays from arrays.xml, we can start using the values.

Use the Selected Theme

In addition to setting a theme in AndroidManifest.xml as we did earlier, we can set a theme via its ID in the onCreate() function of MainActivity. To do this, we need to grab the theme ID from the SharedPreferences class as we've done otherwise, convert that from a text value into a resource ID, then call setTheme(). Again, remember that your theme values and IDs may differ depending on which themes you're using:

```
val prefs =
  PreferenceManager.getDefaultSharedPreferences(this)
```

```
val themeId = when (prefs.getString("theme", "AppTheme")) {
  "Crew" -> R.style.Crew
  "FTD" -> R.style.FTD
  "GPG" -> R.style.GPG
  "Hazel" -> R.style.Hazel
  "Kotlin" -> R.style.Kotlin
  else -> R.style.AppTheme
}

setTheme(themeId)
```

The most important thing here is to make sure the setTheme() function call is completed *before* you call setContentView(). Failing to do so will cause your theme setting to not be picked up properly.

This code is set and it does what we need, but it only does so when the MainActivity is created, which is currently on app startup. To make this more dynamic and not require users to restart their app completely to change the theme, we need to add some logic inside SettingsFragment.

Handle Preference Changes

Inside the onCreatePreferences() function, we can retrieve any of the preferences we've set up and watch for changes to the values via an OnPreferenceChangeListener object. This is another spot where Kotlin is wonderful, as we don't have to create a full OnPreferenceChangeListener class or even worry about explicitly overriding the onPreferenceChange() function, but instead we can just add a Preference.OnPreferenceChangeListener reference with a block of code that's the body of that class's one function. This is similar to how we implemented the OnClickListener back in Add Players to GameViewModel, on page 79.

We can get an instance of our DropDownPreference via the findPreference() function in a similar manner to the findViewById() function using the key value:

```
val themePreference = findPreference<DropDownPreference?>("theme")
```

Once we have that instance, we can (safely) assign the onPreferenceChangeListener on the themePreference value. I say "safely" because themePreference is nullable, so we only want to do the assignment if themePreference is not null. The code block attached to the OnPreferenceChangeListener only does one thing, re-create the current Activity, then returns a value of true:

```
themePreference?.onPreferenceChangeListener =
  Preference.OnPreferenceChangeListener { _, _ ->

    activity?.recreate()

    true
  }
```

Note that I omitted both parameters to this function, as we're not using them. The two parameters would normally be the changed Preference and an Any object that's representing the new value. We don't need either one here, but we will be using them in a bit when changing the theme mode.

In case you're not aware since we haven't mentioned it so far, the Any class in Kotlin is equivalent to an Object class in Java. It's the base-level type and can be used with any (hence the name) object of any type.

Go ahead and run your app and try switching between a few themes. Adding that call to re-create the Activity saves us from having to completely close and reopen the app each time we want a new theme. Next up is switching between light and dark modes, which is a similar (and slightly easier) process.

Add Night Mode Support

One of the latest trends with apps and websites is the introduction of dark themes. With Android 10, dark theme support was finally baked into the OS, giving your entire phone a darker look and feel.

In our code, we can either force a mode for the app on the user (though we're letting them pick which mode they prefer) or we can use the current setting from the system. By having the combination of the Theme.MaterialComponents.DayNight parent style and using mode values from AppCompatDelegate, we can change the entire mode of our app automatically.

The key to making this all work is the AppCompatDelegate.setDefaultNightMode() function. This function brings in a mode ID value and instantly switches the app to use the selected mode. In our case, we're concerned with three values: MODE_NIGHT_NO, MODE_NIGHT_YES, and MODE_NIGHT_FOLLOW_SYSTEM. You can think of these being light, dark, and system, respectively. What we need to do is add those three choices into the SettingsFragment, then respond as we did with the theme, where we change the mode based on the value that's been set.

It's more complex than the previous approach, but it should make sense given what we did before. First up is to added a new <ListPreference> tag with more array values.

Add the Preference with Entries

With both Theme settings preferences, we could have gone with either a <DropDownPreference> or a <ListPreference>, as both serve similar purposes. I decided to use one of each as examples, but feel free to choose whichever preference you prefer. Also, as both preferences serve similar purposes, their attributes are going to be the same, albeit with different values:

```
<ListPreference
  android:defaultValue="System"
  android:entries="@array/theme_modes"
  android:entryValues="@array/theme_mode_values"
  android:key="themeMode"
  android:title="@string/theme_mode"
  app:useSimpleSummaryProvider="true" />
```

We again need to add two more <string-array> sets in arrays.xml:

```
<string-array name="theme_modes">
  <item>Light</item>
  <item>Dark</item>
  <item>System Default</item>
</string-array>
<string-array name="theme_mode_values">
  <item>Light</item>
  <item>Dark</item>
  <item>System</item>
</string-array>
```

While I didn't do so here, you could also use string resource values for all of these items. This is the better approach, but I kept these values as the strings themselves to make things clearer for this chapter. You'll definitely want to go with string resource values if your app will have any language translations, though.

With the <ListPreference> and array values added, we can add another OnPreferenceChangeListener to SettingsFragment.

React to Preference Changes

Things start out the same way as when we did this before. We get an instance of the ListPreference:

```
val themeModePreference = findPreference<ListPreference?>("themeMode")
```

Then we add an OnPreferenceChangeListener to handle when the preference changes:

```
themeModePreference?.onPreferenceChangeListener =
  Preference.OnPreferenceChangeListener { _, newValue ->
    //We'll finish this in a second.
  }
```

Inside this code block, we need to take the newValue and determine which mode the user wants. We can again use a when { ... } block to make this determination, then call AppCompatDelegate.setDefaultNightMode() to assign it. Doing this will actually change the app's theme instantly without the need for an Activity re-creation. We also want to set a default value in the code here since that would make more sense to read than android:defaultValue=*-1*:

```
themeModePreference?.setDefaultValue(
  AppCompatDelegate.MODE_NIGHT_FOLLOW_SYSTEM
)

themeModePreference?.onPreferenceChangeListener =
  Preference.OnPreferenceChangeListener { _, newValue ->
    val nightMode = when (newValue?.toString()) {
      "Light" -> AppCompatDelegate.MODE_NIGHT_NO
      "Dark" -> AppCompatDelegate.MODE_NIGHT_YES
      else -> AppCompatDelegate.MODE_NIGHT_FOLLOW_SYSTEM
    }

    AppCompatDelegate.setDefaultNightMode(nightMode)
    true
  }
```

Right now, the mode is only set when we change it in the Settings page. We also need to add some code to MainActivity to use the saved value upon startup.

Set the Theme Mode on App Startup

We're taking the same approach as we did with the app theme here, just with a different method call in the end.

```
val nightMode = when (prefs.getString("themeMode", "")) {
  "Light" -> AppCompatDelegate.MODE_NIGHT_NO
  "Dark" -> AppCompatDelegate.MODE_NIGHT_YES
  else -> AppCompatDelegate.MODE_NIGHT_FOLLOW_SYSTEM
}
AppCompatDelegate.setDefaultNightMode(nightMode)
```

It's probably better to add this code prior to the setContentView() call like we did with the setTheme() call, but changing the mode is done on demand, so it's not as big of an issue.

Now, if you've run the app, you may have noticed that the slots or game buttons are barely visible in dark mode. This is because we're setting colors meant for a light-themed app in all scenarios. While that worked great when we only had the light theme, we could use something more flexible for various colors throughout the app.

Handle Theme Mode Colors in the App

Back when we added the slots in Update Slot Bindings, on page 87, we had ternary statements to choose the color of each element:

```
android:tint=
  "@{slot.lastRolled ? @color/colorPrimary : @android:color/black}"
```

Instead, we want to change this to use a color state list resource file. We first did this back in Add Color to the Switch, on page 75.

In our case, we want to use the app's primary color when the slot was last rolled. Unfortunately, we can't access the lastRolled property directly, but we *can* use lastRolled to set the view's isActivated flag. Before we get to how to set that flag, the color state list will look like this:

```
<selector xmlns:android="http://schemas.android.com/apk/res/android">
  <item android:color="?attr/colorPrimary"
        android:state_activated="true" />

  <item android:color="?android:attr/textColorPrimary" />
</selector>
```

Now, back to isActivated. We need to add another function to our BindingAdapters.kt file like we did back in Create Binding Adapters, on page 88. Luckily, it's a simple-enough function that sets a single property:

```
@BindingAdapter("slotLastRolled")
fun bindSlotLastRolled(view: View, lastRolled: Boolean) {
  view.isActivated = lastRolled
}
```

With that added, we can now add app:slotLastRolled="@{slot.lastRolled}" to all three view tags in layout_coin_slot.xml and then change each of the colors. We started with something like this:

```
android:tint=
  "@{slot.lastRolled ? @color/colorPrimary : @android:color/black}"
```

And we can change it to something like this instead:

```
android:tint="@color/coin_slot_color"
```

Along the same lines, we want to convert the Roll and Pass buttons to use color state lists. Plus, we can change the other colors for the buttons (text and drawable) to use attribute values instead of hardcoded @color resource values. This will allow the app to automatically change those colors depending on which theme is selected.

Create two new color state list resources inside the res/color directory: roll_button_color.xml and pass_button_color.xml. Each one will have a color when android:state_activated="*true*" and use the ?android:attr/textColorPrimary= attribute otherwise.

roll_button_color.xml looks like this:

```
<?xml version="1.0" encoding="utf-8"?>
<selector xmlns:android="http://schemas.android.com/apk/res/android">
  <item
    android:color="@android:color/darker_gray"
    android:state_enabled="false" />
  <item
    android:color="?attr/colorPrimaryDark"
    android:state_pressed="true"/>
  <item android:color="?attr/colorPrimary"/>
</selector>
```

And pass_button_color.xml looks like this:

```
<?xml version="1.0" encoding="utf-8"?>
<selector xmlns:android="http://schemas.android.com/apk/res/android">
    <item
        android:color="@android:color/darker_gray"
        android:state_enabled="false" />
    <item
        android:color="?attr/colorAccent"/>
</selector>
```

I added in the android:state_pressed= <item> with the Roll button to give a bit of extra feedback when the user taps that button. It's an optional piece but shows how we can combine different state attributes in a single color state list.

Then we can head back to fragment_game.xml to use the new color state list files. While we're in there, let's also update the android:drawableTint= and android:textColor= attributes. The full Roll <Button> tag with the updated attributes will look like this:

```
<Button
  android:layout_width="0dp"
  android:layout_height="wrap_content"
  android:layout_weight="3"
  android:backgroundTint="@color/roll_button_color"
  android:drawableEnd="@drawable/mdi_dice_6_black_24dp"
  android:drawableTint="?android:attr/textColorPrimaryInverse"
  android:enabled="@{vm.canRoll}"
  android:onClick="@{() -> vm.roll()}"
  android:padding="10dp"
  android:text="@string/roll"
  android:textColor="?android:attr/textColorPrimaryInverse" />
```

Before we finish up here, we need a couple of quick changes to the FAB on the Pick Players view. The image tint should now use the inverse of the primary text color, just as we did with the Roll and Pass buttons. We also want to manually set the background tint color to use the accent color from our theme rather than the default colorAccent value.

The full FAB XML (with the app:tint= attribute update) looks like this:

```
<com.google.android.material.floatingactionbutton.FloatingActionButton
  android:id="@+id/buttonPlayGame"
  android:layout_width="wrap_content"
  android:layout_height="wrap_content"
  android:layout_margin="16dp"
  android:contentDescription="@string/play_button"
  android:src="@drawable/ic_baseline_play_arrow_24"
  app:backgroundTint="?android:attr/colorAccent"
  app:layout_constraintBottom_toBottomOf="parent"
  app:layout_constraintEnd_toEndOf="parent"
  app:tint="?android:attr/textColorPrimaryInverse" />
```

With both the theme and theme mode preferences in place, including all their logic and subsequent layout updates, we can move on to the last preference. This preference will take users to a new view which tells users something about what went into building the app.

Add an About the App Section

The intent here is to give users some information about the app: who made it, why it was made, and some credits on the icons we used outside of Google's Material Design library (such as icons from https://materialdesignicons.com/). To do this, we're going to create AboutFragment with the info. My version looks like the image shown on page 189.

I'm not too worried if your AboutFragment has all the same information as mine, as you've done almost all of this before. If you want to see the entire XML for this file, head over to the code and look at fragment_about.xml inside the chapter-7/app-code folder. The parts here that are new are the (clickable) links in the first and third sections.

To add these links, we're going to use both HTML and Android's SpannableString class. But before we get to implementing this view, let's first build an empty fragment, then the navigation to get there.

You've created fragments before, so go ahead and do so now; we'll add to the onCreateView() function soon.

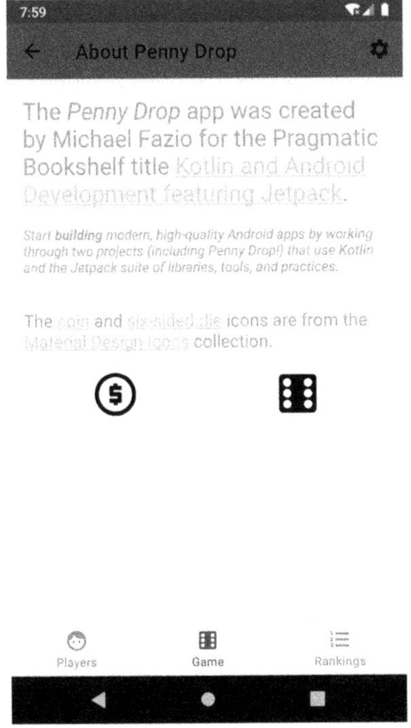

Handle Navigation to AboutFragment

Adding this fragment to the navigation graph is the same as all the others—add a new entry to nav_graph.xml:

```
<?xml version="1.0" encoding="utf-8"?>
<navigation xmlns:android="http://schemas.android.com/apk/res/android"
  xmlns:app="http://schemas.android.com/apk/res-auto"
  android:id="@+id/nav_graph"
  app:startDestination="@id/gameFragment">

    <!-- Other <fragments ... /> still live up here. -->

    <fragment
      android:id="@+id/aboutFragment"
      android:name="dev.mfazio.pennydrop.fragments.AboutFragment"
      android:label="About Penny Drop" />
</navigation>
```

Start on AboutFragment

We're going to mainly be working in AboutFragment in this section, so it'll save you some trouble to switch the app:startDestination= value to *@id/aboutFragment* temporarily. Just make sure you switch it back after you're done.

Next, we want to navigate here whenever a user clicks the About Penny Drop preference in our Settings page. First, we add a generic <Preference> inside the About the App category we created earlier (plus some string resource values):

```
<PreferenceCategory android:title="About the App">
➤   <Preference
➤     android:key="credits"
➤     android:summary="@string/about_app_summary"
➤     android:title="@string/about_penny_drop" />
</PreferenceCategory>
```

Next, we get our Preference and set the onPreferenceClickListener similarly to how we did with the theme preferences:

```
val creditsPreference = findPreference<Preference?>("credits")

«Unrelated code»

creditsPreference?.onPreferenceClickListener =
  Preference.OnPreferenceClickListener { _ ->
    this.findNavController().navigate(R.id.aboutFragment)
    true
  }
```

Since we added AboutFragment to the nav graph, this will handle the navigation to the About view for us while keeping the rest of the navigation setup working. The only issue with this setup is that our top bar is missing a back arrow to tell users they can return to their previous view. In our case, that means a nice way to return to the Settings view from the About view. It works with the phone's back button, but we should give them a way to do this within the app.

Head over to MainActivity, and at the end of the onCreate() function, we want to configure the App Bar to work with our navigation. In particular, we want it to recognize where we are and display a back arrow when we're not on one of the main views (Players, Game, Rankings).

It's possible to explicitly list all the Fragment classes that are considered top-level (meaning they won't display an up arrow), but we can handle this in a more efficient way. We'll create a new AppBarConfiguration and send it the menu value assigned to our bottom nav. Then we can configure the App Bar with this configuration, and the Navigation library will take care of the rest.

```
val appBarConfiguration = AppBarConfiguration(bottomNav.menu)
setupActionBarWithNavController(
  this.navController,
  appBarConfiguration
)
```

The only slight issue with this approach is that the label in the App Bar is now using the android:label= values inside nav_graph.xml. As a result, you'll want to go change all those values to be more readable versions (as string resources, of course), like this:

```
<fragment
  android:id="@+id/pickPlayersFragment"
  android:name="dev.mfazio.pennydrop.fragments.PickPlayersFragment"
  android:label="@string/pick_players" />
```

Here, @string/pick_players is the string resource value "Pick Players". The last piece here is to make sure the back button does what we want. Inside MainActivity, we want to override the onSupportNavigateUp() function to use the navController. We need to make sure the navController has been initialized (as it's marked with lateinit), then we tell it to handle the up navigation.

```
override fun onSupportNavigateUp(): Boolean =
  (this::navController.isInitialized &&
   this.navController.navigateUp()) || super.onSupportNavigateUp()
```

When we head into both the Settings and About views, they'll have a back arrow to show users they can return to where they were previously.

Now that we can get to the AboutFragment, we need to display things properly. Again, most of this is the same as we've done before, but adding clickable links requires some extra work.

Add Clickable Links in TextViews

As I mentioned at the start of this chapter, we've got a couple of options for adding links to a <TextView>. The simplest way is to write our string resource as HTML and to add the formatting there. Things like links and text decorations (bold, italics, and so on) end up being much quicker using this approach. If we create a string resource like this (in your code, this can be a single long line):

```
<string name="penny_drop_created_by">The <i>Penny Drop</i> app was
  created by Michael Fazio for the Pragmatic Bookshelf title
  <a href="https://pragprog.com/titles/mfjetpack/">
    "Kotlin and Android Development featuring Jetpack"
  </a>.</string>
```

This will cause the HTML to be rendered as you'd expect, as shown in the image on page 192.

The *Penny Drop* app was created by Michael Fazio for the Pragmatic Bookshelf title Kotlin and Android Development featuring Jetpack.

The only missing piece is that the link isn't clickable. It renders as a normal-looking web link, but it doesn't do anything when you tap on it. To enable that, we set the movementMethod property on the TextView:

```
view.findViewById<TextView>(R.id.about_credits)?.apply {
  //Makes the links clickable.
  this.movementMethod = LinkMovementMethod.getInstance()
}
```

Now when you click the link we added, it'll take you to the web page. We want the same action with the icon credits section, but this time we'll use a SpannableString to do so.

A SpannableString allows us to change pieces of text in a variety of ways, such as setting background/foreground colors, styling, and in our case, turning these pieces of text into links. We do so by creating a SpannableString from a String (in our case, a string resource), then we call setSpan() one or more times for a given substring (the numbers we send in represent the start/end index values).

Each call will contain a CharacterStyle class which takes some action on that substring of code. In our case, we use URLSpan objects with the correct web page address to create the links. Once those are added, we assign the SpannableString instance to the text property on our TextView.

Also, make sure you set the movementMethod property so the links are clickable here as well.

```
view.findViewById<TextView>(R.id.about_icon_credits)?.apply {
  val spannableString =
    SpannableString(getString(R.string.penny_drop_icons))

  spannableString.setSpan(
    URLSpan(
      "https://materialdesignicons.com/icon/currency-usd-circle-outline"
    ), 4, 8, 0
  )

  spannableString.setSpan(
    URLSpan("https://materialdesignicons.com/icon/dice-6"), 13, 26, 0
  )
```

```
  spannableString.setSpan(
    URLSpan("https://materialdesignicons.com"), 46, 67, 0
  )

  this.text = spannableString

  //Makes the links clickable.
  this.movementMethod = LinkMovementMethod.getInstance();
}
```

In most cases, you're going to be better off using HTML to create links and other basic formatting in a <TextView>, but if you do need extra control, the SpannableString class is there to help out.

With that, the About page is ready to go and our Settings screen is complete. There are other Preference types we haven't touched on here, so feel free to check out the official docs for more information.[2]

Summary and Next Steps

The Penny Drop app is now feature complete. Seven chapters, a whole bunch of pages, and we now have a beautifully working app ready to delight users around the world. Well, while that may be a *bit* of an overstatement, it's still a cool app, plus now you know how to take advantage of Kotlin and Jetpack to build an Android app!

Next up will be the Android Baseball League app, but before we close out Penny Drop, I'll call out a few things we could do to make the app even better.

New Game Dialog

It'd really be handy to give users a quick way to start a new game. Adding a dialog to start a new game quickly when either a game has ended or the user first starts the app would go a long way for app usability. While I don't want to dig into every piece of how to do this, let's have a look at the quick version.

Add a listener to currentGame inside GameFragment, then when the current game has ended, display an AlertDialog to the user like this:

```
val dialog = AlertDialog.Builder(activity)
  .setTitle("New Game?")
  .setIcon(R.drawable.mdi_dice_6_black_24dp)
  .setMessage("Same players or new players?")
  .setPositiveButton("Same Players") { _, _ ->
      gameViewModel.startWithSamePlayers()
  }
```

2. https://developer.android.com/guide/topics/ui/settings/components-and-attributes

```
    .setNegativeButton("New Players") { _, _ ->
        goToPickPlayers()
    }
    .setNeutralButton("Cancel") { _, _ ->
        /* This will just close the dialog */
    }.create()
dialog.show()
```

The dialog for creating a new game would be similar, just without the "Same Players" option. Also, make sure you call the show() function at the end or nothing will happen!

Save Pick Players Values

Along the same lines, we could save users some time by saving the names of the last players in a game, even after the app is closed. At the very least, having the main player's name saved from game to game would be helpful.

We could put this in the database, or we could even add a preference on our Settings screen for the default first player name. This value could also be set the first time they start a game, using the primary player name they enter there.

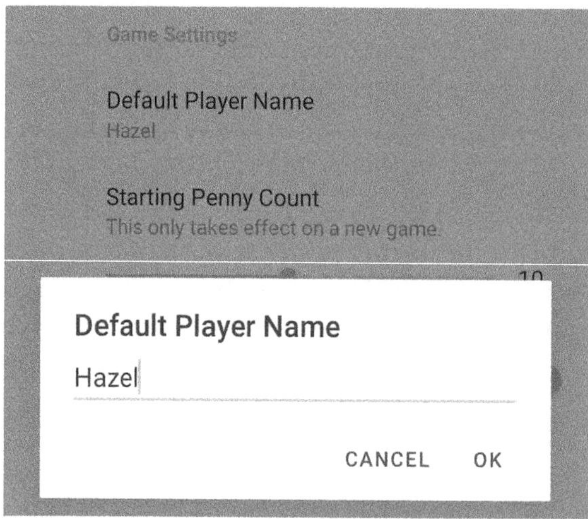

Handle Duplicate AI in a Game

One open bug in our game is that while we can't add the same AI player multiple times to a single game, we don't restrict users from doing so. In fact, if they try to do that, their game will crash.

You could do a few things here: change how AI players are saved to allow them to be included in a game multiple times, update GameStatus to include gamePlayerNumber as a primary key, or add filtering so only non-selected AI are available in the AI drop-down.

All of these solutions will require some extra work, but we could use something better than what we have now. I decided to exclude this from being directly covered in the book since we'd get more sidetracked than I'd like.

Reset Settings to Default

Another useful UX feature is to allow users a quick way to revert settings to their default value. If they want to go back to what the app started with as far as starting penny count and themes, we could either replace the Settings link in the App Bar of the Settings screen or add another Preference to reset everything.

You've seen how to add both a new menu link and a new Preference, plus handle click events, so the only new piece would be setting the value. You can do this by either calling findPreference() for each preference then assigning a new value to value or by using the Editor object on the SharedPreferences class:

```
// You can set the value directly on the Preference itself.
themeModePreference?.value = "System"

// Or you can use the SharedPreferences object to edit values.
val prefs =
  PreferenceManager.getDefaultSharedPreferences(this.context)

prefs.edit()?.also {
  it.putInt("pennyCount", Player.defaultPennyCount)
  it.apply()
}
```

Enable "Hazel" Mode

I had to include this because whenever we play a real-life version of Penny Drop, my daughter, Hazel, always seems to roll a ton of sixes. I don't know why this is the case, but it's a pretty consistent pattern at this point. For the app, it could check if the player's name is Hazel and if so, send in a new isHazel parameter to rollDie(). If that's the case, we roll a D8 (eight-sided die) and call it a six if the value is 6 or greater:

```
private fun rollDie(sides: Int = 6, isHazel: Boolean = false) =
  Random.nextInt(1, sides + 1 + if (isHazel) 2 else 0).let { roll ->
      if (roll > 6) 6 else roll
  }
```

Yes, this is silly, but the code is fun and she really does roll *a ton* of sixes.

Add an App Icon

All this work and we never set a proper icon for the app! That was intentional, since it's not related to what you were learning in each chapter. If you want to see how to do this, we add one right away to the ABL app. Check it out in Add an App Icon, on page 202.

Add Unit and/or UI Testing

This would be an *excellent* idea! So much so that it's what we're doing over in Chapter 14, Unit Test Your App with JUnit, on page 329, and Chapter 15, Test Your App's UI with Espresso, on page 351.

But until it's time to add some tests (you're welcome to go there now if you like), we're done with Penny Drop. Now it's onto the "official" Android Baseball League app, where we take what we learned here and turn it up a level.

Part II

Android Baseball League

It's time to jump into the world of the Android Baseball League, a league created just for this book. Seriously, all the players, teams, box scores, and everything else with the league were created for this. Now it's your turn to build the official Android Baseball League app (as official as an app for an imaginary league can be, that is.)

Things will get tougher here, but you can handle it. You'll take what you learned with Penny Drop and apply it here while also using additional Jetpack libraries and Kotlin coroutines (more in-depth this time).

CHAPTER 8

Initialize the Android Baseball League App

Welcome to the Android Baseball League! Founded in 2018, the Android Baseball League (or ABL for short) is our focus for the next half-dozen chapters. We are tasked with building the official app for the league so everyone's able to find out all about their favorite teams and players.

As you probably can guess, the ABL isn't a real league, but it *is* the focus of Part II of this book. It's time for us to build an advanced app with some more-complicated features.

We'll start with what you learned in Penny Drop, then add on from there. As a result, the pace is going to pick up and I'm not going to be (re-)explaining everything that we covered in the previous app. I *will* reference chapters from Part I when we hit upon certain concepts again, plus you can always reference the source code located on PragProg.com if you get stuck.

Welcome to the Official ABL App

The ABL app is a showcase for the league's teams and players. Users can find the current games (and any games for the year), who's leading the league in both batting and pitching categories, and the roster of any of the ABL's fourteen teams. Users can even set up things like a favorite team and whether or not they want to style the app based on that team.

As I mentioned, most of the chapters here will start with something similar to what we did with Penny Drop but then add on from there. We'll navigate via a menu (a navigation drawer here rather than a bottom nav), but then also see how to send data between destinations and how to create deep links. We'll save data to a local database for access in our screens, but then we'll also grab data from a web service to get up-to-date scoreboard data. We'll display a list of players, but then see how Paging helps to handle a *long* list of players.

We'll do most of the familiar setup within this chapter and do it quickly; I want to get you a working app as soon as possible without adding anything too new. We'll create the app, add in our dependencies, set up a number of images (team logos, league logo) including the app's logo, add some supporting types, and build out a screen.

Then each of the following chapters will add an additional screen (until Chapter 13, Send Info to and from the Android Baseball League App, on page 305, at least).

First things first, we need to create our app. Fire up Android Studio and we'll get started.

Create the App

Once Android Studio is open, create a new project with an Empty Activity (we'll be adding things manually again), and call it Android Baseball League. You can use your own package name as you wish (I like dev.mfazio.abl), and have an SDK of at least API level 26. This will make sure some newer Android features are available to us.

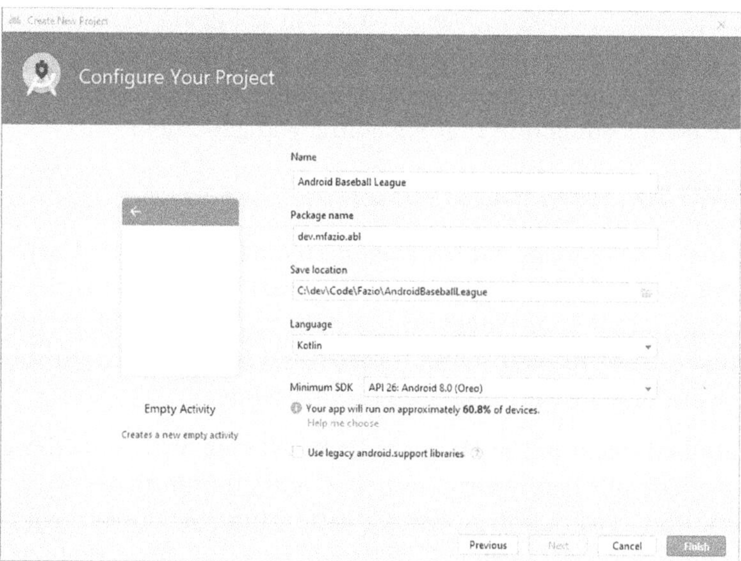

After the new project is indexed and the Gradle sync is complete, we have a nice empty MainActivity with which to work. Before we move on to any specific views, we have some extra dependencies we'll be using.

Add Dependencies

In this chapter, we'll add a new grid via the RecyclerView library and a <ConstraintLayout> in each grid item. Those dependencies are a great place to start, but we'll be adding more as we build out the ABL app. The dependencies block should look like the following:

```
dependencies {
  implementation "org.jetbrains.kotlin:kotlin-stdlib-jdk8:$kotlin_version"
  implementation "androidx.appcompat:appcompat:$app_compat_version"
  implementation
    "androidx.constraintlayout:constraintlayout:$constraint_layout_version"
  implementation "androidx.core:core-ktx:$core_version"
  implementation "androidx.navigation:navigation-fragment-ktx:$nav_version"
  implementation "androidx.navigation:navigation-ui-ktx:$nav_version"
  implementation
    "androidx.recyclerview:recyclerview:$recycler_view_version"
  implementation "com.google.android.material:material:$material_version"

  // Test dependencies down here
}
```

Three pieces of note here: first, we need to add the kotlin-kapt plugin to support data binding. Add it to the plugin block at the top of the app's build.gradle file. That block now looks like this:

```
plugins {
  id 'com.android.application'
  id 'kotlin-android'
➤ id 'kotlin-kapt'
}
```

Second, if it's not set this way by default, we want to use the kotlin-stdlib-jdk8 version of the Kotlin Standard Library. Make sure your app is using this as well.

The third piece is that all the dependencies added here have version variables (located in the project's build.gradle file). We're following the same pattern as we did with Penny Drop, and again, all dependencies with their versions can be found in Appendix 3, Gradle Dependencies, on page 395.

Finally, before you leave the app's build.gradle file, add the buildFeatures block to the top of the android block:

```
android {
➤ buildFeatures {
➤   dataBinding = true
➤ }
  //Rest of the 'android' block is down here.
}
```

Sync up your project to make sure all the dependencies are added, then we can get some assets ready.

Add Image Assets

The ABL app has quite a few more images in it than Penny Drop did, so to make your life easier, I'm including some images in the code on PragProg.com. This includes team logos, helper images, and the ABL logo itself. All the images you need here are under the images/abl directory.

Seriously, just copy/paste all the Drawable XML files in the images/abl/team-logos folder within the code into the drawables directory.

In addition, get all of the sizes of mke_flag.png in that same folder. I took an existing PNG and split it into six different resolutions (ldpi to xxxhdpi), one of which the app will use for a given device. We'll have other images to copy over later, but just getting the logos will be sufficient for now.

Heads up that the drawable-[dpi] folders should go into the src/main/res directory *alongside* the drawables directory, rather than into the drawables directory (like the other team logos).

Finally, in the same directory where we grabbed the other images, you'll want abl-logo-shifted.svg, as we're going to turn that into our app's icon.

Add an App Icon

The abl-logo-shifted.svg is what we'll use to create a new Image Asset, which in this case is the launcher icon for our app.

I've also included the normal abl-logo.svg in there, but I recommend the "shifted" version since it looks better when converted to an app icon. You can always try both versions out to see which one you prefer.

Once you have the icon on your local machine (not added to the project), right-click the res folder and choose New > Image Asset. This will display the Asset Studio, as shown in the first image on page 203.

In here, make sure the Asset Type under Source Asset is set to Image, and choose the abl-logo.shifted.svg file. You can rename the logo if you wish, or just overwrite the existing ic_launcher. Do *not* trim the logo (as this removes the shifting I mentioned), but resize the image to around 65%, as shown in the second image on page 203.

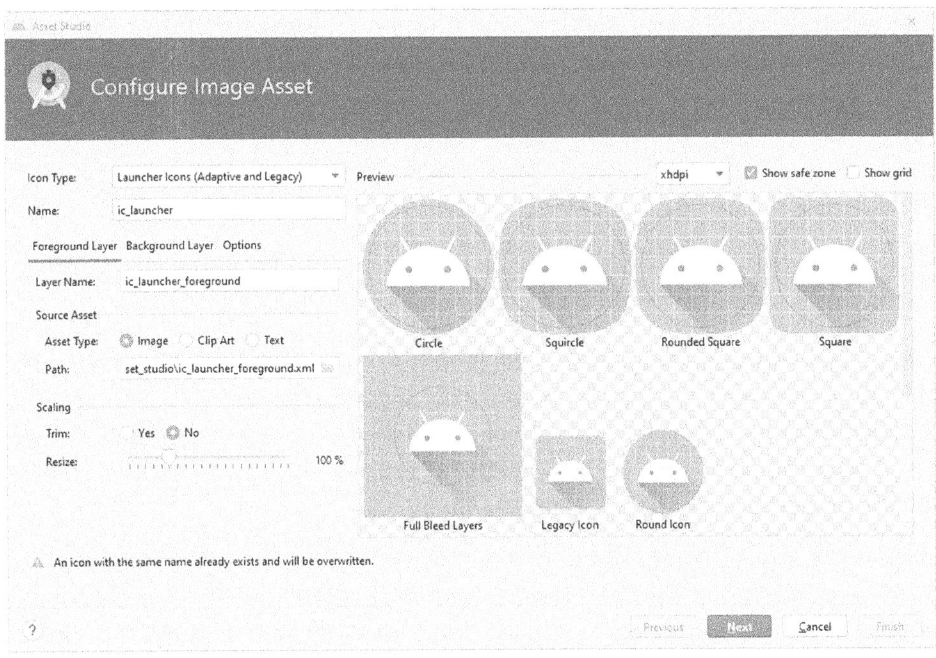
Asset Studio
Configure Image Asset
Icon Type:
Launcher Icons (Adaptive and Legacy)
Preview
xhdpi
Show safe zone
Show grid
Name:
ic_launcher
Foreground Layer
Background Layer
Options
Layer Name:
ic_launcher_foreground
Source Asset
Asset Type:
Image
Clip Art
Text
Path:
set_studio\ic_launcher_foreground.xml
Scaling
Trim:
Yes
No
Resize:
100 %
Circle
Squircle
Rounded Square
Square
Full Bleed Layers
Legacy Icon
Round Icon
An icon with the same name already exists and will be overwritten.
?
Previous
Next
Cancel
Finish

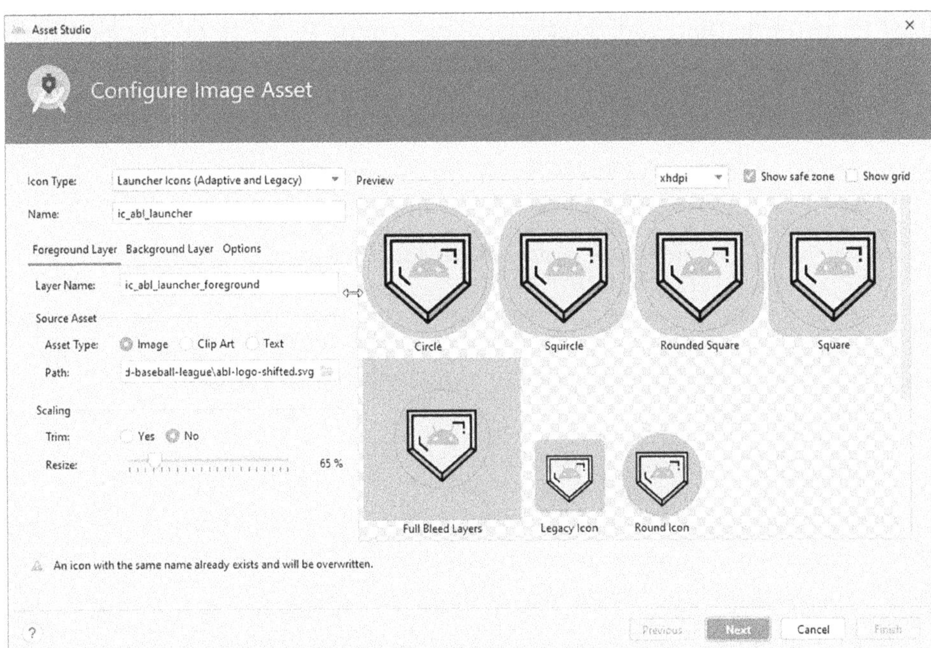
Asset Studio
Configure Image Asset
Icon Type:
Launcher Icons (Adaptive and Legacy)
Preview
xhdpi
Show safe zone
Show grid
Name:
ic_abl_launcher
Foreground Layer
Background Layer
Options
Layer Name:
ic_abl_launcher_foreground
Source Asset
Asset Type:
Image
Clip Art
Text
Path:
d-baseball-league\abl-logo-shifted.svg
Scaling
Trim:
Yes
No
Resize:
65 %
Circle
Squircle
Rounded Square
Square
Full Bleed Layers
Legacy Icon
Round Icon
An icon with the same name already exists and will be overwritten.
?
Previous
Next
Cancel
Finish

In the Background Layer section, you'll probably want to change the Asset Type to Color instead of Image to avoid the default blueprint-style background:

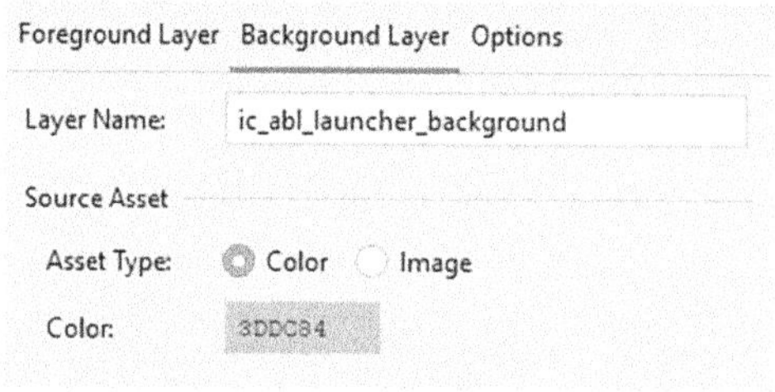

Foreground Layer Background Layer Options
Layer Name: ic_abl_launcher_background
Source Asset
Asset Type: Color Image
Color: 3DDC84

Once the background is ready, hit the Next button, then Finish. If you changed the name of the launcher icon, go into AndroidManifest.xml and replace the android:icon= and android:roundIcon= values with the new name. If you didn't change the name and the image is called "ic_launcher", you're all set (since *@mipmap/ic_launcher* is the default value).

Also, if you want the app name to display as anything other than the project name you entered at the start, you can change android:label= inside AndroidManifest.xml to something else. I changed mine to ABL since Android Baseball League is too long for an app drawer.

Just for confirmation, your <application> tag should look something like this:

```
<application
  android:allowBackup="true"
  android:icon="@mipmap/ic_abl_launcher"
  android:label="@string/app_short_name"
  android:roundIcon="@mipmap/ic_abl_launcher_round"
  android:supportsRtl="true"
  android:theme="@style/Theme.AndroidBaseballLeague">
  <activity android:name=".MainActivity">
    <intent-filter>
      <action android:name="android.intent.action.MAIN" />

      <category android:name="android.intent.category.LAUNCHER" />
    </intent-filter>
  </activity>
</application>
```

Once the icon is updated, you can run the app to see the change. Heads up that it *may* take an uninstall and reinstall for the icon to change. It should look something like the image shown on page 205.

With the icon added, we can start building out our app. First up is some initial MainActivity setup.

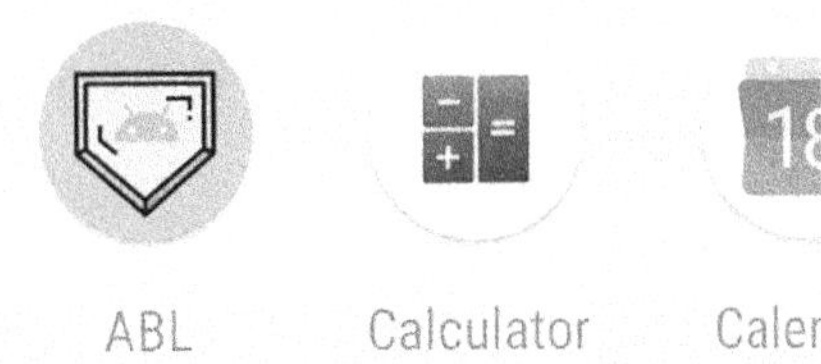

Configure the Activity

As was the case with Penny Drop, MainActivity is the primary hub handling Fragment classes but not a ton else. That's especially true as we're starting out since we're only concerned with some basic navigation.

For navigation, we need a <FragmentContainerView> and a navigation graph. Given that we're only concerned with a single fragment in this chapter, we don't even need to update code in MainActivity. Instead, we'll save that for the next chapter, Chapter 9, Navigate via Navigation Drawer, on page 215.

Add the FragmentContainerView

The <FragmentContainerView> is basically the same as Penny Drop. For now, we're going to have the <FragmentContainerView> take up the entire screen, meaning our activity_main.xml layout file looks like this:

```
<?xml version="1.0" encoding="utf-8"?>
<androidx.constraintlayout.widget.ConstraintLayout
  xmlns:android="http://schemas.android.com/apk/res/android"
  xmlns:app="http://schemas.android.com/apk/res-auto"
  xmlns:tools="http://schemas.android.com/tools"
  android:layout_width="match_parent"
  android:layout_height="match_parent"
  tools:context=".MainActivity">

  <androidx.fragment.app.FragmentContainerView
    android:id="@+id/containerFragment"
    android:name="androidx.navigation.fragment.NavHostFragment"
    android:layout_width="0dp"
    android:layout_height="0dp"
    app:defaultNavHost="true"
    app:layout_constraintBottom_toBottomOf="parent"
    app:layout_constraintEnd_toEndOf="parent"
    app:layout_constraintStart_toStartOf="parent"
    app:layout_constraintTop_toTopOf="parent"
    app:navGraph="@navigation/nav_graph" />

</androidx.constraintlayout.widget.ConstraintLayout>
```

All that's missing now is the navigation/nav_graph.xml file, which is minimal at this point. So minimal that it doesn't even get its own section in the book, just the following code block:

```
<?xml version="1.0" encoding="utf-8"?>
<navigation xmlns:android="http://schemas.android.com/apk/res/android"
  xmlns:app="http://schemas.android.com/apk/res-auto"
  xmlns:tools="http://schemas.android.com/tools"
  android:id="@+id/nav_graph"
  app:startDestination="@id/teamsFragment">
  <fragment
    android:id="@+id/teamsFragment"
    android:name="dev.mfazio.abl.teams.TeamsFragment"
    android:label="@string/teams">
  </fragment>
</navigation>
```

Once you add the teams string resource, this is good. Well, except that TeamsFragment doesn't yet exist. Let's do that.

Add the First Fragment

The TeamsFragment will contain a nice 2x7 grid of all the teams in the Android Baseball League. It'll look something like this:

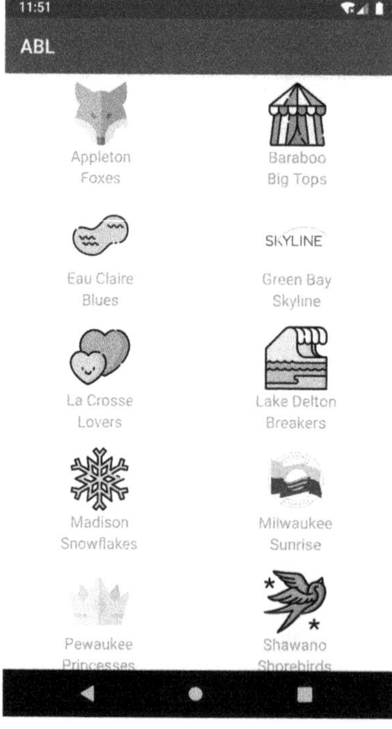

A heads up that I'm structuring things differently with the code in this app. Instead of splitting files up by their type (for example, activities, viewmodels, and so on), we'll split them by subject (for example, teams, leaders, and so on).

Before we create TeamsFragment, we're going to create a few supporting classes that'll be used in different ways on this screen.

Add Team-Related Classes

We need three additional classes for our Teams grid:

- Team—contains various info about each team in the ABL.
- UITeam—contains UI-specific values for each team in the ABL.
- Division—an enum class with the two parts of the ABL: East and West.

A core piece of our app is the Team class. This class holds the team ID, location, nickname, and division for each team. Plus, we have space in here to save wins and losses as well as team rankings in both their division and the ABL overall.

Since a Division is part of Team, let's add that quickly. Create the teams package and add a new enum class called Division that looks like this:

```
enum class Division { East, West, Unknown }
```

Then we can add the Team class:

```
data class Team(
  val id: String,
  val city: String,
  val nickname: String,
  val division: Division,
  val wins: Int = 0,
  val losses: Int = 0,
  val leagueRank: Int = -1,
  val divisionRank: Int = -1
)
```

The Team class itself is done, but I want to add all the teams here in a companion object. Since the teams aren't likely to change, I'm not bothering with putting them into a database or loading them dynamically from an API. While something *could* change with a team, it's guaranteed to not be a frequent occurrence, and we can always update the app when that happens.

We hard-code each team inside the companion object with their team ID, city, nickname, and division values filled in:

```
companion object {
  val Appleton = Team("APL", "Appleton", "Foxes", Division.East)
  val Baraboo = Team("BOO", "Baraboo", "Big Tops", Division.West)
```

```
  val EauClaire = Team("EC", "Eau Claire", "Blues", Division.West)
  val GreenBay = Team("GB", "Green Bay", "Skyline", Division.East)
  val LaCrosse = Team("LAX", "La Crosse", "Lovers", Division.West)
  val LakeDelton = Team("LD", "Lake Delton", "Breakers", Division.West)
  val Madison = Team("MSN", "Madison", "Snowflakes", Division.West)
  val Milwaukee = Team("MKE", "Milwaukee", "Sunrise", Division.East)
  val Pewaukee = Team("PKE", "Pewaukee", "Princesses", Division.East)
  val Shawano = Team("SHW", "Shawano", "Shorebirds", Division.East)
  val SpringGreen = Team("SG", "Spring Green", "Thespians", Division.West)
  val SturgeonBay = Team("SB", "Sturgeon Bay", "Elders", Division.East)
  val Waukesha = Team("WAU", "Waukesha", "Riffs", Division.East)
  val WisconsinRapids =
    Team("WR", "Wisconsin Rapids", "Cranberries", Division.West)
}
```

Next, we can get the UITeam class created. I decided to add this class to hold the logo and team colors for each team rather than have those values inside the Team class. That way we don't have UI-specifc attributes cluttering up a Team when they're not needed.

The UITeam instances will each hold an original Team object as well as a team logo and colors. We'll also include a few helper values to get things like locations and names without having to go through the team property. The class looks like this:

```
data class UITeam(
  val team: Team,
  val logoId: Int,
  val primaryColorId: Int,
  val secondaryColorId: Int,
  val tertiaryColorId: Int
) {
  val teamId = team.id
  val location = team.city
  val nickname = team.nickname
  val teamName = "$location $nickname"
  val division = team.division
}
```

I'm taking almost the same approach with UITeam as I did with Team in that we're hard-coding all the teams inside the class's companion object. But this time I'm putting all of them into a single List<UITeam> rather than creating individual values for each one since that's what we need for the Teams grid.

Each UITeam in the companion object will look similar to this:

```
  companion object {
    val allTeams = listOf(
        UITeam(
          Team.Appleton,
```

```
            R.drawable.fi_ic_fox,
            R.color.appletonPrimary,
            R.color.appletonSecondary,
            R.color.appletonTertiary
        ),
        //Other teams continue on down here
    )
}
```

For the full list of UITeam instances, check out the code. As for the Appleton Foxes we see in the preceding code, we already copied over the logo earlier, but we need to get those three colors in place. Again, you can just copy over all the UITeam colors from the supplied code. Either way, all the team colors live inside colors.xml and are similar to this:

```
<color name="appletonPrimary">#FF4F19</color>
<color name="appletonSecondary">#3A3A41</color>
<color name="appletonTertiary">#FFC173</color>
```

Now that the three supporting types are ready, we can move on to creating the TeamsFragment and everything that goes with it.

Add TeamsFragment

Create TeamsFragment however you wish inside the teams package with an associated layout file. I'm calling my layout file fragment_teams_grid.xml since it tells us more about that view, but that's totally optional.

We're going to work on the TeamsFragment code itself last since we need to set up other pieces first. So first up is the fragment's layout file.

The associated layout file (no matter what you call it) will contain a single <RecyclerView> tag and no more. We're taking the same general approach that we did with Penny Drop, in particular in the section Add the RecyclerView, on page 152.

```
<?xml version="1.0" encoding="utf-8"?>
<androidx.recyclerview.widget.RecyclerView
  xmlns:android="http://schemas.android.com/apk/res/android"
  xmlns:tools="http://schemas.android.com/tools"
  android:id="@+id/teamsGrid"
  android:name="dev.mfazio.abl.TeamsFragment"
  android:layout_width="match_parent"
  android:layout_height="match_parent"
  android:layout_gravity="center"
  tools:context=".teams.TeamsFragment"
  tools:listitem="@layout/teams_grid_item" />
```

Again, we'll come back to the actual code for TeamsFragment later, as we're getting everything set up prior. Next up is the layout for each item in the grid.

Add the Grid Item Layout XML

The teams_grid_item.xml layout file will contain three pieces—the team's logo, location, and nickname, all in a column. We'll also be binding a UITeam object to each item soon, so that'll be included in the layout as a <variable>.

You've done almost all of this before, so we can get to the code right away. I just want to mention that I'm using the Waukesha Riffs as the "tools" team here so the layout editor has something to display. Here's teams_grid_item.xml:

```
<?xml version="1.0" encoding="utf-8"?>
<layout xmlns:android="http://schemas.android.com/apk/res/android"
  xmlns:app="http://schemas.android.com/apk/res-auto"
  xmlns:tools="http://schemas.android.com/tools">

  <data>
    <variable
      name="team"
      type="dev.mfazio.abl.teams.UITeam" />
  </data>

  <androidx.constraintlayout.widget.ConstraintLayout
    android:layout_width="match_parent"
    android:layout_height="wrap_content"
    android:layout_margin="8dp">

    <ImageView
      android:id="@+id/teamLogo"
      android:layout_width="64dp"
      android:layout_height="64dp"
      android:contentDescription="@string/team_logo"
      android:src="@{team.logoId}"
      app:layout_constraintEnd_toEndOf="parent"
      app:layout_constraintStart_toStartOf="parent"
      app:layout_constraintTop_toTopOf="parent"
      tools:src="@drawable/fi_ic_electric_guitar" />

    <TextView
      android:id="@+id/teamLocation"
      android:layout_width="wrap_content"
      android:layout_height="wrap_content"
      android:text="@{team.location}"
      android:textSize="16sp"
      app:layout_constraintEnd_toEndOf="parent"
      app:layout_constraintStart_toStartOf="parent"
      app:layout_constraintTop_toBottomOf="@id/teamLogo"
      tools:text="Waukesha" />
```

```
    <TextView
      android:id="@+id/teamNickname"
      android:layout_width="wrap_content"
      android:layout_height="wrap_content"
      android:text="@{team.nickname}"
      android:textSize="16sp"
      app:layout_constraintEnd_toEndOf="parent"
      app:layout_constraintStart_toStartOf="parent"
      app:layout_constraintTop_toBottomOf="@id/teamLocation"
      tools:text="Riffs" />

  </androidx.constraintlayout.widget.ConstraintLayout>
</layout>
```

The one piece that needs some extra work is the android:src="@{team.logoId}" attribute. Yes, I know, we've set an image source on an <ImageView> before, but what we've done here won't work.

I should say, it won't work without a binding adapter. The android:src= attribute is expecting a @drawable reference rather than a bound ID like we're doing here. Luckily, we can keep our code just like this yet make the ImageView display properly with a new @BindingAdapter function.

Create a class called BindingAdapters inside a util package (or something similar). Here, we need to add a single @BindingAdapter function called setImageViewResource().

This function brings in as parameters the ImageView and a resource ID, in our case the ID of the team's logo. Then we'll set the image resource on the ImageView using that logo's ID:

```
@BindingAdapter("android:src")
fun setImageViewResource(imageView: ImageView, resourceId: Int) {
  imageView.setImageResource(resourceId)
}
```

By making the value parameter into the @BindingAdapter annotation "android:src", we're effectively overloading that property to handle additional values. This means @drawable references still work just as you'd expect, but now data binding values work as well. We keep our layout files nice and readable without being constrained by the OS.

With that added, we can move on to the Adapter class.

Add a RecyclerView Adapter

With both the <RecyclerView> and item layout files created, we can get our Adapter class created. This is very similar to what you did before in Create a Custom ListAdapter, on page 160.

Create a class called TeamsGridAdapter inside the teams package. This class inherits from RecyclerView.Adapter and has an inner class which is a child of RecyclerView.ViewHolder.

This is a simpler adapter than we had with Penny Drop, so I won't worry about explaining anything here. The entire TeamsGridAdapter looks like this:

```
class TeamsGridAdapter(
  private val teams: List<UITeam>
) : RecyclerView.Adapter<TeamsGridAdapter.TeamViewHolder>() {

  override fun onCreateViewHolder(
    parent: ViewGroup,
    viewType: Int
  ): TeamViewHolder =
    TeamViewHolder(
      DataBindingUtil.inflate(
        LayoutInflater.from(parent.context),
        R.layout.teams_grid_item,
        parent,
        false
      )
    )

  override fun onBindViewHolder(
    holder: TeamViewHolder,
    position: Int
  ) {
    holder.bind(teams[position])
  }

  override fun getItemCount(): Int = teams.size

  inner class TeamViewHolder(
    private val binding: TeamGridItemBinding
  ) : RecyclerView.ViewHolder(binding.root) {

    fun bind(item: UITeam) {
      binding.apply {
        team = item
        executePendingBindings()
      }
    }
  }
}
```

Now that the TeamsGridAdapter class is completed, we can get back to TeamsFragment to get it connected to the grid.

Configure the Teams Grid

In TeamsFragment, we need to do three things: inflate the view, set the layoutManager property, and then connect the adapter. This is basically the same as what we did with Penny Drop's Rankings screen, but we need a different layoutManager since this screen is a grid instead of a list.

We need to create a GridLayoutManager set to two "spans" (columns, in our case) and vertically aligned. Then we get an instance of the TeamsGridAdapter in place with UITeam.allTeams sent in. Given that, the entire TeamsFragment looks like this:

```
class TeamsFragment : Fragment() {
  override fun onCreateView(
      inflater: LayoutInflater,
      container: ViewGroup?,
      savedInstanceState: Bundle?
  ): View? {
    val view =
      inflater.inflate(R.layout.fragment_teams_grid, container, false)

    // Set the adapter
    if (view is RecyclerView) {
      with(view) {
        layoutManager = GridLayoutManager(
          context,
          2, //Span Count (columns)
          GridLayoutManager.VERTICAL,
          false) //Reverse layout

        adapter = TeamsGridAdapter(UITeam.allTeams)
      }
    }
    return view
  }
}
```

That's it! Go ahead and run the app; it should look something like the image shown on page 214.

Assuming things look right, you're good to move along. If not, check out the associated code. We're moving a lot faster in this part of the book, so it's easier to miss something.

Summary and Next Steps

We're rolling on app number two, the official Android Baseball League app! While a lot of this was review from Penny Drop, we included a few new things and, more importantly, set ourselves up for the rest of this part of the book.

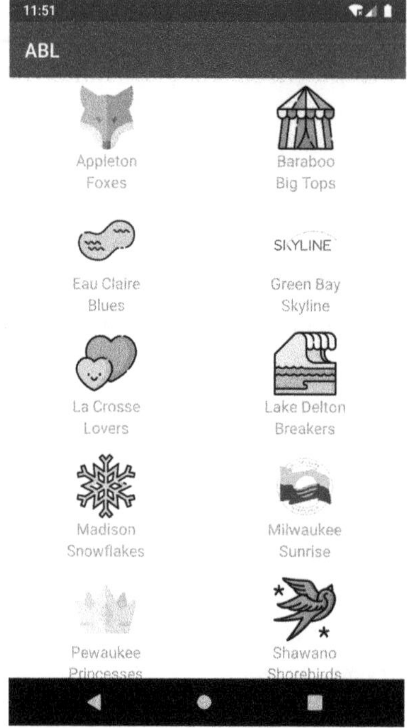

We've got an app, it has a lot of the images we need (including an app icon), and we can see all fourteen of the ABL teams.

The next four chapters are all going to follow a consistent model: we build out something we've done before, then we add on something new.

First up is Navigation and the addition of a navigation drawer. The initial setup will be very similar to the bottom nav we used in the last app, but we're going to take it a step farther with actions, Safe Args for navigating with type safety, and even deep links. We'll do all that while we add a new Standings screen to the app as well as views for each individual team.

CHAPTER 9

Navigate via Navigation Drawer

We've got the ABL app up and running; now we need to give people a way to move around. After all, they need to have a way to see where their beloved Spring Green Thespians are in the standings or if Justin Witz is still leading the league in steals.

Whereas in Penny Drop we only had a few screens, with the ABL app we're looking at five distinct areas plus both Settings and About the App screens. Due to this increased number of destinations, the bottom nav structure doesn't work well for us anymore. We're going to add a *navigation drawer* to the app, which is a panel that slides out from the side of the screen and gives users multiple places to go, as shown in the image on page 216.

You should see that the nav drawer is in many ways similar to a bottom nav, but we're going to add more onto that user experience. Along with the standard navigation from the drawer, we'll also have a way to go directly from one page to a separate page not found in the drawer. We can also send type-safe parameters into that separate page. We can even jump directly to that page (or any other) from outside the app.

We're focusing on individual ABL teams, where they fall in the league standings, and all the advanced navigation features that get us to each of these locations. Let's start out by adding the navigation drawer to our app.

Add the Navigation Drawer

We likely won't need any additional dependencies here for the nav drawer since we added the `androidx.navigation` library last chapter and apps now by default include the Material Design Components library. If either are missing, though, add them now. We can then jump over to `activity_main.xml` to add in the nav drawer.

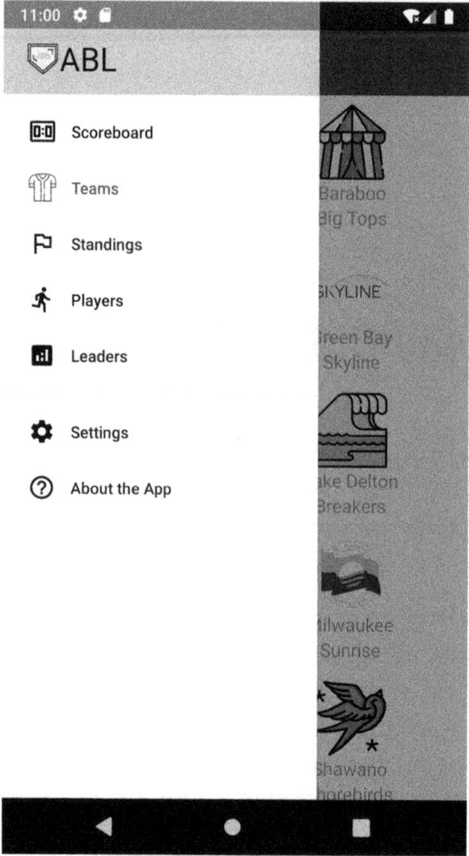

Update activity_main.xml

From a UI perspective, we're adding in the nav drawer to our existing MainActivity layout, and we're additionally going to be changing the layout a decent amount. The parent view of the screen is now going to be a <DrawerLayout> with a <Toolbar> and a <FragmentContainerView> inside:

```
<androidx.drawerlayout.widget.DrawerLayout
  xmlns:android="http://schemas.android.com/apk/res/android"
  xmlns:app="http://schemas.android.com/apk/res-auto"
  xmlns:tools="http://schemas.android.com/tools"
  android:id="@+id/drawer_layout"
  android:layout_width="match_parent"
  android:layout_height="match_parent"
  tools:context=".MainActivity">

  <!-- Contents are in here. -->

</androidx.drawerlayout.widget.DrawerLayout>
```

The <Toolbar> and <FragmentContainerView> are both wrapped in a <LinearLayout> and are together taking up the entire window:

```
<LinearLayout
  android:layout_width="match_parent"
  android:layout_height="match_parent"
  android:orientation="vertical">

  <androidx.appcompat.widget.Toolbar
      android:id="@+id/toolbar"
      android:layout_width="match_parent"
      android:layout_height="wrap_content"
      android:paddingTop="24dp"
      android:background="?attr/colorPrimary"
      android:theme=
        "@style/ThemeOverlay.MaterialComponents.Dark.ActionBar" />

  <androidx.fragment.app.FragmentContainerView
      android:id="@+id/containerFragment"
      android:name="androidx.navigation.fragment.NavHostFragment"
      android:layout_width="match_parent"
      android:layout_height="match_parent"
      app:defaultNavHost="true"
      app:navGraph="@navigation/nav_graph" />
</LinearLayout>
```

Finally, the <NavigationView>, which lives inside the <DrawerLayout> but *not* the <LinearLayout>, slides out over the screen:

```
<com.google.android.material.navigation.NavigationView
  android:id="@+id/nav_view"
  android:layout_width="wrap_content"
  android:layout_height="match_parent"
  android:layout_gravity="start"
  android:fitsSystemWindows="true"
  app:headerLayout="@layout/nav_header"
  app:menu="@menu/navigation" />
```

You've seen most of this before, in particular the <FragmentContainerView>, but I do want to highlight the couple of new items.

The android:fitsSystemWindows="*true*" attribute on the nav drawer tells the device to adjust that view based on system components, in this case the status bar at the top of the screen. By adding this, the nav drawer will move down to be displayed properly.

Having the android:theme= property on the <Toolbar> is likely new as well. You may notice that the listed theme is similar to what we've seen before in the themes.xml file, which is where we're headed next.

Since we're adding a <Toolbar> manually, we need to make sure the app's theme doesn't try to add one for us by changing the app theme's parent to a NoActionBar variant:

```
<style name="Theme.AndroidBaseballLeague"
       parent="Theme.MaterialComponents.DayNight.NoActionBar">
  <!-- Style properties are in here -->
</style>
```

Also, while we're in themes.xml, we want to add two new <item> tags. These tags work together to make the status bar display on top of the nav drawer, but with the nav drawer's color:

```
<item name="android:windowDrawsSystemBarBackgrounds">true</item>
<item name="android:windowTranslucentStatus">true</item>
```

The last piece that's new from activity_main.xml is app:headerLayout="*@layout/nav_header*". This attribute gives the nav drawer a nice header item at the top of the drawer with its own layout file.

Add nav_header.xml

In our case, this header will be the ABL logo (with the letters *ABL*) and an Android green background. If you need the logo, it's in the code under chapter-9/images. Once the logo's ready, the header layout file looks like this:

```
<androidx.constraintlayout.widget.ConstraintLayout
  xmlns:android="http://schemas.android.com/apk/res/android"
  xmlns:app="http://schemas.android.com/apk/res-auto"
  android:layout_width="match_parent"
  android:layout_height="wrap_content"
  android:padding="16dp"
  android:background="@color/androidGreen">

  <ImageView
    android:layout_width="wrap_content"
    android:layout_height="28dp"
    android:layout_marginTop="20dp"
    android:layout_marginStart="4dp"
    android:contentDescription="@string/abl_logo"
    android:scaleType="fitStart"
    android:src="@drawable/ic_abl_logo_with_text"
    app:layout_constraintBottom_toBottomOf="parent"
    app:layout_constraintStart_toStartOf="parent"
    app:layout_constraintTop_toTopOf="parent" />

</androidx.constraintlayout.widget.ConstraintLayout>
```

Padding and some margins are in place to move the image down a bit so it displays nicely below the status bar, but nothing new other than android:scaleType=*fitStart*. This scaling makes sure the image fits inside its container properly and also aligns with the top-left corner.

With those two layout files complete, we can add in our one missing file, menu/navigation.xml.

Create the Navigation Menu

This is similar to the menu we created in Build the App's Navigation, on page 15. The biggest difference this time is that we're going to have two <group> tags splitting the nav drawer into sections. We're actually able to add all our menu items at once for the app, even if they don't yet have the associated fragments. This way the nav drawer can look right without worrying about making a bunch of Fragment classes. The entire navigation.xml looks like this:

```
<?xml version="1.0" encoding="utf-8"?>
<menu xmlns:android="http://schemas.android.com/apk/res/android">
  <group android:id="@+id/mainMenuGroup">
    <item
      android:id="@+id/scoreboardFragment"
      android:icon="@drawable/mdi_scoreboard_outline"
      android:title="@string/scoreboard" />
    <item
      android:id="@+id/teamsFragment"
      android:icon="@drawable/ic_jersey"
      android:title="@string/teams" />
    <item
      android:id="@+id/standingsFragment"
      android:icon="@drawable/ic_baseline_outlined_flag_24"
      android:title="@string/standings" />
    <item
      android:id="@+id/playersFragment"
      android:icon="@drawable/ic_baseline_directions_run_24"
      android:title="@string/players" />
    <item
      android:id="@+id/leadersFragment"
      android:icon="@drawable/ic_baseline_analytics_24"
      android:title="@string/leaders" />
  </group>
  <group android:id="@+id/settingsMenuGroup">
    <item
      android:id="@+id/settingsFragment"
      android:icon="@drawable/ic_baseline_settings_24"
      android:title="@string/settings" />
```

```
    <item
      android:id="@+id/aboutTheAppFragment"
      android:icon="@drawable/ic_baseline_help_outline_24"
      android:title="@string/about_the_app" />
  </group>
</menu>
```

Everything's good here other than the plethora of missing images. All of those can be found in the source code under chapter-9/images/nav-images. Copy all of those into your project's drawables folder and peek at navigation.xml to make sure all the images resolve properly.

Now that our layout files are all good, we can head back to MainActivity to connect everything up. This time, we're going to use *view binding* to do that.

Add viewBinding

Now, it's not really related to navigation, but I want to bring in the view binding feature here. Since we're grabbing each of the components from activity_main.xml, view binding will make things easier on us.

In a lot of ways, view binding will look similar to what we do with data binding when, for example, we associate a ViewModel class with a layout. Instead of calling findViewById() to get a layout element, we can instead reference that element as a property on the generated binding class.

If you're unclear on what I mean here, don't worry. It should make more sense once we get to configuring everything inside MainActivity. But before we can do anything there, we need to turn view binding on inside the app's build.gradle file. We already have the dataBinding flag inside the buildFeatures block, but now we need to add viewBinding:

```
buildFeatures {
  dataBinding = true
  viewBinding = true
}
```

That's actually all we need to do to enable view binding in our app (after a Gradle sync, of course)—no need to include generic <layout> tags or any extra dependencies. I recommend using view binding any time you simply want to skip findViewById() calls in an Activity or Fragment class and if you don't need binding expressions in a layout file. Keep in mind that view binding is faster than data binding and less work to get ready, so decide which approach is needed for each use case.

Update MainActivity

We've already seen how we can connect the <FragmentContainerView> inside a MainActivity class while building Penny Drop, but this time we also need to add our <Toolbar> and do a bit to get the nav drawer configured.

Since we already enabled view binding, we can start using it right away. The beginning of the onCreate() function now looks like this:

```
super.onCreate(savedInstanceState)
val binding = ActivityMainBinding.inflate(layoutInflater)

setContentView(binding.root)
```

Seems familiar enough, right? And while it's a bit more code than we had before, using our <Toolbar> with the Activity is a single, clear line:

```
setSupportActionBar(binding.toolbar)
```

Had we not included view binding, we instead would have had a block like this:

```
val toolbar = findViewById<Toolbar>(R.id.toolbar)
setSupportActionBar(toolbar)
```

While it's not exactly a huge code savings, the first line is definitely nicer to deal with and clearer to read. We'll see a few more examples soon, but first we need to get our navController. Don't forget to declare navController at the top of the class as a lateinit var.

```
val navHostFragment = supportFragmentManager
  .findFragmentById(R.id.containerFragment) as NavHostFragment
this.navController = navHostFragment.navController
```

Unfortunately, view binding doesn't help us here since we need to interact with the supportFragmentManager, but the rest of the configuration is simplified nicely.

In particular, we have to set up two components with the navController value. The navigation drawer (via binding.navView) and the <Toolbar> (via a appBarConfiguration value) both need to be associated with the NavController:

```
binding.navView.setupWithNavController(this.navController)

this.appBarConfiguration =
  AppBarConfiguration(binding.navView.menu, binding.drawerLayout)
setupActionBarWithNavController(this.navController, appBarConfiguration)
```

Again, make sure the appBarConfiguration lateinit var is declared after navController.

The last thing we need to do in MainActivity is override the onSupportNavigateUp() function. This function is what allows our nav drawer button to work.

We make sure the navController is initialized and, if so, call the navigateUp() function on navController. If either of those return false, we fall back to the default onSupportNavigateUp() function:

```
override fun onSupportNavigateUp(): Boolean =
  (this::navController.isInitialized &&
    this.navController.navigateUp(this.appBarConfiguration)
  ) || super.onSupportNavigateUp()
```

With that set, we can finally run our app. Fire it up and take a peek:

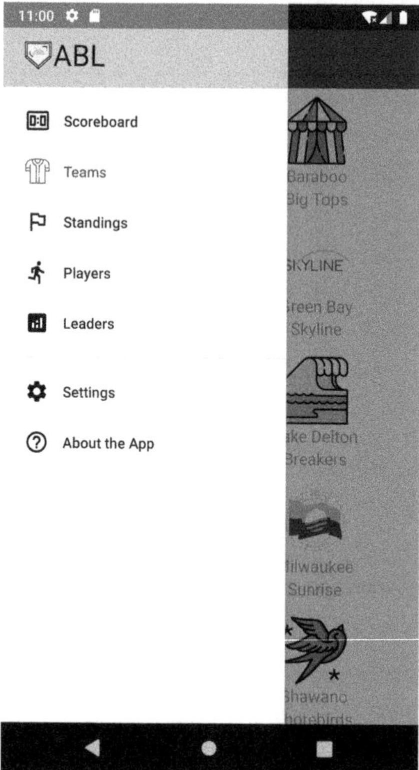

Looks pretty snazzy, right? Note that the highlighting is automatically handled for us, as it was with the bottom nav, since our fragment IDs match up. Only problem is that the nav drawer doesn't do much of anything yet because we only have a single view in the app. Let's change that by getting the Standings page added.

Add Fragments (Standings and Single Team)

We want two new fragments to support what we're doing with Navigation in this chapter: StandingsFragment and SingleTeamFragment. We'll link to the Standings-Fragment in the nav drawer and SingleTeamFragment as a separate (non-nav drawer) destination that we access from both StandingsFragment and Teams-Fragment.

All the code you want to copy can be found in the chapter-9/code-to-copy directory.

Add StandingsFragment

The Standings page is going to be another RecyclerView list, but with a twist: we're going to add some headers into the list to split up the rows. Specifically, we're adding headers to split the East and West divisions of the ABL. The Standings page at the end will look like this:

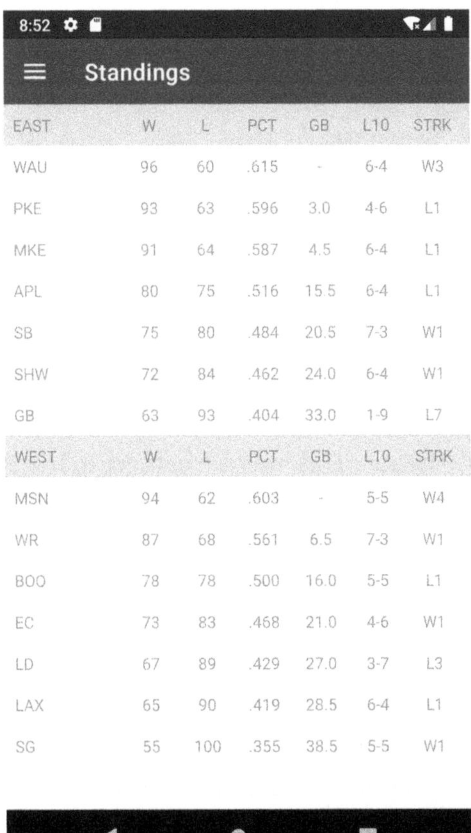

Now, while I'd love to show you how all of this works, we have navigating to do. Given that, just go ahead and copy everything in the standings package into your project. That includes the following classes: StandingsAdapter, StandingsFragment, StandingsListItem, StandingsViewModel, TeamStanding, and UITeamStanding. Also, you need the fragment_standings.xml, standings_header.xml, and standings_team_item.xml files from the res/layout directory.

Feel free to look through these files/classes at your leisure, because they're definitely useful and a great extension of our work in Chapter 6, Build a List with RecyclerView, on page 151.

One bit of info: I included some mock team standings data inside the TeamStanding class so you've got something to display on the Standings page. This will be removed in Chapter 10, Load and Save Data with Coroutines and Room, on page 235, once we call the APIs to get our data.

Two more required changes—we need some extra string resource values:

```
<string name="wins_w">W</string>
<string name="losses_l">L</string>
<string name="percentage_abbr">PCT</string>
<string name="games_back_abbr">GB</string>
<string name="last_ten_abbr">L10</string>
<string name="streak_abbr">STRK</string>
```

Also, the fromTeamId() function is missing from the UITeam class. Add that in and make sure to include the @JvmStatic annotation since we'll be using this function in data binding expressions later:

```
@JvmStatic
fun fromTeamId(teamId: String?) =
  allTeams.firstOrNull { uiTeam -> uiTeam.teamId == teamId }
```

With those files copied over and the function added, add the StandingsFragment <fragment> tag to nav_graph.xml. This way we can get to the StandingsFragment from the nav drawer (and yes, I'm making the StandingsFragment my start location for now):

```
<navigation xmlns:android="http://schemas.android.com/apk/res/android"
  xmlns:app="http://schemas.android.com/apk/res-auto"
  xmlns:tools="http://schemas.android.com/tools"
  android:id="@+id/nav_graph"
  app:startDestination="@id/standingsFragment">
➤ <fragment
➤   android:id="@+id/standingsFragment"
➤   android:name="dev.mfazio.abl.standings.StandingsFragment"
➤   android:label="@string/standings" />
  <fragment
    android:id="@+id/teamsFragment"
    android:name="dev.mfazio.abl.teams.TeamsFragment"
    android:label="@string/teams" />
</navigation>
```

Once you have that in place, run the app to make sure your standings page looks like the one we saw at the beginning of this section. If that's good, we'll move on to the SingleTeamFragment.

Add SingleTeamFragment

We're going to do something similar here in that we're just copying files over from the code. This time it's SingleTeamFragment and SingleTeamViewModel inside the teams package, plus the fragment_single_team.xml layout file from res/layout.

Also, we need string resource values for @string/view_roster and @string/in_abl:

```
<string name="view_roster">View Roster</string>
<string name="in_abl"> in ABL </string>
```

In addition, we need the updated version of the BindingAdapters.kt file in the util directory. Here, we're adding a setBackgroundTint() @BindingAdapter that can take a color ID (similar to what we did with the logos in Add the Grid Item Layout XML, on page 210) and assign it to the background of a <Button>. This is a handy little function to have, so I recommend checking it out:

```
@BindingAdapter("android:backgroundTint")
fun setBackgroundTint(view: View, colorId: Int) {
  view.background.setTintList(
    ContextCompat.getColorStateList(view.context, colorId)
  )
}
```

There we go—I saved you the trouble of opening that file, but now it's time for more navigating!

Pass Data with Safe Args

You may have noticed that the SingleTeamFragment class isn't happy right now because it doesn't know about SingleTeamFragmentArgs or that navArgs() function. Also note that the problematic line looks suspiciously close to how we grab a ViewModel class.

In Android, the "traditional" way to send data between locations is via a Bundle, where you add key/value pairs and either send them directly into a class or as part of an Intent. Instead of doing that, we're going to take advantage of the Navigation Safe Args plugin.

This plugin allows us to send typed values between destinations rather than String values we have to convert into something else manually. We then can reference a NavArgs class that's generated for us to use the values.

Before we try to use NavArgs anywhere, we need to add in a classpath dependency and a plugin reference.

Add the Safe Args Plugin

This is one of the rare occasions where we add a dependency to our *project* build.gradle file rather than the app-level file, since we're bringing in a new plugin. Alongside the Kotlin and Gradle classpath dependencies, we need to include the Safe Args plugin:

```
dependencies {
  classpath "com.android.tools.build:gradle:$gradle_version"
  classpath "org.jetbrains.kotlin:kotlin-gradle-plugin:$kotlin_version"
  classpath
    "androidx.navigation:navigation-safe-args-gradle-plugin:$nav_version"
}
```

Notice that we don't even need a new version variable here since we just use the existing Navigation version. Once the dependency is added, then we can include one more plugin in the app's build.gradle file:

```
plugins {
  id 'com.android.application'
  id 'kotlin-android'
  id 'kotlin-kapt'
  id 'androidx.navigation.safeargs.kotlin'
}
```

With those added, sync up Gradle, and head into navigation/nav_graph.xml to add some Actions.

Add Navigation Actions

Navigation actions are a way to get from one destination to another. In our case, we're going to add a way to move from both the TeamsFragment and StandingsFragment to the SingleTeamFragment.

To do this, we add an <action> tag *inside* one of our <fragment> tags, like so:

```
<fragment
  android:id="@+id/standingsFragment"
  android:name="dev.mfazio.abl.standings.StandingsFragment"
  android:label="@string/standings">
  <action
    android:id="@+id/actionGoToTeam"
    app:destination="@id/singleTeamFragment" />
</fragment>
```

Now, that's great, except we can't go to the SingleTeamFragment without any extra info since we won't know which team to reference. This is where the Safe Args come in; we can add <argument> tags to an <action> to include parameters:

```
<fragment
  android:id="@+id/standingsFragment"
  android:name="dev.mfazio.abl.standings.StandingsFragment"
  android:label="@string/standings">
  <action
    android:id="@+id/actionGoToTeam"
    app:destination="@id/singleTeamFragment">
➤   <argument
➤     android:name="teamId"
➤     app:argType="string" />
➤   <argument
➤     android:name="teamName"
➤     app:argType="string" />
  </action>
</fragment>
```

Now, the action will work here, but we need to allow the SingleTeamFragment class to receive those args. This means we need a new <fragment> tag with some <argument> tags in it:

```
<fragment
  android:id="@+id/singleTeamFragment"
  android:name="dev.mfazio.abl.teams.SingleTeamFragment"
  android:label="{teamName}"
  tools:layout="@layout/fragment_single_team">
  <argument
    android:name="teamId"
    app:argType="string" />
  <argument
    android:name="teamName"
    app:argType="string" />
</fragment>
```

A couple of takeaways here: the <argument> tags match up between the <action> and <fragment> (meaning both tags contain the same <argument> tags), plus we can even use one of those <argument> values in an attribute of the <fragment> tag. The android:label=*"{teamName}"* means that whatever we send in as a teamName argument, that's what will be displayed in the toolbar when the screen is shown.

If we want to get here from the TeamsFragment, we can copy the same <argument> tags into that <fragment> tag. Hopefully this sounds to you like a poor approach since we're copying and pasting values, but don't worry, we have a better way we can do this.

The Navigation library has the concept of *global actions*, which can be accessed from anywhere. This means we declare the <action> once, then reference it from any location we choose. To add a global action, we just need to create a stand-alone <action> tag in nav_graph.xml. The entire (final) file looks like this:

```
<navigation xmlns:android="http://schemas.android.com/apk/res/android"
  xmlns:app="http://schemas.android.com/apk/res-auto"
  xmlns:tools="http://schemas.android.com/tools"
  android:id="@+id/nav_graph"
  app:startDestination="@id/standingsFragment">

➤ <action
➤   android:id="@+id/actionGoToTeam"
➤   app:destination="@id/singleTeamFragment">
➤   <argument
➤     android:name="teamId"
➤     app:argType="string" />
➤   <argument
➤     android:name="teamName"
➤     app:argType="string" />
➤ </action>

  <fragment
    android:id="@+id/standingsFragment"
    android:name="dev.mfazio.abl.standings.StandingsFragment"
    android:label="@string/standings" />
  <fragment
    android:id="@+id/teamsFragment"
    android:name="dev.mfazio.abl.teams.TeamsFragment"
    android:label="@string/teams" />
  <fragment
    android:id="@+id/singleTeamFragment"
    android:name="dev.mfazio.abl.teams.SingleTeamFragment"
    android:label="{teamName}"
    tools:layout="@layout/fragment_single_team">
    <argument
      android:name="teamId"
      app:argType="string" />
    <argument
      android:name="teamName"
      app:argType="string" />
  </fragment>
</navigation>
```

Last word of warning: global actions only work if the navigation graph has an ID property, so don't forget to include that.

With the navigation graph complete, we're ready to get back into our Kotlin code to get moving around. Make sure SingleTeamFragment compiles without any errors, and notice how we're using args.teamId in the binding logic. That's all we need to use Safe Args in a destination.

Navigating via Actions

We want to add navigation logic for our SingleTeamFragment to both the Teams grid and Standings screen, both of which are handled in similar ways. We'll start out with the StandingsAdapter since the code is already present, but commented out.

In the bind() function inside the StandingsListTeamViewHolder class, we're binding a UITeamStanding object to our layout. We also have a block of code wrapped in a comment that we can now add in:

```
fun bind(standingsTeamItem: StandingsListItem.TeamItem) {
  binding.uiTeamStanding = standingsTeamItem.uiTeamStanding
  //TODO: Uncomment this code when you're ready.
  binding.clickListener = View.OnClickListener { view ->
    val action = NavGraphDirections.actionGoToTeam(
      standingsTeamItem.uiTeamStanding.teamId,
      standingsTeamItem.uiTeamStanding.teamName
    )
    view.findNavController().navigate(action)
  }
}
```

That code will assign the clickListener for a Standings list item and send the user to the SingleTeamFragment class, complete with the team name and ID. The Safe Args plugin generates that NavGraphDirections class for us, making the call itself nice and straightforward.

Uncomment the code and run your app. You should now be able to click a team in the Standings page and it'll take you to their Team page, as shown in the image on page 230.

The bind() function in TeamsGridAdapter is basically the same thing:

```
fun bind(item: UITeam) {
  binding.apply {
    team = item
    setClickListener { view ->
      val action = NavGraphDirections.actionGoToTeam(
        item.teamId,
        item.teamName
      )
      view.findNavController().navigate(action)
    }
  }
}
```

We can follow this same pattern whenever we want to get to a certain page in the app from another place within the app. But what happens if we want

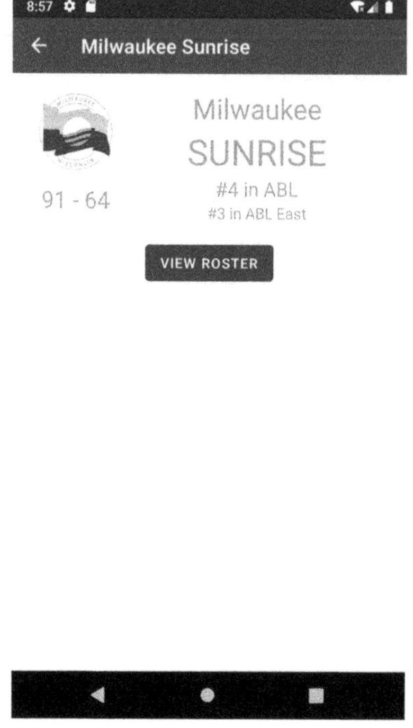

to get to a certain page from *outside* the app? That's where *deep links* come into play.

Navigate Directly via a Deep Link

Deep links are a way to go directly to any destination in our app, even ones not in the nav drawer. The Navigation library supports two types of deep links: explicit and implicit.

Explicit deep links are used with things like app widgets or notifications, for example. We build up the pieces of the link, complete with any arguments we need, and head over to the destination. We don't have a good spot for an explicit deep link now, but we'll add one in Chapter 13, Send Info to and from the Android Baseball League App, on page 305.

Implicit deep links, on the other hand, are URIs (uniform resource identifiers, generally web links) that map to a destination. For example, we can have a link like https://link.mfazio.dev/teams/GB?teamName=Green%20Bay%20Skyline that will take us to the Skyline team page.

The navigation component helps us out here by allowing us to add <deepLink> tags in nav_graph.xml, then reference that nav graph in our AndroidManifest.xml file.

Add an Implicit Deep Link

Inside nav_graph.xml, add a new <deepLink> tag inside the Single Team <fragment> tag:

```
<fragment
  android:id="@+id/singleTeamFragment"
  android:name="dev.mfazio.abl.teams.SingleTeamFragment"
  android:label="{teamName}"
  tools:layout="@layout/fragment_single_team">
  <argument
    android:name="teamId"
    app:argType="string" />
  <argument
    android:name="teamName"
    app:argType="string" />
➤ <deepLink
➤   app:uri="https://link.mfazio.dev/teams/{teamId}?teamName={teamName}" />
</fragment>
```

Then in AndroidManifest.xml, we can add a <nav-graph> tag to our main <activity> tag:

```
<activity android:name=".MainActivity">
  <intent-filter>
    <action android:name="android.intent.action.MAIN" />

    <category android:name="android.intent.category.LAUNCHER" />
  </intent-filter>
➤ <nav-graph android:value="@navigation/nav_graph" />
</activity>
```

Once those are in place, you can now click a link from outside the ABL app and have it take you into the app. You can go to https://abl.mfazio.dev/deep-links for all the team links. In my case, I tapped the Pewaukee Princesses link, which gave me the Open with pop-up, as shown in the first image on page 232.

After selecting the ABL option, we're taken to the ABL app and in the case of my link to the Pewaukee Princesses team page, as shown in the second image on page 232.

Notice how the top-left corner is a back arrow instead of the nav drawer "hamburger" menu? By using a deep link within a navigation graph, we're taken directly into our navigation graph and the graph hierarchy is preserved.

Now, in our case, that means we go back to the start destination if we press the back button. If we were to have a more complex navigation graph, we'd pop into the flow with the same back stack as when someone navigated there in the first place. All of that is handled automatically for us, too.

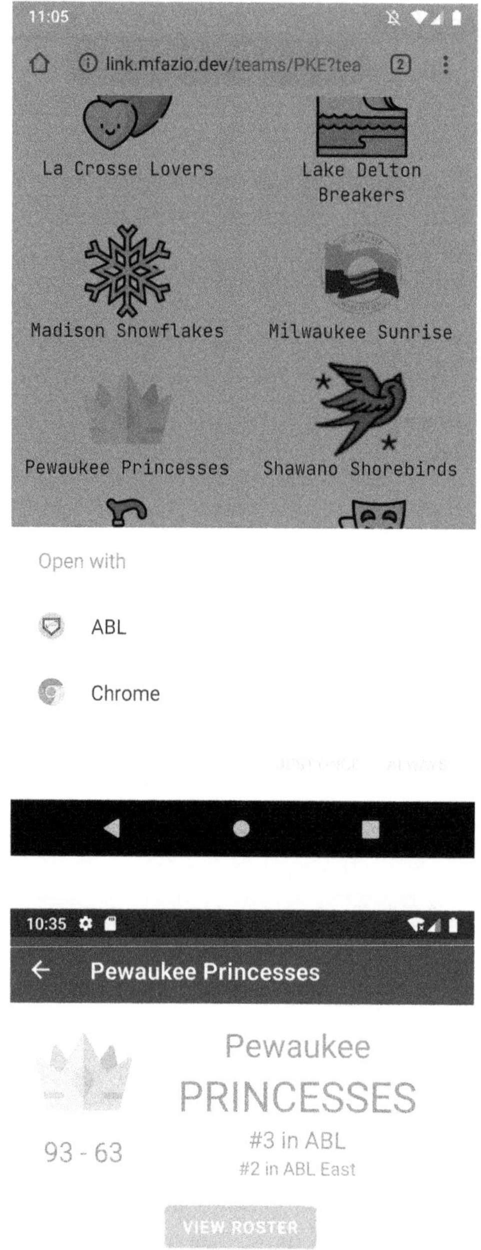

You can do something similar to test out any team links. Also, feel free to add extra `<deepLink>` tags for the other two pages.

Having deep links is handy when people want to share a particular spot in your app or need to jump back quickly to a certain destination. However, the process of getting there can be a bit annoying, in particular that Open with dialog. We can remove that step by turning this deep link into an Android App Link.

Turn a Deep Link into an Android App Link

On a high level, Android App Links associate your website and web links with your app. This is done by both adding deep links in the app (to give the links somewhere to go) and verifying those links. The latter part is handled by adding a verification file on your website to tell the device that the site and your app are connected.

That verification file is called a *Digital Asset Links file* and lists info about your app to be used during verification. That file contains a relation type and a target, the latter containing a namespace ("android_app"), package name ("dev.mfazio.abl"), and SHA256 certificate fingerprint.

The last piece can be obtained automatically by using the Java keytool (replacing app-release-key with the name of your keystore file):

```
keytool -list -v -keystore app-release-key.keystore
```

If you're lost with that keystore file, that's OK—we haven't talked about those at all. If you're curious, check out Google's App Signing overview.[1] The main point here is that you need to get the fingerprint from your app keystore so the app can be verified. A full sample Digital Asset Links file looks like this:

```
[
  {
    "relation": [
      "delegate_permission/common.handle_all_urls"
    ],
    "target": {
      "namespace": "android_app",
      "package_name": "dev.mfazio.abl",
      "sha256_cert_fingerprints": [...]
    }
  }
]
```

I excluded the sample fingerprint purely for space, but it'll be a combination of hexadecimal numbers joined by colons. A sample file can also be found in the code in the assetlinks.json file.

1. https://link.mfazio.dev/app-signing

Once we have our file created, then we need to push it out to our website. In our example, I used link.mfazio.dev as my URL, so I would need to upload the Digital Asset Links file to https://link.mfazio.dev/.well-known/assetlinks.json.

Keep in mind that this process needs to be duplicated on every subdomain that you want to use in an Android App Link.

Need a quick summary of this section? Android App Links are deep links that are verified and can skip the disambiguation (Open with) dialog. It's a bit of extra work but definitely offers a better user experience.

Summary and Next Steps

We can now get around our app! The nav drawer will give us a smooth way to hit all the pieces of the app we'll be building out in the next few chapters.

Plus, we have quick routes to get directly to a destination in our app with actions. Using actions with Safe Args make the navigation experience great, as we're working with actual objects rather than only String values that require some kind of conversion and are prone to mistakes.

Finally, with deep links and Android App Links, we can give users direct access to parts of our app that wouldn't be immediately accessible otherwise. We'll expand on these in later chapters for sure.

Next up is one of the most valuable chapters in the book. We're going to reach *outside* our app to pull in data from external APIs and use them to display info in the app. We'll update the Standings page we added here to use that data, as well as add a new Scoreboard screen to display the past, present, and future games in the Android Baseball League. Room + Retrofit + Coroutines will make this happen, and it's going to be a blast.

CHAPTER 10

Load and Save Data with Coroutines and Room

Everything we've done in this book so far has been focused on working within an app, but now it's time to reach out and bring in some external data. We're going to be calling out to the Android Baseball League APIs to get up-to-date scores, standings, and statistics.

In particular, we'll pull in data for the current games and standings in the league. We did the initial work on the latter screen in Add Fragments (Standings and Single Team), on page 222, but that was with mocked-up data. The Scoreboard page is new (and frankly, complicated), so you'll again pull in the code rather than us going through all of it.

Having current data is going to be great, but we could really use some place to hang onto it. That means we need a Room database to store all our data, so let's get that created first.

Create a Database

The first part of the process here is going to be very familiar if you've gone through Chapter 5, Persist Game Data with Room, on page 115, so I'll try to speed through things to get to the new stuff.

Before you do anything, add in the Room dependencies:

```
➤ implementation "androidx.room:room-ktx:$room_version"
➤ implementation "androidx.room:room-runtime:$room_version"
  implementation "com.google.android.material:material:$material_version"

➤ kapt "androidx.room:room-compiler:$room_version"
```

Then, inside a new data package, create an abstract BaseballDatabase class that inherits from RoomDatabase. It'll start out pretty empty, but we'll go through and add pieces in as we go along. For now, it looks like this:

```
@Database(
  entities = [],
  exportSchema = false,
  version = 1
)
abstract class BaseballDatabase : RoomDatabase() {
  companion object {
    @Volatile
    private var Instance: BaseballDatabase? = null

    fun getDatabase(context: Context, scope: CoroutineScope):
      BaseballDatabase = Instance ?: synchronized(this) {
        val instance = Room.databaseBuilder(
          context,
          BaseballDatabase::class.java,
          "BaseballDatabase"
        ).build()

      Instance = instance

      instance
    }
  }
}
```

The DB is in place, so now we need some classes to work with it. We'll convert the TeamStanding class to an @Entity, plus we'll create both DAO and Repository classes. Let's start with TeamStanding since we'll be using it in the other classes.

Convert TeamStanding to an Entity

Thankfully, this isn't going to take much work. We need to mark the class as an @Entity, add an @PrimaryKey, and a few @TypeConverter functions.

First, the class changes, which look like this:

```
@Entity(tableName = "standings")
data class TeamStanding(
  val teamId: String,
  val division: Division,
  val wins: Int = 0,
  val losses: Int = 0,
  val winsLastTen: Int = 0,
  val streakCount: Int = 0,
  val streakType: WinLoss = WinLoss.Unknown,
  val divisionGamesBack: Double = 0.0,
  val leagueGamesBack: Double = 0.0
) {
```

```
    @PrimaryKey(autoGenerate = true)
    var id: Long = 0

    companion object {
      // Mock data's still here, we're going to put it in the DB in a bit.
      // We can remove it once we're loading data from the APIs.
    }
}
```

Room won't know what to do with Division or WinLoss, so we need a Converters class with the @TypeConverter functions, as I mentioned earlier. That class lives in the data package and looks like this:

```
class Converters {
  @TypeConverter
  fun fromDivision(division: Division?) =
    division?.ordinal ?: Division.Unknown.ordinal

  @TypeConverter
  fun toDivision(divisionOrdinal: Int?) =
    if (divisionOrdinal != null) {
      Division.values()[divisionOrdinal]
    } else {
      Division.Unknown
    }

  @TypeConverter
  fun fromWinLoss(winLoss: WinLoss?) =
    winLoss?.ordinal ?: WinLoss.Unknown.ordinal

  @TypeConverter
  fun toWinLoss(winLossOrdinal: Int?) =
    if (winLossOrdinal != null) {
      WinLoss.values()[winLossOrdinal]
    } else {
      WinLoss.Unknown
    }
}
```

We have conversion methods to and from each type, and both fall back to their Unknown value in case of a conversion failure.

With the Converters class done for now and the TeamStanding class now an @Entity, we can add them both to our database:

```
@Database(
  entities = [TeamStanding::class],
  exportSchema = false,
  version = 1
)
@TypeConverters(Converters::class)
abstract class BaseballDatabase : RoomDatabase() {
  companion object {
```

```
    @Volatile
    private var Instance: BaseballDatabase? = null

    fun getDatabase(context: Context, scope: CoroutineScope):
      BaseballDatabase = Instance ?: synchronized(this) {
        val instance = Room.databaseBuilder(
          context,
          BaseballDatabase::class.java,
          "BaseballDatabase"
        ).build()

      Instance = instance

      instance
    }
  }
}
```

With that done, we can move on to the Repository and DAO classes.

Add the BaseballDao Class

As a reminder, the DAO is either an interface or abstract class that will pull data in from our Room database, while the Repository is a standard class where we get data to the rest of the app. The DAO is only concerned with Room, while the Repository can reference multiple data sources. This will become more important once we're calling out to an API.

First, we need to create the BaseballDao class with a few functions related to TeamStanding objects. We want the ability to insert new TeamStanding records, update those records, and retrieve them from the database. The BaseballDao class will currently look like this:

```
@Dao
abstract class BaseballDao {
  @Insert
  abstract suspend fun insertStandings(standings: List<TeamStanding>)

  @Update
  abstract suspend fun updateStandings(standings: List<TeamStanding>)

  @Query("SELECT * FROM standings")
  abstract fun getStandings(): LiveData<List<TeamStanding>>

  @Query("SELECT * FROM standings")
  abstract suspend fun getCurrentStandings(): List<TeamStanding>
}
```

Yes, I know I have two functions that are running the same query, and no, it's not ideal. That's being done due to getStandings() returning the standings data wrapped in a LiveData object. We really only want to use LiveData with our UI, so I'm adding a second function in here for use in our Repository.

Honestly, I don't love this approach, but it does make sense when you think about how LiveData isn't intended for use in the background. Plus, if you try to just grab the LiveData version and get the value out of it, you'll get null.

Last thing with that extra function: it's marked with the suspend modifier so that we grab the data on a non-UI thread. This way the UI isn't locked up for users, but we can handle the data as we'd expect. If we didn't include this modifier, we'd get an error about running queries on the UI thread. You *can* enable UI-thread queries, but please don't. It's a protection that's in place for a reason.

With the DAO set, we can use it within a new BaseballRepository class.

Add the BaseballRepository Class

Right now, we just need to initialize the BaseballRepository class and add a single function to get Standings data. Remember that we send in the BaseballDao class as a constructor parameter to use within the class. Here's the BaseballRepository class as it currently stands:

```
class BaseballRepository(private val baseballDao: BaseballDao) {

  fun getStandings(): LiveData<List<TeamStanding>> =
    baseballDao.getStandings()

  companion object {
    @Volatile
    private var instance: BaseballRepository? = null

    fun getInstance(baseballDao: BaseballDao) =
      this.instance ?: synchronized(this) {
        instance ?: BaseballRepository(baseballDao).also {
          instance = it
        }
      }
  }
}
```

With the DAO and Repository ready to go, we can start adding data to our database. For now, it'll be handy to have some Standings data again, so we'll insert that mock data we were referencing last chapter.

Add BaseballDao and Mock Data to BaseballDatabase

The BaseballDao is added as an abstract fun to BaseballDatabase with no extra work on our part. As far as the mock data, we'll take the same approach we did in the past and use a RoomDatabase.Callback to add things in. We can insert the mock standings when the database is created and then it'll be available for us to display. Those two additions look like this:

```
@Database(
  entities = [TeamStanding::class],
  exportSchema = false,
  version = 1
)
@TypeConverters(Converters::class)
abstract class BaseballDatabase : RoomDatabase() {
  abstract fun baseballDao(): BaseballDao

  companion object {
    @Volatile
    private var Instance: BaseballDatabase? = null

    fun getDatabase(context: Context, scope: CoroutineScope):
      BaseballDatabase = Instance ?: synchronized(this) {
        val instance = Room.databaseBuilder(
          context,
          BaseballDatabase::class.java,
          "BaseballDatabase"
        ).addCallback(object : RoomDatabase.Callback() {
          override fun onCreate(db: SupportSQLiteDatabase) {
            super.onCreate(db)
            scope.launch {
              Instance
                ?.baseballDao()
                ?.insertStandings(TeamStanding.mockTeamStandings)
            }
          }
        }).build()

        Instance = instance

        instance
      }
  }
}
```

With those changes in place, we can move on to updating the Standings page to use data from the database.

Load Standings Data from the Database

Right now, we're converting the mock Standings into LiveData to be used on the page. Instead, we need an instance of BaseballRepository, then we can call getStandings() to get TeamStanding objects from the database. Make sure you change the base class to AndroidViewModel, since we need a context to retrieve a database.

We do want to continue mapping the TeamStanding objects into UITeamStanding objects, but now we'll do that inside a Transformations.map() block. Here's what StandingsViewModel looks like now:

```
class StandingsViewModel(application: Application) :
  AndroidViewModel(application) {

  private val repo: BaseballRepository

  val standings: LiveData<List<UITeamStanding>>

  init {
    repo = BaseballDatabase
      .getDatabase(application, viewModelScope)
      .baseballDao()
      .let { dao ->
          BaseballRepository.getInstance(dao)
      }

    standings =
      Transformations.map(repo.getStandings()) { teamStandings ->
        teamStandings.mapNotNull { teamStanding ->
          UITeamStanding.fromTeamIdAndStandings(
            teamStanding.teamId,
            teamStandings
          )
        }
      }
  }
}
```

Go ahead and run the app now, it should look the same as it did before. You can verify that it's using the data from the database by changing values within Android Studio's Database Inspector. Now that the mock data is in there and our Standings page is working with our database, we can move on to pulling data from an external API. To do this, we're going to use a library called Retrofit.

Work with Retrofit

While we've gotten away with developing offline apps so far, that's very rarely the case in the real world. Don't get me wrong, everything we've done so far is valuable (both here and with Penny Drop), but calling APIs is a critical piece of building an app.

If you're not familiar, Retrofit[1] is an open source library created by Square, Inc.,[2] and has become a de facto "official" Android library—so much so that the official Google tutorials use Retrofit for any API calls.

I'm going to cover the basics with setting up a Retrofit service here. If you're more interested in just using the service rather than building it, skip ahead

1. https://square.github.io/retrofit/
2. https://squareup.com/

to the next section: Add the ABL API Client, on page 244. We're going to be using the ABL API client for our app rather than what I'm showing you here, so you won't actually be using the code we write. But as Retrofit is so widely used, I figure it's worth covering.

Build a Retrofit Service

The core piece of a Retrofit implementation is the Service interface. Here, you define each of your APIs by listing the HTTP method (GET, POST, and so on), the API path, any query parameters, and the return type. Again, the great thing about Retrofit is that you're always working with objects rather than having to manually convert things each time.

For example, the getStandings() function that we'll use in a bit is set up in the following manner. It's a GET request with a single query parameter (currentDate) and a return type of TeamStandingApiModel. The currentDate parameter allows us to request the standings as they were for any date in the year. The currentDate parameter is optional, so it should be marked as a nullable LocalDate? object.

Also, thanks to Kotlin, we can mark our Retrofit functions with the suspend modifier and call them inside coroutines in our code. The AndroidBaseballLeagueService with the getStandings() function looks like this:

```
interface AndroidBaseballLeagueService {
  @GET("standings")
  suspend fun getStandings(
    @Query("currentDate") currentDate: LocalDate? = null
  ): List<TeamStandingApiModel>
}
```

All of our endpoint functions in AndroidBaseballLeagueService will follow a similar setup. Additional features are available to us, like adding a path variable, which you can see in the getSinglePlayer() function:

```
@GET("players/{playerId}")
suspend fun getSinglePlayer(
  @Path("playerId") playerId: String,
  @Query("currentDate") currentDate: LocalDate? = null
): BoxScoreItemsApiModel
```

Once all the endpoints you want are added to the service, we can set up the Retrofit builder. In our case, this is a two-part process. We need a JSON converter and then the Retrofit object builder.

For the JSON converter, I'm choosing Moshi,[3] another great library from our friends at Square. For anyone that's used GSON before, Moshi is effectively GSON v3.0, as it was started by two of the three main GSON maintainers. If you don't know about GSON, don't worry about it, as it's deprecated.

By adding Moshi as a Converter.Factory in our Retrofit service, data can be automatically converted from JSON text into objects. We can even add adapters to our Moshi converter for certain data types, like dates:

```
class MoshiLocalDateAdapter {
  @ToJson
  fun toJson(date: LocalDate?): String?
    = date?.let { dateFormat.format(it) }

  @FromJson
  fun fromJson(dateString: String?): LocalDate?
    = dateString?.let { LocalDate.parse(it, dateFormat) }
}
```

With adapters like the one above, the Moshi builder would look like this:

```
val moshi = Moshi.Builder()
  .add(MoshiLocalDateAdapter())
  .add(MoshiLocalDateTimeAdapter())
  .build()
```

With that, we're able to build the Retrofit object. Now, this isn't the service we'll be using in our Android app but rather the Retrofit class used to create the service from the interface we defined.

As I mentioned, Moshi can be added as a Converter.Factory to the Retrofit object, and we can add other Converter.Factory classes like this one:

```
class DateTimeQueryConverterFactory : Converter.Factory() {
  override fun stringConverter(
    type: Type,
    annotations: Array<Annotation>,
    retrofit: Retrofit
  ): Converter<*, String>? = when (type) {
    LocalDate::class.java ->
      Converter<LocalDate, String> { date -> dateFormat.format(date) }
    LocalDateTime::class.java ->
      Converter<LocalDateTime, String> {
        dateTime -> dateTimeFormat.format(dateTime)
      }
    else -> super.stringConverter(type, annotations, retrofit)
  }
}
```

3. https://link.mfazio.dev/moshi

With everything set up, the Retrofit builder gives us the Retrofit object, where can call the create() function to get our concrete service.

Using the ABL API Client we'll add soon, we get the service via a getDefaultABLService() function I added to the client. This gives us a quick way to get an instance of the AndroidBaseballLeagueService without having to worry about doing any setup in the app:

```
fun getDefaultABLService(
  baseUrl: String = "https://abl.mfazio.dev/api/"
): AndroidBaseballLeagueService {
  val moshi = Moshi.Builder()
    .add(MoshiLocalDateAdapter())
    .add(MoshiLocalDateTimeAdapter())
    .build()

  val retrofit = Retrofit.Builder()
    .addConverterFactory(MoshiConverterFactory.create(moshi))
    .addConverterFactory(DateTimeQueryConverterFactory())
    .baseUrl(baseUrl)
    .build()

  return retrofit.create(AndroidBaseballLeagueService::class.java)
}
```

Now, this was admittedly a *very* quick overview of Retrofit, but hopefully it gave you an idea of what's going on here. If you want to see more, I've put the source code for the ABL API client into a public GitHub Repo[4] as well as this book's source code.

It's now time for us to add the ABL API client and start using it in our app.

Add the ABL API Client

By using the ABL API client, you'll save a bunch of time with setting up services and creating all the required API models containing the response data. The only thing that leaves for us in the app is to call the services and convert the API models to our internal models.

To use the client, we need to include a new repository in both the buildscript and allprojects repositories blocks within the project's build.gradle file:

```
buildscript {
  ext { ... }
  repositories {
```

4. https://github.com/MFazio23/ABL-API-Client

```
    google()
    jcenter()
➤   maven { url 'https://jitpack.io' }
  }
  dependencies { ... }
}

allprojects {
  repositories {
    google()
    jcenter()
➤   maven { url 'https://jitpack.io' }
  }
}
```

We then can add the ABL API Client and Retrofit dependencies (plus their version variables, of course):

```
implementation "com.squareup.retrofit2:retrofit:$retrofit_version"
implementation "dev.mfazio:abl-api-client:$abl_client_version"
```

Normally, we wouldn't need the Retrofit dependency at all, but we're going to use the HttpException class from there later on, so it's a requirement in our case.

Also, make sure your project's build.gradle file has jcenter() in the allprojects repositories block, as that's where I deployed the client. It should already be there, but just in case it's not, add it now.

Once the dependencies are added, sync up the project and we can move on to using the client. We will make a quick stop in AndroidManifest.xml to add a couple of permisions, then back to the BaseballRepository class to start with the client.

Load Data from External APIs

Web service calls may be the task most improved by moving to Kotlin + Jetpack (plus Retrofit, which we just covered). You used to have to build a new child class of AsyncTask, override the functions there, hope you didn't accidentally leak the context somewhere, and then finally update the UI once the processing was done.

Now? We've got coroutines, LiveData, and suspend functions to make everything smoother and clearer. Also, the type-safe suspend functions from Retrofit make calling APIs so much smoother.

Load Standings Data via the ABL API Client

Inside AndroidManifest.xml, we need to give the app permission to access the internet and check the current network state of the device. We do this by adding one <uses-permission> tag near the top of our <manifest> container tag:

```
<manifest xmlns:android="http://schemas.android.com/apk/res/android"
  package="dev.mfazio.abl">

➤  <uses-permission android:name="android.permission.INTERNET" />

  <application ...>
    «Application tag attributes»
  </application>
</manifest>
```

Next up is the BaseballRepository. There isn't much in here right now, but we do at least have a function to get the Standings LiveData from the database. Now it's time for us to add an updateStandings() function that uses the ABL API Client.

The first order of business is to add the ABL API Client to our Repository. This is done by adding an instance of AndroidBaseballLeagueService in our companion object, which we get from the getDefaultABLService() function:

```
companion object {
➤  private val apiService = getDefaultABLService()

  @Volatile
  private var instance: BaseballRepository? = null

  fun getInstance(baseballDao: BaseballDao) =
    this.instance ?: synchronized(this) {
      instance ?: BaseballRepository(baseballDao).also {
        instance = it
      }
    }
}
```

Once we have the apiService in BaseballRepository, we can call the getStandings() function to get the current league standings. We'll be doing this inside the updateStandings() function.

At a high level, updateStandings() pulls data in from the Standings API, and if there's data, the API models are converted into TeamStanding objects to be entered into the database. Then our UI is updated automatically via the LiveData object we set up last chapter.

The conversion logic for Standings objects lives in an APIConverters.kt file. Here, there's an extension function called convertToTeamStandings(). We're going to need to convert API models to our internal models both here and with the Scoreboard page, so go ahead and grab the APIConverters.kt file from the source code.

We could cover its contents here, but it's just a bunch of map and when blocks. Those are certainly useful, but they're nothing new and I'd rather we focus on the new pieces.

Once you have the file copied over and the apiService instance added, we can implement updateStandings():

```
suspend fun updateStandings() {
  val standings = apiService.getStandings()

  if(standings.any()) {
    baseballDao.updateStandings(
      standings.convertToTeamStandings(
        baseballDao.getCurrentStandings()
      )
    )
  }
}
```

Calling the Standings API, converting that data to our @Entity model, and sending it to the DAO to be saved only takes eleven lines of code. Also, all of this is done on a background thread, so the user is never interrupted in any way. This all works because both our current function and the getStandings function are marked with the suspend modifier.

That is all we need to get the data from the API, so now it's time to call that getStandings() function. Inside StandingsViewModel, we want a new function called refreshStandings(), which calls out to repo.updateStandings() inside a launch block:

```
fun refreshStandings() {
  viewModelScope.launch {
    repo.updateStandings()
  }
}
```

Then we can call that function inside StandingsFragment at the end of the onCreateView() function:

```
override fun onCreateView(
  inflater: LayoutInflater,
  container: ViewGroup?,
  savedInstanceState: Bundle?
): View? {
  «Binding code is still up here.»
```

```
  standingsViewModel.refreshStandings()

  return binding.root
}
```

Now our Standings data will be updated whenever the StandingsFragment is created, like when a user chooses the Standings page in the nav drawer. The only issue here is that the data isn't updated unless a user navigates away from the Standings page and back to it. We could make this better (without too much work) by adding the ability to swipe down from the top to refresh.

Refresh Data on Swipe

We need a new library dependency here:

```
implementation
  "androidx.swiperefreshlayout:swiperefreshlayout:$swipe_refresh_version"
```

Then, inside fragment_standings.xml, wrap the existing <RecyclerView> tag in a new <SwipeRefreshLayout> tag. That outer tag now holds all the XML namespaces as well. The whole file looks like this:

```
<?xml version="1.0" encoding="utf-8"?>
<androidx.swiperefreshlayout.widget.SwipeRefreshLayout
  xmlns:android="http://schemas.android.com/apk/res/android"
  xmlns:app="http://schemas.android.com/apk/res-auto"
  xmlns:tools="http://schemas.android.com/tools"
  android:id="@+id/standingsSwipeRefreshLayout"
  android:layout_width="match_parent"
  android:layout_height="match_parent">

  <androidx.recyclerview.widget.RecyclerView
    android:id="@+id/standingsList"
    android:layout_width="match_parent"
    android:layout_height="match_parent"
    android:layout_gravity="center"
    app:layoutManager="LinearLayoutManager"
    tools:context=".standings.StandingsFragment"
    tools:listitem="@layout/standings_team_item" />

</androidx.swiperefreshlayout.widget.SwipeRefreshLayout>
```

Inside StandingsFragment, we want to switch to using view binding so we can more easily bind the StandingsAdapter to our RecyclerView:

```
override fun onCreateView(
  inflater: LayoutInflater,
  container: ViewGroup?,
  savedInstanceState: Bundle?
): View? {
```

```
➤   val binding = FragmentStandingsBinding.inflate(inflater)

    val standingsAdapter = StandingsAdapter()

➤   binding.standingsList.adapter = standingsAdapter

    standingsViewModel.standings.observe(viewLifecycleOwner) { standings ->
        standingsAdapter.addHeadersAndBuildStandings(standings)
    }

    standingsViewModel.refreshStandings()

    return binding.root
}
```

Then we add an OnRefreshListener to our newly added SwipeRefreshLayout that calls standingsViewModel.refreshStandings() whenever the view is swiped down. Plus, we need to set the isRefreshing property to false once the data loads, which means we should set that inside the existing observe() block. Those additions look like this:

```
val binding = FragmentStandingsBinding.inflate(inflater)

val standingsAdapter = StandingsAdapter()

binding.standingsList.adapter = standingsAdapter

➤ binding.standingsSwipeRefreshLayout.setOnRefreshListener {
➤   standingsViewModel.refreshStandings()
➤ }

standingsViewModel.standings.observe(viewLifecycleOwner) { standings ->
  standingsAdapter.addHeadersAndBuildStandings(standings)
➤ binding.standingsSwipeRefreshLayout.isRefreshing = false
}

standingsViewModel.refreshStandings()

return binding.root
```

We now have given users a way to update the data on this screen without having to navigate anywhere else without too much work. I know it was a bit of a detour, but it'll definitely improve the user experience of the app, as shown in the image on page 250.

Everything's in place to display the updated data since we already set up the LiveData previously. That's a great advantage of the setup saving API data to a Room DB: we always pull data from the same spot no matter the original source. Plus, having the data stored in the database allows for data to be available offline.

Speaking of offline, did your app crash when attempting a refresh? Was the error log utterly unhelpful?

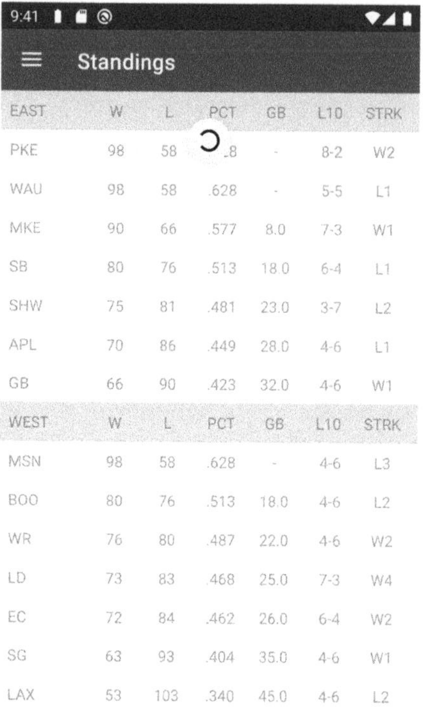

9:41
Standings
EAST W L PCT GB L10 STRK
PKE 98 58 .8 - 8-2 W2
WAU 98 58 .628 - 5-5 L1
MKE 90 66 .577 8.0 7-3 W1
SB 80 76 .513 18.0 6-4 L1
SHW 75 81 .481 23.0 3-7 L2
APL 70 86 .449 28.0 4-6 L1
GB 66 90 .423 32.0 4-6 W1
WEST W L PCT GB L10 STRK
MSN 98 58 .628 - 4-6 L3
BOO 80 76 .513 18.0 4-6 L2
WR 76 80 .487 22.0 4-6 W2
LD 73 83 .468 25.0 7-3 W4
EC 72 84 .462 26.0 6-4 W2
SG 63 93 .404 35.0 4-6 W1
LAX 53 103 .340 45.0 4-6 L2

Handle Offline Scenarios

Retrofit has a downside: if you don't have network connectivity, you'll end up with an unhandled exception, which can crash your app. As a result, we need to make sure to catch and handle any exceptions that may come up.

We want to catch different exceptions that pop up, and if we can give the user more info about what just happened, that's always helpful. So we'll catch a few different types of exceptions, then return a ResultStatus to our ViewModel classes, which will display a Toast message if there's an error.

Add API Result Types

To support this process, we need a few new things in our BaseballRepository class. First, we need a ResultStatus enum class that tells the ViewModel classes what happened with the call:

```
enum class ResultStatus {
  Unknown,
  Success,
  NetworkException,
  RequestException,
  GeneralException
}
```

Then we want a new inner class called ApiResult to hold both a result and the ResultStatus. We can set this class to take in a generic type so it can be used with any of our API requests.

The T parameter listed in the class represents that generic type. Note that any variable could be used in place of T; that's just a convention since it's representing a type. The code looks like this:

```
inner class ApiResult<T>(
  val result: T? = null,
  val status: ResultStatus = ResultStatus.Unknown
) {
  val success = status == ResultStatus.Success
}
```

Add a Function to Safely Call APIs

Finally, we have our safeApiRequest() function that calls one of our service endpoints and returns the result if we didn't get an exception. If we did get an exception, we catch it and return a different ResultStatus type. This function brings in a separate suspend function call as a parameter, which we then call within the safeApiRequest() function:

```
private suspend fun <T> safeApiRequest(
  apiFunction: suspend () -> T
): ApiResult<T> =
  try {
    val result = apiFunction()
    ApiResult(result, ResultStatus.Success)
  } catch (ex: retrofit2.HttpException) {
    ApiResult(status = ResultStatus.RequestException)
  } catch (ex: IOException) {
    ApiResult(status = ResultStatus.NetworkException)
  } catch (ex: Exception) {
    ApiResult(status = ResultStatus.GeneralException)
  }
```

We have three separate exception types we're catching here since that allows us to give the user a bit more info. A Retrofit HttpException tells us there's an issue with the request itself, while an IOException says there was likely some kind of network or connectivity issue. We also want the fallback of catching any Exception since we never want the app crashing due to not being able to update data.

Be Careful with Catching Exceptions

Adding a catch for the top-level Exception can be dangerous, at least in the sense of it hiding errors in your code.

Make sure you're doing something useful with the exception when it's caught and start by catching more specific Exception types (like IOException) so you can take the proper action for your app.

With the safeApiRequest() function added, we can use it inside updateStandings():

```
suspend fun updateStandings(): ResultStatus {
  val standingsResult = safeApiRequest {
    apiService.getStandings()
  }

  return if (
    standingsResult.success &&
    standingsResult.result?.any() == true
  ) {
    baseballDao.updateStandings(
      standingsResult.result.convertToTeamStandings(
        baseballDao.getCurrentStandings()
      )
    )
    ResultStatus.Success
  } else {
    standingsResult.status
  }
}
```

Yes, this added some complexity to our API call, but now we're protected against scenarios where a user's phone is offline for any reason, which we know will happen. With that ready, we can start using those ResultStatus values.

Handle Request Exceptions on the UI

Inside the StandingsViewModel class, we need to make two changes. We need a new MutableLiveData value called errorMessage and we need to update refreshStandings() to handle the returned ResultStatus. The errorMessage value goes near the top of the StandingsViewModel class:

```
val errorMessage = MutableLiveData("")
```

The refreshStandings() function update isn't too bad either, but the main piece here is taking a ResultStatus value and converting it to an error message. I decided to do this inside the UIExtensions.kt file as an extension function on ResultStatus:

```
fun ResultStatus.getErrorMessage(application: Application) = when (this) {
  ResultStatus.NetworkException ->
    application.resources.getString(R.string.network_exception_message)
  ResultStatus.RequestException ->
    application.resources.getString(R.string.request_exception_message)
  ResultStatus.GeneralException ->
    application.resources.getString(R.string.general_exception_message)
  else -> null
}
```

This code needs some new string resource values, but otherwise it's ready to use. Then, inside StandingsViewModel, we need to call that new getErrorMessage() function:

```
fun refreshStandings() {
  viewModelScope.launch {
    repo.updateStandings().getErrorMessage(getApplication())
      ?.let { message -> errorMessage.value = message }
  }
}
```

With the errorMessage LiveData value now ready, we can add a new observe() call on it. Here, we use that error message text to display a Toast message to the user. Also, we want to let the swipe refresh layout know that we're done refreshing when we get a new error message:

```
standingsViewModel.errorMessage
  .observe(viewLifecycleOwner) { errorMessage ->
    if(!errorMessage.isNullOrEmpty()) {
      Toast.makeText(context, errorMessage, Toast.LENGTH_LONG).show()
    }
    binding.standingsSwipeRefreshLayout.isRefreshing = false
  }
```

Now if a user doesn't have connectivity or our APIs are down, we display an error Toast message instead of crashing the app. The StandingsFragment is now complete, so we can get to adding our new Scoreboard page.

Add a New Fragment (Scoreboard)

The Scoreboard shows users the games on a given day, complete with teams, scores, winning/losing/upcoming pitchers, and if a game is in progress, even baserunners. It's by far the most complicated page from a UI/XML perspective in the app, and the good news is that you don't have to make it!

Instead, we're going to copy code over again. You're certainly welcome to check out what's in the code, because it *is* interesting, but there's far too much going on to fit into this chapter. Honestly, building the UI would be a forty-page chapter on its own, and nobody wants that.

All the code you need is in the chapter-10/code-to-copy directory, and there's quite a bit to add to your app, so pay close attention to the list:

- Everything in the scoreboard package.
- All the layout XML files prefixed with the word *scoreboard* and fragment_scoreboard.xml.
- The five drawable XML files inside the scoreboard-images folder (or under res/drawable).
- The five string resource values prefixed with *scoreboard_*.
- The Extensions.kt and UIExtensions.kt files from the util package.
- An entry for the ScoreboardFragment class in nav_graph.xml.
- The ScheduledGame @Entity to BaseballDatabase.
- Extra @TypeConverter functions inside data.Converters.
- The fromTeamIds() function inside UITeam.

There are a lot of moving parts here, so you'll probably want to build the app. Unfortunately, it won't build successfully yet because we're missing the getGamesForDate() functions in our Repository and DAO classes.

Add Functions to Get Scoreboard Data

The easy function here is in BaseballDao since it's almost exactly like @Query functions we've written before:

```
@Query("SELECT * FROM games WHERE gameId LIKE :dateString")
abstract fun getGamesForDate(
  dateString: String
): LiveData<List<ScheduledGame>>
```

The only real difference is the LIKE part of the SQL query. To filter for a date, we check that the beginning of the gameId value for a ScheduledGame matches the date we want. While I could have added another field that contains just the date for matching purposes, I wanted to give you an example of a LIKE expression in a Room query.

Due to having LIKE in our query, we can add a wildcard parameter (%) in the dateString value we send into the DAO function. This causes our Repository function to look like this:

```
fun getGamesForDate(date: LocalDate): LiveData<List<ScheduledGame>> =
  baseballDao.getGamesForDate("${date.toGameDateString()}%")
```

See how the % is at the end of the date string? That means that our query should accept any value in that place. In practice, this means a date string of "20201115" will match values such as "2020111509-LD-WAU" and "2020111517-MKE-SHW".

Now that we can get some data out of our database, we can build the app to make sure everything works, then move on to actually loading some data (since the blank Scoreboard page isn't too interesting). Make sure you include the ScoreboardFragment in your navigation graph, as well, or we won't even be able to get to the blank Scoreboard page.

Load Scoreboard Data from the API

Sadly, Room doesn't come with upsert functionality (update if present, insert otherwise) out of the box, so we need to implement it ourselves. Inside BaseballDao, we need a new function called insertOrUpdateGames() that goes through each of the ScheduledGame objects we sent in and either inserts or updates each one in the DB.

To update a game, we want to grab it from the database by the game ID since we have that value on our API result (and not the database ID). That function looks like this:

```
@Query("SELECT * FROM games WHERE gameId = :gameId")
abstract fun getGameByGameId(gameId: String): ScheduledGame?
```

We're returning a nullable ScheduledGame? object from this function since we may or may not find the game we're looking for. This comes in handy with our insertOrUpdateGames() since we can use a null value as the determining factor of whether or not we update or insert the ScheduledGame.

If we find an existing game, we call updateGame() and send in a copy of the current game we're considering but with the id variable set to the ID from the database. If the game *doesn't* exist in the database, we can then insert it as a new record. The logic for insertOrUpdateGames(), along with the associated @Insert and @Update functions, looks like this:

```
@Insert
abstract suspend fun insertGame(game: ScheduledGame)

@Update
abstract suspend fun updateGame(game: ScheduledGame)

@Transaction
open suspend fun insertOrUpdateGames(games: List<ScheduledGame>) {
  games.forEach { game ->
    getGameByGameId(game.gameId)?.let { dbGame ->
      updateGame(game.apply { id = dbGame.id })
    } ?: insertGame(game)
  }
}
```

With the DAO functions complete, we can add updateGamesForDate() to BaseballRepository:

```
suspend fun updateGamesForDate(date: LocalDate): ResultStatus {
  val gamesResult = safeApiRequest {
    apiService.getGames(requestedDate = date)
  }

  return if (gamesResult.success && gamesResult.result?.any() == true) {
    baseballDao.insertOrUpdateGames(
      gamesResult.result.convertToScheduledGames()
    )
    ResultStatus.Success
  } else {
    gamesResult.status
  }
}
```

The convertToScheduledGames() function is likely missing or commented out in your APIConverters.kt file, so copy/uncomment that from the code along with all the extension functions on classes starting with ScheduledGame:

- List<ScheduledGameApiModel>.convertToScheduledGames()
- ScheduledGameStatusApiModel.toScheduledGameStatus()
- ScheduledGameApiModel.getScoreboardPlayerInfo()
- ScheduledGamePitcherApiModel.convertPitcherToScoreboardPlayerInfo()
- ScheduledGamePitcherApiModel.convertCloserToScoreboardPlayerInfo()
- ScheduledGameBatterApiModel.convertCurrentBatterToScoreboardPlayerInfo()

We're almost set with the Scoreboard screen—next up is the refreshScores() function inside ScoreboardViewModel. The code should be here already but commented out for you. Add it back in and notice that it's basically the same as what we did in StandingsViewModel:

```
private fun refreshScores(date: LocalDate) {
  //TODO: Add this in once the Repository has updateGamesForDate(...)
  viewModelScope.launch {
    repo.updateGamesForDate(date).getErrorMessage(getApplication())
      ?.let { message ->
        errorMessage.value = message
      }
  }
}
```

What's cool about this function is that we can send whichever date we wish into this function and it'll give us back games for that day (excluding Christmas—they get the day off). This way we can scroll through the schedule on the screen and refresh the scores for each day to give updated results.

With that, everything's ready to go now with the Scoreboard screen. Run your app again and make sure you can navigate to the Scoreboard page. It should look something like this:

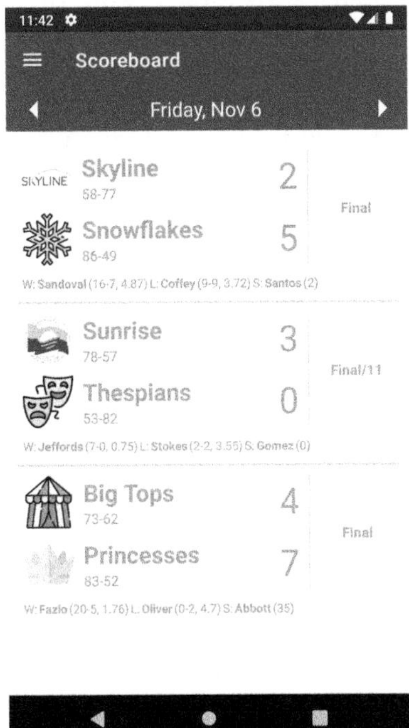

If things look good, then you're all set here and we can wrap things up in a bit. But before you go, take a peek at goToDate() to see how we're handling date changes. Everything is keyed on the selectedDate; when that value changes, we then load up new games due to the Transformations.switchMap() call being assigned to the games value.

By linking everything to the selectedDate, we have a single approach for both loading and refreshing data. If, in the future, we want to allow users to jump directly to any date, there's very little extra work we'll need to do in here.

Summary and Next Steps

We've moved outside of our app and are bringing information in. Almost every app we work on nowadays will have some kind of API or web service component, so know you'll be doing things like this with most modern Android development.

Having a backing Room database to go with our APIs made our app more resilient since we can bring data back to our users even when they don't have any connection. By taking a bit of care in how we call our services, we can give users a solid offline experience.

Using coroutines enabled both of those parts by allowing us to easily call both the APIs and the database without interrupting the user or UI. Rather than having to add a bunch of extra code to support asynchronous logic, coroutines make things so much smoother.

Next up is in a way part two of this same idea—we're going to pull in player data from the APIs but with a slightly different approach. Now, instead of just grabbing everything for the league or a given day, we're going to split up a list of data into pages. This way we only grab the players currently displayed in the list rather than everyone in the league with each request.

To do this, we're going to use Jetpack's Paging library, which will help us in this process. Paging helps us keep our data usage down and helps make our app more resilient when displaying lists of data.

CHAPTER 11

Display Data with Paging

Welcome to the beta chapter! That means this is the chapter most likely to have changed multiple times by the time you're reading it.

The reason is that we're going to be using version 3 of Jetpack's Paging library. This version is in beta as I'm writing this, which means the library is *not* totally solidified and *may* change.

Then why on earth would I choose to have us use this library? It's because this is the proper version going forward and the one you want to use. I'd rather have you learn the new approach and have to tweak a bit of what you know rather than have to completely upgrade your screen(s). Just know things are more likely to break and need to be changed here than we're used to elsewhere in the book.

Now, with that warning out the way, let's get to the good parts about paging! The Paging library helps you to more easily display long lists of data while limiting the number of network calls being made. We can avoid having to load all 420 ABL players at once when we're just looking for Nick Adam (who's near the top of the list alphabetically). We'll also have the ability to search the list based on player names while still paging out the results, as shown in the image on page 260.

Paging also works beautifully with Room, where the library will automatically pull in players from our local database as needed to fill out a page, then allow our API calls to happen in the background. Plus, this way we can still display all the players we had already loaded when a user is offline.

Before we get to the Players screen shown in the preceding image, we want to get two new screens in here that go hand-in-hand with the Players list: league leaders and individual player pages. These two pages aren't directly

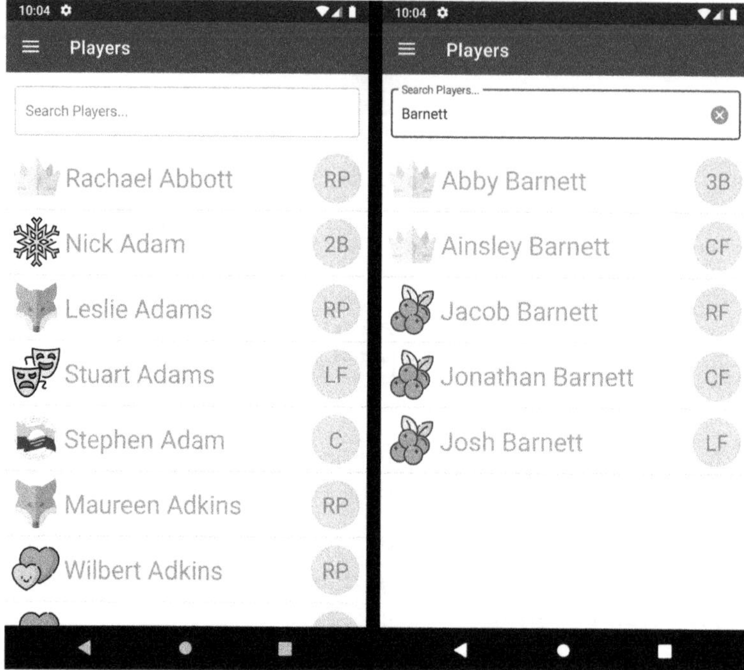

connected to paging but tie in well with the Players screen, so we're including them here. Plus, the construction of those pages has a few interesting parts.

Add Two New Fragments (Leaders and Single Player)

We've got a bunch of code to copy over to set up these screens. All the code needed for both views can be found in the Code folder under chapter-11/code-to-copy. You want to grab everything inside the leaders and players packages (except for PlayerListItem and PlayersAdapter), and both Player and PlayerStats need to be part of the entities list in BaseballDatabase:

```
entities = [
➤   Player::class,
➤   PlayerStats::class,
    ScheduledGame::class,
    TeamStanding::class
]
```

The BaseballRepository and BaseballDao classes can be copied over as well, as they contain the new functions for these two pages plus everything else we've added up to this point. The same is true for both data/Converters.kt and util/APIConverters.kt.

Then get all the layout files: fragment_leaders.xml, fragment_leaders_list.xml, fragment_single_player.xml, leader_list_item.xml, single_player_stat_with_label.xml, and single_player_stats.xml. Don't grab the player-related layout files yet, as we'll be writing that code later.

Finally, get the drawable/basic_circle.xml and navigation/nav_graph.xml resource files, plus strings.xml, unless you *really* want to write some string resource values yourself.

Before you move on, make sure to update all initializations of the BaseballRepository class since that now requires the BaseballDatabase as a parameter rather than BaseballDao. We'll address why later on in the chapter, but make that change now so you can build your project.

Finally, include the View Pager dependency (plus version variable):

```
implementation "androidx.viewpager2:viewpager2:$view_pager_version"
```

Everything should be good to go now, so fire up the app and take a look at both screens. You can open up the Leaders screen (note that you can swipe between Batting and Pitching leaders) and click a player to see their info. The Leaders screen plus a Single Player screen should look something like this:

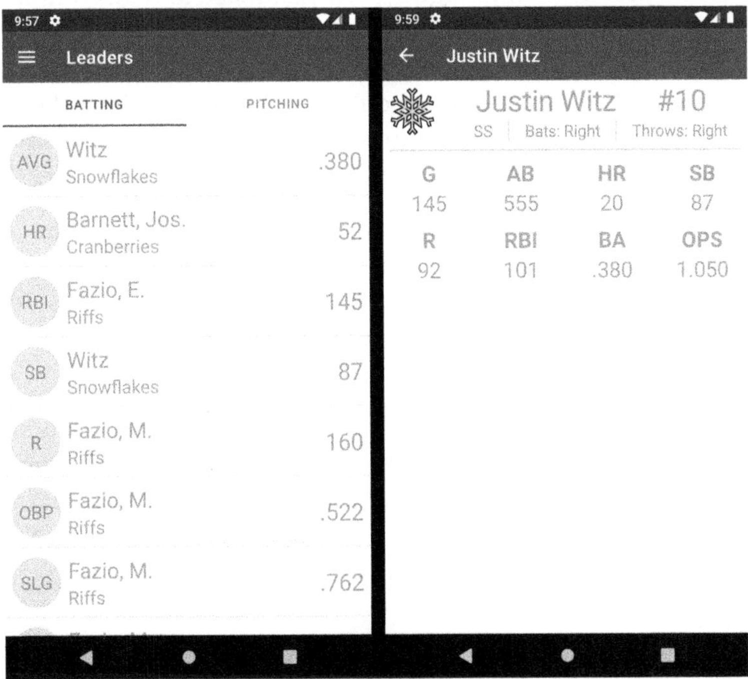

Since we're not writing the code for these screens, I want to call out a couple of items that may be interesting to you.

Calculate League Leaders on the Leaders Screen

As I mentioned, the Leaders screen contains both the Batting and Pitching leaders, listed out in different tabs. This is done by using a combination of a <TabLayout> tag and a <ViewPager2> tag. These work together to display both the top tabs and the proper view depending on which tab is selected. A TabLayoutMediator instance handles switching things within LeadersFragment, and since both tabs are displayed the same way, we can use a single layout contained in fragment_leaders_list.xml.

A bit more is done with the Tabbed Swipe view on the Leaders screen, so I recommend checking out the code for yourself. Using the ViewPager2 library saves us so much trouble with displaying multiple tabs of information, leaving us only some configuration and data loading to handle.

Now, that data loading (along with the conversion process) isn't simple but hopefully will at least be logical. On a high level, we load PlayerWithStats objects from the database, then grab the top player for each stat category. Easy, right?

Well, not as easy as you'd think. Issue number one is that we won't necessarily have all the players in the league in our database at a given time, and we don't want to download everyone to calculate leaders, as that would defeat the purpose of having paging. Instead, we can use the getBattingLeaders() and getPitchingLeaders() API functions to get only the players who lead the ABL in at least one category. We put them into our database (along with their stats) and then we can pull them out to calculate the leaders for each category.

That calculation could be a bunch of copied and pasted lines that get all the players, sort them by whatever category we want, then with the top player in the list, we get the data we need for a Leader list item on the screen. This approach would certainly be valid, but we've got the power of Kotlin at our disposal, so why not take advantage?

Each of the leader categories (batting and pitching) are basically doing the same thing, so both of those functions are similar single expressions that do what I just described. The trick here is that we can put all the stat categories into a big list and map the players on each category. The function that populates battingLeaders looks like this:

```
battingLeaders =
  Transformations.map(repo.getBattersWithStats()) { battersWithStats ->
    battingStatCategories.mapIndexed { index, handler ->
      battersWithStats
```

```
      ?.sortedWith(handler.statComparator)
      ?.firstOrNull()?.let { batterWithStats ->
        LeaderListItem(
          index.toLong(),
          batterWithStats.player,
          handler.category,
          handler.formattedStatValue(batterWithStats),
          UITeam.fromTeamId(
            batterWithStats.player.teamId
          )?.nickname ?: "N/A"
        )
      }
  }.filterNotNull()
}
```

I hope this makes some sense at a high level since we've done similar things before, but this mystery handler object may be throwing you off. That's an object with a stat category *plus* functions to compare stats and format the stat for the UI. For example, the PlayerStatHandler object for batting average looks like this:

```
PlayerStatHandler(
  category = "AVG",
  statComparator = { batterA, batterB ->
    -batterA.stats.batterStats.battingAverage.compareTo(
      batterB.stats.batterStats.battingAverage
    )
  },
  formattedStatValue = { batter ->
    batter.stats.batterStats.battingAverage.toBattingPercentageString()
  }
)
```

That's a String value and two *lambda functions*, both of which are used in our mapping function. In this case, we display a label of "AVG", sort players by their batting average (the negative sign in front makes it descending), and then format the batting average properly (for example, .300 for a 30% hitter).

I wanted to include this section because it shows not only a more advanced way to map data we get from the database but also how we can use higher-order functions to send logic around inside variables.

Review Concepts from the Single Player Screen

This is admittedly the less exciting of the two screens since we've already covered the concepts in this page previously. We get a playerId value from the SinglePlayerFragmentArgs class, load the PlayerWithStats object from the database, *then* convert the stats from that object into PlayerStatWithLabel objects which are used on the front end.

This is a great review of different things we've done so far: LiveData with Transformations calls, Repository/DAO/DB call sequences, data binding, and even the nice Toast error message. But now it's time to move on to something new.

Add a New Fragment (Players)

As I've mentioned, Paging will save users a bunch of bandwidth when displaying players from the ABL. Plus, loading data from the database automatically will require nothing more than a single DAO call on our end. Before we get into things, add in the single Paging dependency with an associated version variable:

```
implementation "androidx.paging:paging-runtime-ktx:$paging_version"
```

Now, we already have the Room dependency in here, but make sure you're using at least version 2.3 (even if it's an alpha version). That's required to have Room work nicely with Paging.

The base pieces of this screen will also be similar to what we've seen with other list pages, in particular the PlayersAdapter class. We'll end up copying that over later from the Code directory, but heads up that the only real difference here is our use of the PagingDataAdapter base class rather than ListAdapter.

The first step here is to get a new PlayerListItem class created. This class is the model we'll be using for each of our rows in the Players list, so either copy that over or add it in manually:

```
@Entity(tableName = "player_list_items")
data class PlayerListItem(
  @PrimaryKey val playerId: String,
  val playerName: String,
  val teamId: String,
  val position: Position
)
```

Yes, the PlayerListItem class is an @Entity we're saving in the database, and no, I didn't forget about the Player class. The reason I'm introducing a new @Entity here is because this way we can have a database table that is only connected to the Players screen. Since we're using the Player class in other places, the order in which data is loaded can get messed up and cause issues when grabbing new data. This isolation avoids any such issues for us and lets the Paging library have full control.

Make sure you add PlayerListItem to the entities array attached to BaseballDatabase, then we can move on to PlayersFragment.

The PlayersFragment starts out very much like other views with some NavArgs, a ViewModel class, and an adapter. The Fragment code and the UI are connected up via view binding, and we're even going to add in a nice divider to each list item.

The first version of the class looks something like this:

```
class PlayersFragment : Fragment() {

  private val playerListArgs: PlayersFragmentArgs by navArgs()

  private lateinit var playersAdapter: PlayersAdapter

  override fun onCreateView(
    inflater: LayoutInflater,
    container: ViewGroup?,
    savedInstanceState: Bundle?
  ): View {
    val binding = FragmentPlayersBinding.inflate(inflater)

    this.playersAdapter = PlayersAdapter()

    with(binding.playersList) {
      adapter = playersAdapter
      addItemDecoration(
        DividerItemDecoration(
          context,
          LinearLayoutManager.VERTICAL
        )
      )
    }

    return binding.root
  }
}
```

We can just copy over the XML files we need, fragment_players.xml and player_list_item.xml, plus the PlayersAdapter class. The only new and noteworthy piece here is inside fragment_players.xml, where we're including a <TextInputLayout> containing a <TextInputEditText> field. This will be our search box that we'll implement near the end of the chapter.

Make sure to also include the PlayersFragment in the nav_graph.xml file, otherwise there will be errors in PlayersFragment:

```
<fragment
  android:id="@+id/playersFragment"
  android:name="dev.mfazio.abl.players.PlayersFragment"
  android:label="@string/players">
```

```
  <argument
    android:name="teamId"
    android:defaultValue="@null"
    app:argType="string"
    app:nullable="true" />
</fragment>
```

Now, this screen isn't interesting yet since we don't have any of the player list items in the database currently. Let's start by setting up the calls within BaseballRepository and BaseballDao, then we'll create a new PlayerListRemoteMediator class, and finally end by setting up PlayerListViewModel.

Handle Paging Data in the App

Now we're getting into the core of this chapter and all the cool, new features. This is also the part that may need to change depending on if anything changes with the Paging library in the future, so heads up in case anything isn't working as you'd expect. Let's start off with something more comfortable and add in our BaseballDao functions.

Manage PlayerListItem Objects in the Database

We need three new functions related to PlayerListItem objects: getPlayerListItems(), insertPlayerListItems(), and deleteAllPlayerListItems(). None of these new functions contain anything new except that we're returning a PagingSource object from our @Query function:

```
@Query(
"""
    SELECT * FROM player_list_items
    WHERE (:teamId IS NULL OR teamId = :teamId)
    AND (:nameQuery IS NULL OR playerName LIKE :nameQuery)
    ORDER BY playerId
"""
)
abstract fun getPlayerListItems(
    teamId: String? = null,
    nameQuery: String? = null
): PagingSource<Int, PlayerListItem>

@Insert(onConflict = OnConflictStrategy.REPLACE)
abstract suspend fun insertPlayerListItems(
  playerListItems: List<PlayerListItem>
)

@Query("DELETE FROM player_list_items")
abstract suspend fun deleteAllPlayerListItems()
```

Notice how we don't have an @Update function? That's because the Paging library will be prepending or appending data, unless a refresh occurs where everything is cleared from the database table and reloaded. This means we never actually update existing records, only add new ones.

However, the PlayerListItem objects aren't enough on their own; we also need to keep track of which page contains each item. To do this, we're adding in a PlayerKeys class and a few things to go with it.

Track Paging with PlayerKeys

The Paging library will combine the PlayerListItem and PlayerKeys classes to figure out where a player belongs on the screen. Along those lines, we could have combined those two classes together in the first place. But I didn't do that for two reasons: I wanted to highlight the PlayerKeys class and how that fits into Paging, plus having two classes makes more sense from a separation-of-concerns perspective.

None of the PlayerKeys pieces are complicated, thankfully. The class, which connects a PlayerListItem (via playerId) to the previous and next pages, looks like this:

```
@Entity(tableName = "player_keys")
data class PlayerKeys(
  @PrimaryKey val playerId: String,
  val previousKey: Int?,
  val nextKey: Int?
)
```

Sticking with the theme of separation, we're going to create a new PlayerKeysDao interface for all PlayerKeys interaction. We actually could refactor BaseballDao into separate classes if we wished (Players, Stats, Games/Standings, and so on), but that comes down to personal and/or team preference.

We're going to have three functions here that are similar to the PlayerListItem ones: getPlayerKeysByPlayerId(), insertKeys(), and deleteAllPlayerKeys(). The new PlayerKeysDao looks like this:

```
@Dao
interface PlayerKeysDao {

  @Query("SELECT * FROM player_keys WHERE playerId = :playerId")
  suspend fun getPlayerKeysByPlayerId(playerId: String): PlayerKeys?

  @Insert(onConflict = OnConflictStrategy.REPLACE)
  suspend fun insertKeys(keys: List<PlayerKeys>)

  @Query("DELETE FROM player_keys")
  suspend fun deleteAllPlayerKeys()

}
```

Make sure to add the playerKeysDao() function and PlayerKeys (and PlayerListItem, if you haven't yet) class reference to the BaseballDatabase:

```
@Database(
  entities = [
    Player::class,
    PlayerListItem::class,
    PlayerKeys::class,
    PlayerStats::class,
    ScheduledGame::class,
    TeamStanding::class
  ],
  exportSchema = false,
  version = 1
)
@TypeConverters(Converters::class)
abstract class BaseballDatabase : RoomDatabase() {
  abstract fun baseballDao(): BaseballDao
  abstract fun playerKeysDao(): PlayerKeysDao

  companion object {
    «Initialization logic is still here.»
  }
}
```

With that, we're set to use the PlayerKeys class in our RemoteMediator class. This is the spot where we'll handle loading data from both the API and database and adding that data to the players list.

Handle Local and Remote Data with PlayerListRemoteMediator

The PlayerListRemoteMediator class is the core of our Paging functionality, as it takes care of figuring out which data needs to be displayed next in the list. Plus, it loads data from the ABL APIs and stores them in the database, which we'll pull out later. You can think of the "Mediator" part of the name being that it handles coordination between new (API) and existing (DB) data.

The primary function in our RemoteMediator class is the load() function, which brings in the LoadType (Prepend, Append, or Refresh) and a PagingState. That PagingState holds the previously loaded pages, where we are in the list, and the PagingConfig used for the list (which we'll initialize when we set things up later).

Our version of the RemoteMediator class takes in AndroidBaseballLeagueService and BaseballDatabase instances to handle all our data needs. We also include both teamId and nameQuery parameters, which can be used to filter the data. The general structure of the PlayerListRemoteMediator class looks like this:

```
@ExperimentalPagingApi
class PlayerListRemoteMediator(
    private val apiService: AndroidBaseballLeagueService,
    private val baseballDatabase: BaseballDatabase,
    private val teamId: String? = null,
    private val nameQuery: String? = null
) : RemoteMediator<Int, PlayerListItem>() {

  override suspend fun load(
    loadType: LoadType,
    state: PagingState<Int, PlayerListItem>
  ): MediatorResult {
    //This is coming up next.
  }
}
```

That @ExperimentalPagingApi annotation on the class is because the RemoteMediator class is currently marked as experimental and is subject to change. Hopefully by the time you're working on this, no such addition will be needed, but it is for the time being.

The load() function has two parts: loading the proper page (via a PlayerKeys instance) and then inserting/updating keys and data in the database. Once both parts are done (unless there's an issue with the keys), we return a MediatorResult to tell the BaseballRepository (where this class is used) how everything went.

Calculate the Current Page

The logic to get the current page depends on which LoadType we need to handle. Determining the LoadType is done for us by the Paging library, we just need to either get a key value or tell the Paging library that we're done loading data. The block to handle all three scenarios looks like this:

```
val page = when (loadType) {
  LoadType.PREPEND -> {
    val keys = loadKeysForFirstPlayer(state)
      ?: return MediatorResult.Error(
        InvalidObjectException("Keys should not be null for $loadType.")
      )

    keys.previousKey ?:
      return MediatorResult.Success(endOfPaginationReached = true)
  }
  LoadType.APPEND -> {
    val keys = loadKeysForLastPlayer(state)

    keys?.nextKey
      ?: return MediatorResult.Success(endOfPaginationReached = false)
  }
```

```
    LoadType.REFRESH -> {
      val keys = loadKeysForClosestPlayer(state)

      keys?.nextKey ?: startingPageIndex
    }
}
```

If the code's throwing you off, think about it this way: PREPEND wants to figure out which page to start adding to the top of the list and needs the top-most loaded page key. APPEND is doing the opposite with finding the last loaded item, then returning which page should come after it, and REFRESH is figuring out where we are to know on which page to start loading brand-new data.

The three loadKeys functions are all handling the logic of finding the PlayerKeys associated with the item in question: top, bottom, or current. Since they're all doing similar things, the logic is also similar in each case:

```
private suspend fun loadKeysForFirstPlayer(
  state: PagingState<Int, PlayerListItem>
) = state.pages.firstOrNull { it.data.isNotEmpty() }
  ?.data?.firstOrNull()?.let { player ->
    baseballDatabase
      .playerKeysDao()
      .getPlayerKeysByPlayerId(player.playerId)
  }

private suspend fun loadKeysForLastPlayer(
  state: PagingState<Int, PlayerListItem>
) = state.pages.lastOrNull { it.data.isNotEmpty() }
  ?.data?.lastOrNull()?.let { player ->
    baseballDatabase
      .playerKeysDao()
      .getPlayerKeysByPlayerId(player.playerId)
  }

private suspend fun loadKeysForClosestPlayer(
  state: PagingState<Int, PlayerListItem>
) = state.anchorPosition?.let { position ->
  state.closestItemToPosition(position)?.playerId?.let { playerId ->
    baseballDatabase
      .playerKeysDao()
      .getPlayerKeysByPlayerId(playerId)
  }
}
```

The one missing piece with the keys is that startingPageIndex variable, which in our case equals zero since that's the first page from our API.

```
companion object {
  private const val startingPageIndex = 0
}
```

Load and Save API Data

Next up is the data handling section of the load() function, which always starts with an API call and ends with some database interaction. We call the function right after the page logic:

```
override suspend fun load(
  loadType: LoadType,
  state: PagingState<Int, PlayerListItem>
): MediatorResult {
  val page = when (loadType) {
    //Page logic is still in here.
  }

  return loadAndSaveApiData(page, state, loadType == LoadType.REFRESH)
}
```

The loadAndSaveApiData() is an expression returning a try/catch block, which is valid in Kotlin. We're doing this to catch any Exception that may be thrown in our logic since we never want that to crash our app. Instead, we return an instance of MediatorResult.Error containing the exception. While we're not doing anything with it in our app, you could use that Exception to give your users more info about what went wrong or maybe log diagnostics for troubleshooting.

```
private suspend fun loadAndSaveApiData(
  page: Int,
  state: PagingState<Int, PlayerListItem>,
  isRefresh: Boolean
): MediatorResult =
  try {
    // Implementing this is coming next.
  } catch (ex: Exception) {
    MediatorResult.Error(ex)
  }
```

Calling the API in here is simpler than when we're in BaseballRepository since we're not having to handle any errors with the request (as that's already done by the outer try/catch block). That leaves us to grab the data, convert the result into a List<Player>, and check if that's the end of the pagination (meaning we've reached the end of our list from the API). We can then use those results when working with the database. The API logic looks like this:

```
private suspend fun loadAndSaveApiData(
  page: Int,
  state: PagingState<Int, PlayerListItem>,
  isRefresh: Boolean
): MediatorResult =
  try {
```

```
    val apiResponse = apiService.getPlayers(
      page,
      state.config.pageSize,
      nameQuery,
      teamId
    )

    val players = apiResponse.convertToPlayers()

    val endOfPaginationReached = players.isEmpty()

    //This will be the database logic.

  } catch (ex: Exception) {
    MediatorResult.Error(ex)
  }
```

Once we have our <Player> converted from the API result, we can get it into the database. Here, we figure out the proper keys for a PlayerListItem, then insert the PlayerKeys, PlayerListItem, and Player instances into the database. The latter table isn't being used here, but we've got the data, so why not save it?

Similar to how we mark functions that reference multiple tables with the @Transaction annotation, we want to make sure all of the actions here are completed or none of them are. This one block is the entire reason that we changed the BaseballRepository to reference BaseballDatabase rather than BaseballDao. Apologies for the hassle, but having withTransaction is really handy here to make sure we aren't left with inconsistent data:

```
baseballDatabase.withTransaction {
  // The steps in here are coming up next.
}
```

The next three code snippets all go inside that withTransaction block. The first check is to see if we're refreshing the list, and if so, we want to clear out both the player_list_items and player_keys tables:

```
if (isRefresh) {
  baseballDatabase.playerKeysDao().deleteAllPlayerKeys()
  baseballDatabase.baseballDao().deleteAllPlayerListItems()
}
```

Then we need to figure out the previous and next keys for pages, plus map all the incoming players to PlayerKeys instances:

```
val previousKey = if (page == startingPageIndex) null else page - 1
val nextKey = if (endOfPaginationReached) null else page + 1
val keys = players.map { player ->
  PlayerKeys(player.playerId, previousKey, nextKey)
}
```

Finally, we put those new PlayerKeys into the database along with the PlayerListItem and Player instances. That logic looks like this:

```
baseballDatabase.playerKeysDao().insertKeys(keys)
baseballDatabase.baseballDao().insertOrUpdatePlayers(players)
baseballDatabase.baseballDao().insertPlayerListItems(
  players.map { player ->
    PlayerListItem(
      player.playerId,
      player.fullName,
      player.teamId,
      player.position
    )
  }
)
```

Once the transaction block is completed, we need to send a Success message back telling if we're at the end of the pages or not. Remember that we don't use the return keyword here since we're in an expression block:

```
MediatorResult.Success(endOfPaginationReached = endOfPaginationReached)
```

With that, the PlayerListRemoteMediator is ready for use! For that, we're going to head over to BaseballRepository to configure things.

Load Paging Data with Flow

The function in question inside BaseballRepository is getPlayerListItems(), which returns a Kotlin Flow object containing PagingData. Before we see how this class gets the PagingData, let's chat a bit about Flow.

A Kotlin Flow is a data stream that's computed asynchronously with values that can be returned separately from one another. Contrast this with LiveData that has to be returned all together as a single item or collection.

In practice, we can use a Flow object in a similar way to LiveData, but Flow instances also work particularly well with Paging (as we can continually send in new pages of data). Flow has additional great features that we won't be using here, like the ability to map and filter data just like a "normal" list/sequence of data.

We'll see more about the differences with using Flow versus LiveData once we're into PlayerListViewModel, but first we need to use the PlayerListRemoteMediator within a new Pager instance.

We send the Pager instance three parameters here: a PagingConfig instance with the pageSize, a reference to the PlayerListRemoteMediator, and a pagingSourceFactory.

That last piece is a function that returns a PagingSource instance. That's the same class we're returning from BaseballDao.getPlayerListItems(), so we can create a lambda function to return the result of a call to that function. The Pager class looks like this:

```
Pager(
  config = PagingConfig(
    pageSize = defaultPageSize
  ),
  remoteMediator = PlayerListRemoteMediator(
    apiService,
    baseballDatabase,
    teamId,
    nameQuery
  ),
  // Yes, this is actually a function.
  pagingSourceFactory = {
    baseballDao.getPlayerListItems(teamId, dbNameQuery)
  }
)
```

We still need dbNameQuery, which allows us to use a LIKE expression in our query:

```
val dbNameQuery = if (nameQuery != null) "%$nameQuery%" else null
```

Then, the last piece here is with the Pager object we created. We're going to return a Flow object from the Pager object, which can be done by referencing the flow property on the Pager object. The entire function (with the @ExperimentalPagingApi annotation on top) looks like this:

```
@ExperimentalPagingApi
fun getPlayerListItems(
  teamId: String?,
  nameQuery: String?
): Flow<PagingData<PlayerListItem>> {
  val dbNameQuery = if (nameQuery != null) "%$nameQuery%" else null
  return Pager(
    config = PagingConfig(
      pageSize = defaultPageSize
    ),
    remoteMediator = PlayerListRemoteMediator(
      apiService,
      baseballDatabase,
      teamId,
      nameQuery
    ),
```

```
    pagingSourceFactory = {
      baseballDao.getPlayerListItems(teamId, dbNameQuery)
    }
  ).flow
}
```

Don't forget to add the defaultPageSize variable and set it to whatever you'd like within the companion object:

```
companion object {
  private val apiService = getDefaultABLService()
  private const val defaultPageSize = 25

  @Volatile
  private var instance: BaseballRepository? = null

  fun getInstance(baseballDatabase: BaseballDatabase) =
    this.instance ?: synchronized(this) {
      instance ?: BaseballRepository(baseballDatabase).also {
        instance = it
      }
    }
}
```

This value should be something that allows API calls to finish quickly enough for users to not see any stuttering but still avoid making too many API calls. It's a balance that depends on how much data comes in with each item, and you'll want to tweak this number to see what works best for you.

With that complete, it's now time to create PlayerListViewModel, which will reference this getPlayerListItems() function.

Bring In Data via PlayerListViewModel

On a base level, this is the same as previous ViewModel classes. Here's most of the class right away:

```
@ExperimentalPagingApi
class PlayerListViewModel(application: Application) :
  AndroidViewModel(application) {

  private val repo: BaseballRepository

  init {
    repo = BaseballDatabase
      .getDatabase(application, viewModelScope)
      .let { db ->
        BaseballRepository.getInstance(db)
      }
  }
```

```
  fun getPlayerListItems(
    teamId: String? = null,
    nameQuery: String? = null
  ): Flow<PagingData<PlayerListItem>> {
    // This is coming up next
  }
}
```

The getPlayerListItems() function's primary purpose is to call the getPlayerListItems() function from BaseballRepository and send that to the PlayersFragment. And since we're returning a Flow object, we can cache it for later use:

```
repo.getPlayerListItems(teamId, nameQuery).cachedIn(viewModelScope)
```

In addition to that little bit of caching, we want to save off the result of this function in the view model. That way, if the same data is requested with the same filter parameters (team and the name query), we return the same result. So we're saving the last query values as well as the data coming back from the repository, just in case. The whole PlayerListViewModel then looks like this:

```
@ExperimentalPagingApi
class PlayerListViewModel(application: Application) :
  AndroidViewModel(application) {

  private val repo: BaseballRepository

➤ private var currentTeamId: String? = null
➤ private var currentNameQuery: String? = null

➤ private var currentPlayerListItems:
➤   Flow<PagingData<PlayerListItem>>? = null

  init {
    repo = BaseballDatabase
      .getDatabase(application, viewModelScope)
      .let { db ->
        BaseballRepository.getInstance(db)
      }
  }

  fun getPlayerListItems(
    teamId: String? = null,
    nameQuery: String? = null
  ): Flow<PagingData<PlayerListItem>> {
➤   val lastResult = currentPlayerListItems

➤   return if (
➤     teamId == currentTeamId &&
➤     nameQuery == currentNameQuery &&
➤     lastResult != null
➤   ) {
➤     lastResult
➤   } else {
```

```
        currentNameQuery = nameQuery
        currentTeamId = teamId

        val newResult = repo
          .getPlayerListItems(teamId, nameQuery)
          .cachedIn(viewModelScope)

        currentPlayerListItems = newResult

        newResult
      }
    }
  }
```

With the PlayerListViewModel all set, we're left with the PlayersFragment and its RecyclerView.

Display Paging Data in a RecyclerView List

We have three tasks to complete in PlayersFragment: bind the playersList RecyclerView, implement a searchPlayers() function, and bind the playerSearchBoxText text box. We're starting off with the RecyclerView since we've done it before, and if you copied PlayersFragment from the Code directory, you can skip this part:

```
override fun onCreateView(
  inflater: LayoutInflater,
  container: ViewGroup?,
  savedInstanceState: Bundle?
): View {
  val binding = FragmentPlayersBinding.inflate(inflater)

  this.playersAdapter = PlayersAdapter()

  with(binding.playersList) {
    adapter = playersAdapter
    addItemDecoration(
      DividerItemDecoration(context, LinearLayoutManager.VERTICAL)
    )
  }

  // Bind the text box

  // Search for players

  return binding.root
}
```

The player search functionality is different than how we worked with LiveData in the past, but it's nothing you can't handle.

Search for Players

With previous RecyclerView lists, we would call observe() on a LiveData that would update a list whenever we got new data. With the PlayersFragment class, we're going to be doing the same thing but with a slightly different approach. Instead of linking to LiveData and letting that plus Room handle everything, we're now going to use the collectLatest() function from getPlayerListItems() to get our data. Calling collectLatest() gives us the data from inside our Flow object so we can send it to the playersAdapter and the RecyclerView:

```
playersListViewModel
  .getPlayerListItems(playerListArgs.teamId, nameQuery)
  .collectLatest { playerListItems ->
    if(::playersAdapter.isInitialized) {
      playersAdapter.submitData(playerListItems)
    }
  }
```

Since we're calling a suspend fun here, collectLatest(), this all needs to live in a coroutine scope. This call being in a coroutine, as always, helps by moving the call to a background thread so we're not locking up the UI. But an additional advantage here is that we can save off the Job from that scope, which can then be canceled in the case where we send another request. This way we can avoid having multiple calls going on at once.

Declare the playersListViewModel and currentJob variables:

```
private var currentJob: Job? = null
```

And add the @ExperimentalPagingApi annotation to the class:

```
➤ @ExperimentalPagingApi
  class PlayersFragment : Fragment()
```

We can then build out the rest of the searchPlayers() function:

```
➤ private fun searchPlayers(nameQuery: String? = null) {
➤   currentJob?.cancel()

➤   currentJob = lifecycleScope.launch {
      playersListViewModel
        .getPlayerListItems(playerListArgs.teamId, nameQuery)
        .collectLatest { playerListItems ->
          if(::playersAdapter.isInitialized) {
            playersAdapter.submitData(playerListItems)
          }
        }

➤   }
➤ }
```

We only need to call searchPlayers() when we have a change to the query (or the teamId variable changes). If something updates the PlayerListItem records in the database or we need new data, all of that will be displayed automatically, just like when we used LiveData. We call searchPlayers() at the end of the onCreateView() function, which is sufficient until the user wants to query for a player's name.

Speaking of a user search, our last bit of work is to interact with that Search Players box on the top of the list. Here, we're going to listen for a Go action or a Clear action. Go actions include a user hitting the check mark button on their keyboard or an Enter key either on a physical keyboard or equivalent on a device's virtual keyboard. The Clear action will happen when a user clicks the X icon on the right side of the text box.

The Go listeners are added to the playerSearchBoxText item from our binding object. In both cases, if we get the action we're expecting, we call searchPlayers() with the text value from the text box and return true to tell the listener on TextInputEditText we've done something with the event or else false to say we're ignoring that action. The entire binding block looks like this:

```
with(binding.playerSearchBoxText) {
  setOnEditorActionListener { _, actionId, _ ->
    if (actionId == EditorInfo.IME_ACTION_GO) {
      searchPlayers(text.toString().trim())
      true
    } else {
      false
    }
  }

  setOnKeyListener { _, keyCode, event ->
    if (event.action == KeyEvent.ACTION_DOWN &&
        keyCode == KeyEvent.KEYCODE_ENTER) {
      searchPlayers(text.toString().trim())
      true
    } else {
      false
    }
  }
}
```

The Clear action works in a similar manner with the setEndIconOnClickListener() function on binding.playerSearchBox. Now, the <TextInputLayout> has an app:endIconMode= property, set to *clear_text*, that would handle this for us. The only issue with this automatic approach is that we can't easily add additional actions, in particular the ability to search when clearing the data, so we'll have to handle things manually:

```
binding.playerSearchBox.setEndIconOnClickListener {
  binding.playerSearchBoxText.text?.let { text ->
    text.clear()
    searchPlayers()
  }
}
```

With that, we're able to search for players on our screen while still maintaining proper paging, and our Players screen is done. Make sure you're calling searchPlayers() at the end of onCreateView() or it's going to seem like we did nothing at all, and that'd be really sad.

Filter Players by Team

One last update before we wrap up the chapter. Inside fragment_single_team.xml, a <variable> called viewRosterButtonClickListener is attached to the View Roster button but previously had nowhere to go. Now it does.

Inside SingleTeamFragment, we want to bind a new View.OnClickListener to that viewRosterButtonClickListener variable and navigate to the Players screen when it's clicked. Inside the onCreateView() function and the large apply block, we have the following code:

```
viewRosterButtonClickListener = View.OnClickListener { view ->
  val action = NavGraphDirections.actionGoToTeamRoster(
    args.teamId
  )

  view.findNavController().navigate(action)
}
```

Now when someone clicks a View Roster button on any team's screen, they'll go the Players screen but only with the players on that team, as shown in the image on page 281.

Summary and Next Steps

Our Players screen is complete and fully integrated with the Paging library. We're able to continually show more players to users without any stuttering or slowdown in the list but without having to grab all the data up front. Users get a better experience while probably using less data than they would have otherwise. Plus, you got an introduction into using Flow, which can do even more than what we covered here.

What else could we do with these three new screens or Paging in general? Maybe you want to expand the user's page, where tapping a leader instead shows the top 10/20/50/100 players in that category. Or you could add in

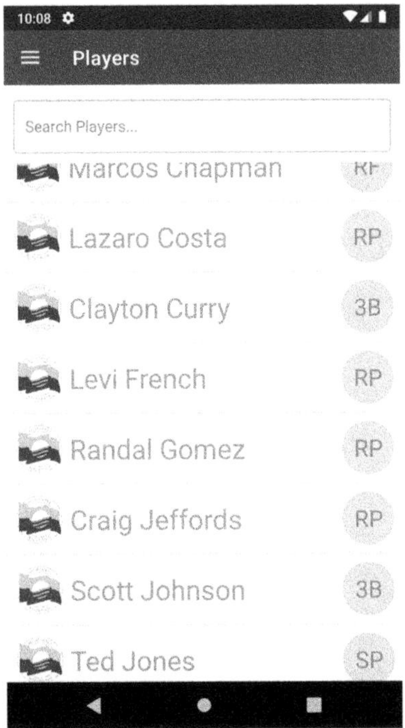

a page with play-by-play data, again using the Paging library to only load the plays you are viewing at a given time. Any list where we could have a great deal (or even theoretically infinite amount) of data will benefit from the Paging library.

Next up is getting the Settings page ready for users. This time, we're going to build it out completely in code, unlike in Chapter 7, Customize an App with Settings and Themes, on page 169. We're going to add some syncing between our app and a server, plus learn all about the Palette library for pulling colors from images.

CHAPTER 12

Personalize the Android Baseball League App

The ABL app is nearly complete. All the main screens are ready, we're pulling in data from the ABL APIs, and the app is easy to navigate. We could safely stop here and have a lovely app for all the ABL fans out there, but why not add a bit of polish?

Back in Chapter 7, Customize an App with Settings and Themes, on page 169, we used a Settings page to give users some more options about how their games of Penny Drop would be played. Also, they could change up the look and feel of the app as they wished. We could certainly do that here, and honestly *would* in most cases, but we'll skip a lot of that theming for now to highlight some new concepts.

In this chapter, we're going back to the PreferenceFragmentCompat class to allow users to customize their app. But this time, we're going to look at a few different things.

Users will be able to set their favorite team, do a little styling based on that team (but without a theme, as you'll see), and even set a starting point for the app. We'll do all of this without writing any XML, too, at least for the Settings screen. Plus, once that's all ready, we'll back up the user's settings to the server.

Before we dig into that Settings screen, let's get a few theme-related things set. We want to use Android green as our primary color (since that's the same color used for the ABL) and otherwise include some extra colors taken from the ABL logo. Add the following colors to your res/values/colors.xml file:

```
<color name="androidGreen">#00DE7A</color>
<color name="darkAndroidGreen">#006f3d</color>
<color name="ablTan">#afad97</color>
<color name="darkAblTan">#9b977e</color>
```

Then, in your themes files (both normal and night), make sure you're pointing to a NoActionBar parent. Then update the brand colors as well as the status/navigation bar colors:

```
<!-- Primary brand color. -->
<item name="colorPrimary">@color/androidGreen</item>
<item name="colorPrimaryVariant">@color/darkAndroidGreen</item>
<item name="colorOnPrimary">@android:color/white</item>
<!-- Secondary brand color. -->
<item name="colorSecondary">@color/ablTan</item>
<item name="colorSecondaryVariant">@color/darkAblTan</item>
<item name="colorOnSecondary">@android:color/black</item>
<!-- Status bar color. -->
<item name="android:statusBarColor" tools:targetApi="l">
  ?attr/colorPrimaryVariant
</item>
<!-- Navigation bar color. -->
<item name="android:navigationBarColor" tools:targetApi="l">
  ?attr/colorPrimary
</item>
```

If you need to confirm your changes, both files are in the code-to-copy directory. Our app looks more on-brand now, so we can move on to some new things in our Settings page.

Build a Settings Screen via Code

I mentioned that a code-built Settings screen was possible back in Add the Preferences Resource File, on page 172, and this feels like a perfect time to create one. Before we do anything, though, we need to get the Preferences dependency in here:

```
implementation "androidx.preference:preference-ktx:$preference_version"
```

After adding the version variable and syncing, we want a new class in a new settings package called SettingsFragment.

Create the SettingsFragment Class

As we did before, this will be a child class of the PreferenceFragmentCompat class and include an onCreatePreferences() function:

```
class SettingsFragment : PreferenceFragmentCompat() {

  override fun onCreatePreferences(
    savedInstanceState: Bundle?,
    rootKey: String?
  ) {
    // Next up
  }
}
```

The difference this time is that we aren't adding in the xml/preferences.xml file but instead will do everything inside onCreatePreferences(). This means we create the Preference types in here rather than calling findPreference() like we did with Penny Drop. To start, we need a PreferenceScreen object to which we can add all our settings.

We use the createPreferenceScreen() function to get that PreferenceScreen object, which takes in preferenceManager.context. The preferenceManager value comes from the PreferenceFragmentCompat class and is a Kotlin shortcut for the getPreferenceManager() function on the Java side of things. Once we have the PreferenceScreen object, then we can assign that back to the preferenceScreen variable on PreferenceFragmentCompat:

```
override fun onCreatePreferences(
    savedInstanceState: Bundle?,
    rootKey: String?
  ) {
➤   val ctx = preferenceManager.context
➤   val screen = preferenceManager.createPreferenceScreen(ctx)

    // The individual preferences will be added in here.

➤   preferenceScreen = screen
  }
```

The reason I created the ctx value is because we're going to be using it when adding each Preference to the screen, so having a shorter name will make the code easier to read. Before we add any Preference objects to this screen, let's allow ourselves to navigate here by adding a new <fragment> tag in nav_graph.xml:

```
<fragment
  android:id="@+id/settingsFragment"
  android:name="dev.mfazio.abl.settings.SettingsFragment"
  android:label="@string/settings"/>
```

Once that's in, we can run the app at any time. Of course, the Settings page won't have anything yet, so why don't we go do that?

Add the Favorite Team Preference

Since we're looking at some customization here, we're going to start by allowing users to set their favorite ABL team in the app. We could use this for all sorts of customizations in the app, though in this chapter all we're worried about is a little color change (which we'll handle in a bit).

The favorite team setting will be a DropDownPreference (same as the App Theme setting in Penny Drop) containing all the teams in the ABL. We also want to include a None option in case they just love the league and don't want to focus on a single team. This preference follows the same pattern we'll use with the rest of the preferences in that we're using const string values for the preference keys, all of which go in the companion object:

```
companion object {
  const val favoriteTeamPreferenceKey = "favoriteTeam"
}
```

We then use that key when initializing the favoriteTeamPreference (which also needs a lateinit var at the top of the class):

```
class SettingsFragment : PreferenceFragmentCompat() {
➤ private lateinit var favoriteTeamPreference: DropDownPreference

  override fun onCreatePreferences(
    savedInstanceState: Bundle?,
    rootKey: String?
  ) {
    val ctx = preferenceManager.context
    val screen = preferenceManager.createPreferenceScreen(ctx)

➤   this.favoriteTeamPreference = DropDownPreference(ctx).apply {
➤     key = favoriteTeamPreferenceKey
➤     title = getString(R.string.favorite_team)
➤     entries = (listOf("None")
➤       + UITeam.allTeams.map { it.teamName }).toTypedArray()
➤     entryValues = (listOf("")
➤       + UITeam.allTeams.map { it.teamId }).toTypedArray()
➤     setDefaultValue("")
➤     summaryProvider = ListPreference.SimpleSummaryProvider.getInstance()
➤   }

➤   screen.addPreference(favoriteTeamPreference)

➤   preferenceScreen = screen
  }

  companion object {
➤   const val favoriteTeamPreferenceKey = "favoriteTeam"
  }
```

It may look a bit confusing how entries and entryValues are being set. On a base level, we're using all the UITeam objects we created in the past, plus the default value of "None" I mentioned previously. We can append List objects together with a + sign to create a brand-new List with the elements from both lists. That's why we're using listOf() with single values of "None" or an empty string.

As we did before, we use the SimpleSummaryProvider to display the currently selected entry (the value in entries) on the main settings page. The setting then looks like one of these two:

Favorite Team
None

Favorite Team
Pewaukee Princesses

Well, that's helpful but not too fun, is it? Why don't we spruce things up a bit with a logo here. Preferences have a built-in icon that we can use whenever a favorite team is set.

Add a Logo to the Favorite Team Preference

We're once again using functionality that we saw with Penny Drop, this time the onPreferenceChangeListener() function. The idea here is to check if a team ID was set on the preference, then we get the logo for that team and add it to the preference as the icon property. Finally, to inform the Preference library that we should change the stored preference value, we return true from the function. The whole block looks like this:

```
favoriteTeamPreference.onPreferenceChangeListener =
  Preference.OnPreferenceChangeListener { _, newValue ->
    val teamId = newValue?.toString()

    if (teamId != null) {
      favoriteTeamPreference.icon = getIconForTeam(teamId)
    }

    true
  }
```

Nothing too crazy here, but we do need an implementation for that getIconForTeam() function. This is a private method in SettingsFragment that gets the UITeam object for the given teamId, then uses the logoId property to get a Drawable:

```
private fun getIconForTeam(teamId: String) =
  UITeam.fromTeamId(teamId)?.let { team ->
    ContextCompat.getDrawable(requireContext(), team.logoId)
  }
```

This is how we can get a Drawable resource easily within our code. Note that the requireContext() function is a shortcut for either ensuring the context variable is not null or throwing an Exception.

Now, this approach will work perfectly for any situation where a user chooses their favorite team, but if we come back into the screen, the favorite team icon will be missing since we aren't displaying it with the previously set value. We can handle that by overriding the onBindPreferences() function:

```
override fun onBindPreferences() {
  favoriteTeamPreference.icon =
    getIconForTeam(favoriteTeamPreference.value)
}
```

There, now both when a team is favorited and subsequent trips to the Settings screen will properly show the team logo, like so:

Much better! Little touches like these make the app feel more put together. Speaking of which, now that we know a user's favorite team, we can style the app to match that team's colors.

I want to mention that the *correct* way to handle this would be to add multiple themes like we saw in Add Themes, on page 178. But as we already did that before, I want to show you another option for colors: Palette.

Extract Colors with Palette

The Palette library allows us to take an image and pull colors out of it to use within our app. Ever run a music app on your Android device and notice how the window changes color? That's Palette in action.

Palette analyzes your image and gives you a Palette object with the dominant, vibrant, and muted colors on it. There's only one dominant color, but the latter two types have normal, light, and dark variants that are included in a Palette. I wrote a sample app that creates a Palette from an image and displays them under the image. When I used the cover of this book on the app, I got something that looked like the image shown on page 289.

Pretty cool, right? Well, unless you're viewing this page in black and white, then you'll just have to trust me here. The darker gray is picked up as the dominant color (a similar gray is dark muted), while the vibrant colors are all variations of the blue on the cover. Do notice that while the cover is primarily white, it's thankfully not included in the cover's Palette.

Going back to our current app, I think a fun sample of what we can do with Palette is to change the color of the navigation bar, which is the bar that normally has your back/home/recent apps buttons or maybe just the gesture bar (if you're using gesture navigation). This will make the Scoreboard page for a fan of the Skyline look something like the image shown on page 290 (again, people seeing in black and white have to trust me that this works).

Before we start using Palette, we need to get the library added to our project:

```
implementation "androidx.palette:palette-ktx:$palette_version"
```

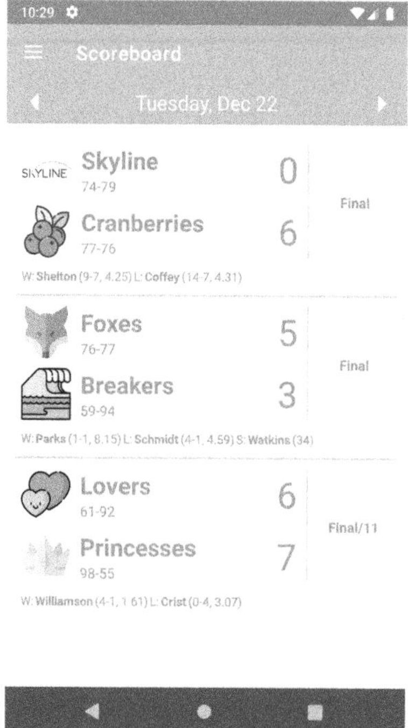

The process here is very similar to how we handled the icon next to the Favorite Team preference: we need to perform the UI update either when the value is set or when the screen is opened. Since we're changing the navigation bar color for every screen, this means we need to make the change as the app starts up with MainActivity. Let's start by getting a Palette for a given team.

Generate a Palette for a Favorite Team

On a base level, Palette's code looks something like this—we send a Bitmap into the from() function on the Palette class to get a Palette.Builder type, then we generate() a Palette object from there. In our case, we need to load the team's logo (via ContextCompat.getDrawable(), as we did earlier), convert that into a Bitmap, then send that into the Palette.from() call. The whole sequence (plus a lookup of a UITeam via teamId) looks like this:

```
fun getTeamPalette(context: Context, teamId: String?) =
  fromTeamId(teamId)?.let { team ->
    ContextCompat.getDrawable(context, team.logoId)
      ?.toBitmap()
      ?.let { logoBitmap ->
        Palette.from(logoBitmap).generate()
      }
  }
```

Now that we can get a Palette for a UITeam, we can return to SettingsFragment to use that function and set the navigation bar color.

Modify the Nav Bar Color When Picking a Favorite Team

First up is to create a new setNavBarColorForTeam() function, which will take in a teamId, find the dominant color, and set the navigation bar to that color.

In this function, we retrieve the team's Palette, pull out the dominantSwatch value, then its rgb property to get the color we need. Not all Palette objects have all the colors assigned, though, so all these checks must be null-safe, and we may not have a color in the end. As a result, we also want to include a backup, or default, color. We'll start with setNavBarColorForTeam(), which looks like this:

```
private fun setNavBarColorForTeam(teamId: String?) {
  val color = UITeam.getTeamPalette(requireContext(), teamId)
    ?.dominantSwatch
    ?.rgb
    ?: getDefaultColor()

  activity?.window?.navigationBarColor = color
}
```

That getDefaultColor() function is weird since we're grabbing out the colorPrimary resource value from the current theme. To do this, we're using a TypedValue object, which gets a value from the resolveAttribute() function but as an out value. This means we send in the TypedValue object and it's changed by the function as a side effect (though that's the point of the function). We then return the data property on that TypedValue object:

```
private fun getDefaultColor(): Int {
  val colorValue = TypedValue()

  activity?.theme?.resolveAttribute(
    R.attr.colorPrimary,
    colorValue,
    true
  )

  return colorValue.data
}
```

This is definitely not an approach you'll use too often, but if you want to get a resource value from a theme, it's at least possible this way.

Now that setNavBarColorForTeam() is created, we can use it in the existing favoriteTeamPreference.onPreferenceChangeListener() function:

```
favoriteTeamPreference.onPreferenceChangeListener =
  Preference.OnPreferenceChangeListener { _, newValue ->
    val teamId = newValue?.toString()

    setNavBarColorForTeam(teamId)

    if (teamId != null) {
      favoriteTeamPreference.icon = getIconForTeam(teamId)
    }

    true
  }
```

This is great for when the favorite team is initially set, but we also need to handle when users open up the app later on and they already have their favorite team. In that scenario, we need to go over to MainActivity to make changes.

Modify the Nav Bar Color on App Startup

Inside onCreate(), we need to do the same thing as when a user sets their favorite team in the first place but with two differences here: we can use this for the Context object, and we get the teamId value via a SharedPreferences object.

Using this for the Context works because AppCompatActivity is the great-great-great-great-great-great-great-grandchild class of Context. That may be too many "great"s, as I'm better with Android than I am with ancestry.

To get the SharedPreferences object, we need to include the following line inside onCreate():

```
val prefs = PreferenceManager.getDefaultSharedPreferences(this)
```

Then, once we have our SharedPreferences, we can get the Favorite Team preference value from there. If we don't find that setting yet (like when the app first starts up), we can send null into the getTeamPalette() function since it can handle null scenarios without issue. The call to set the nav bar color looks like this:

```
UITeam.getTeamPalette(
  this,
  prefs.getString(SettingsFragment.favoriteTeamPreferenceKey, null)
)
  ?.dominantSwatch
  ?.rgb
  ?.let {
      window.navigationBarColor = it
  }
```

Now when users start up the app and have a favorite team selected, or when they choose their favorite team, the nav bar will change to the dominant color on the team's logo. Again, it would be better to use a theme to change colors like this, but it's a good way to see how Palette works in an app.

Given the color change, we have another helpful feature we can add for users. Let's get a new setting in here to allow them to decide if they want the colors to change in the first place.

Toggle the Favorite Team Nav Bar Colorization

Back in the SettingsFragment, we need a new SwitchPreferenceCompat called favoriteTeamColorPreference, which we'll use to know if we should toggle the nav bar color when a favorite team is set. Add the lateinit var declaration at the top of SettingsFragment:

```
private lateinit var favoriteTeamPreference: DropDownPreference
private lateinit var favoriteTeamColorPreference: SwitchPreferenceCompat
```

Then add the Preference declaration *before* the favoriteTeamPreference.onPreferenceChangeListener block (making sure to declare the string resource):

```
this.favoriteTeamColorPreference = SwitchPreferenceCompat(ctx).apply {
  key = favoriteTeamColorsPreferenceKey
  title = getString(R.string.team_color_nav_bar)
  setDefaultValue(false)
}
```

Don't forget to add favoriteTeamColorsPreferenceKey to your companion object, then we can add another onPreferenceChangeListener() here. This function checks if newValue is true, and if so, will set the nav bar color for the selected team if it's set. Otherwise, it sends in null to setNavBarColorForTeam(), which uses the default Android green color:

```
favoriteTeamColorPreference.onPreferenceChangeListener =
  Preference.OnPreferenceChangeListener { _, newValue ->
    val useFavoriteTeamColor = newValue as? Boolean

    setNavBarColorForTeam(
        if(useFavoriteTeamColor == true) {
            favoriteTeamPreference.value
        } else null
    )

    true
  }
screen.addPreference(favoriteTeamColorPreference)
```

If it's not familiar, the as? syntax is a *safe cast operator*, which means we get the nullable version of type listed to the right of the operator (here, it's a

Boolean?). Since we could get null back here, we use == true to skip the first block when useFavoriteTeamColor is either false or null.

Adding this toggle also requires us to change the body of favoriteTeamPreference.onPreferenceChangeListener to include the toggle's value:

```
favoriteTeamPreference.onPreferenceChangeListener =
  Preference.OnPreferenceChangeListener { _, newValue ->
    val teamId = newValue?.toString()

    if (favoriteTeamColorPreference.isChecked) {
      setNavBarColorForTeam(teamId)
    }

    if (teamId != null) {
      favoriteTeamPreference.icon = getIconForTeam(teamId)
    }

    true
  }
```

The same thing is true in MainActivity:

```
if (
  prefs.getBoolean(SettingsFragment.favoriteTeamColorsPreferenceKey, false)
) {
  UITeam.getTeamPalette(
      this,
      prefs.getString(SettingsFragment.favoriteTeamPreferenceKey, null)
  )
      ?.dominantSwatch
      ?.rgb
      ?.let {
          window.navigationBarColor = it
      }
}
```

To summarize the current state of the SettingsFragment code, we create both favoriteTeamPreference and favoriteTeamColorPreference, then set each listener and add that Preference to the screen. This will likely also work in a different order, but order does sometimes matter, as we'll see when we add a PreferenceCategory to our Settings screen.

For now, we're going to add in a few more Preference items, including a couple inside a PreferenceCategory.

Add and Group Additional Preferences

We're going to include two new standard Preference items in here, plus two Preference links. All four are Preference objects, but the former two are actually saved by the Preferences library as you expect and the latter two will take the user to new screens. Once we get everything added, the Settings screen will look like this:

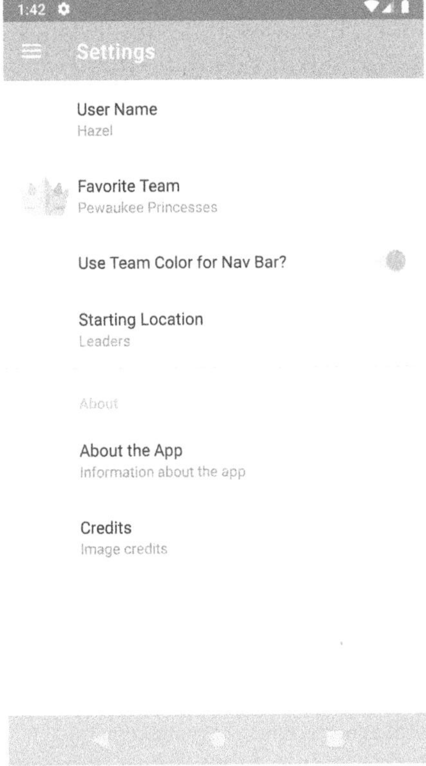

Add the User Name Preference

The User Name Preference is how we're going to associate a user with their settings on the API side. It's not a particularly good approach for a production app, but it'll at least give you a way to identify users when backing up settings. We'll cover this backup process in more detail in the next section, Reliably Complete Background Work with WorkManager, on page 299.

It turns out this EditTextPreference just needs a few bits of configuration to get working, including a lateinit var declaration up top and a usernamePreferenceKey const val in the companion object. The code to create and add this Preference is here:

```
this.usernamePreference = EditTextPreference(ctx).apply {
  key = usernamePreferenceKey
  title = getString(R.string.user_name)
  summaryProvider = EditTextPreference.SimpleSummaryProvider.getInstance()
}
screen.addPreference(usernamePreference)
```

The OnPreferenceChangeListener property will be added in the next section, so we can ignore it for now. Next up is the startingScreenPreference, which saves the ID of the screen a user wants to start on in the app. Once again, we're focused on allowing the app to work however the user wishes, and having a configurable starting location is a great way to do that.

Allow the User to Choose Their Starting Location

This DropDownPreference works similarly to the Favorite Team Preference in that we have a set of values used as entries and entryValues. The Map we'll use for those properties is in a new StartingLocationHelper.kt file inside the settings package:

```
val startingScreens = mapOf(
  "Leaders" to R.id.leadersFragment,
  "Players" to R.id.playersFragment,
  "Scoreboard" to R.id.scoreboardFragment,
  "Standings" to R.id.standingsFragment,
  "Teams" to R.id.teamsFragment
)
```

The actual preference code ends up looking like this, excluding the required lateinit var and const val declarations:

```
this.startingScreenPreference = DropDownPreference(ctx).apply {
  key = startingScreenPreferenceKey
  title = getString(R.string.starting_location)
  entries = startingScreens.keys.toTypedArray()
  entryValues = startingScreens.keys.toTypedArray()
  summaryProvider = ListPreference.SimpleSummaryProvider.getInstance()
  setDefaultValue(R.id.scoreboardFragment.toString())
}
screen.addPreference(startingScreenPreference)
```

We don't need an OnPreferenceChangeListener yet since we aren't taking any action when this is set, only when the app starts up. The other code we *do* need here is again in two spots. First, the StartingLocationHelper.kt file needs a new function called getSelectedStartingScreen(). This function either gets the starting screen setting from a SharedPreference parameter or defaults to the Scoreboard page:

```
fun getSelectedStartingScreen(prefs: SharedPreferences) =
prefs.getString(
  SettingsFragment.startingScreenPreferenceKey,
  null
).let { startId -> startingScreens[startId] ?: R.id.scoreboardFragment }
```

Next, we're on to MainActivity, where we'll update our navigation graph with the setting value. What we do is get the current navigation graph and set a new startDestination based on the value we get back from getSelectedStartingScreen()

```
val navGraph = navController.navInflater.inflate(R.navigation.nav_graph)
navGraph.startDestination = getSelectedStartingScreen(prefs)
navController.graph = navGraph
```

The next step is to add in the two link Preferences, About the App and Credits, both of which will live in the About category.

Categorize Preferences and Navigate to Other Fragments

Since we already dealt with displaying HTML on a Fragment with Penny Drop, you can go ahead and copy the files we need for both views from the Code/code-to-copy folder. In particular, you want everything in the settings package, plus the fragment_about_the_app.xml, fragment_image_credits.xml, and image_credit_item.xml files. Also included are a few new string resource values.

As always, feel free to take a peek at the code you copied over, as it's pretty cool. The two screens will look like this:

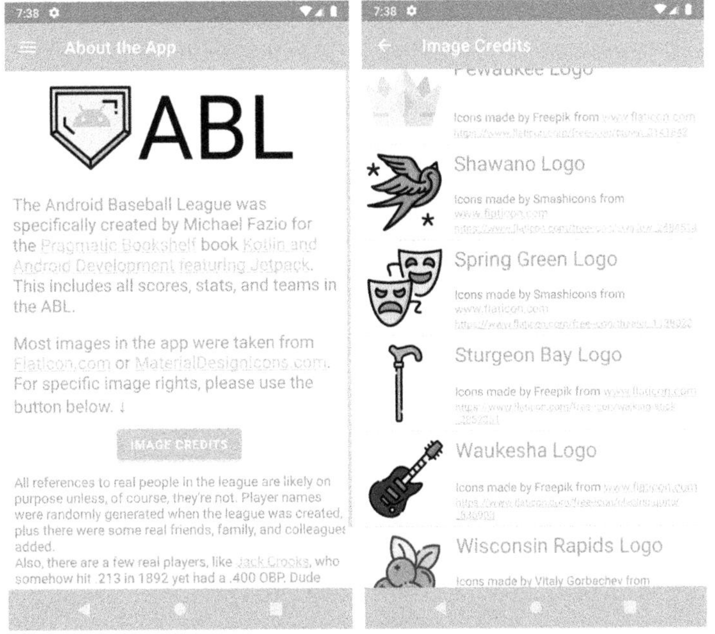

Now that we have the two screens, we can get the links added into the Settings page. The first thing we need on that page is the aboutCategory, where we'll add the Preference links. That category looks like this:

```
val aboutCategory = PreferenceCategory(ctx).apply {
  key = aboutPreferenceCategoryKey
  title = getString(R.string.about)
}
screen.addPreference(aboutCategory)
```

Take note that we're adding the PreferenceCategory to the screen now, *then* adding the other Preference objects I create. If it's not added to screen first, you'll get an exception, and nobody wants that.

Both link Preference items are set up in the same fashion, with a few properties being set and an onPreferenceClickListener to handle navigation. Note in the navigation flow that we're using this@SettingsFragment to reference the SettingsFragment class rather than the Preference itself. The code for both Preference items looks like this:

```
val aboutTheAppPreference = Preference(ctx).apply {
  key = aboutTheAppPreferenceKey
  title = getString(R.string.about_the_app)
  summary = getString(R.string.info_about_the_app)
  onPreferenceClickListener = Preference.OnPreferenceClickListener { _ ->
    this@SettingsFragment.findNavController().navigate(
      R.id.aboutTheAppFragment
    )
    true
  }
}
aboutCategory.addPreference(aboutTheAppPreference)

val creditsPreference = Preference(ctx).apply {
  key = creditsPreferenceKey
  title = getString(R.string.credits)
  summary = getString(R.string.image_credits)
  onPreferenceClickListener = Preference.OnPreferenceClickListener { _ ->
    this@SettingsFragment.findNavController().navigate(
      R.id.imageCreditsFragment
    )
    true
  }
}
aboutCategory.addPreference(creditsPreference)
```

The last thing we need to do here is make sure both screens are in the navigation graph. Add two new <fragment> tags after the <action> tags:

```
<fragment
  android:id="@+id/aboutTheAppFragment"
  android:name="dev.mfazio.abl.settings.AboutTheAppFragment"
  android:label="@string/about_the_app"
  tools:layout="@layout/fragment_about_the_app" />
<fragment
  android:id="@+id/imageCreditsFragment"
  android:name="dev.mfazio.abl.settings.ImageCreditsFragment"
  android:label="@string/image_credits"
  tools:layout="@layout/fragment_image_credits" />
```

With that, the Settings page for this app is done, or at least as far as what we're doing in this chapter. We still have one more thing we want to do in here, and that's back up a user's settings to our server. We're going to use that User Name Preference as a simplistic way to tie Settings to a particular user, but the important part here is that we'll be taking advantage of WorkManager to make that API call.

Reliably Complete Background Work with WorkManager

The WorkManager library/API is a great way to schedule tasks that should run in the background and complete even if the app is closed or the device is restarted. WorkManager will handle the tasks it's given in a way that the OS can handle, meaning that older versions of the Android OS can still use the library using existing features. This gives us a higher level of backward compatibility in our app without needing to worry about implementation details.

I'll show you how to implement a Worker, which will be used by WorkManager to back up Settings. Once we're done there, I'll highlight a few of the other features WorkManager can offer for other use cases. Add in the WorkManager dependency:

```
implementation "androidx.work:work-runtime-ktx:$work_version"
```

First up with WorkManager is a new SaveSettingsWorker class that will handle that backup process.

Handle Asynchronous Work with CoroutineWorker

The SaveSettingsWorker is going to take in a username plus the current settings, which we'll then use to call the saveAppSettings() function on the ABL API client.

Normally with WorkManager we would use the Worker class as our base class. But thanks to some Kotlin extensions, we have the CoroutineWorker class and its suspend version of doWork(). This way we can make our API call within that coroutine scope instead of having to pass scopes or contexts all around.

To get our input parameters, we need to reference inputData, the Data object on CoroutineWorker. The Data class holds input data of varying types, which we can then pull out in our code. For example, to get the userName value, we would make a call like this:

```
val userName = inputData.getString(userNameKey)
```

The last piece with the SaveSettingsWorker and the doWork() function is the Result return type. This informs the WorkManager whether or not the work was completed successfully. While we're not using this yet (since we're not worried about taking any action upon a sync failure), it's available as needed. The entire SaveSettingsWorker looks like this:

```
class SaveSettingsWorker(appContext: Context, params: WorkerParameters) :
  CoroutineWorker(appContext, params) {
  override suspend fun doWork(): Result = try {
    val userName = inputData.getString(userNameKey)

    if (userName != null) {
      Log.i(TAG, "Saving user settings for $userName")
      getDefaultABLService().saveAppSettings(
        AppSettingsApiModel(
          userName,
          inputData.getString(favoriteTeamKey) ?: "",
          inputData.getBoolean(favoriteTeamColorCheckKey, false),
          inputData.getString(startingScreenKey) ?: ""
        )
      )
    }

    Result.success()

  } catch (ex: Exception) {
    Log.e(TAG, "Exception saving settings to API")
    Result.failure()
  }

  companion object {
    const val TAG = "SaveSettingsWorker"
    const val userNameKey = "userName"
    const val favoriteTeamKey = "favoriteTeam"
    const val favoriteTeamColorCheckKey = "favoriteTeamColorCheck"
    const val startingScreenKey = "startingScreenKey"
  }
}
```

A few items of interest here:

- The entire function is an expression with a try block, where we catch all Exception types, meaning this code can never crash the app.
- The TAG value is a way to separate out our log messages. Using a const val with the class's name is a normal Android convention.
- We *could* have reused the const val keys from SettingsFragment, but having keys owned by SaveSettingsWorker seemed to be a better approach. This way SaveSettingsWorker owns the keys for values coming in and out of its doWork() function, keeping them in the same spot where they're used.

Now that SaveSettingsWorker is ready to be used, we can go back into SettingsFragment and use it. We need a new function, unsurprisingly called saveSettings(), that brings in all of our settings with fallbacks to the current values on each Preference:

```
private fun saveSettings(
  userName: String? =
    usernamePreference.text,
  favoriteTeam: String? =
    favoriteTeamPreference.value,
  useFavoriteTeamColor: Boolean? =
    favoriteTeamColorPreference.isChecked,
  startingScreen: String? =
    startingScreenPreference.value
) { }
```

Inside the function we'll make sure userName is *not* null, then build and enqueue() our work request. To do this, we get an instance of WorkManager and use the OneTimeWorkRequestBuilder class to build our work request. Any parameters we need for the work request are added via the setInputData() function on the builder. Here's the inside of the saveSettings() function:

```
if(userName != null) {
  WorkManager.getInstance(requireContext()).enqueue(
    OneTimeWorkRequestBuilder<SaveSettingsWorker>()
      .setInputData(
        workDataOf(
          SaveSettingsWorker.userNameKey to userName,
          SaveSettingsWorker.favoriteTeamKey to favoriteTeam,
          SaveSettingsWorker.favoriteTeamColorCheckKey to
            useFavoriteTeamColor,
          SaveSettingsWorker.startingScreenKey to startingScreen
        )
      ).build()
  )
}
```

With WorkManager, we can either have one-time requests like the preceding one or we can set up periodic work that's run every so often. Please note that PeriodicWorkRequest work can only be executed at a minimum interval of every fifteen minutes, so this isn't intended for something that runs every ten, twenty, or thirty seconds. If you want something that runs more often, like a Scoreboard updater, you would want to go a different route (for example, repeated coroutine calls).

With saveSettings() ready to go, we need to add in our calls to the function. What we're going to do is call saveSettings() each time a Preference is changed, excluding the usernamePreference (which we'll address in a bit) and the two "link" preferences.

For the other three Preference items, we either need to add a call to saveSettings() to the existing OnPreferenceChangeListener or create a new OnPreferenceChangeListener (in the case of startingScreenPreference).

With each saveSettings() call, we'll send in newValue for the changing value. We have to do this because the Preference values are only changed *after* the OnPreferenceChangeListener is completed. For example, the startingScreenPreference will contain the following code block:

```
onPreferenceChangeListener =
  Preference.OnPreferenceChangeListener { _, newValue ->
    saveSettings(
        startingScreen = newValue?.toString()
    )

    true
  }
```

We can reference the parameter we care about by name, as we did here with startingScreen, and the rest will use the current values as fallback (since those aren't changing). Go ahead and make the necessary changes to the other two Preference items, which will be similar to this:

```
favoriteTeamPreference.onPreferenceChangeListener =
  Preference.OnPreferenceChangeListener { _, newValue ->
    val teamId = newValue?.toString()
    if (favoriteTeamColorPreference.isChecked) {
      setNavBarColorForTeam(teamId)
    }

    if (teamId != null) {
      favoriteTeamPreference.icon = getIconForTeam(teamId)
    }

    saveSettings(
      favoriteTeam = teamId
    )

    true
  }
```

Now that we're saving a user's settings to the server, we probably should add a way to load them back out, or this entire addition will be educational but useless.

Load User Settings via API

The loadSettings() function will be the one that's called whenever the usernamePreference value is changed. Since we may not have settings on the server for a given user, we'll save the current settings if the attempt to load them fails.

The core of this function is a call to the API, where we use that result to set all our preferences as if the user was setting the values manually. We also wrap the entire call in a try...catch block in case of any failure statuses being returned from the API call. The catch block is also where we'll make the saveSettings() call to initialize settings for a given user. The entire (somewhat large) loadSettings() function looks like this:

```
private fun loadSettings(userName: String? = null) {
  viewLifecycleOwner.lifecycleScope.launch {
    if (userName != null) {
      try {
        val apiResult = ablService.getAppSettingsForUser(userName)

        with(favoriteTeamPreference) {
          value = apiResult.favoriteTeamId
          icon = getIconForTeam(apiResult.favoriteTeamId)
        }

        setNavBarColorForTeam(
          if (apiResult.useTeamColorNavBar) {
            apiResult.favoriteTeamId
          } else null
        )

        favoriteTeamColorPreference.isChecked =
          apiResult.useTeamColorNavBar

        startingScreenPreference.value =
          getScreenId(apiResult.startingLocation).toString()

      } catch (ex: Exception) {
        Log.i(
          TAG,
          """Settings not found.
          |This may just mean they haven't been initialized yet.
          |""".trimMargin()
        )
        saveSettings(userName)
      }
    }
  }
}
```

Unless you added in TAG to do logging earlier, you'll need that in the companion object, as we did in SaveSettingsWorker:

```
const val TAG = "SettingsFragment"
```

Calling the loadSettings() function is the easy part, since we just need to add a new OnPreferenceChangeListener to usernamePreference:

```
this.usernamePreference = EditTextPreference(ctx).apply {
  key = usernamePreferenceKey
  title = getString(R.string.user_name)
  summaryProvider =
    EditTextPreference.SimpleSummaryProvider.getInstance()
  onPreferenceChangeListener =
    Preference.OnPreferenceChangeListener { _, newValue ->
      loadSettings(newValue?.toString())

      true
    }
}
```

With that, the SettingsFragment class is all set, so let's review everything we did, shall we?

Summary and Next Steps

We now have ourselves a nice Settings page, completed in code, that can dynamically style our app and reliably save user settings to the server. Palette is a great way to react to images in the app we may not know about ahead of time and give users a more personalized look to the app. WorkManager is the perfect way to take some kind of action in our app that we want to finish even if the app is closed out or even if the device is restarted.

Next up is our last "normal" chapter of the book (since the following two are focused on testing), where we're going to work on bringing in and sending out data from the app. This includes notifications (in particular, push notifications), the ability to share links and info about certain players and teams, and how we can retrieve large amounts of data via the Download Manager library.

CHAPTER 13

Send Info to and from the Android Baseball League App

Here we are, the last "standard" chapter of the book! We're going to put some finishing touches on the Android Baseball League app, in particular notifications and sharing. On the notifications side, we're going to look at both local and push (server-triggered) notifications, while sharing will be a quick overview of the Android Sharesheet and what we can do there. Let's get to it!

Alert Users with Notifications

Ah, notifications, one of the biggest make-or-break features of an app. We know users have little patience for apps that frequently crash or don't work as intended, as they should. Misuse of notifications is an excellent way to ensure people delete your app without hesitation. That being said, well-used notifications can be a perfect way to engage users and increase app usage.

Proper use of notifications could be its own chapter (or multiple chapters), but that's not what we're worrying about here. Instead, we're going to focus on how you get those notifications to display when you *do* want to use them.

My one piece of advice regarding when to display a notification is to always consider whether or not the alert you're sending to a user is worth their time. In particular, keep in mind if it's worth it to *them* and not just something you want them to know.

With that said, we can get to the implementation process. For the sake of simplicity, all notifications are going to be launched in a new page that we hit from the Settings screen. This way you can go there, tap an item in the list, and it'll give you the notification you want.

Add the Notifications Setting Screen

The link to the Notifications screen will be found at the bottom of the Settings screen, like this:

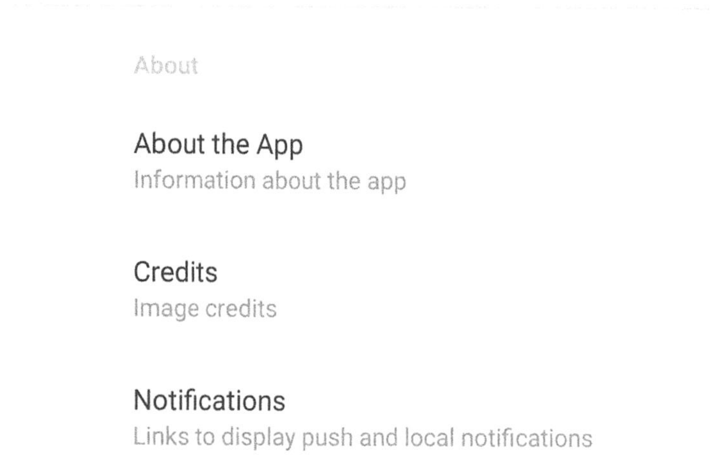

About

About the App
Information about the app

Credits
Image credits

Notifications
Links to display push and local notifications

I've prepared most of the code you need for that screen in the chapter-13/code-to-copy folder—everything in the notifications folder/package as well as the new version of SettingsFragment and all the resource files in the res folder. The latter has some updates to existing resource files, so you can either do a straight copy or compare with what you have and make any changes manually.

Once those are all moved over, go ahead and run the app to make sure things are set up correctly. Our Notifications page will be empty for now, which is totally fine. That's our next step.

Configure Our First Local Notification

The first notification we're going to include is to display an update about a particular player while allowing a user to click the notification to get to that player's page.

Inside NotificationsFragment, there's a currently empty listOf<NotificationItem> that we'll be filling in with all our notification configurations, which will then display on the Notifications page. I figured this was an easy enough way to allow you to kick off notifications whenever you wanted within the app without being too invasive elsewhere.

The first NotificationItem in the list looks like this:

```
NotificationItem(
  1,
  "Local - Player",
  "Displays a local notification for Rolando Lopez, " +
  "which when clicked, takes a user to his player page.",
  NotificationType.Local
) { ctx, _ ->
  // This is the next part.
}
```

You can always open the NotificationItem class to see all the properties, but here's a quick overview: we put in an ID of some kind, a title and description for the notification (the latter of which is on two lines in the preceding code, in case it looks weird), and a NotificationType of either local or push.

Note also the action block at the end where we'll do all the Notification-related work, as the other settings are related to how we display that item in the list. The action block brings in a Context object and a CoroutineScope, the latter being used for push notifications later in this chapter.

Inside that block, we have a three step process: create a PendingIntent that handles the action when a user taps a notification, build the Notification itself, and notify() the NotificationManagerCompat class that the notification should be displayed.

The PendingIntent here is an example of an *explicit deep link* that I mentioned back in Navigate Directly via a Deep Link, on page 230. I told you we didn't have a good spot to include explicit deep links before, but now we've got a perfect place for them, as the notifications will take users to different locations.

We use the NavDeepLinkBuilder class to help create the PendingIntent object we need, which takes in a few properties before building. Since we're keeping the deep link as part of our navigation flow, we need to send in not only a destination but the navigation graph we use. We can also include a few arguments so that our existing NavArgs are populated as we expect. The NavDeepLinkBuilder logic looks like this:

```
val pendingIntent = NavDeepLinkBuilder(ctx)
  .setGraph(R.navigation.nav_graph)
  .setDestination(R.id.singlePlayerFragment)
  .setArguments(Bundle().apply {
    putString("playerId", "lopezrol")
    putString("playerName", "Rolando Lopez")
  }).createPendingIntent()
```

The one "gotcha" here is that to set arguments, we need to create a new Bundle object, then add String values to that. Besides that, the NavDeepLinkBuilder saves us the trouble of setting up the Intent manually. With the PendingIntent ready, we can build out the Notification itself.

We have a fair number of properties we can set on a Notification object, so know that what we're doing certainly isn't an exhaustive list. That being said, you're likely to use most of these properties with every local notification you would see in an app. The list is as follows:

- Content Title: the main header that displays on the notification. Comes from the string resources.
- Content Text: the text body. Comes from the string resources.
- Small Icon: the icon displayed on the notification and on the status bar.
- Content Intent: the PendingIntent we just created.
- Auto Cancel: a flag saying whether or not to automatically dismiss a notification after being tapped.

Nothing here is new for us, as we're used to drawable and string resource values and we saw how to create the PendingIntent already. The one piece that *is* especially noteworthy is how we set up the NotificationCompat.Builder. The second parameter that's sent in is a channelId, referring to a *notification channel*. We can talk through what that means in a bit, but first, here's the full code to not only build the Notification but then display it:

```
val channel = ABLNotificationChannel.Players

val notification =
  NotificationCompat.Builder(ctx, channel.channelId)
    .setContentTitle(ctx.getString(R.string.lopez_notification_title))
    .setContentText(ctx.getString(R.string.lopez_notification_text))
    .setSmallIcon(R.drawable.ic_baseline_directions_run_24)
    .setContentIntent(pendingIntent)
    .setAutoCancel(true)
    .build()

NotificationManagerCompat.from(ctx).notify(
  1, //This ID can be used to update/remove an existing notification
  notification
)
```

This is all we need to do in here for the notification, but don't bother trying it out yet, as it likely won't work. The notification channel is the way Android groups notifications and is a key piece when dealing with newer devices.

Group Notifications with Notification Channels

Notification channels allow developers to separate notifications into particular buckets and assign default priorities and sounds to those notifications. Maybe more importantly, it allows for finer user control of notifications in an app. If a user isn't interested in being notified about any players, they can turn off the Player notification channel and will never receive those notifications. Or, if they prefer, they can instead just turn down the importance level so they get the notifications but without sound or an alert.

We can set whichever channels we want, but they need to be set up when the user first opens our app. So we need to include a new createNotificationChannels() function inside MainActivity. This function will go through all the ABLNotificationChannel entries and add a new channel for each one. Please do take a peek at that enum class to see what's going on, then we can get to adding things inside MainActivity.

The code here will convert the ABLNotificationChannel objects into Android's NotificationChannel type, then grab the Notifications system service to add those channels. The entire function looks like this:

```
private fun createNotificationChannels() {
  if (Build.VERSION.SDK_INT >= Build.VERSION_CODES.O) {
    val channels = ABLNotificationChannel.values().map { channel ->
      NotificationChannel(
        channel.channelId,
        channel.channelName,
        channel.importance
      ).apply {
        description = channel.channelDescription
      }
    }

    (getSystemService(Context.NOTIFICATION_SERVICE) as NotificationManager)
      .createNotificationChannels(channels)
  }
}
```

I wrapped all the logic inside the version check, as notification channels are unavailable below API Level 26 (Android 8.0 Oreo); so we want to avoid using them on those older devices. Now, as our minimum SDK version for this app is already API Level 26, this is technically unnecessary—but still good for you to know, so it's staying in there.

It's not an issue if this function is run multiple times, as it'll update the channels as needed if anything changes in the code (or leave things as is). So we can include the call to createNotificationChannels() somewhere inside onCreate().

Without using notification channels, none of our notifications would work on devices running at least API level 26. We can make them as generic or specific as we wish, but the main intent is to give users control over when they get alerts.

With those notification channels added, we can now test out our first notification, which looks like this on the screen when tapped:

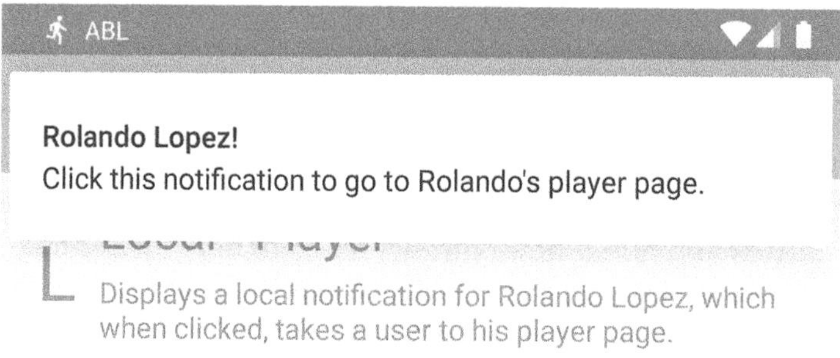

And like this when you pull down the notification shade:

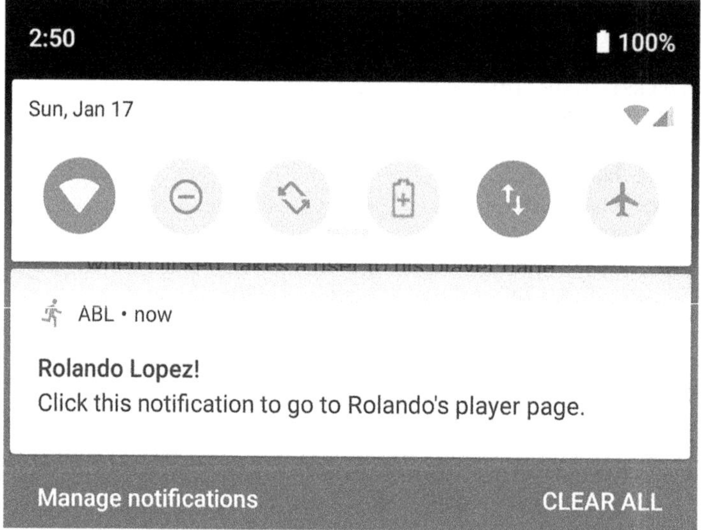

Plus, if we go into the App Info and choose Notifications, we're presented with all the channels that were just added, as shown in the image on page 311.

We're now well on our way with notifications in the app, so let's get a few more included.

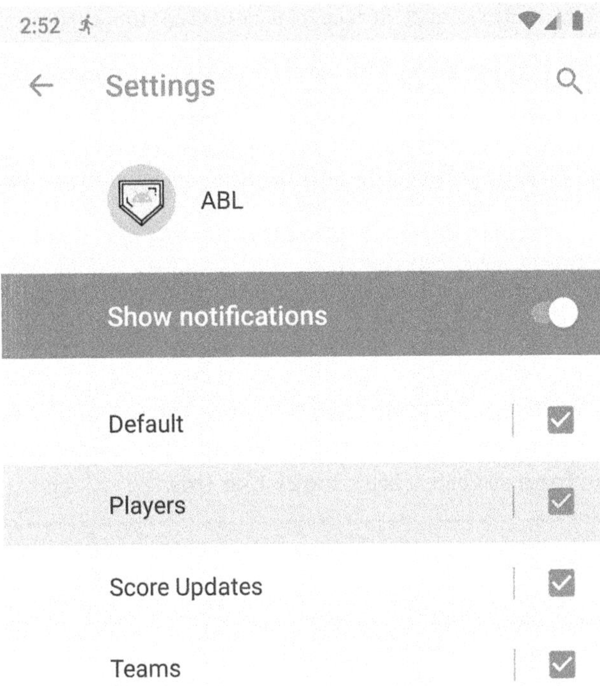

Add Additional Local Notifications

The other two notifications we're adding highlight how to use a long notification description and an additional action on the notification. Notification 2 takes a user to the team page of the Pewaukee Princesses, but this time we're going to set an additional longer description when the notification's expanded. The initial setup is structurally the same but with some different values:

```
NotificationItem(
  2,
  "Local - Team",
  "Displays a local notification for the Pewaukee Princesses, " +
    "which when clicked, takes a user to their team page.",
  NotificationType.Local
) { ctx, _ ->
  val pendingIntent = NavDeepLinkBuilder(ctx)
    .setGraph(R.navigation.nav_graph)
    .setDestination(R.id.singleTeamFragment)
    .setArguments(Bundle().apply {
      putString("teamId", "PKE")
      putString("teamName", "Pewaukee Princesses")
    }).createPendingIntent()
```

Then we get some longText and add that along with a BigTextStyle:

```
val longText = ctx.getString(R.string.pke_notification_long_text)

val channel = ABLNotificationChannel.Teams
val notification =
  NotificationCompat.Builder(ctx, channel.channelId)
    .setContentTitle(ctx.getString(R.string.pke_notification_title))
    .setContentText(ctx.getString(R.string.pke_notification_short_text))
    .setSmallIcon(R.drawable.fi_ic_crown)
    .setStyle(NotificationCompat.BigTextStyle().bigText(longText))
    .setContentIntent(pendingIntent)
    .setAutoCancel(true)
    .build()
```

By including the setStyle() piece, we can have a larger description when the notification is expanded. Do notice how I kept in the setContentText() call, though, as this keeps a shorter description by default. The non-expanded version, using the value from setContentText(), looks like this:

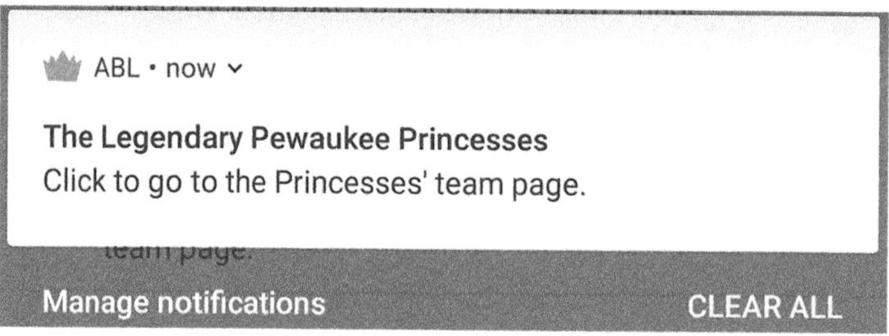

Then, once the user expands the notification, it looks like this:

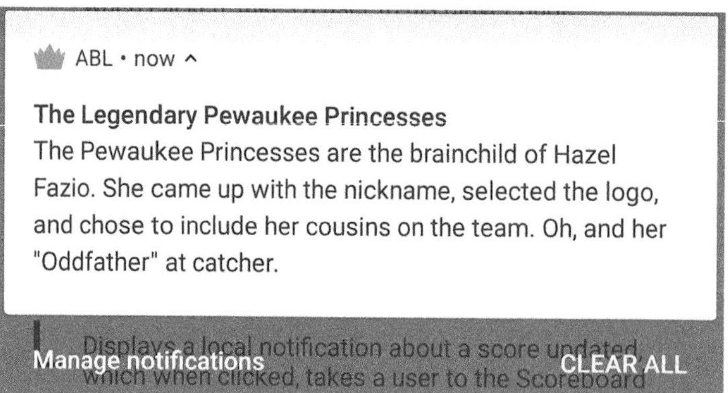

If you want to check the code for this notification and see the full implementation for the next one, be sure to check out the chapter-13 directory.

Notification 3 skips the longer text and instead adds a secondary action (shown as Standings) to the notification, which shows up as an extra link at the bottom. This way, tapping the notification itself takes a user to the Scoreboard page, while tapping the action we add will take them to the

Standings page. We include that option with the addAction() step of the NotificationCompat.Builder process.

We need a secondary PendingIntent for that action, which looks like this:

```
val scoreboardPendingIntent = NavDeepLinkBuilder(ctx)
  .setGraph(R.navigation.nav_graph)
  .setDestination(R.id.scoreboardFragment)
  .createPendingIntent()

val standingsPendingIntent = NavDeepLinkBuilder(ctx)
  .setGraph(R.navigation.nav_graph)
  .setDestination(R.id.standingsFragment)
  .createPendingIntent()
```

Then, we include the addAction() call when building our Notification:

```
val notification =
  NotificationCompat.Builder(ctx, channel.channelId)
    .setContentTitle(ctx.getString(R.string.scoreboard_notification_title))
    .setContentText(ctx.getString(R.string.scoreboard_notification_text))
    .setSmallIcon(R.drawable.mdi_scoreboard_outline)
    .setContentIntent(scoreboardPendingIntent)
    .addAction(
      R.drawable.ic_baseline_outlined_flag_24,
      ctx.getString(R.string.standings),
      standingsPendingIntent
    )
    .setAutoCancel(true)
    .build()
```

Don't be alarmed if the icon we specified on the action isn't displayed. It hasn't been since Android 7.0, but the icon is still included in the addAction() function in case you're building an app which will work on older devices. Also note that if you click the action, the setAutoCancel() flag won't be used and the notification will remain in the user's status bar.

You now have a few examples of local notifications that are triggered within an app. The next step of the process is to move to *push notifications*, which are messages sent to a device from a remote location. We're going to use what we did here while reacting to these cloud-based messages.

Send Cloud-Based Alerts with Push Notifications

I want to make the scope of this section very clear from the get-go: we're focusing on the *client-side* of push notifications, meaning the app that consumes the messages. The server-side piece is out of scope for this book, so I've added some logic to the ABL APIs that we can use when building our handlers. I would have liked to add both sides of push notifications in here, but we're already 325+ pages into the book, so I'm instead making that piece a free blog for everyone.[1]

For our push notifications, we're using Google's Firebase platform and in particular the Firebase Cloud Messaging library, and we have a bit of setup we need to go through before we can get rolling.

Configure Firebase Cloud Messaging

As I've already registered the ABL app (with the dev.mfazio.abl package name) with Firebase, you can just use the same google-services.json file that I have. That file is in the chapter-13/code-to-copy folder and should be copied into the app's top-level directory, next to the app's build.gradle file.

Speaking of build.gradle, we also have changes to make in both of those. Starting with the project's file, we need new gms_version and firebase_version version variables as well as a classpath dependency:

```
dependencies {
  classpath "com.android.tools.build:gradle:$gradle_version"
  classpath "org.jetbrains.kotlin:kotlin-gradle-plugin:$kotlin_version"
  classpath
    "androidx.navigation:navigation-safe-args-gradle-plugin:$nav_version"
➤ classpath "com.google.gms:google-services:$gms_version"

  // NOTE: Do not place your application dependencies here; they belong
  // in the individual module build.gradle files
}
```

Then in the app's build.gradle, we need a new plugin:

```
plugins {
  id 'com.android.application'
  id 'kotlin-android'
  id 'kotlin-kapt'
  id 'androidx.navigation.safeargs.kotlin'
➤ id 'com.google.gms.google-services'
}
```

We also need a new dependency. While it's not totally necessary in this case, I'm going to use the Firebase Bill of Materials *platform* dependency to make each Firebase dependency use the same version. Again, it's not super-useful now, as we only have a single dependency here; but it's likely you'll want more in a real app, so I wanted to make you aware that this exists:

1. https://blog.mfazio.dev/abl/push-notifications

```
implementation platform(
  "com.google.firebase:firebase-bom:$firebase_version"
)

//All our other dependencies are still here

implementation "com.google.firebase:firebase-messaging-ktx"
```

Now that the dependencies are in place, the last steps are to update the AndroidManifest.xml and add an ABLFirebaseMessagingService class as well so the app knows how to handle incoming messages. While we're in AndroidManifest.xml, we'll also set up a few notification defaults.

Inside the <application> tag after the <activity> tag, we need to add a new <service> tag with the *com.google.firebase.MESSAGING_EVENT* intent filter. Here, we'll list the FirebaseMessagingService child class we're creating next section:

```
<service
  android:name=".notifications.ABLFirebaseMessagingService"
  android:exported="false">
  <intent-filter>
    <action android:name="com.google.firebase.MESSAGING_EVENT" />
  </intent-filter>
</service>
```

In addition, we can set a few defaults for incoming push notifications by adding some <meta-data> tags below our new <service> tag:

```
<meta-data
    android:name=
      "com.google.firebase.messaging.default_notification_icon"
    android:resource="@drawable/ic_abl_launcher_foreground" />
<meta-data
    android:name=
      "com.google.firebase.messaging.default_notification_color"
    android:resource="@color/androidGreen" />
<meta-data
    android:name=
      "com.google.firebase.messaging.default_notification_channel_id"
    android:value="@string/default_notification_channel_id" />
```

The preceding settings will use the ABL logo as the icon by default, the Android green color we use for the ABL logo, and the default notifications channel (which we've set as a string resource). We can always override these settings from the server if we wish.

Now that we've got our configurations set, we can start building out ABLFirebaseMessagingService, which is the main spot for handling incoming push notifications. This class will be used whenever we receive a foreground notification (meaning our app is currently being seen/used) or if we get a data notification (which we'll cover later).

Handle Push Notifications with FirebaseMessagingService

First off, go ahead and add in ABLFirebaseMessagingService to the notifications package:

```
class ABLFirebaseMessagingService : FirebaseMessagingService() {
  override fun onMessageReceived(message: RemoteMessage) {
    // Coming up!
  }
}
```

FirebaseMessagingService has other functions as well, but we only care about the onMessageReceived() function. It takes in a RemoteMessage containing all the info about the push notification so we can then respond. In our case, that response is to display a notification ourselves as we did inside the NotificationsFragment.

We'll set up ABLFirebaseMessagingService to handle both Player and Team push notifications. Since both types of push notifications are handled effectively the same way, we want to prep a NotificationConfig object, then send that into a generic notification block. This means that when onMessageReceived() is called, we send the RemoteMessage into a function which creates a NotificationConfig instance, then we use that to fill in the pieces for NotificationCompat generation.

This should be clearer once we get all the pieces in place. The first one will be createNotificationConfig(), which takes in both a Context object and the current RemoteMessage. We then check the destination property on that message and use that to figure out which type of notification we'll be sending (or null if we can't determine the right type).

The logic here looks like this:

```
private fun createNotificationConfig(
  ctx: Context,
  message: RemoteMessage
): NotificationConfig? =
  when (message.data["destination"]) {
    ctx.getString(R.string.notification_destination_player) ->
      NotificationConfig(
        id = 10,
        channel = ABLNotificationChannel.Players,
        titleInput = message.data["playerName"] ?: "N/A",
        textInput = message.data["playerName"] ?: "N/A",
        smallIconId = R.drawable.ic_baseline_directions_run_24,
        destinationId = R.id.singlePlayerFragment,
        arguments = mapOf(
```

```
                "playerId" to (message.data["playerId"] ?: ""),
                "playerName" to (message.data["playerName"] ?: "")
            )
        )
    ctx.getString(R.string.notification_destination_team) ->
        NotificationConfig(
            id = 11,
            channel = ABLNotificationChannel.Teams,
            titleInput = message.data["teamName"] ?: "N/A",
            textInput = message.data["teamName"] ?: "N/A",
            smallIconId = R.drawable.ic_baseline_outlined_flag_24,
            destinationId = R.id.singleTeamFragment,
            arguments = mapOf(
                "teamId" to (message.data["teamId"] ?: ""),
                "teamName" to (message.data["teamName"] ?: "")
            )
        )
    else -> null
}
```

Using the when block, we set the notification's ID, channel, title, body text, icon, destination, and parameters. Also, I included named parameters here for the sake of clarity since it's hard to tell what each piece means at a glance. They're not required but can be helpful at times like these.

If you look at the pieces in here, they should look familiar when compared to the previous notification work we've done in this chapter. With that function added, we can go back to implementing onMessageReceived().

This function, after making sure we have valid Context and NotificationConfig objects, creates a PendingIntent object for a NotificationCompat object, which is then sent via a NotificationManagerCompat:

```
override fun onMessageReceived(message: RemoteMessage) {
  baseContext?.let { ctx ->
    createNotificationConfig(ctx, message)?.let { config ->
      val pendingIntent = NavDeepLinkBuilder(ctx)
        .setGraph(R.navigation.nav_graph)
        .setDestination(config.destinationId)
        .setArguments(Bundle().apply {
          config.arguments.forEach {
            (key, value) -> putString(key, value)
          }
        }).createPendingIntent()

      val notification =
        NotificationCompat.Builder(ctx, config.channel.channelId)
          .setContentTitle(ctx.getString(
```

```
          R.string.generic_push_title,
          config.titleInput
        ))
        .setContentText(ctx.getString(
          R.string.generic_push_description,
          config.textInput
        ))
        .setStyle(NotificationCompat.BigTextStyle().bigText(
          ctx.getString(
            R.string.generic_push_description,
            config.textInput
          )
        ))
        .setSmallIcon(config.smallIconId)
        .setContentIntent(pendingIntent)
        .setAutoCancel(true)
        .build()

      NotificationManagerCompat.from(ctx).notify(config.id, notification)
    }
  }
}
```

This may look like a lot of logic, but it should more or less be review now. The biggest difference from the previous notification is that we're using that NotificationConfig object to fill in all the pieces here. Also, the ctx.getString() calls are more complex since we're sending in a parameter to the string resource value. This is a handy technique you can use any time you're using string resources in code.

With that, this class it done. As I mentioned, a number of other functions are available from FirebaseMessagingService, but we didn't need them for our use. I do want to mention the onNewToken() function, which is called whenever we're assigned a new notification token. This can be handy if we want to save a given user's notification token along with their user account. We're not doing that here, but we *are* going to grab that token another way, then add it to our server requests when we want to send push notifications to ourselves.

Send Push Notifications to Your Device

We're heading back to the NotificationsFragment class for three additional items. Each one will get one of the notification tokens I mentioned before, then send out a notification request to our server. In turn, the server will tell Firebase to send a notification to your device. That notification token is used to identify the device, so this way you only have to worry about sending a message to yourself during testing.

To get a token to send to the server, we'll use the FirebaseMessaging class and its token property. That property has a function called addOnCompleteListener(), which is called after the token request is completed (successfully or not). Inside there, we make sure the call succeeded, then send our request to the server. If the call didn't succeed, we just bail out.

Since we're doing the same thing for all three notifications, we want a separate function to handle this logic. getTokenAndSendRequest() will grab a token and, if successful, call the request suspend function we're sending into getTokenAndSendRequest(). We also will need a CoroutineScope since we're making an API call. By making request a parameter, we can have custom logic in a block to be run while using the same getTokenAndSendRequest() function.

Things will likely be clearer if we look at the code. Add in a TAG for logging, then we can complete getTokenAndSendRequest(). Here's the entirety of that function:

```
private fun getTokenAndSendRequest(
  coroutineScope: CoroutineScope,
  request: suspend (token: String) -> Unit
) {
  FirebaseMessaging.getInstance().token.addOnCompleteListener { task ->
    if (!task.isSuccessful) {
      Log.w(
        TAG,
        "Fetching FCM registration token failed.",
        task.exception
      )
      return@addOnCompleteListener
    }

    val token = task.result ?: "N/A"

    coroutineScope.launch {
      request(token)
    }
  }
}
```

The request property is then defined inside each NotificationItem as a block after the function call:

```
NotificationItem(
  4,
  "Push - Player",
  "Requests a push notification from the server for Juan Pablo Siller. " +
    "If the app is still open when received, it will display a dialog. " +
    "If the app is closed, it will display a notification.",
  NotificationType.Push
) { _, coroutineScope ->
  getTokenAndSendRequest(coroutineScope) { token ->
```

```
        ablService.sendNotificationToPhone(
          NotificationTypeApiModel.Player,
          token,
          "sillejua",
          false
        )
    }
}
```

The other two push notifications will look more or less the same as this one. We configure the NotificationItem, then add a body containing getTokenAndSendRequest() plus our API call. However, I'm adding in a delay to these two notifications. This will allow you time to minimize the app if you wish to test out different push notification scenarios.

Minimizing the app is important because of how Android handles push notifications. If the app is in the foreground, we use the ABLFirebaseMessagingService to handle the message. But if the app's in the background, then we're presented with a notification handled by the OS. If we want to skip that possibility and instead always go to ABLFirebaseMessagingService, we can send a push notification from the server as a "data" notification. This tells the device to not display a notification automatically but instead have the app always handle it. It's your choice with how you want to deal with push notifications on the server side.

Back in our list of NotificationItem objects, we can include the two delayed notifications. Note that the latter one is also a data notification:

```
NotificationItem(
  5,
  "Push - Team (Delayed)",
  "Requests a push notification (after a small delay) " +
    "from the server for the Waukesha Riffs. " +
    "The delay exists to allow for minimizing of the app " +
    "in order to get the notification in the status bar.",
  NotificationType.Push
) { _, coroutineScope ->
  getTokenAndSendRequest(coroutineScope) { token ->
    delay(3000)
    ablService.sendNotificationToPhone(
      NotificationTypeApiModel.Team,
      token,
      "WAU",
      false
    )
  }
},
NotificationItem(
  6,
```

```
    "Push - Player (Delayed, Data)",
    "Requests a push notification (after a small delay) " +
      "from the server for Hazel Fazio. " +
      "This is a \"data-only\" push notification, " +
      "meaning the onMessageReceived(...) function will always be used.",
    NotificationType.Push
  ) { _, coroutineScope ->
    getTokenAndSendRequest(coroutineScope) { token ->
      delay(3000)
      ablService.sendNotificationToPhone(
        NotificationTypeApiModel.Player,
        token,
        "faziohaz",
        true
      )
    }
  }
```

Now we can check out the difference with push notification handling between foreground (left) and background (right):

The left side is our handling from within ABLFirebaseMessagingService and the right side uses the configuration set inside the server code. It's certainly handy to have the OS automatically handle displaying a notification for a backgrounded app, but it's also valuable to have the option to handle things ourselves.

With that, we're set with both local and push notifications. You can do so much more than what we did here, but this is a great starting point to add notifications to your own apps. Just don't annoy your users! Before we leave this chapter behind, recall that this chapter is about sending data in *and* out of the app. We've more than covered the "in" part of that, but what about the "out" side of things? For that, we're going to look at Sharing inside Android and how we can quickly send (deep) links to our friends.

Share Links with Android Sharesheet

You've probably seen this before: an app has the two-line, three-dot Share icon and clicking it gives you something like the image shown on page 322.

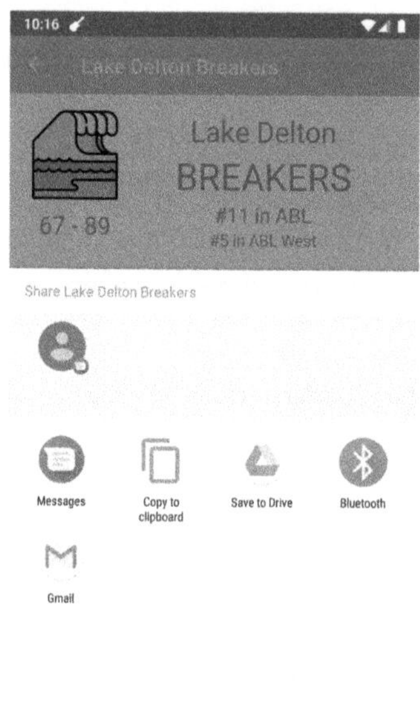

We're going to add sharing to both Team and Player pages, which requires a Share button and a bit of logic in each page's ViewModel. You should have copied it into your project at the beginning, but if not, add in a new Share vector asset:

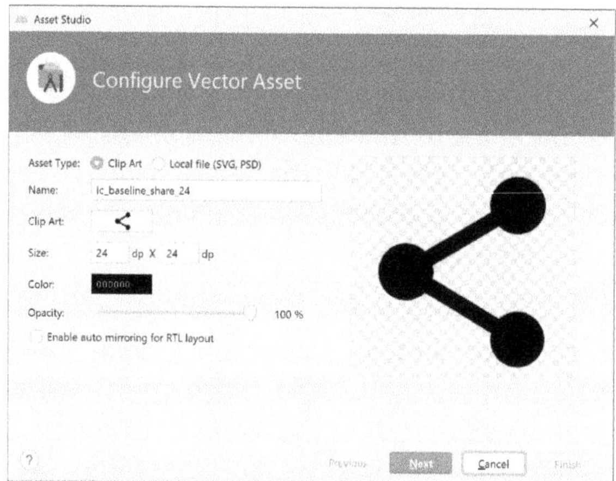

Then we need to add the Share button to both players and teams. We'll start with fragment_single_player.xml since it's the simpler of the two:

```
<Button
  android:id="@+id/singlePlayerShareButton"
  android:layout_width="wrap_content"
  android:layout_height="wrap_content"
  android:layout_margin="16dp"
```

```
  android:paddingVertical="8dp"
  android:paddingHorizontal="16dp"
  android:onClick="@{vm.sharePlayer}"
  android:text="@string/share"
  app:icon="@drawable/ic_baseline_share_24"
  app:layout_constraintStart_toStartOf="parent"
  app:layout_constraintEnd_toEndOf="parent"
  app:layout_constraintTop_toBottomOf="@id/singlePlayerStats" />
```

The vm.sharePlayer() function doesn't exist yet, which is fine, we'll do that in a bit. First, we want to get the XML updated for Single Team as well. This includes adding the new button and rearranging the View Roster button:

```
<Button
  android:id="@+id/teamViewRoster"
  android:layout_width="0dp"
  android:layout_height="wrap_content"
  android:layout_marginTop="16dp"
  android:backgroundTint="@{vm.team.primaryColorId}"
  android:onClick="@{viewRosterButtonClickListener}"
  android:text="@string/view_roster"
  app:icon="@drawable/ic_baseline_directions_run_24"
  app:layout_constraintEnd_toStartOf="@id/teamShareTeam"
  app:layout_constraintStart_toStartOf="parent"
  app:layout_constraintTop_toBottomOf="@id/teamDivisionStandings" />

<Button
  android:id="@+id/teamShareTeam"
  android:layout_width="0dp"
  android:layout_height="wrap_content"
  android:layout_margin="16dp"
  android:onClick="@{vm.shareTeam}"
  android:text="@string/share"
  app:icon="@drawable/ic_baseline_share_24"
  app:layout_constraintTop_toBottomOf="@id/teamDivisionStandings"
  app:layout_constraintStart_toEndOf="@id/teamViewRoster"
  app:layout_constraintEnd_toEndOf="parent"/>
```

By the way, I know that we're taking two different approaches here for the android:onClick= attributes, and that's on purpose. It's intended to show you two approaches you can take when adding click handlers in your code. Speaking of click handlers, we need to implement those inside the ViewModel classes. We can start with SinglePlayerViewModel.

Here, the sharePlayer() function will grab the current playerWithStats value and (if it's not null), use that to build out an Intent. This Intent object will set up an action that sends text to another app. We can use our deep link URLs we created in Navigate Directly via a Deep Link, on page 230, with this, as they will take users right to a given page. We then use the Intent.createChooser() function and startActivity() to display the Sharesheet. Here's the whole function:

```
fun sharePlayer(view: View) {
  playerWithStats.value?.player?.let { player ->
    val encodedPlayerName = URLEncoder.encode(player.fullName, "UTF-8")
    val sendIntent = Intent().apply {
      action = Intent.ACTION_SEND
      putExtra(
        Intent.EXTRA_TEXT,
        "https://link.mfazio.dev/players/${player.playerId}" +
          "?playerName=$encodedPlayerName"
      )
      type = "text/plain"
    }

    val shareIntent =
      Intent.createChooser(sendIntent, "Share ${player.fullName}")

    view.context.startActivity(shareIntent)
  }
}
```

Notice how we're encoding the player name to remove spaces from the link. If we don't do this, some links may break for the person receiving the message. Also, we can use the incoming view's Context to start the share Activity instead of having to open up the application value that came from AndroidViewModel.

As you could probably guess, the shareTeam() function inside SingleTeamViewModel looks pretty similar:

```
fun shareTeam(view: View) {
  team.value?.let { team ->
    val encodedTeamName = URLEncoder.encode(team.teamName, "UTF-8")
    val sendIntent = Intent().apply {
      action = Intent.ACTION_SEND
      putExtra(
        Intent.EXTRA_TEXT,
        "https://link.mfazio.dev/teams/${team.teamId}" +
          "?teamName=$encodedTeamName"
      )
      type = "text/plain"
    }

    val shareIntent =
      Intent.createChooser(sendIntent, "Share ${team.teamName}")

    view.context.startActivity(shareIntent)
  }
}
```

We could always add more to these sharing calls, such as sharing images or video clips, but the base will look like the code above. The Android Developers page[2] has more in-depth info about the Sharesheet in case you find yourself with a more advanced use case.

Summary and Next Steps

The Android Baseball League app is complete! We started the app with nothing and now have a fine-looking application all about our (not quite real) baseball league. This chapter was about sending data into and out of the ABL app, primarily in the form of notifications. Hopefully you now see how you can use both local and push notifications to enhance your users' experience. Just don't bug them too much!

We also touched upon sharing within an app here at the end. It wasn't nearly as in-depth, but it didn't need to be. In most cases, a simple text link is all that someone would want and will handle what you need.

What's next? For the ABL app, nothing, at least not in this book. We've got some testing coming up in the next two chapters, which is excellent, but we're using the Penny Drop app for both of those. I do hope you enjoyed building out the ABL app—it was definitely a special one for me to build along with you.

2. https://link.mfazio.dev/sharing

Part III

Test Your App

Now that we've built two apps, we need to make sure they're working. Unit and UI testing help users love your app and reassure you that the app is doing what you want.

CHAPTER 14

Unit Test Your App with JUnit

Ah, unit testing. That lovely way of letting the computer keep you from making boneheaded mistakes and help you speed up your development process. It may seem particularly scary with Android development, but some great tools are available to us, which makes all of this easier to digest.

Full disclosure: these next two chapters are in no way intended as a full-scale testing overview nor an exhaustive list of Android testing tips and tricks. Instead, I just want to offer you a few tools you can use to ensure that your app is doing what you expect. Given what we'll be covering here and in the next chapter, you'll be able to get yourself a solid test suite.

However, if you want more information or are unfamiliar with how to test software applications in general, the offical Android docs have a bunch of information and a few codelabs to go through. I'd highly recommend checking those out if you want additional info past what I give you here.[1]

Now, I'm assuming you're coming here after finishing one (likely Penny Drop) or both of the apps. If for some reason you haven't, that's OK, but you'll want to use the code we sent along with the book to have something to test. The first half of this chapter is using the resulting code after Chapter 4 when we've added in the GameHandler but before adding in any Room features in Chapter 5. This makes ViewModel testing easier. Once we get to the second half of the chapter, we'll change over to the end code after Chapter 7. I'll let you know when we switch codebases.

In this chapter, we're going to cover how to get basic unit tests in place, then we'll dig into how to test out ViewModel classes with LiveData objects. Finally, we'll see how to test out our PennyDropDao class with a local Room DB.

1. https://link.mfazio.dev/testing

Add Unit Tests

We're starting at the base testing level, a JUnit *unit test*. If you're unfamiliar, unit testing is where we validate that a single piece of our code is working. This is a general software development concept rather than an Android concept and is used with all kinds of applications.

JUnit is the testing framework used for most Android unit testing, and the dependency is already in your application. It's used so often when building an app that the default Android template includes it. JUnit gives us a number of annotations and functions to use when testing to help write tests and make them more readable.

In particular, we're going to be using the @Test, @Before, and @BeforeClass annotations in our tests. The @Test annotation marks a function as a unit test, letting Android Studio know it's a single test that should be run. By doing this, the IDE can then run each test from the UI and give you a list of succeeded and/or failed tests.

The @Before and @BeforeClass annotations (along with their counterparts @After and @AfterClass) help set up your tests. These annotations allow code to be run before and after every test or all tests, respectively, in case we need the same setup for each scenario. We'll see how these work when we start testing GameViewModel.

While the default project template did give us the JUnit dependency and a bare-bones ExampleUnitTest class, we've got a few more libraries we want to add.

- androidx.test:core-ktx: the core AndroidX testing library with a number of features, in particular the getApplicationContext() function we'll see later in the chapter.
- androidx.test.ext:junit-ktx: contains Kotlin-specific extension functions/types for JUnit testing, like the AndroidJUnit4 class (which we'll use later).
- androidx.arch.core:core-testing: testing helpers for tests using Architecture Components, in our case the GameViewModel.

Add in the latest version of each of these libraries with their associated version variables in the project's build.grade file, just as we've done so many times in this book. After you sync your project, open up the test directory in the project.

It'll have the same package name as the app, but Android Studio shows the word *test* in parentheses like this:

dev.mfazio.pennydrop (test)

In here, Android Studio was kind enough to create the ExampleUnitTest class with a single unit test. If you're familiar with JUnit, go ahead and delete the class. If JUnit and/or unit testing is new for you, take a look at the addition_isCorrect() test function, *then* delete the class. Instead, we're going to build out GameHandlerTests, which will focus on the GameHandler.pass() function.

Add the First Unit Test

Add the new class, then create a new function called "Test nextPlayer() via pass() function". No, really, that's what we're calling this function (I mean, I technically can't make you, but stick with me here). It'll look like this:

```
@Test
fun `Test nextPlayer() via pass() function`() {
  // We'll fill this in soon.
}
```

I'm guessing your reaction here is either one of surprise or confusion. With test classes (and *only* test classes) in Kotlin, we can create functions with names including spaces and symbols. You *technically* can include emoji, but please don't. Plus, Android Studio will yell at you for it.

```
@Test
// Please, PLEASE don't do this.
fun `Test nextPlayer() via pass() function 😨`() {
```

Having the ability to put a human-readable sentence as a function name instead of a camel-cased testNextPlayerViaPassFunction() is helpful when looking through a class but really shines when we use the test summary view in Android Studio. This window comes up when we run a test (generally inside the Run tab at the bottom of the IDE) and lists all the test you've just run. It shows you the test class, each test's name, and the state of each test.

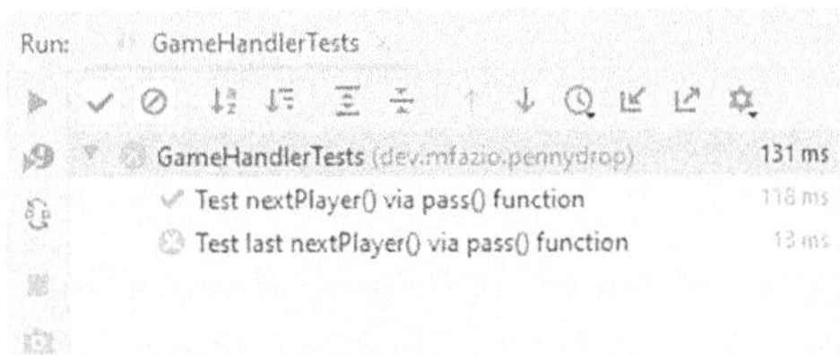

From here, we can see which tests are passing and which are failing. Plus, if we ever have a particularly long-running test suite, we can use the second button (the play button with the red circle + white exclamation point) to only rerun the failed tests. While it doesn't do all that much for us with just a couple of tests, it's very handy when you have multiple classes each with multiple tests.

Backticks in Kotlin

While I was very clear about how backticks should only be used for function names in test classes, we can hit a scenario where we need to use them in normal classes.

The possibility is there of having a Java method with the same name as a keyword in Kotlin (for example, in, is, object, and so on) and would be normally impossible to call from the Kotlin side of things. But we can escape the method name in our Kotlin code using backticks:

```
item.`is`(ready)
```

This isn't likely to happen, but it is possible to ensure full compatability between Java and Kotlin code, so be aware that this functionality exists.

As you can read from our function name, we're going to make sure the nextPlayer() function works but do so via the pass() function. The reason we're not testing the pass() function directly is because it's private inside GameHandler.

While we *could* change its visibility to public, it's not really intended as a public method. The argument could be made that we shouldn't be unit testing a non-public function, but I like it as an example here, so we're going to do so. Plus, the pass() function doesn't do much other than call nextPlayer(), so it's a valid test of pass(), which for reference looks like this:

```
fun pass(players: List<Player>, currentPlayer: Player) =
  TurnResult(
    previousPlayer = currentPlayer,
    currentPlayer = nextPlayer(players, currentPlayer),
    playerChanged = true,
    turnEnd = TurnEnd.Pass,
    canRoll = true,
    canPass = false
  )
```

Our test has three stages: setup, action, and assertion. We need to prep a List<Player>, call GameHandler.pass(), then validate the results. The setup portion has two parts—the List<Player> plus the two players we care about, the current player and next player:

```
val testPlayers = listOf(
  Player("Michael", true),
  Player("Emily", true),
  Player("Hazel", true),
  Player("Riverboat Ron", false, selectedAI = AI.basicAI[5])
)

val currentPlayer = testPlayers.first { it.playerName == "Emily" }
val nextPlayer = testPlayers.first { it.playerName == "Hazel" }
```

With those in place, we then call GameHandler.pass() and check the results. A nice bit of Kotlin syntax for this scenario is an also block. That'll run the function, then give us the result to test inside the block.

```
GameHandler.pass(testPlayers, currentPlayer).also { result ->
  // Assertions will go in here.
}
```

We're going to use JUnit's Assert class to check the results. This class contains a number of functions to make sure values are what we'd expect and alert the JUnit framework if not. In our case, we're going to start with two functions: assertTrue() and assertEquals(). The former confirms that the value sent in as a parameter is true, while the latter checks that the second parameter (the TurnResult from GameHandler.pass()) is equal to the first (expected) parameter.

We're going to include four assertions in our test: the player changed, the turned ended with a Pass action, the currentPlayer we sent in is now the previous player, and the nextPlayer we set up is now rolling. Including those four tests looks like this:

```
GameHandler.pass(testPlayers, currentPlayer).also { result ->
  assertTrue(result.playerChanged)
  assertEquals(TurnEnd.Pass, result.turnEnd)
  assertEquals(currentPlayer, result.previousPlayer)
  assertEquals(nextPlayer, result.currentPlayer)
}
```

With those three parts of the function in place, we can run the test. You should have green arrows to the left of your function names, or you can right-click a function to run it. Once it starts, the Run window will pop up with the summary pane that I mentioned earlier. If your test succeeds (which it should here), then you're done with this one! If not, the main pane inside the Run window should tell you why you have an error, which assertions failed, and hints about what you can do, as you can see in the example shown on page 334.

```
java.lang.AssertionError:
Expected :Player(playerName=Hazel, isHuman=true, selectedAI=null)
Actual   :Player(playerName=Michael, isHuman=true, selectedAI=null)
<Click to see difference>

<1 internal call>
    at org.junit.Assert.failNotEquals(Assert.java:835) <2 internal calls>
    at dev.mfazio.pennydrop.GameHandlerTests.checkNextPlayer(GameHandlerTests.kt:47)
    at dev.mfazio.pennydrop.GameHandlerTests.Test last nextPlayer() via pass()
 function(GameHandlerTests.kt:39) <31 internal calls>
```

Add One More Test

Before we move on to the GameViewModelTests class, let's get a second test in here. It'll be almost the exact same test, except now we're choosing the last Player in the List<Player>. This makes sure when the player that's last in the turn order passes, play wraps back around to the first player. The test looks like this:

```
@Test
fun `Test last nextPlayer() via pass() function`() {
  val testPlayers = listOf(
    Player("Michael", true),
    Player("Emily", true),
    Player("Hazel", true),
    Player("Riverboat Ron", false, selectedAI = AI.basicAI[5])
  )

  val currentPlayer =
    testPlayers.first { it.playerName == "Riverboat Ron" }
  val nextPlayer = testPlayers.first { it.playerName == "Michael" }

  GameHandler.pass(testPlayers, currentPlayer).also { result ->
    assertTrue(result.playerChanged)
    assertEquals(TurnEnd.Pass, result.turnEnd)
    assertEquals(currentPlayer, result.previousPlayer)
    assertEquals(nextPlayer, result.currentPlayer)
  }
}
```

Go ahead and run the test to make sure it works as written. It should be good since it's almost the same test as the previous one. That these test are so similar should also tell you that there's a smarter way to handle things.

Clean Up the Test Code

Since the test players are the same in both tests, we can do that ahead of time in a function called setUpTestPlayers(), marked with the @BeforeClass and @JvmStatic annotations. Plus, the actual call to GameHandler.pass() is the same in both tests, so we can move that to a separate function.

The setUpTestPlayers() function that we're adding will be run before all the tests due to the @BeforeClass annotation. This is useful to ensure that your data is prepared the same way for each test (as we don't want one unit test to influence another test).

Since @BeforeClass is run before the class is created, we actually end up putting it in a companion object. Plus, due to interacting with JUnit (which is a Java library) we need to include the @JvmStatic.

This function (along with the declaration of the testPlayers variable) looks like this:

```
companion object {
  private lateinit var testPlayers: List<Player>

  @BeforeClass
  @JvmStatic
  fun setUpTestPlayers() {
    this.testPlayers = listOf(
      Player("Michael", true),
      Player("Emily", true),
      Player("Hazel", true),
      Player("Riverboat Ron", false, selectedAI = AI.basicAI[5])
    )
  }
}
```

Now, when we run either of our tests, they can reference the testPlayers variable. Also, this means our upcoming checkNextPlayer() function can also reference testPlayers. checkNextPlayer() now handles the call to GameHandler.pass() along with all the assertions, while each test is left to send in the proper values for currentPlayer and nextPlayer:

```
private fun checkNextPlayer(currentPlayer: Player, nextPlayer: Player) =
  GameHandler.pass(testPlayers, currentPlayer).also { result ->
    assertTrue(result.playerChanged)
    assertEquals(TurnEnd.Pass, result.turnEnd)
    assertEquals(currentPlayer, result.previousPlayer)
    assertEquals(nextPlayer, result.currentPlayer)
  }
```

With that function added, we can change the previous two tests to look like this:

```
@Test
fun `Test nextPlayer() via pass() function`() {
  val currentPlayer = testPlayers.first { it.playerName == "Emily" }
  val nextPlayer = testPlayers.first { it.playerName == "Hazel" }
```

```
  checkNextPlayer(currentPlayer, nextPlayer)
}

@Test
fun `Test last nextPlayer() via pass() function`() {
  val currentPlayer =
    testPlayers.first { it.playerName == "Riverboat Ron" }
  val nextPlayer = testPlayers.first { it.playerName == "Michael" }

  checkNextPlayer(currentPlayer, nextPlayer)
}
```

With both of the functions, we *could* shrink them down even more to be like this:

```
fun `Test nextPlayer() via pass() function`() =
  checkNextPlayer(
    testPlayers.first { it.playerName == "Emily" },
    testPlayers.first { it.playerName == "Hazel" }
  )
```

However, I'm not a big fan of this syntax for two reasons. One, it's not nearly as clear what each of those first() blocks represents. By having values with the names currentPlayer and nextPlayer, your test becomes more readable when looking quickly. Two, JUnit tests are supposed to return Unit (which is like void in Java) and we're returning a TurnResult object from checkNextPlayer(). This latter issue isn't a big one, but readabilty is valuable with tests (and code in general).

We now have a couple of unit tests in place for the app and they're actually useful. Ensuring that the player order works correctly is a key component in the app, and were we to change the app's code in a way that breaks that functionality, we'd want to know immediately. You can feel free to add any other unit tests here as you see fit, as it'd be a great exercise to make sure you understood what we just did.

But the issue now is that we don't have a ton that can be unit tested easily in the app. A lot of what we do lives within ViewModel classes and the PennyDropDatabase. So next up is some tests against GameViewModel, looking at the startGame() and roll() functions.We'll work on PennyDropDatabase (and more accurately PennyDropDao) later.

Test a ViewModel Class

Testing a ViewModel takes what we did in the previous section and adds a bit more complexity. Instead of just the response from a function, we now have to deal with LiveData and Observer objects. Luckily, the libraries we added at the beginning of the chapter will make our life easier here.

Add a new class inside the test folder called GameViewModelTests. This class at the end will contain two tests: one checking GameViewModel.startGame() and the other dealing with GameViewModel.roll(). Before we get into the tests, though, let's get all the setup work out of the way.

Set Up the Test Class

Most of this class will look the same at a high level as GameHandlerTests in that we have a setup function with the @Before annotation and two @Test functions with a number of assertions. In addition to those parts, we have an extra @Rule annotation to let the system know how to handle LiveData.

That annotation is @get:Rule, which tells JUnit to use the listed value as a TestRule. In our case, it's an instance of the InstantTaskExecutorRule class, which is a rule telling architecture components (like LiveData) to run immediately and synchronously in the same thread. This causes those components to be a touch slower but much easier to test, which is a tradeoff we're willing to make here.

```
@get:Rule
val instantExecutorRule = InstantTaskExecutorRule()
```

With that rule added, we can set up the GameViewModel instance we'll be using in both tests. We're using the same private lateinit var modifiers as we did in the last test class and a similar setup function:

```
private lateinit var gameViewModel: GameViewModel
private lateinit var testPlayers: List<Player>

@Before
fun initializeViewModel() {
  this.gameViewModel = GameViewModel()

  this.testPlayers = listOf(
    Player("Michael", true),
    Player("Emily", true),
    Player("Hazel", true),
    Player("Riverboat Ron", false, selectedAI = AI.basicAI[5])
  )
}
```

With those pieces set, we're now ready to move on to our tests.

Add a ViewModel Test

The first test is called *Test StartGame on GameViewModel.* Our test structure here will be a bit different than what we did in GameHandlerTests in that we're going to include some assertions, *then* call the functions, *then* run more assertions. We're checking the starting state of a GameViewModel instance to make sure everything is initialized correctly before we start a game. Then, once we start the game, we check again to make sure things are changed as we expect.

Both before and after we start the game, we want to look at the current state of the slots. We check if there are six slots, five of which can be filled, and that none of them start filled. If the slots variable is null, then we want to instantly fail the test, as something is already wrong. The start of the function looks like this:

```
fun `Test StartGame on GameViewModel`() {
  this.gameViewModel.slots.value?.let { slots ->
    assertEquals(6, slots.size)
    assertEquals(5, slots.count { it.canBeFilled })
    assertEquals(0, slots.count { it.isFilled })
  } ?: fail("The slots on GameViewModel are null.")

  // This will have the rest of the test in a bit.
}
```

The fact that we're able to chain the fail() call right to the null check keeps this entire piece wrapped up in a single expression and saves us from having to create a bunch of extra values and if conditions.

Next up we have the rest of the assertions that I mentioned earlier. Take particular note of the canRoll and canPass assertions in the upcoming block, as they use the same approach to null safety as we have in the past. Instead of just checking gameViewModel.canRoll.value for true or false and having to mess with null scenarios, we can use == false to make sure those fields aren't starting as true *or* null.

```
assertNull(this.gameViewModel.currentPlayer.value)

assertTrue(this.gameViewModel.canRoll.value == false)
assertTrue(this.gameViewModel.canPass.value == false)

assertEquals("", this.gameViewModel.currentTurnText.value)
assertEquals("", this.gameViewModel.currentStandingsText.value)
```

With the initialization assertions in place, it's time to call startGame(). We send in the testPlayers variable we set up before the test, then move on to our other assertions. We're doing the same set of assertions here but with the values we now expect:

```
this.gameViewModel.startGame(this.testPlayers)

this.gameViewModel.slots.value?.let { slots ->
  assertEquals(6, slots.size)
  assertEquals(5, slots.count { it.canBeFilled })
  assertEquals(0, slots.count { it.isFilled })
} ?: fail("The slots on GameViewModel are null.")

assertEquals(
  "Michael",
  this.gameViewModel.currentPlayer.value?.playerName
)

assertTrue(this.gameViewModel.canRoll.value == true)
assertTrue(this.gameViewModel.canPass.value == false)

assertEquals(
  "The game has begun!\n",
  this.gameViewModel.currentTurnText.value
)
assertNotEquals("", this.gameViewModel.currentStandingsText.value)
```

Once you've got those three code blocks together in your test function, give it a run. It should succeed, but if not, use the output pane inside the Run window to get some hints on what's wrong. One test is now done and we can move on to the other.

Add a Second ViewModel Test

This next test, called *Test Roll on GameViewModel*, will start a new game, execute a single roll, and check the results. For this test, instead of directly accessing the value property on the LiveData objects, we're instead going to add a number of Observer objects to listen for updates. This is the better approach to take with LiveData testing since it's how you're using LiveData objects in your app.

The only issue with using Observer objects is that we should be removing them when we're done. It's not a big problem if it's only a single test that uses them, but if we have a test suite with a hundred tests using Observer objects, we're going to see a performance impact. Removing the objects in itself isn't a big issue, but it's annoying to have to do that manually with each property we're checking.

Luckily, the Android Developers team shared a super-useful helper function called getOrAwaitValue() that we can use. An issue's out there to add this function to the official library, but in the meantime, I have no problem using this great function they created (and that I tweaked slightly).

Inside a new file called LiveDataTestExtensions.kt, I'm adding the getOrAwaitValue() function. The quick summary of the function is that it creates a new observer on the LiveData object, then waits for up to two seconds for a value to be assigned. If a value is assigned, it's returned from the function. If not, the function returns null.

The key piece here is that we're removing the Observer no matter the result, meaning we don't have to worry about it in our test class. Here's the entire function:

```
fun <T> LiveData<T>.getOrAwaitValue(
  time: Long = 2,
  timeUnit: TimeUnit = TimeUnit.SECONDS
): T? {
  var data: T? = null

  val latch = CountDownLatch(1)

  val observer = object : Observer<T> {
    override fun onChanged(newValue: T?) {
      data = newValue
      latch.countDown()
      this@getOrAwaitValue.removeObserver(this)
    }
  }

  this.observeForever(observer)

  if(!latch.await(time, timeUnit)) {
    this@getOrAwaitValue.removeObserver(observer)
    return null
  }

  return data
}
```

Without digging in too much, the CountDownLatch holds up the processing of this function until either the timer runs out (which we've set for two seconds) or the observer returns a value.

With this function added, we can use it inside our test function. The assertions here will be similar to the previous GameViewModel test, as we're checking the same LiveData objects but now after a single roll has occurred.

The first piece to check is probably the most critical, the slots. After checking that the slots even exist in the first place, we get the last rolled slot to make sure *it* exists, then check the number of filled slots based on which slot was rolled. If we rolled a six, none of the slots should be filled. Otherwise, one of them should be. Here's the first part of the function, including the calls to start a game and roll:

```
fun `Test Roll on GameViewModel`() {
  this.gameViewModel.startGame(this.testPlayers)

  this.gameViewModel.roll()

  this.gameViewModel.slots.getOrAwaitValue()?.let { slots ->
    assertNotNull(slots)

    val lastRolledSlot = slots.firstOrNull { it.lastRolled }

    assertNotNull(lastRolledSlot)

    val expectedFilledSlots = if (lastRolledSlot?.number == 6) 0 else 1
    assertEquals(expectedFilledSlots, slots.count { it.isFilled })
    if (expectedFilledSlots > 0) {
        assertEquals(slots.firstOrNull { it.isFilled }, lastRolledSlot)
    }
  } ?: fail("Slots should not be null")
  // More assertions to come!
}
```

With the help of getOrAwaitValue(), our assertions aren't all that different than the first test in this class. However, it's a much more accurate test of how we'll be using all these LiveData objects.

The rest of the tests continue along in similar fashion. We make sure the currentPlayer keeps the same value (since we know it won't have changed after a single roll), both canRoll and canPass should be true, and we do a bit of checking at the contents of the game info text at the bottom of the screen.

Since the current player has rolled, we can not only check to make sure it's the right person but also that they have the proper number of pennies. Keep in mind that we're assuming each player starts the game with the default ten pennies. Here are the current player checks:

```
this.gameViewModel.currentPlayer.getOrAwaitValue()?.let { player ->
  assertEquals("Michael", player.playerName)
  assertEquals(9, player.pennies)
} ?: fail("No current player was found.")
```

Both canRoll and canPass have a single call to assertTrue():

```
this.gameViewModel.canRoll.getOrAwaitValue()?.let { canRoll ->
  assertTrue(canRoll)
} ?: fail("canRoll should not be null.")

this.gameViewModel.canPass.getOrAwaitValue()?.let { canPass ->
  assertTrue(canPass)
} ?: fail("canPass should not be null.")
```

The bottom text takes more work since we don't know the exact text that'll be there. In both cases, we'll use the contains() function on the text values to see if the text we're looking for is somewhere in that value. The currentTurnText variable is expecting text with the current player's name and what they rolled, which we can get by finding the lastRolledSlot:

```
this.gameViewModel.currentTurnText.getOrAwaitValue()?.let { turnText ->
  val lastRolledSlot =
    this.gameViewModel.slots.value?.firstOrNull { it.lastRolled }

  assertTrue(
    turnText.contains("Michael rolled a ${lastRolledSlot?.number}")
  )
} ?: fail("No current turn text was found.")
```

Similarly, the currentStandingsText will check to make sure all the players are listed with their correct penny counts:

```
this.gameViewModel.currentStandingsText
  .getOrAwaitValue()?.let { standingsText ->
    assertTrue(standingsText.contains("Michael - 9 pennies"))
    assertTrue(standingsText.contains("Emily - 10 pennies"))
    assertTrue(standingsText.contains("Hazel - 10 pennies"))
    assertTrue(standingsText.contains("Riverboat Ron - 10 pennies"))
  } ?: fail("No current standings text was found.")
```

That's all we need to do in this test class! We're verifying all the values from our LiveData are correct while properly using Observer objects. This is definitely helpful for Penny Drop, except with the code as we wrote it in Chapter 5 and later, all the LiveData was coming from PennyDropDatabase. To test this flow out, and PennyDropDao in particular (since that's where our logic lives), we need to do a bit more work.

Test a Data Access Object (DAO)

Testing a DAO takes some extra work in addition to what we did in the previous two classes, as now we're dealing with Room. Also, this is the first time we're going to be making *instrumented tests* or tests that run on an Android device, either a real device or an emulator. While working with a Room DB doesn't require you to run the test on a device, doing so makes sure you're using the same version of SQLite from an Android device. If you run these tests on your local machine, you may see errors that wouldn't actually happen on the app.

Writing instrumented tests has a downside, though. They're significantly slower since you have to wait for the device to be ready and the test to be deployed out to the device. Ideally, you should make as many tests as possible local since they're faster, and save the instrumented tests for when you really need them.

We're going to be writing two tests here, one focusing on PennyDropDao.insertPlayer() and the other on PennyDropDao.startGame(). The former test will show you the pieces you need to get a test running, while the latter shows how to take advantage of the getOrAwaitValue() function we wrote in the last section. The first thing we need to do here is get things ready for testing.

Prepare for the Tests

The previous two sections were built using code from Chapter 4, Update LiveData with Conditional Game Logic, on page 91, to avoid having to deal with the database calls. Now, since we're going to be testing those same database calls, we're going to use the code as completed after Chapter 7, Customize an App with Settings and Themes, on page 169. Go ahead and either take your code from after Chapter 7 or the code archive from the PragProg site.

We need to include some new dependencies in the app's build.gradle, all of which will be androidTestImplementation dependencies. If you still have some of the testImplemenation dependencies in your file, that's fine, but they won't be used for any instrumented tests. The end of your dependencies block will look like this:

```
androidTestImplementation
  "junit:junit:$junit_version"
androidTestImplementation
  "androidx.arch.core:core-testing:$arch_core_version"
androidTestImplementation
  "androidx.test:core-ktx:$androidx_test_version"
androidTestImplementation
  "androidx.test.ext:junit-ktx:$test_junit_ext_version"
androidTestImplementation
  "androidx.test:runner:$androidx_test_version"
```

All of these dependencies we saw before, other than the AndroidX Test Runner library, which gives us the AndroidJUnit4 we'll see in a bit. After you've synced your project, create a new class called PennyDropDaoTests in the androidTest source folder. This will again have the same package as your app and will be highlighted in green but with "androidTest" in parentheses.

We have an annotation on this class, @RunWith(AndroidJUnit4::class), which tells JUnit which class to use as a runner. The AndroidJUnit4 class allows us to run JUnit tests on a device (either physical or virtual) without the need for any code changes. Also, we're once again using the InstantTaskExecutorRule here to make calls run sequentially.

We'll need to do some prep here, as we're working with a DAO and a database for our tests. We define both private lateinit var database and dao variables, which are PennyDropDatabase and PennyDropDao objects (respectively) that we then assign in the initializeDatabaseAndDao() function. We set up a new in-memory database before each test using the @Before annotation and Room.inMemoryDatabaseBuilder() function. Just as we did in Add Data During Database Creation, on page 124, we send a Context object and a class reference to PennyDropDatabase into the builder function. But this time, instead of adding a callback function, we set two other properties via builder functions.

The allowMainThreadQueries() function lets the test app run database queries on the UI thread, as we're not concerned with ANR (App Not Responding) issues for a user during a unit test.

The other function we add in is setTransactionExecutor() with a call to Executors.newSingleThreadExecutor() inside. This is added because we have @Transaction functions in the DAO. Without this, transactions will never be completed and the unit tests will run indefinitely or crash unsuccessfully. Either way, you're going to want this in here when dealing with @Transaction functions.

Similarly to how we removed each of the Observer classes from LiveData in the previous section's tests, we want to close the database here after each test is run and before we build a new database. We can do that by adding the @After annotation to a function. This annotation is the bookend to @Before, as it's run after each individual unit test. In our case, we just need to call database.close() and we're good.

The set up test class (without any tests) currently looks like this:

```
@RunWith(AndroidJUnit4::class)
class PennyDropDaoTests {

  @get:Rule
  var instantExecutorRule = InstantTaskExecutorRule()

  private lateinit var database: PennyDropDatabase
  private lateinit var dao: PennyDropDao

  @Before
  fun initializeDatabaseAndDao() {
    this.database = Room.inMemoryDatabaseBuilder(
      ApplicationProvider.getApplicationContext(),
      PennyDropDatabase::class.java
    )
      .allowMainThreadQueries()
      .setTransactionExecutor(Executors.newSingleThreadExecutor())
      .build()
```

```
    this.dao = this.database.pennyDropDao()
  }

  @After
  fun closeDatabase() = database.close()

  //Tests coming soon!
}
```

Create an Android Unit Test

Now that everything's ready, we can get our tests created. First up is testInsertingNewPlayer(), which will insert a new player, retrieve that player from the database, and check to make sure everything matches up.

Note the name of the function and in particular that I didn't use the backtick approach from the last section. This is because Android test functions must have standard function names that can be called on a device.

Something new with these DAO tests is that the test code will be called inside a runBlocking block. This allows us to have suspend functions in our code, such as the insertPlayer() function.

Inside the runBlocking block, we follow a similar process to our other tests. The only additional piece here is that we're going to verify that the player doesn't exist in the database to start. Once we insert the player, then we get the player back out of the database and check a few properties. The test code looks like this:

```
@Test
fun testInsertingNewPlayer() = runBlocking {
  val player = Player(5, "Hazel")

  assertNull(dao.getPlayer(player.playerName))

  val insertedPlayerId = dao.insertPlayer(player)

  assertEquals(player.playerId, insertedPlayerId)

  dao.getPlayer(player.playerName)?.let { newPlayer ->
    assertEquals(player.playerId, newPlayer.playerId)
    assertEquals(player.playerName, newPlayer.playerName)
    assertTrue(player.isHuman)
  } ?: fail("New player not found.")
}
```

The great part about the available Android testing tools here is that this test really doesn't look much different than our previous tests save for the runBlocking block. But since we set up the test in the androidTest folder, it runs against a device instead of locally.

What's especially neat about the AndroidJUnit4 test runner is that we could run this test the same way locally as well as on a device and the test runner will handle it for us. Again, we prefer doing an Android test here to make sure we're using the right version of SQLite, but there's minimal work needed to run the same test locally versus on a device.

Create a Second Android Unit Test

Our other test, testStartGame(), is going to be similar to the Test StartGame on GameViewModel test we did in the previous section. We set up some test data, start the game, then check the values. We do have additional sets of assertions here due to the split between a game, players, and the game statuses, but the concepts are the same. The setup and call look like this:

```
@Test
fun testStartGame() = runBlocking {
  val players = listOf(
    Player(23, "Michael"),
    Player(12, "Emily"),
    Player(5, "Hazel"),
    Player(100, "Even Steven", false, AI.basicAI[4])
  )
  val pennyCount = 15

  val gameId = dao.startGame(players, pennyCount)

  //Assertions are coming up
}
```

The main piece we're checking here is the game and associated players. We use the getOrAwaitValue() extension function from before to grab the current GameWithPlayers class. Once we have the object, we can use a with() block to reference the Game object repeatedly. Then we grab the List<Player> and verify that the players on our original list are all included in the list we got back. Note that we're not checking to ensure no extra players are in the gamePlayers list, as that should be an additional test. The entire section (which is wrapped in a let block) looks like this:

```
dao.getCurrentGameWithPlayers().getOrAwaitValue()?.let { gameWithPlayers ->
  with(gameWithPlayers.game) {
    assertEquals(gameId, this.gameId)
    assertNotNull(startTime)
    assertNull(endTime)
    assertNull(lastRoll)
    assertTrue(canRoll)
    assertFalse(canPass)
  }
```

```
    val gamePlayers = gameWithPlayers.players

    players.forEach { player ->
      assertTrue(gamePlayers.contains(player))
    }
} ?: fail("No current game with players found.")
```

While we already verified the players returned from getCurrentGameWithPlayers(), we can do an extra check of getPlayer() after the above block if we want:

```
players.map { it.playerName }.forEach { playerName ->
  assertNotNull(dao.getPlayer(playerName))
}
```

With both the Game and List<Player> objects validated, we only have the GameStatus objects left. Here, we use a similar approach with getOrAwaitValue() on LiveData plus a number of assertions inside the let block. Since we're dealing with a List here, we're going to use all() a few times to assert every value in the gameStatuses list:

```
val playerIds = players.map { it.playerId }
dao.getCurrentGameStatuses().getOrAwaitValue()?.let { gameStatuses ->
  assertTrue(gameStatuses.all { it.gameId == gameId })
  assertTrue(gameStatuses.all { playerIds.contains(it.playerId) })
  assertTrue(gameStatuses.all { it.pennies == pennyCount })
  assertEquals(1, gameStatuses.count { it.isRolling })
  assertEquals(
    players.first().playerId,
    gameStatuses.first { it.isRolling }.playerId
  )
} ?: fail("No current game with players found.")
```

Once everything's in place, go ahead and run your tests. If they all pass, great! You're done and can head to the Summary and Next Steps section. But if not, here are a few suggestions for you.

Troubleshooting Android Unit Tests

I'll be honest here—instrumented tests can be more trouble than a standard unit test. With the extra layer of complexity due to testing on a device, more can go wrong with a test outside of what you're trying to assert.

First off, when running an Android instrumented test, you need to have the app installed on the device you want to use for testing. Luckily, if the app isn't there already, Android Studio will install it for you. Unluckily, if there are any conflicts between the installed app and the app you're trying to test, it can cause a problem. In particular, if the database structure for the app on the device differs from the version you're testing, you'll get a conflict and the tests will fail before they begin.

Second, I ran into an issue when getting the tests in here where it was telling me some duplicated files were being found: "More than one file was found with OS independent path 'META-INF/AL2.0'." If you run into this, you can exclude those files from your project with a packagingOptions block in your app's build.gradle file:

```
packagingOptions {
  exclude 'META-INF/AL2.0'
  exclude 'META-INF/LGPL2.1'
}
```

Third, be aware that if there are uncaught exceptions in a unit test, sometimes the test will keep running without telling you that anything failed. You'll know once the test has run far too long for what it's trying to verify. For example, the current player check shouldn't take a minute and a half. If that's the case, try splitting up your test into smaller pieces to see what is causing the issue (this is a good approach for development in general).

Past that, there will probably be some quirks with tests going forward, especially when libraries get updated. Since I can't see the future, I'll just say good luck and happy testing!

Summary and Next Steps

Again, this wasn't a complete overview of unit testing on Android or testing techniques/ideas/dogma, but I hope you now have a few tools in your arsenal to get some automated testing in your app. Having even a moderate amount of unit test coverage in your app will help speed up development and make your app more reliable, as you'll know right away when something breaks during development.

One principle of testing I want to share is this: most of your tests should be local unit tests, then have some Android instrumented tests, and have a smaller amount yet of UI tests (which we'll cover next chapter). Small unit tests are much, much faster than getting onto a device and can confirm a lot with an app without taking too much time.

How many of each type of test and the "proper" amount of test coverage varies from app to app, though, so make sure you understand what your app needs and where tests will be the most valuable.

Before we move on to the UI testing in the next chapter, I want to mention one more thing. If you're writing AndroidViewModel tests in the future but want to keep them local (making them faster to execute), a library is available called Robolectric.

Robolectric is a framework that creates a simulated Android environment for local testing. It's way faster than needing some kind of actual device and allows you to run `AndroidViewModel` tests (or any tests requiring an Android app context) without a device. You can run the same tests both on a device and locally without needing to change a thing. For more info about Robolectric, check out their site at http://robolectric.org/.

Next up is the other testing chapter focusing on UI testing with Espresso. The Espresso testing library makes UI testing and view interaction so much smoother and readable, plus optimizations under the hood make the tests as fast as possible. Head on over to the next chapter to see how we can use Espresso to verify our app's views automatically.

CHAPTER 15

Test Your App's UI with Espresso

Welcome to the second half of our testing section! Here we're taking the unit testing concepts from last chapter and we're moving them to the screen. This chapter is all about simulating users playing Penny Drop and making sure things work. You'll even be able to see your tests being run on your device in real time, which is always neat.

We started last chapter with post–Chapter 4 code, then moved to the "final" Penny Drop codebase, which is what we had after Chapter 7. Here, we're going to also use that post–Chapter 7 code without any of the test code from last chapter. That way we can focus on what's being used for each chapter and type of test.

The high-level plan for this chapter is to set up our dependencies, give a quick overview of Espresso, then write two test classes: PickPlayersFragmentTests and GameFragmentTests.

Add UI Tests

While this chapter does indeed focus on the UI and user interaction with the app, things are thankfully going to look pretty similar to last chapter. This includes the test format (setup, run, assert) and the dependencies. The androidTestImplmentation dependencies look like this:

```
androidTestImplementation "junit:junit:$junit_version"
androidTestImplementation "androidx.test:core-ktx:$test_core_version"
androidTestImplementation "androidx.test.ext:junit-ktx:$test_ext_version"
androidTestImplementation
  "androidx.test.espresso:espresso-core:$espresso_version"
androidTestImplementation
  "org.jetbrains.kotlinx:kotlinx-coroutines-test:$coroutines_version"
```

The only new dependency here is for Espresso, Jetpack's UI testing library. Espresso simulates user interactions with an app, then runs assertions on those actions in a succinct, readable syntax. Under the hood, Espresso is using the Hamcrest library to help with matching elements—in fact, a number of the pieces we see with Espresso UI tests are Hamcrest Matcher objects.

Rather than spending time explaining more about Espresso and Hamcrest, let's get a simple test in place for the PickPlayersFragment, namely a test to see if the Play Game FAB exists.

Add PickPlayersFragmentTests

Create the PickPlayersFragmentTests class inside the androidTest folder (same place we had PennyDropDaoTests) and annotate the class with @RunWith(AndroidJUnit4::class). Then we're going to add a JUnit rule as we did before, but this time it's ActivityScenarioRule. This rule tells the tests to create and launch an Activity before each test, which in our case is MainActivity. The initial class setup looks like this:

```
@RunWith(AndroidJUnit4::class)
class PickPlayersFragmentTests {

  @get:Rule
  var activityScenarioRule = activityScenarioRule<MainActivity>()

  // We've got more coming up soon.
}
```

Adding that Rule effectively gives us an @Before function without needing to write any extra code. We do need to do a bit more before each test is run, though, since the app starts on the Game screen. The goToPickPlayersFragment() does what we need, taking us over to the PickPlayersFragment. We can use the activityScenarioRule to get the current activity, then reference the activity to navigate:

```
@Before
fun goToPickPlayersFragment() {
  activityScenarioRule.scenario.onActivity { activity ->
      activity
        .findNavController(R.id.containerFragment)
        .navigate(R.id.pickPlayersFragment)
  }
}
```

Now we can add our test, which makes sure it can find the Play Game FAB (the round button with the Play icon) on the Pick Players screen. The way this works with Espresso is that we find the item by ID, then check() that some condition is true—in our case, checking the visibility of the button via the isDisplayed() function. The code looks like this:

```
@Test
fun testFindFab() {
  onView(withId(R.id.buttonPlayGame)).check(matches(isDisplayed()))
}
```

The onView() function finds a view based on the criteria sent into it, which in our case is the ID of the FAB. Once we have the view, we then check() that the view matches() the condition of being displayed. This is the general flow for Espresso; we get a View via one or more ViewMatcher objects, then optionally perform some kind of ViewAction, then finally confirm one or more ViewAssertion objects.

Espresso Cheat Sheet

The Android Developers team created an awesome cheat sheet for Espresso functions and common test pieces you'll be using. I *highly* recommend you have it up when you're writing Espresso tests. That's just what I did when I was writing the tests you'll see here in our chapter.

The cheat sheet can be found at https://link.mfazio.dev/espresso-cheat-sheet. They also have a PDF version of the sheet in case you want to save a copy for later or need to print it out to put on your wall.

Now that we've got the basics down and know the general structure, let's move on to something more complicated—adding a couple of players, then starting a game.

Test Adding Players to a Game

Next up is the testAddingNamedPlayers() function. With this test, we're going to have Espresso type some names into player fields, close out the keyboard, then click the Play Game button. Once we're on the Game screen, we're going to verify a few things to make sure our player names were entered correctly. Note that we're not checking *everything* on the Game screen, as we'll save that for the GameFragmentTests later in the chapter.

Typing in a player's name is a two-step process; we need to find the <EditText> element, then perform() a typeText() ViewAction with some kind of String value. We can find the <EditText> element by using the allOf() Matcher, which takes a variable number of inputs and says if they all are true.

In this case, we want the ID of the <include> tag and the R.id.edit_text_player_name resource value. More specifically, we use the withParent() matcher around the latter ID to find that element, since R.id.edit_text_player_name is a child view inside the <include> view. That leaves us with a matcher that looks like this:

```
onView(
  allOf(
    withId(R.id.edit_text_player_name),
    withParent(withId(parentId))
  )
).perform(typeText(text))
```

Typing a player's name in is something we'll do in multiple tests across multiple test classes, so it makes sense to have a TestHelpers.kt file in our androidTest folder with a few handy functions. This particular function is uncreatively named typeInPlayerName(parentId: Int, text: String), and we'll be using it a bunch. We'll see two more helper functions in the rest of the chapter.

Espresso Is for Developers

As you may be able to tell from the examples so far, Espresso is intended to be used by developers who are familiar with an app's code. Accessing elements by ID would be nigh impossible without being able to read the code, and while you *can* access view components via text, it's far less useful, and text values like that are prone to errors.

The test will type in two players' names, then close the keyboard and click the Play Game button. The closeSoftKeyboard() piece is critical here because otherwise the test runner won't be able to see the Play Game button to click it, and the test will fail. The first two-thirds of our test (setup + action) look like this:

```
@Test
fun testAddingNamedPlayers() {
  typeInPlayerName(R.id.mainPlayer, "Michael")
  typeInPlayerName(R.id.player2, "Emily")
  closeSoftKeyboard()

  onView(withId(R.id.buttonPlayGame)).perform(click())

  // Verifying things in a bit.
}
```

The typeInPlayerName() function, which lives in the TestHelpers.kt file (if you haven't created that file yet, do so now), can be referenced here since it's in the same package as the PickPlayersFragmentTests. Also, there's no need to create a class just to hold a few helpful functions, we can instead put them into a file and use them directly. Even if they live in a separate package, that still works; we just need to import that package in our file.

You *could* run this test right now, and I'm betting it would succeed since we're not yet asserting anything, though it could still fail if there's an issue with the test code itself.

We're going to add three assertions, all of which look similar to what we did in findTestFab(). We want to make sure the current player's name is Michael (or whatever you sent in for player one in the test) and that both entered players are in the standings text box with ten pennies (since the game has started but no actions have been taken).

With all three assertions, we use the withText() ViewMatcher to verify the displayed text is accurate. The current player name assertion is particularly familiar:

```
onView(
  withId(R.id.textCurrentPlayerName)
).check(
  matches(
    withText("Michael")
  )
)
```

Hopefully the pieces of this assertion are clearer being split out like that. We're doing the same thing with the current standings, but since we're performing two checks on the same View, we can use the allOf() object Matcher to check both items at once. Each assertion will use containsString() to make sure the players and coin values are at least somewhere in the standings text:

```
onView(withId(R.id.textCurrentStandingsInfo)).check(
  matches(
    allOf(
      withText(containsString("Michael - 10 pennies")),
      withText(containsString("Emily - 10 pennies"))
    )
  )
)
```

Now that the full test is in place, go ahead and run it to make sure it works. It *should*, but if not, check the test output console to see what hints it gives you as to why things aren't working right now. Once it's ready to go, it's time for test number three, adding a third player.

Test Adding a Third Player

This test adds an extra step to our previous test, as we need to enable the third player to be in the game. In the previous test, both players are included by default (since you have to have two people in a game of Penny Drop for it to be interesting), but now we want to get that third player in there.

We do so by clicking the check box to the left of the Player Name input, which turns out to be a very similar process to typing into that Player Name input. We find the parent element (the player row), then get the check box and perform() a click(). As we'll be reusing this functionality again as well, it should also go into TestHelpers.kt:

```
fun clickPlayerCheckbox(parentId: Int) {
  onView(
    allOf(
      withId(R.id.checkbox_player_active),
      withParent(withId(parentId))
    )
  ).perform(click())
}
```

Now we do the same process as we did before but with the additional checkbox click, another typing command, and one more bit of validation:

```
@Test
fun testAddingThreeNamedPlayers() {
  typeInPlayerName(R.id.mainPlayer, "Michael")
  typeInPlayerName(R.id.player2, "Emily")

  clickPlayerCheckbox(R.id.player3)

  typeInPlayerName(R.id.player3, "Hazel")

  closeSoftKeyboard()

  onView(withId(R.id.buttonPlayGame)).perform(click())

  onView(withId(R.id.textCurrentPlayerName))
    .check(matches(withText("Michael")))

  onView(withId(R.id.textCurrentStandingsInfo)).check(
    matches(
      allOf(
        withText(containsString("Michael - 10 pennies")),
        withText(containsString("Emily - 10 pennies")),
        withText(containsString("Hazel - 10 pennies"))
      )
    )
  )
}
```

Run this test as well, and once it's working, we can get one more test created in this class.

Test Adding an AI Player

We're going to once again add a third player, but this time it's one of our AI players in that slot. This means instead of typing in the third player's name, we need to hit the Player/AI <SwitchCompat>, open the AI name <Spinner>, and click one of the items.

The first two steps are done in a similar way to how we click the FAB, but finding data in a <Spinner> requires use of the onData() function. Here, instead of looking at views in our layout, we're instead looking at data in some kind of list. This is generally used with <RecyclerView> lists, but we can also use it with our <Spinner>.

We call onData() and look for AI types, then we pick the one at position 3 (or whichever AI we want) and click it. Once we're into the next screen, we do our checks as we did before with the third check being for the selected AI, in this case Fearful Fred. Here's the full version of that test:

```
@Test
fun testAddingThirdAIPlayer() {
  typeInPlayerName(R.id.mainPlayer, "Michael")
  typeInPlayerName(R.id.player2, "Emily")

  closeSoftKeyboard()

  clickPlayerCheckbox(R.id.player3)

  onView(
    allOf(
      withId(R.id.switch_player_type),
      withParent(withId(R.id.player3))
    )
  ).perform(click())

  onView(
    allOf(
      withId(R.id.spinner_ai_name),
      withParent(withId(R.id.player3))
    )
  ).perform(click())

  //AI Position #3 is Fearful Fred
  //Also, note the use of backticks with the `is` function
  onData(`is`(instanceOf(AI::class.java))).atPosition(3).perform(click())

  onView(withId(R.id.buttonPlayGame)).perform(click())

  onView(withId(R.id.textCurrentPlayerName))
    .check(matches(withText("Michael")))
```

```
  onView(withId(R.id.textCurrentStandingsInfo)).check(
    matches(
      allOf(
        withText(containsString("Michael - 10 pennies")),
        withText(containsString("Emily - 10 pennies")),
        withText(containsString("Fearful Fred - 10 pennies"))
      )
    )
  )
}
```

We're all set now with testing PickPlayersFragment! Certainly, we could add more tests of value here, but we at least know we can add both human and AI players to a game and things appear to initialize correctly. I say "appear" since we don't know for sure what's going on in the database and something could be funky, but that's why we wrote database and ViewModel tests last chapter.

Next up is the GameFragmentTests class, where we'll make sure slots start as they should and everything is updated correctly after a roll.

Add More UI Tests

Create the GameFragmentTests class just like you did with PickPlayersFragmentTests, adding it to the androidTest folder of your project. Then, once again add the activityScenarioRule and annotate the class with @RunWith(AndroidJUnit4::class). In addition, add a second annotation called @ExperimentalCoroutinesApi. This annotation allows us to use, without a warning, the runBlockingTest TestCoroutineScope. This is a handy scope to use (for tests only) because it allows us to call suspend functions while skipping any delays in our code. We're using it here for our @Before function startNewGameBeforeEachTest(), as running this function normally causes timing issues with starting a game and checking values.

I would have liked to use runBlockingTest in Create an Android Unit Test, on page 345, but at the time of writing, there's a bug in the library that keeps runBlockingTest from working with transactions. Maybe by the time you're working on this it's fixed, since it's a better approach for automated testing, and if so, you can swap out the functions in the last chapter.

Getting back to the startNewGameBeforeEachTest(), the entire function looks like this:

```
@Before
fun startNewGameBeforeEachTest() = runBlockingTest {
  startGame(activityScenarioRule.scenario)
}
```

That startGame() function lives over in TestHelpers.kt and is performing the same actions as we saw in the PickPlayersFragmentTests.testAddingThreeNamedPlayers() test function earlier, just without any assertions. We go to the PickPlayersFragment, add a couple of players, and click the Play Game button:

```
@ExperimentalCoroutinesApi
fun startGame(scenario: ActivityScenario<MainActivity>) = runBlockingTest {
  scenario.onActivity { activity ->
    activity.findNavController(R.id.containerFragment)
      .navigate(R.id.pickPlayersFragment)
  }

  typeInPlayerName(R.id.mainPlayer, "Michael")
  typeInPlayerName(R.id.player2, "Emily")

  clickPlayerCheckbox(R.id.player3)

  typeInPlayerName(R.id.player3, "Hazel")

  closeSoftKeyboard()

  onView(withId(R.id.buttonPlayGame)).perform(click())
}
```

While we could have used this function for the PickPlayersFragmentTests.testAddingThreeNamedPlayers() test, I prefer how the steps are shown in that test since we're testing the process of setting up a game. Here, we're testing what happens *after* you start up a game, so I'm fine hiding those implementation details.

With the setup complete, we can move on to the first test—ensuring all slots are present but empty.

Check the Starting Slots

Since we're checking all six slots in similar ways, we can add each one to a Map, then loop through them. Having this map will allow us to run multiple check() calls on each slot:

```
private val coinSlotMap = mapOf(
  "1" to R.id.coinSlot1,
  "2" to R.id.coinSlot2,
  "3" to R.id.coinSlot3,
  "4" to R.id.coinSlot4,
  "5" to R.id.coinSlot5,
  "6" to R.id.coinSlot6
)
```

The test will then be running two or three check() calls on each of those pieces: make sure the bottom slot number text matches the key value in the Map.Entry, the coin icon is not displayed, and if we're dealing with slots 1–5, that slot 6 is below the given slot on the screen.

We've done each of these pieces before other than testing layout locations, which is done via *position assertions*. Expresso has a number of included position assertions that confirm the alignment of elements on the screen. In our case, we're using the isCompletelyBelow() function to confirm slot 6 is below the slot we're currently verifying. Given that, our test function looks like this:

```
@Test
fun checkStartingSlots() {
  coinSlotMap.forEach { (slotNumber, slotId) ->
    onView(
      allOf(withId(R.id.slotNumberCoinSlot), withParent(withId(slotId)))
    ).check(matches(withText(slotNumber)))

    onView(
      allOf(withId(R.id.coinImageCoinSlot), withParent(withId(slotId)))
    ).check(matches(not(isDisplayed())))

    if (slotId != R.id.coinSlot6) {
      onView(withId(R.id.coinSlot6))
        .check(isCompletelyBelow(withId(slotId)))
    }
  }
}
```

Hopefully you're starting to see the patterns with Espresso tests. Most tests will follow the same format and use the same functions, and the next test is no exception. However, sometimes the built-in functions aren't enough for what we want to do, which means we then need to look at creating a custom matcher.

Check a Roll Result with a Custom Matcher

We've done a lot of work testing the initial state of a started game, but now we're going to check what happens when a player takes their first turn. While there are challenges here due to the randomness of a roll, checking the first roll simplifies things since we don't need to worry about a player busting (since it's the first roll of a new game) or anyone other than the rolling player having fewer than the default number of pennies.

Still, two pieces add complexity here: verifying which slot was rolled and whether or not that slot is a six (as that causes our assertions to change).

We'll start with the rolled slot issue first since it feeds into how we verify what was rolled. Espresso doesn't have a built-in function to check the color of an element or if an element is activated, so we'll need to do that ourselves. As a reminder, the color change is due to a change in the isActivated property on the generic slot line <View>.

We create a new function, isLastRolled(), that returns a TypeSafeMatcher object. Since TypeSafeMatcher is an abstract class, we can't just initialize an instance, so we're instead going to create an anonymous class object that's returned each time the function is called. We saw this approach first back in Add Data During Database Creation, on page 124.

In the anonymous class object, we override two functions, describeTo() and matchesSafely(), which give us info about the function and whether or not the TypeSafeMatcher we're creating matches successfully. The advantage of using this custom TypeSafeMatcher is that it gives us access to a View object directly rather than just going off of what we see on the screen.

As a result, we can check the isActivated property, which is what we use to mark a slot as the last one rolled. The isLastRolled() function looks like this:

```
private fun isLastRolled() = object : TypeSafeMatcher<View>() {
  override fun describeTo(description: Description?) {
    description?.appendText("The View is activated.")
  }

  override fun matchesSafely(view: View?): Boolean =
    view?.isActivated == true
}
```

I want to mention that renaming the isLastRolled() function to isActivated() makes sense if you're going to be checking that property in any other context. The reason I went with a more view-specific name here is because it tells more about why we're bothering to test that property within the scope of our test.

We've seen a number of times now, but the == true ending to the matchesSafely() check means both false and null will fail the check, which is what we want here. With the custom matcher function in place, we can now use it as we see fit in our code. But first, we need to fill out the action step of our test and a few assertions.

Since our @Before function handles getting us a new game, we just need to click the Roll button to get our test into the state we want. Then we check that the current player didn't change and that they now have nine pennies left (since we know that'll be the case, as you can't bust on the first roll of a game).

The first part of our test looks like this:

```
fun checkSingleRollResult() = runBlockingTest {
  onView(withId(R.id.rollButton)).perform(click())

  onView(withId(R.id.textCurrentPlayerName))
    .check(matches(withText("Michael")))
  onView(withId(R.id.textCurrentPlayerCoinsLeft))
    .check(matches(withText("9")))

  // The last rolled slot check is coming next.
}
```

With those pieces in place, we're on to the complicated part of this test. It wouldn't seem at first like checking the last rolled slot would be too tricky, but again, we're dealing with two different scenarios with slots 1–5 and slot 6. We, though, won't find the last rolled slot a problem anymore since our custom matcher is handling that for us nicely (you'll see how in a second).

Our assertion is intended to find the generic <View> tag piece of our slot by using a three-step matcher inside an allOf() call: make sure the ID is R.id.bottomViewCoinSlot, that it has an isActivated property value of true, and either has a penny displayed or it's coin slot 6. The last part is the toughest part of this lookup, but if we break it down enough, it becomes much more manageable. Before we get there, though, let's look at the view lookup minus the last piece:

```
onView(
  allOf(
      withId(R.id.bottomViewCoinSlot),
      isLastRolled(),
      // We'll check the penny image or slot number in a minute.
  )
)
```

By adding the custom matcher, we can now just use isLastRolled() in the same fashion as the built-in Matcher functions. It takes minimal code and leaves us with a nice, readable test.

By the way, if we were to leave this test as is, it *would* be valid. We're checking that we have a last-rolled slot on the screen and that there's only one, because if there were multiple slots that matched that criteria, Espresso would throw an exception and the test would fail. But by adding the coin/number piece, we help make this test more thorough.

In this last part, we're using the anyOf() Matcher to make sure we have at least one of the following scenarios: the slot <View> has a sibling element where the coin image isDisplayed() or a sibling where the slot number text is "6". We can use the hasSibling() Matcher along with a normal allOf() object Matcher to get the elements we want:

```
anyOf(
  hasSibling(
    allOf(withId(R.id.coinImageCoinSlot), isDisplayed())
  ),
  hasSibling(
    allOf(withId(R.id.slotNumberCoinSlot), withText("6"))
  )
)
```

Note that test is only going to verify that we found a slot with a coin and/or the number 6 but has nothing built-in to make sure it's only one of the two. That would either require an additional test (which I'd recommend) or extra logic in this test to make sure only one of those conditions is true.

Once everything's put together, we have a last check() call that makes sure the onView() view matcher found *something*. We can use the function block variant of check() to get access to a View and a NoMatchingViewException, using both to verify the view exists:

```
onView(
  allOf(
    withId(R.id.bottomViewCoinSlot),
    isLastRolled(),
    anyOf(
      hasSibling(
        allOf(withId(R.id.coinImageCoinSlot), isDisplayed())
      ),
      hasSibling(
        allOf(withId(R.id.slotNumberCoinSlot), withText("6"))
      )
    )
  )
).check { view, noViewFoundException ->
  assertNull(noViewFoundException)
  assertNotNull(view)
}
```

Run the test, make sure your device's screen is on (otherwise the test will fail), and see what happens. Assuming it works, we're done with this chapter! If not, it's time for troubleshooting until your tests are green. Best of luck there since, as I mentioned previously, Android instrumented tests can be tricky.

Summary and Next Steps

We now have two levels of testing in our app: unit testing and UI testing. Plus, the unit tests cover both normal code and database interactions. All of this will help ensure our app is working as we expect and give us happier users.

We can also feel safer making changes in the codebase without (as much) fear of breaking things since our tests will let us know as soon as we do.

So much more is available with testing in Android that we don't have the space for here, but I do hope this gives you an idea of where you can go with your apps. If you're wanting more, head over to the Android Developers docs and codelabs—they have a bunch to offer there that I highly recommend. [1]

And with that, we're done here. You're ready to start building your own dream app (or at least your first app on your own). I do hope you enjoyed both Penny Drop and the Android Baseball League!

1. https://link.mfazio.dev/testing

Part IV

Appendixes

Here's some useful info that didn't fit into the stories of Penny Drop or the Android Baseball League apps but is still worth your while.

The appendixes here will get you up and running with Android Studio plus help troubleshoot your apps. Also included is a handy list of dependencies used in the book with their version numbers.

APPENDIX 1

Install Android Studio

Android Studio is the best way to develop Android apps. Period.

While using Android Studio is optional to work through this book, I highly, *highly* recommend it because it's far and away the best choice.

All that being said, getting Android Studio set up, especially if you're including an emulator, can be a long and sometimes annoying process.

During the first review of this book, every reviewer had the same piece of feedback: "Can you include how to get Android Studio set up in the first place?" If this is your first time with Android Studio, hopefully this appendix helps you skip the trouble those brave souls had and you're able to start building apps sooner.

Already have Android Studio set up? Then why are you here? Go build Penny Drop in Chapter 1, Initialize the Penny Drop App, on page 3, or the Android Baseball League app in Chapter 8, Initialize the Android Baseball League App, on page 199!

Download Android Studio

I want to call out right away that everything in this section is subject to change, more so than the rest of the book. Pages, URLs, and screens are likely to be modified in future versions of Android Studio. But while some details may change, the overall process itself *should* stay relatively similar to this in the future.

With that being said, head over to https://developer.android.com/studio and click the Download Android Studio button, as shown in the image on page 368.

The terms and conditions will likely pop up for Android Studio. Please take the same care reading them as you do with all the other T&C you face on a

daily basis. Once you're done with them, click the "I have read and agree with the above terms and conditions" check box (assuming you do) and click Download Android Studio for [Platform]. The [Platform] will either be Windows or Mac, depending on what you're using. In my case, I'm using Windows for most of my work, including this appendix.

The download will take a while, as Android Studio is almost 900 MB when I'm writing this. My apologies in particular to anyone reading this that has to download it on slow internet in the country.

Once the download completes, open the installer and wait for it to be ready for setup.

Install Android Studio

Once the installer opens, you'll be greeted with the welcome screen.

Hit Next to get to the Choose Components page. There, make sure both Android Studio and Android Virtual Device are selected.

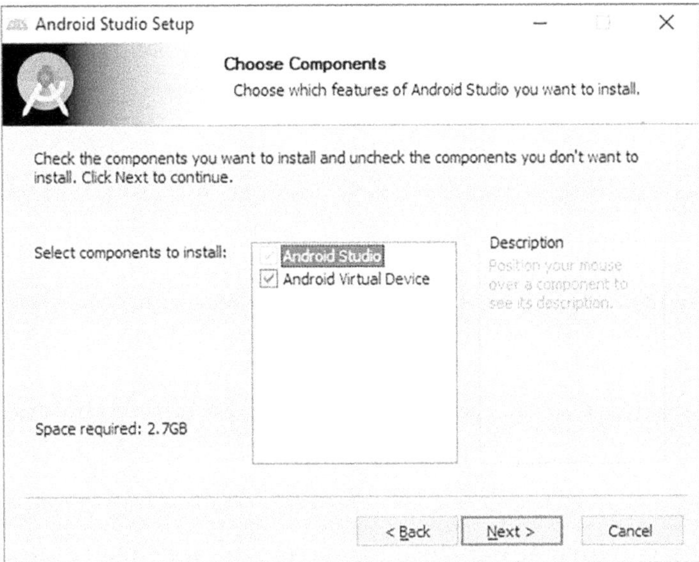

Click Next and choose your Android Studio installation path. Likely the default location will be fine, but it's up to you.

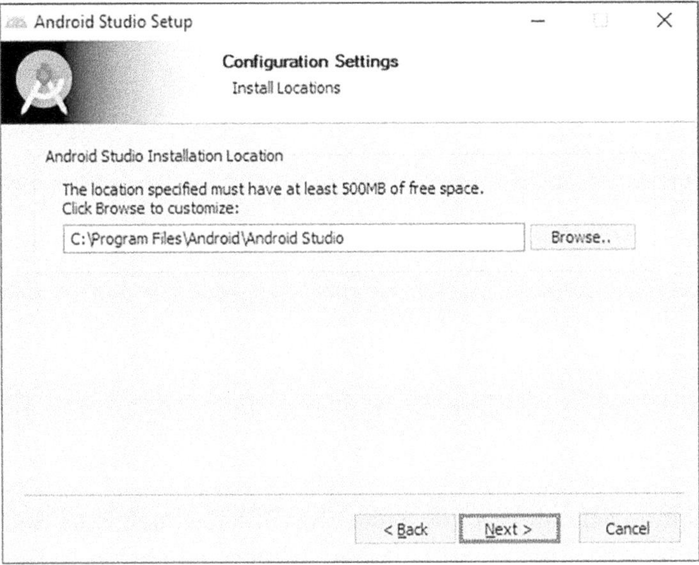

Click Next to move to Choose Start Menu Folder.

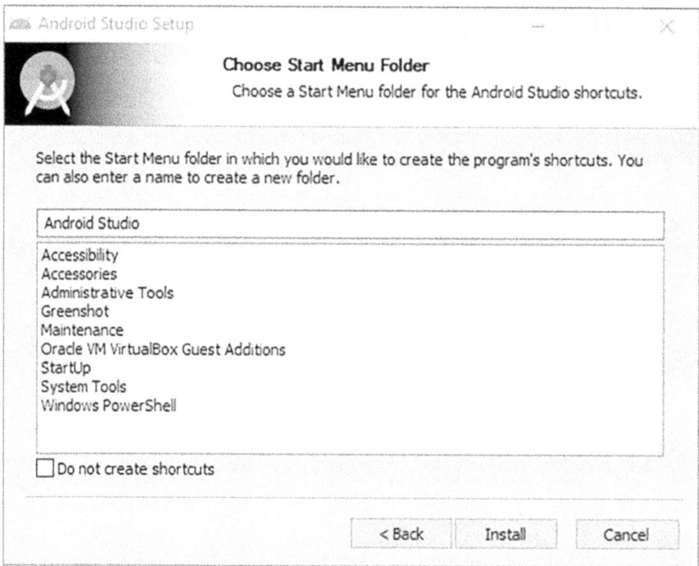

Again, the default here is fine. Click Install to start installing Android Studio.

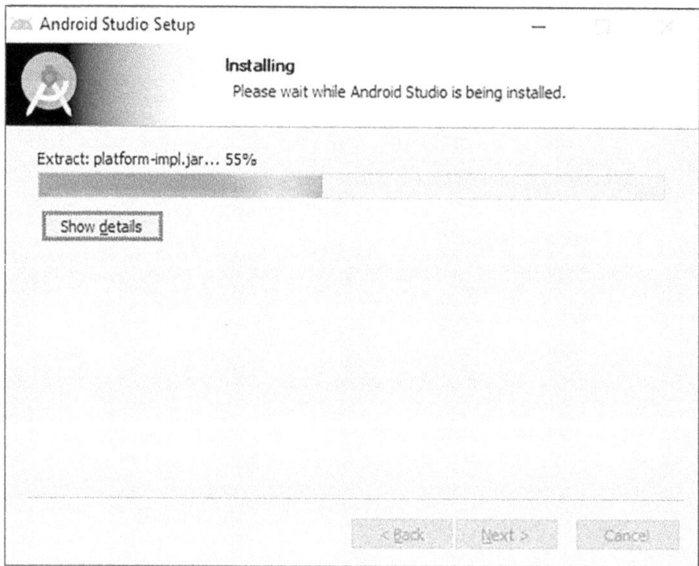

The installation will take a while. Once that finishes, leave the Start Android Studio box checked and click the Finish button, as shown in the image on page 371.

It'll ask if you want to import any previous Android Studio settings. Since I'm assuming you don't have any if you're this far along in this appendix, choose Do not import settings and click OK.

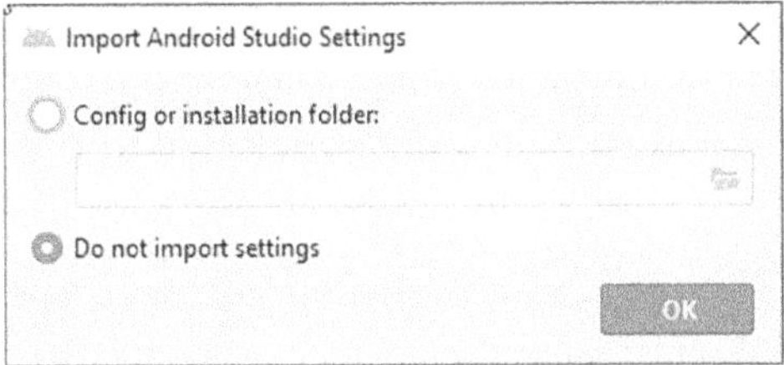

The next popup should be the Data Sharing window, where you can give Google permission to collect usage stats. Click your choice and we'll continue on.

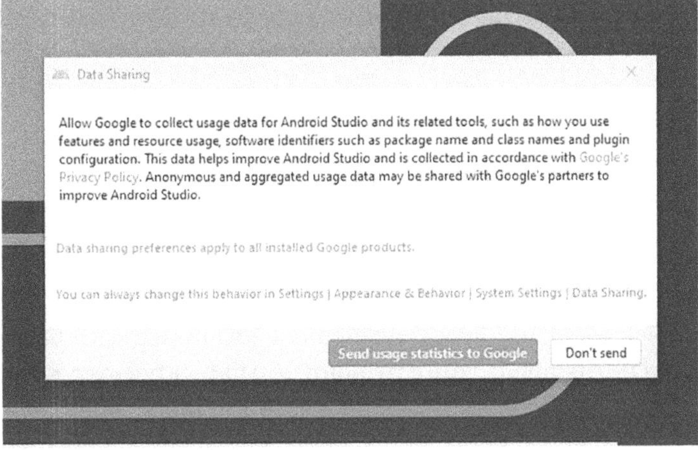

We're now to the Android Studio Setup Wizard, where we'll configure our dev environment and set up an emulated device.

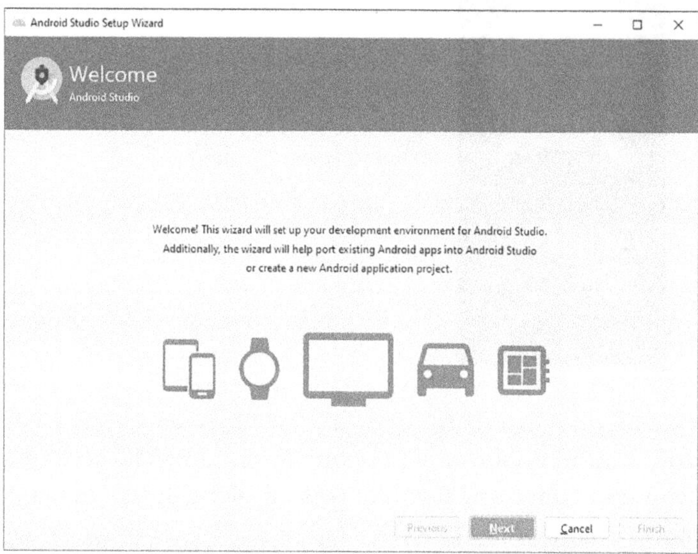

Next up is the Install Type screen, which gives us the choice of Standard or Custom. Normally I'd recommend going with Standard, but we're choosing Custom so you can see each piece that's included in the installation.

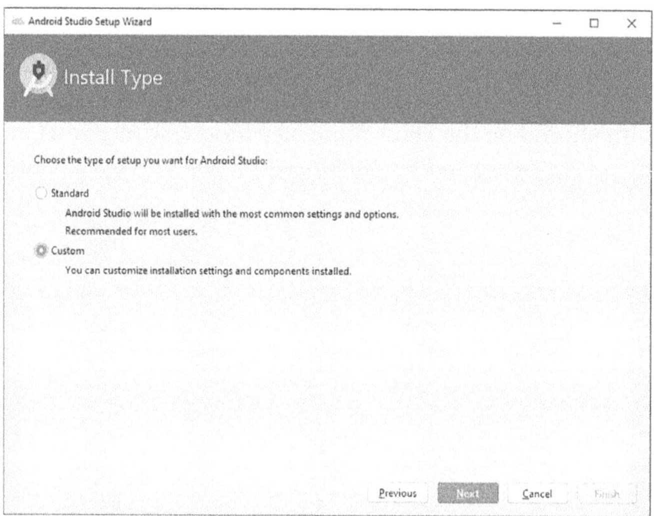

We need to pick the JDK (Java Development Kit) to use with Gradle next. If you have a JDK installed, you can point to that, otherwise stick with the default one from Android Studio, as shown in the image on page 373.

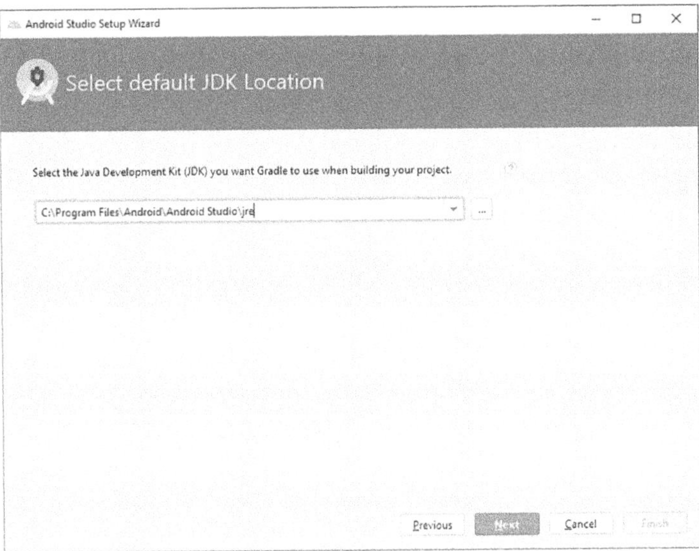

Light theme or dark theme? It's your choice, pick one and continue along.

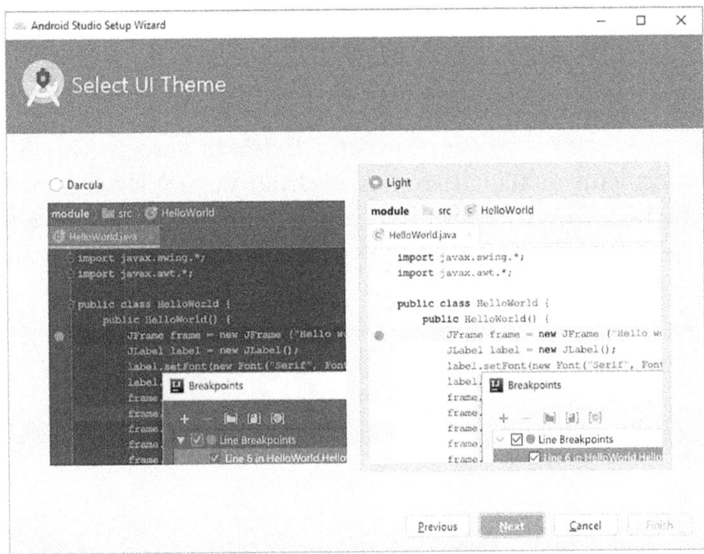

Now we're shown a list of what we can install along with Android Studio:

- Android SDK: the core Android development kit used for building apps. This is required for Android development.
- Android SDK Platform: versions of the Android OS containing new features. This book is written targeting API level 30.

- Performance (Intel HAXM): an extra driver that significantly speeds up the Android Virtual Device we'll be creating. This is optional but highly recommended.
- Android Virtual Device: an emulated device to use for testing.

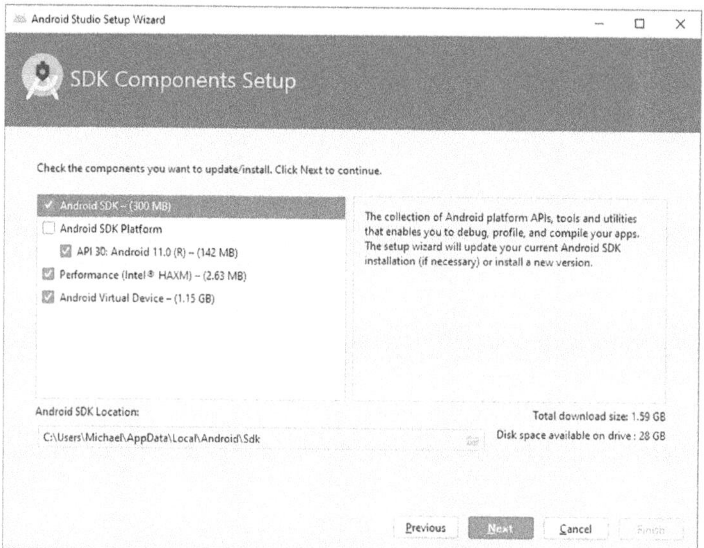

We're then presented with the Emulator Settings screen, which asks how much RAM we want to allocate to our Android Virtual Device (or AVD). Half a gigabyte is the recommended amount here, so that should work fine. If you happen to be developing on a machine with 16+ GB of RAM, you could afford to allocate more.

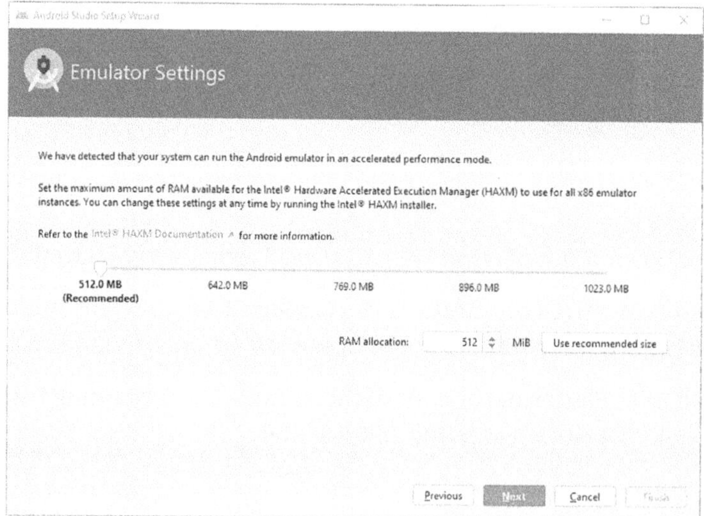

Once you click Next, you'll get the Verify Settings screen with everything that will be downloaded and installed. I recommend looking through the list to see all the pieces that are included.

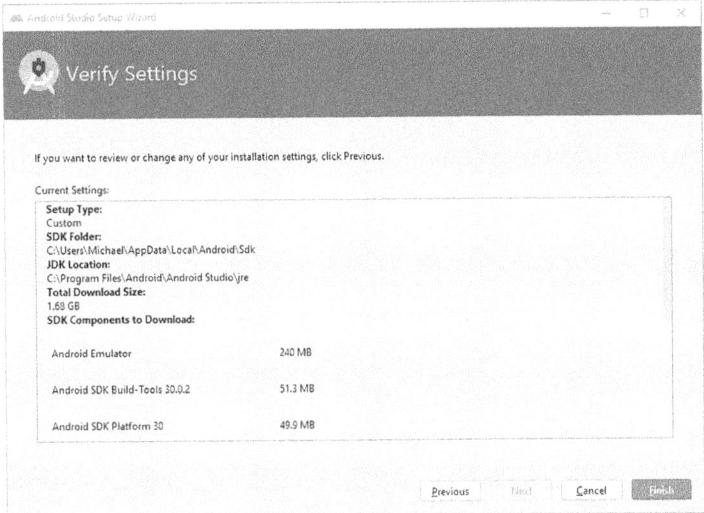

Click Finish and everything will start installing. This will also take a while, so settle in.

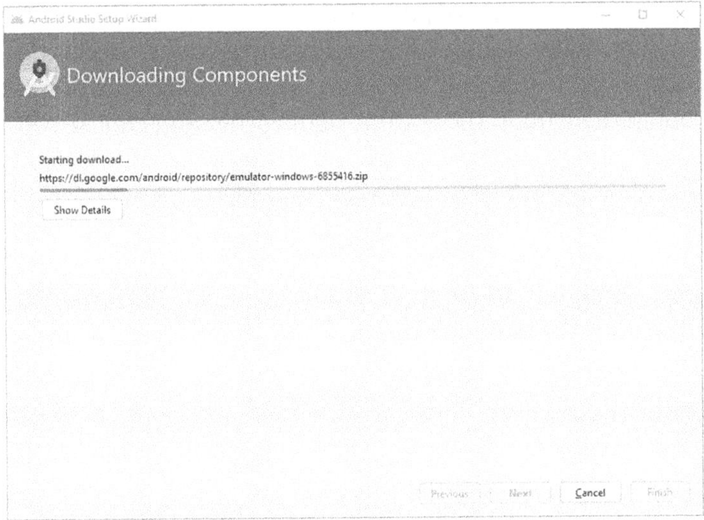

Once everything is done, click the Finish button, and Android Studio will be ready to begin!

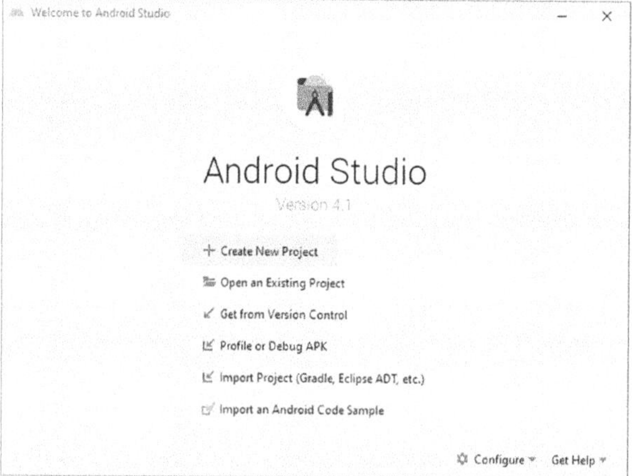

You're now ready to start on Penny Drop, so head over to Chapter 1, Initialize the Penny Drop App, on page 3, to get started. Or if you want another AVD for any reason, continue on to the next section.

Set Up an Android Virtual Device (AVD)

We already set up an AVD as part of the initial setup, but you may want another device or make changes to your existing device. To do that, open the AVD Manager. If you're on the Welcome to Android Studio screen, you can click the Configure menu in the bottom-right corner and choose AVD Manager.

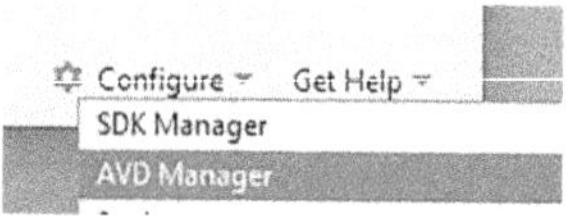

If you're instead already in Android Studio, you can find the AVD Manager under the Tools > AVD Manager menu.

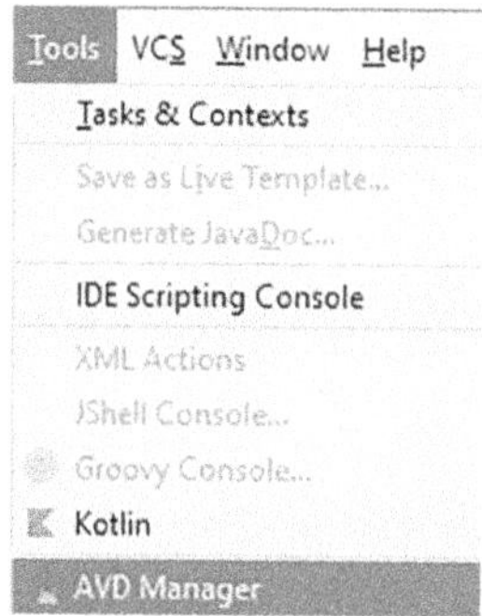

Once there, you're presented with a list of your virtual devices, including their type, name, screen resolution, and info about the OS version.

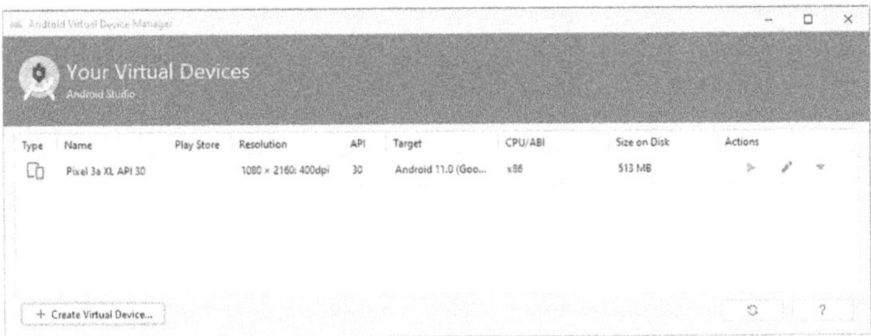

From here, we can open or update an existing AVD or create a brand-new one. Let's go ahead and add a new device now by clicking the + Create Virtual Device... button.

This opens the Virtual Device Configuration page, where we have a list of different devices we can create, including phones, tablets, and even automotive displays. Let's create a new phone, preferably something different than the device created during Android Studio setup.

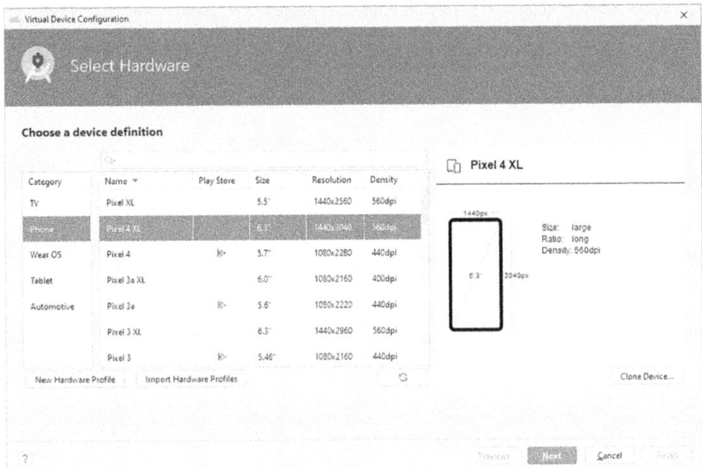

I'm creating a Pixel 4 XL in order to have a higher density device than the Pixel 3a XL that was created during setup. Click Next to go to the System Image screen, which lets you choose which Android version is installed on the AVD, as shown in the image on page 378.

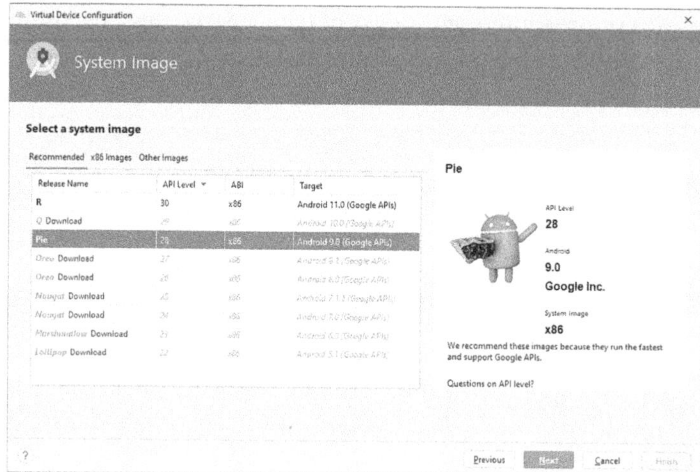

It's a good idea to try out your app on multiple API levels, so I'd suggest choosing something different than the default device. Click Next to verify your AVD configuration.

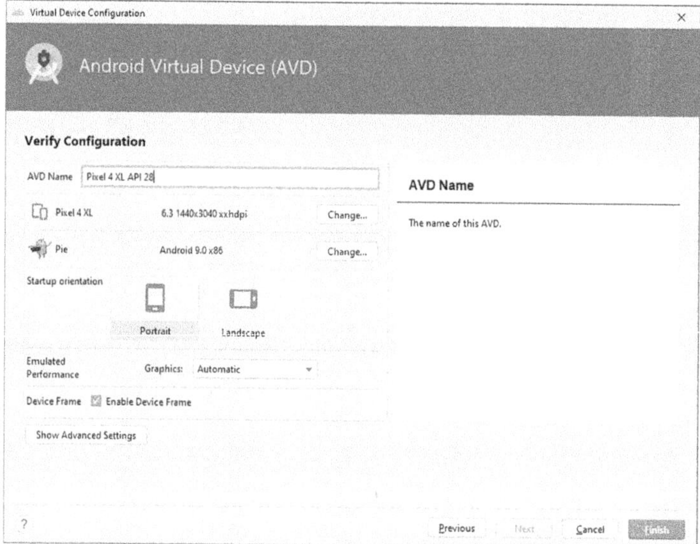

You're welcome to open up the Advanced Settings here to see how the device will be set up, but the default values are probably fine for what you need. Click Finish to create your device.

Once your device is created, you can run it right from the AVD Manager if you wish.

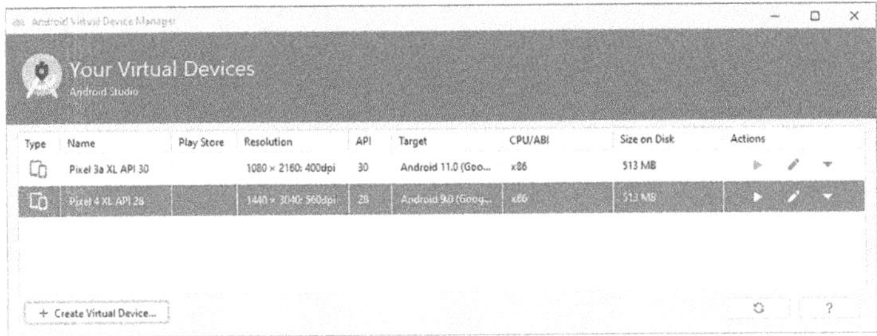

Otherwise, you can head back into Android Studio and choose your device there. In the upper part of the IDE, you can choose which device you want to use when running the app. The drop-down is next to the Play button to run the app.

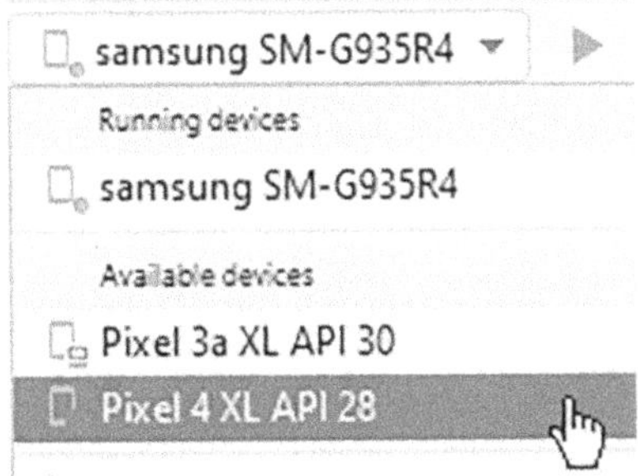

You're all set! Feel free to come back into the AVD Manager if you ever want any extra devices. For now, it's time to get started on an app. Head over to Chapter 1, Initialize the Penny Drop App, on page 3, to build your first app, Penny Drop.

APPENDIX 2

Troubleshooting Your App

When developing an app, at some point you're going to need to get information out of your code. As with most things in app development, we have a few ways to handle this. We can inspect our live code via the Android Studio debugger or log data to an output window. And sometimes, the quickest approach may be a pop-up on the screen.

As a software engineer, I feel obligated to say that debugging is the *proper* approach here. You should be using your debugger to dig into your code and not write any test-only lines of code in your application at any time.

With that said, let's look at reality. Sometimes it's easier to just throw a `Toast` message into the code to see what's happening each time you click a button, or write something to Logcat. And let's be honest, you're probably going to do this anyway, so I might as well tell you how both parts work and how they can be valuable.

We're going to walk through three ways to get information out of your code: debugging, Logcat, and Toast messages. For each approach, I'll explain the proper way to use it and how to use it for troubleshooting issues or to view the current state in your app.

If you're coming here from Binding a Player's Name with Two-Way Binding, on page 68, we're picking up pretty much right where we left off. If not, assume we're in the Penny Drop app, just after the introduction of two-way binding. We've got a list of `NewPlayer` objects that we want to view, and I'm going to show you how to do that with all three approaches. You can then use similar approaches anywhere else in this book or whenever you're developing apps.

Here's what the app looks like at that point:

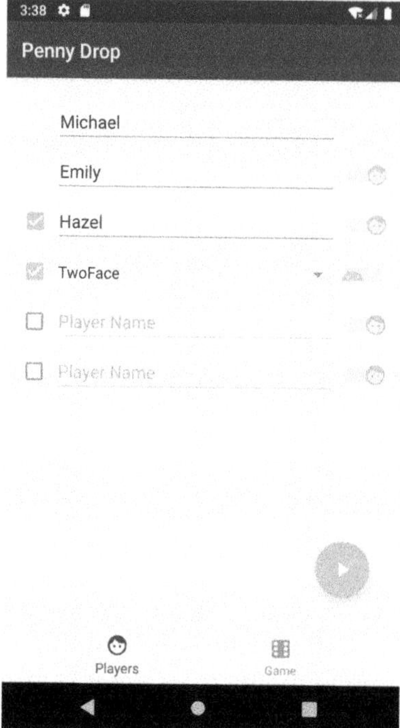

The binding code for the OnClickListener, which lives in the binding inside PickPlayersFragment, will look something like this:

```
this.buttonPlayGame.setOnClickListener {
    // Load info about the players
}
```

We'll be using this block for all three examples, so you're welcome to open the Penny Drop code from the end of Chapter 3. You can find all that code on the book's page on PragProg.com.

Debug Your App

Your debugger is one of the most valuable tools at your disposal when building an app. The debugger allows you to stop your app at any point and look at the current status of the live objects. This may be second nature for some of you, but in case you haven't used a debugger previously, let's talk a bit about how to use it in Android Studio.

The debugger allows us to set *breakpoints* throughout our app, which halts code execution and gives us the ability to look into objects available at that point in time. We can inspect objects we've created as well as ones inside the

Android OS. From there, we can either continue the app's execution or go through the app line by line. We start by adding a breakpoint somewhere in our code, then we either start the app or attach the debugger to an already-running app instance. From there, we can dig in as we wish.

Add a Breakpoint

Breakpoints can be added in Android Studio by clicking the left gutter in your editor. This is the section between the line numbers and the edge of where you're writing your code. When you click here, a red dot will be added.

```
.apply { this: FragmentPickPlayersBinding
    this.vm = pickPlayersViewModel

    this.buttonPlayGame.setOnClickListener { it: View!
        gameViewModel.startGame(
            playersForNewGame: pickPlayersViewModel.players.value
                ?.filter { newPlayer ->
                    newPlayer.isIncluded.get()
                }?.map { newPlayer ->
                    newPlayer.toPlayer()
                } ?: emptyList()
        )
```

Breakpoints can be removed by left-clicking the red dot, while right-clicking gives you a few options. We can disable breakpoints without removing them or add in conditional logic where your breakpoint will only hit if a particular expression is true.

Once you have one or more breakpoints added, we can attach the debugger. This is done by either starting the app in Debug mode or attaching the debugger to a running app.

Attach the Debugger

The simplest way to attach the debugger to an app is to start it up in Debug mode. This is done by clicking the bug icon in the upper part of Android Studio, right next to the Play button you've been using to start up your app.

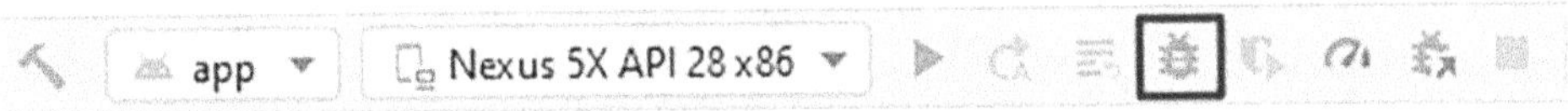

Starting an app in this fashion will tell your app and Android Studio to look for breakpoints and stop code execution when one is hit. If your app is already running and you just want the debug functionality, you can instead use the Attach Debugger to Android Process button. This looks similar to the Debug button, but it has an arrow pointing to the right side of the icon. With either approach, once the app is running with an attached debugger and at least one breakpoint, you're ready to inspect your objects.

Use the Debugger

All we need to do to stop the app is run whichever line(s) of code have a breakpoint. In this case, if the OnClickListener is empty, add a line to get the players in the game from the PickPlayersViewModel: val players = pickPlayersViewModel.players.value. If you're using the example from the end of the chapter, you can leave the code as is. Either way, put the breakpoint on the first line of code in that OnClickListener, add some players to the Pick Players screen, and click the Play FAB. The breakpoint should be hit in Android Studio and your app should stop executing. Your editor inside Android Studio will look something like the image shown on page 385.

If your code is a bit different, that's fine; we're more worried about the breakpoint being hit. When a breakpoint is hit, Android Studio will show you the Debug window at the bottom of your screen. Here, we have a few sections: the frames/threads of the application, variables in the current scope, and a window about the overhead of the debugger.

While the first and last windows have their uses, we're mainly concerned with the Variables section. As a result, I'm going to hide those other windows using the icon in the upper-right section of the Debug window.

The Variables window contains some of the important variables in the current scope (in our case, inside the OnClickListener) with the ability to add other variables as we wish. Click the + button next to the variable list and type in PickPlayersViewModel. Doing this will add our pickPlayersViewModel value as a watched item.

We can then expand this (or any other) item to see any values/variables on the object:

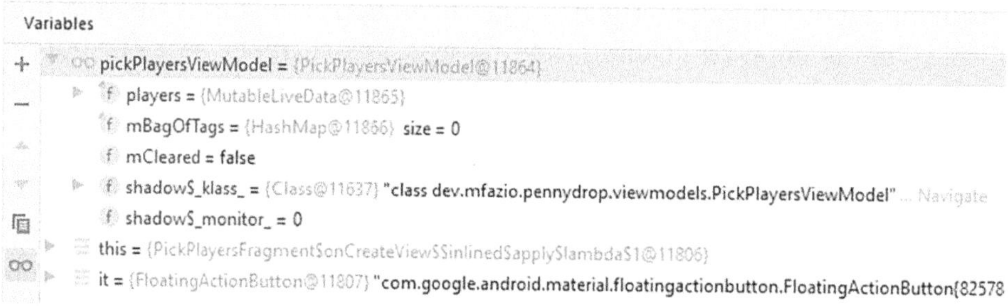

```
Variables
pickPlayersViewModel = {PickPlayersViewModel@11864}
    players = {MutableLiveData@11865}
    mBagOfTags = {HashMap@11866} size = 0
    mCleared = false
    shadow$_klass_ = {Class@11637} "class dev.mfazio.pennydrop.viewmodels.PickPlayersViewModel" ... Navigate
    shadow$_monitor_ = 0
this = {PickPlayersFragment$onCreateView$$inlined$apply$lambda$1@11806}
it = {FloatingActionButton@11807} "com.google.android.material.floatingactionbutton.FloatingActionButton{82578
```

From there, we can continue to dig into values/variables as far as they exist. For example, we can open up the players MutableLiveData value on the PickPlayersViewModel and check the NewPlayer instances inside of it. When an object is being displayed, it uses its toString() function to display information. The ones

you see here for each of the NewPlayer objects are nice to read to due to changes we'll be making later in this chapter, specifically in Create a Better toString(...) Function, on page 389.

The expanded NewPlayer objects will look something like this:

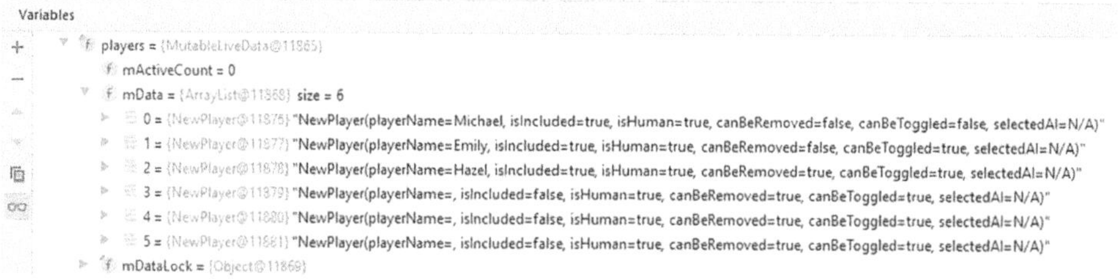

```
Variables
players = {MutableLiveData@11865}
    mActiveCount = 0
    mData = {ArrayList@11868} size = 6
        0 = {NewPlayer@11876} "NewPlayer(playerName=Michael, isIncluded=true, isHuman=true, canBeRemoved=false, canBeToggled=false, selectedAI=N/A)"
        1 = {NewPlayer@11877} "NewPlayer(playerName=Emily, isIncluded=true, isHuman=true, canBeRemoved=false, canBeToggled=true, selectedAI=N/A)"
        2 = {NewPlayer@11878} "NewPlayer(playerName=Hazel, isIncluded=true, isHuman=true, canBeRemoved=true, canBeToggled=true, selectedAI=N/A)"
        3 = {NewPlayer@11879} "NewPlayer(playerName=, isIncluded=false, isHuman=true, canBeRemoved=true, canBeToggled=true, selectedAI=N/A)"
        4 = {NewPlayer@11880} "NewPlayer(playerName=, isIncluded=false, isHuman=true, canBeRemoved=true, canBeToggled=true, selectedAI=N/A)"
        5 = {NewPlayer@11881} "NewPlayer(playerName=, isIncluded=false, isHuman=true, canBeRemoved=true, canBeToggled=true, selectedAI=N/A)"
    mDataLock = {Object@11869}
```

You can do a great deal more with the debugger, but hopefully this part gave you enough information to get started. If you want to learn more about debugging in Android Studio, check out the official Android Developers docs at https://developer.android.com/studio/debug.

Display Messages with the Toast Class

Again, I feel compelled to clarify that Toast messages are intended to be small, brief alerts to users that something just happened. This may be some kind of processing or that they've been logged out of their account. With that being said, they can be handy for troubleshooting as well, similar to something like window.alert() with web development.

In this section, we're going to cover how Toast messages work plus a couple of String-related concepts: a new toString() on a data class and the joinToString() function on a Collection. We're going to use that function to get our player info first, then we'll see how Toast messages work.

Use joinToString() to Get NewPlayer Info

To get the info about the players, we're going to take advantage of two great Kotlin features: null safety (null-safe calls + the null-coalescing operator) and the aforementioned joinToString() function. One of the best things about Kotlin is that it requires you (at compile time) to handle *all* null scenarios in your code.

This helps avoid most situations where a NullPointerException could be thrown, crashing your app and leaving your users frustrated. In this function, we're going to get the List<NewPlayer> from PickPlayersViewModel (by using the nullable value property on the LiveData object), then *safely* call joinToString() (which we'll cover in a minute). This is done by adding a question mark before the call, like so:

```
pickPlayersViewModel.players.value?.joinToString("\n")
```

Since value is nullable, we need to use the ?. (null-safe call) syntax to call joinToString(). However, using this syntax causes that entire line to return a String? (nullable String) rather than a String. If we want to make this expression a String, we can use the *null-coalescing operator* to handle when players.value is null.

In case you haven't seen it yet, the null-coalescing operator, or the *Elvis operator*, allows you to have a fallback when an expression is null. Meaning, if the left side of an expression resolves to null, whatever is on the right side of an Elvis operator will be called instead. In our case, we'll have this expression:

```
val players =
  pickPlayersViewModel.players.value?.joinToString("\n")
    ?: "Unable to get players"
```

The Elvis operator here means we'll use the String value returned from joinToString() unless pickPlayersViewModel.players.value is null, then we'll return "Unable to get players". Now, if joinToString() could return a null value (it can't), it would also fall back to the "Unable to get players" value.

Speaking of the joinToString() function, this function will take each item in a collection, join them using the entered separator character (or a space if none is entered), and return a single String representing that collection. You can add on prefix and postfix values if you wish, which add starting or ending characters onto your string. Finally, you can include a transform block to change each item in the list before including that item in the String. Each item is already being converted into a String for us, meaning we don't have to do so manually inside this transform block, but it's still an option when we need it.

For now, we'll simply join each of the NewPlayer instances with a newline character. With that, we're getting our text, so let's use Toast to display it.

Display Alerts with Toast.makeText(...)

With Android applications, we sometimes want to alert a user about something with a little pop-up style window, but we don't want to keep them from whatever it is they're trying to do. Toast messages are perfect for this; a (usually) small message with a gray background is displayed near the bottom of the app telling the user some kind of information. Other than the message that's displayed, we can control if the message is shown for a short or a long amount of time.

Finally, once we create the Toast message, we need to make sure to call show() or nothing will happen. Usually, we'd use a Toast for giving the user a heads up about something in the app, like they've just been logged out of their account or a web service call failed. In our case, it'll print out the user list we just generated. Suppose we run code like this:

```
val players =
  pickPlayersViewModel.players.value?.joinToString("\n")
    ?: "Unable to get players"
Toast.makeText(activity, players, Toast.LENGTH_LONG).show()
```

Entering a few players, then clicking the FAB will give us output like this:

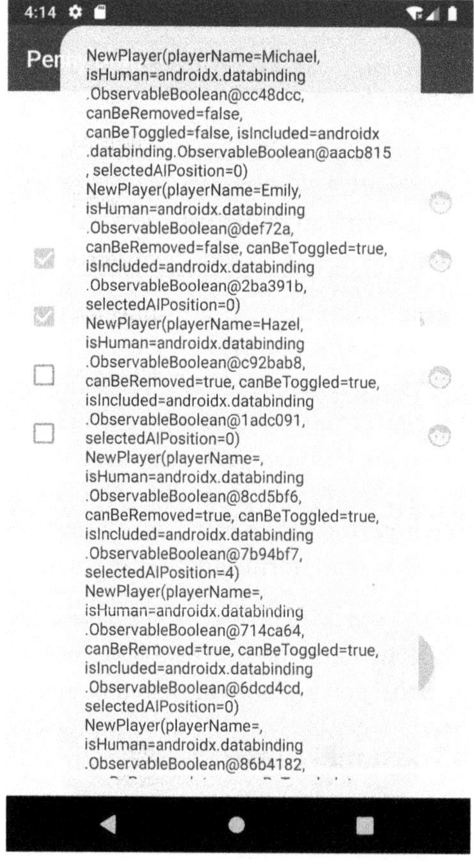

Unfortunately, that's not as helpful as we'd like. It's hard enough to read each NewPlayer instance, but both IsIncluded and IsHuman are ObservableBoolean types, so they don't get the nice human-readable toString() value automatically.

Create a Better toString(...) Function

Since NewPlayer is a data class, we got the nicer looking text with all the properties inside NewPlayer(...) instead of something like dev.mfazio.pennydrop.types.NewPlayer@d1688b3, as we did with the ObservableBoolean properties. To help make this look better, we're going to override the toString() method on NewPlayer. The output will be similar to what we'd get with a data class by default but with the values extracted from both ObservableBoolean properties. We could create one long String with the five fields included, but this seems like a perfect time to show a more complex example of joinToString().

In this case, we're going to create a List of Pair entries. This syntax is going to be almost exactly the same as how you would create a Map, but we're using a List purely because Map doesn't have the joinToString() function on it. Our List will consist of the property name mapped to the property value, which we can then join in the joinToString() function's transform block. Plus, to keep this similar to the default toString() from a data class, we'll add prefix and postfix values to add the title/label "NewPlayer" and wrap the results in parentheses.

```
override fun toString(): String {
  return listOf(
      "playerName" to this.playerName,
      "isIncluded" to this.isIncluded.get(),
      "isHuman" to this.isHuman.get(),
      "canBeRemoved" to this.canBeRemoved,
      "canBeToggled" to this.canBeToggled
  ).joinToString(", ", "NewPlayer(", ")") {(property, value) ->
      "$property=$value"
  }
}
```

Note that both isIncluded and isHuman need to call get() since we care about the Boolean value wrapped inside the ObservableBoolean class. The syntax of { (property, value) -> ... }, called *destructuring declarations*, is a way for us to split the Pair into two distinct values. Rather than call entry.first and entry.second to get at each half of the pair, we have two variables ready for us to use.

One last change we can make to our new toString(): since all we're doing in the function is returning the one expression that's in there, we can just change the function to use expression syntax, getting rid of the need for explicitly listed return types and even the return keyword:

```
override fun toString() = listOf(
    "playerName" to this.playerName,
    "isIncluded" to this.isIncluded.get(),
    "isHuman" to this.isHuman.get(),
    "canBeRemoved" to this.canBeRemoved,
    "canBeToggled" to this.canBeToggled
).joinToString(", ", "NewPlayer(", ")") { (property, value) ->
    "$property=$value"
}
```

Realize that the two previous code blocks are equivalent, but the second one removes a bit of boilerplate code. As always, go with the syntax that makes the most sense for you and your team.

Once we set a couple of names, we can hit the FAB and look at the output:

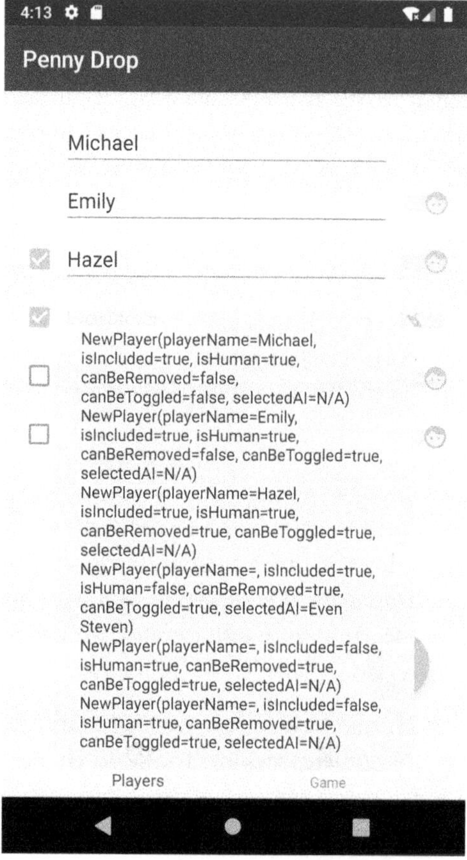

Much better! It's still not the greatest to read, but you can definitely pick out values better this time. This isn't exactly the use case you'd have for a production app, but for the sake of testing things out, it works fine. More importantly, you now know how to use the Toast class to inform users of a small bit of useful information.

Log Messages to Logcat

Logcat is a command-line tool that comes with the Android SDK and takes in system messages, both from the device and apps running on the device. You can use Logcat to see what's going on in your app without disrupting the UI or having to debug. As Logcat is a command-line tool, a bunch of options are available, which you can find at https://link.mfazio.dev/logcat.

For now, we're going to focus on using Logcat within Android Studio. The Logcat window can be found on the bottom of Android Studio, near the Run window button:

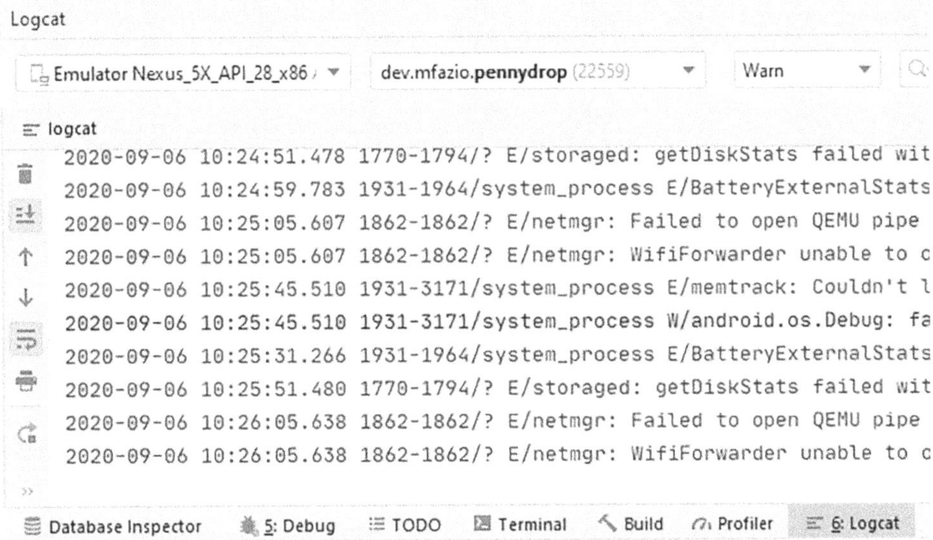

In here, we get information about all kinds of things about our device, no matter if it's a real device or an emulator. We also have the ability to filter for a specific app, only display messages at a certain log level (which correlates to the importance of the message), and search though log messages for certain phrases or regex patterns. Here, we're going to print to Logcat when the Play button is hit, then search for our given TAG.

The TAG variable is a common convention within Android apps for giving your log messages a category. This can be any string value you want, but normally we use the name of the class. In Java, you'd create a static final String called TAG and use that with your log call. However, since Kotlin doesn't have the concept of static types, we're going to instead put the TAG inside a companion object.

If you're not familiar with them, a companion object is an object that is associated with a class. There's only one instance of this object per class (meaning it's a *singleton*), and functions/values/variables in here can be accessed in a similar way to how we would reference static types. Inside the companion object, we're going to use the Java class object for PickPlayerFragment and reference the simpleName variable instead of manually writing out the class name.

```
class PickPlayersFragment : Fragment() {
    //All our other code lives up here.

    companion object {
        private val TAG
            = PickPlayersFragment::class.java.simpleName
    }
}
```

Once the TAG variable has been declared, we can call the Log method of our choosing. A number of methods on the Log correspond to the log level of the message; for more info on these log levels, check out the docs at https://link.mfazio.dev/log. For our testing, we're going to use Log.i() method, which logs a message with an *Info* severity. Info logs are generally used to see what's going on in an app and is a medium-level log. The full log code will look like this:

```
this.buttonPlayGame.setOnClickListener {
    val playerString = pickPlayersViewModel.players.value
        ?.joinToString("\n") ?: "Unable to get players"

    Log.i(TAG, playerString)

    // Other code lives down here.
}
```

Logcat Log Levels

Log levels in Logcat represent the priority of a message. These priorities help tell you how important a message is and allows for filtering within Android Studio. From high to low priority, they are:

- F: Fatal—messages associated with the app crashing.
- E: Error—messages from exceptions in the code, but not ones that crash the app.
- W: Warning—something going wrong in the app, but execution can continue otherwise.

Logcat Log Levels

- I: Info—useful information from the app, doesn't necessarily mean anything is wrong.
- D: Debug—detailed/frequent messages used to look through app processes.
- V: Verbose—overly detailed messages; likely not needed when an app is live.

Using the TAG we created eariler, our FAB will now write an entry to Logcat. The only trouble now is that a lot of values are added to Logcat at an Info level, so ours may be tough to find. But if we go the Logcat search bar and search for PickPlayersFragment, our message will pop right up.

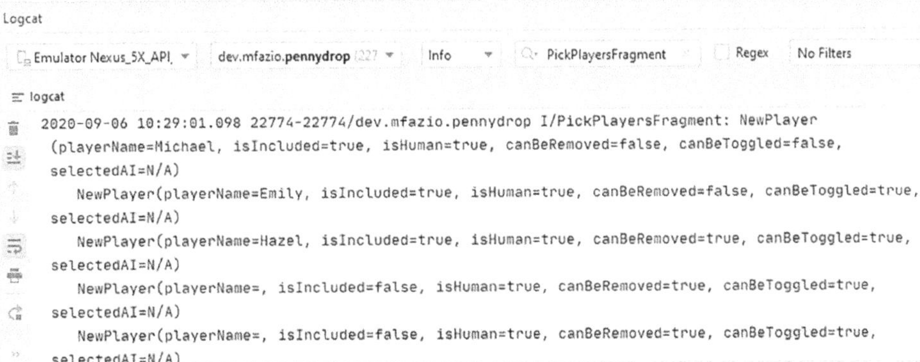

Another issue with checking Logcat logs may be the amount of data written for each item. If you want to change what's displayed for each Logcat entry, you can click the Gear icon on the left side of the Logcat window to display the Configure Logcat Header dialog:

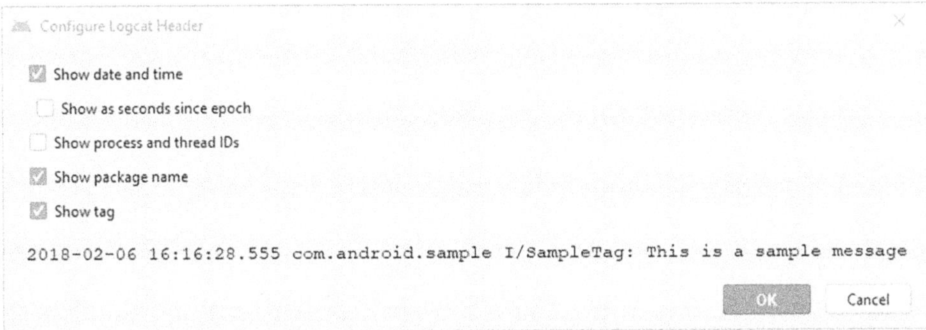

Being able to troubleshoot issues with an application without needing (or being able to use) a debugger holds a lot of value. In fact, if you hook up a device to a computer and open Logcat, you can even see messages being output from current apps on your phone. This can be a valuable tool for fixing issues after your app's been built and is off to real users.

Wrapping Up

Once again, I have to remind you that debugging is the proper approach for figuring out what's going on in your app at runtime. However, having information being output to Logcat is absolutely useful and will help with general diagnostics, even when your app is deployed to users.

Toast messages? They're to inform users of something quickly, but can be handy for displaying a message for yourself when developing. Just make sure you don't leave your testing Toasts in your production app!

If you want more info on each of these topics, the official documentation has articles on each one:

- Debugging: https://link.mfazio.dev/debug
- Logcat: https://link.mfazio.dev/logcat
- Toast: https://link.mfazio.dev/toasts

APPENDIX 3

Gradle Dependencies

Throughout the book, we include many Gradle dependencies to add functionality to our apps. These libraries are an invaluable part of what we create, but keeping them all straight can be tricky.

To help out, I've compiled a list of all the dependencies used in the book along with a bit of info about each one, the actual Gradle file statement, which apps they're used in, and most importantly, the version used in the book.

If you're looking for a certain dependency, whether to figure out what it does or which version we used, here's where you can go.

Classpath Dependencies

These dependencies are included inside the project's build.gradle file and are used along with plugins inside the app's build.gradle file.

Gradle Build Plugin

Gradle handles all the build-related tasks for Android apps.

```
classpath "com.android.tools.build:gradle:$gradle_version"
```

- Book version: 4.1.2
- Apps: Android Baseball League, Penny Drop

Kotlin Language Plugin

The core Kotlin plugin.

```
classpath "org.jetbrains.kotlin:kotlin-gradle-plugin:$kotlin_version"
```

- Book version: 1.4.30
- Apps: Android Baseball League, Penny Drop

Navigation Component – Safe Args Plugin

Adds safe args for navigation between destinations.

```
classpath
  "androidx.navigation:navigation-safe-args-gradle-plugin:$nav_version"
```

- Book version: 2.3.3
- Apps: Android Baseball League

Google Services Plugin

Allows enabling of Google APIs or Firebase services (in our case, push notifications).

```
classpath "com.google.gms:google-services:$gms_version"
```

- Book version: 4.3.5
- Apps: Android Baseball League

Implementation Dependencies

These are the standard dependencies used in the app during runtime. Most dependencies are in this category.

ABL API Client

Adds the ABL API Client, which can be used to more easily make API calls and handle data with those calls.

This requires the JitPack.io repository to be included in the project's build.gradle file.

```
implementation "dev.mfazio:abl-api-client:$abl_client_version"
```

- Book version: 1.1.1
- Apps: Android Baseball League

AndroidX Appcompat

Allows us to access new APIs on older Android versions.

```
implementation "androidx.appcompat:appcompat:$app_compat_version"
```

- Book version: 1.2.0
- Apps: Android Baseball League, Penny Drop

AndroidX Core

Adds Kotlin extensions to common Android libraries.

```
implementation "androidx.core:core-ktx:$core_version"
```

- Book version: 1.3.2
- Apps: Android Baseball League, Penny Drop

Constraint Layout

Gives us the <ConstraintLayout> tag in our apps.

```
implementation
  "androidx.constraintlayout:constraintlayout:$constraint_layout_version"
```

- Book version: 2.0.4
- Apps: Android Baseball League, Penny Drop

Firebase Platform

The overarching Firebase dependency that will give each Firebase library their version.

```
implementation platform("com.google.firebase:firebase-bom:$firebase_version")
```

- Book version: 26.2.0
- Apps: Android Baseball League

Firebase Messaging

Allows for push notifications in the ABL app. Version comes from the Platform dependency.

```
implementation "com.google.firebase:firebase-messaging-ktx"
```

- Book version: 26.2.0
- Apps: Android Baseball League

Kotlin Standard Library

The core Kotlin library; required to do anything with Kotlin. Note that we're using the JDK 8 version of the library.

```
implementation "org.jetbrains.kotlin:kotlin-stdlib-jdk8:$kotlin_version"
```

- Book version: 1.4.30
- Apps: Android Baseball League, Penny Drop

Lifecycle – LiveData

Adds the LiveData class to the app.

```
implementation "androidx.lifecycle:lifecycle-livedata-ktx:$lc_version"
```

- Book version: 2.3.0
- Apps: Android Baseball League, Penny Drop

Lifecycle – ViewModel

Adds the ViewModel class to the app.

```
implementation "androidx.lifecycle:lifecycle-viewmodel-ktx:$lc_version"
```

- Book version: 2.3.0
- Apps: Android Baseball League, Penny Drop

Material Design Components

Brings Material Design components into your Android app.

```
implementation "com.google.android.material:material:$material_version"
```

- Book version: 1.3.0
- Apps: Android Baseball League, Penny Drop

Navigation Component – Fragment

Adds the NavHostFragment class to the app.

```
implementation "androidx.navigation:navigation-fragment-ktx:$nav_version"
```

- Book version: 2.3.3
- Apps: Android Baseball League, Penny Drop

Navigation Component – UI

Handles interaction between the Navigation component and the nav drawer, bottom nav, or app bar.

```
implementation "androidx.navigation:navigation-ui-ktx:$nav_version"
```

- Book version: 2.3.3
- Apps: Android Baseball League, Penny Drop

Paging

Adds supporting classes for smooth paging of RecyclerView lists.

```
implementation "androidx.paging:paging-runtime-ktx:$paging_version"
```

- Book version: 3.0.0-beta01
- Apps: Android Baseball League

Palette

Adds Palette functionality for pulling colors from bitmaps.

```
implementation "androidx.palette:palette-ktx:$palette_version"
```

- Book version: 1.0.0
- Apps: Android Baseball League

Preferences

Adds the PreferenceFragment class and other preference-related classes to the app.

```
implementation "androidx.preference:preference-ktx:$preference_version"
```

- Book version: 1.1.1
- Apps: Android Baseball League, Penny Drop

RecyclerView

Adds the <RecyclerView> tag/class to the app.

```
implementation
  "androidx.recyclerview:recyclerview:$recycler_view_version"
```

- Book version: 1.1.0
- Apps: Android Baseball League, Penny Drop

Retrofit

Adds the Retrofit library to the ABL app for making web service calls.

```
implementation "com.squareup.retrofit2:retrofit:$retrofit_version"
```

- Book version: 2.9.0
- Apps: Android Baseball League

Room – Core

Adds database interaction via Room to the app.

```
implementation "androidx.room:room-runtime:$room_version"
```

- Book version: 2.3.0-beta01
- Apps: Android Baseball League, Penny Drop

Room – Kotlin Extensions and Coroutine Support

Adds support for coroutines and other Kotlin extensions to Room.

```
implementation "androidx.room:room-ktx:$room_version"
```

- Book version: 2.3.0-beta01
- Apps: Android Baseball League, Penny Drop

Swipe Refresh Layout

Adds the ability to pull down from the top of a screen and refresh the screen's contents.

```
implementation
  "androidx.swiperefreshlayout:swiperefreshlayout:$swipe_refresh_version"
```

- Book version: 1.1.0
- Apps: Android Baseball League

ViewPager2

Gives us the `<ViewPager2>` tag in our apps, which allows swiping between multiple views.

```
implementation "androidx.viewpager2:viewpager2:1.0.0"
```

- Book version: 1.0.0
- Apps: Android Baseball League

Work Manager

Adds the Work Manager library for background processing.

```
implementation "androidx.work:work-runtime-ktx:$work_version"
```

- Book version: 2.5.0
- Apps: Android Baseball League

KAPT Dependencies

This is the Kotlin annotation processing dependency. We've only got one (for Room), so this is a short section.

Room KAPT

Adds Room-specific Kotlin annotation processing to the app.

```
kapt "androidx.room:room-compiler:$room_version"
```

- Book version: 2.3.0-beta01
- Apps: Android Baseball League, Penny Drop

Test Dependencies

These are the libraries used for automated testing in your app. The dependencies may be used for normal unit tests and/or Android tests. You can tell which type of test by the Gradle configuration keyword included in each dependency.

AndroidX Core Testing Kotlin Extensions

Adds Kotlin extension functions to various testing libraries.

```
testImplementation "androidx.test:core-ktx:$test_core_version"
androidTestImplementation "androidx.test:core-ktx:$test_core_version"
```

- Book version: 1.3.0
- Apps: Penny Drop

AndroidX Test – Runner

Adds the AndroidJUnit4 test runner class.

```
testImplementation "androidx.test:runner:$test_core_version"
```

- Book version: 1.3.0
- Apps: Penny Drop

Arch Core – Testing

Adds JUnit test rules that can be used with LiveData.

```
testImplementation "androidx.arch.core:core-testing:$arch_core_version"
```

- Book version: 2.1.0
- Apps: Penny Drop

Espresso Core Library

Adds Espresso UI testing to the app.

```
androidTestImplementation
  "androidx.test.espresso:espresso-core:$espresso_version"
```

- Book version: 3.3.0
- Apps: Penny Drop

JUnit

Adds JUnit as an Android test dependency.

```
testImplementation "junit:junit:$junit_version"
androidTestImplementation "junit:junit:$junit_version"
```

- Book version: 4.13.2
- Apps: Penny Drop

JUnit Kotlin Extensions

Adds Kotlin-specific extension functions to JUnit.

```
testImplementation "androidx.test.ext:junit-ktx:$test_ext_version"
androidTestImplementation "androidx.test.ext:junit-ktx:$test_ext_version"
```

- Book version: 1.1.2
- Apps: Penny Drop

KotlinX Coroutines Test

Provides testing utilities for effectively testing coroutines.

```
androidTestImplementation
  "org.jetbrains.kotlinx:kotlinx-coroutines-test:$coroutines_version"
```

- Book version: 1.4.2
- Apps: Penny Drop

Index

E

M

N

O

P

T

U

Thank you!

How did you enjoy this book? Please let us know. Take a moment and email us at support@pragprog.com with your feedback. Tell us your story and you could win free ebooks. Please use the subject line "Book Feedback."

Ready for your next great Pragmatic Bookshelf book? Come on over to https://pragprog.com and use the coupon code BUYANOTHER2021 to save 30% on your next ebook.

Void where prohibited, restricted, or otherwise unwelcome. Do not use ebooks near water. If rash persists, see a doctor. Doesn't apply to *The Pragmatic Programmer* ebook because it's older than the Pragmatic Bookshelf itself. Side effects may include increased knowledge and skill, increased marketability, and deep satisfaction. Increase dosage regularly.

And thank you for your continued support,

Andy Hunt, Publisher

Intuitive Python

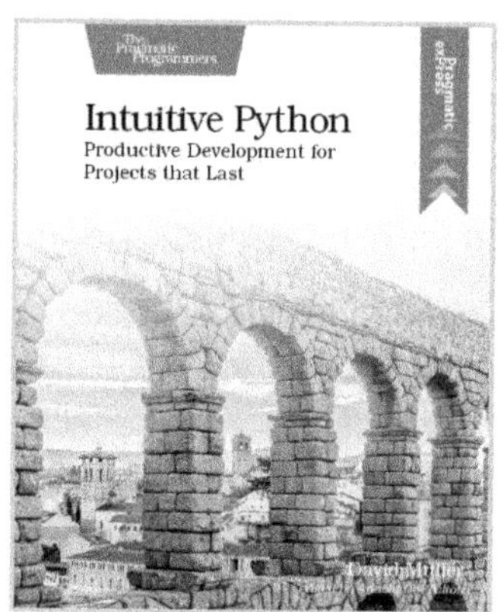

Developers power their projects with Python because it emphasizes readability, ease of use, and access to a meticulously maintained set of packages and tools. The language itself continues to improve with every release: writing in Python is full of possibility. But to maintain a successful Python project, you need to know more than just the language. You need tooling and instincts to help you make the most out of what's available to you. Use this book as your guide to help you hone your skills and sculpt a Python project that can stand the test of time.

David Muller
(140 pages) ISBN: 9781680508239. $26.95
https://pragprog.com/book/dmpython

Modern CSS with Tailwind

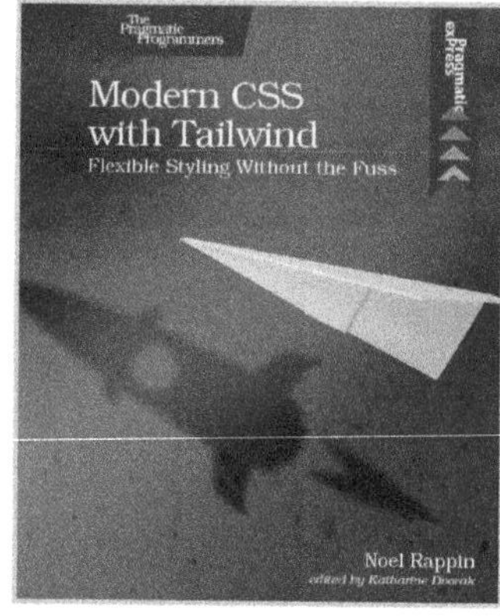

Tailwind CSS is an exciting new CSS framework that allows you to design your site by composing simple utility classes to create complex effects. With Tailwind, you can style your text, move your items on the page, design complex page layouts, and adapt your design for devices from a phone to a wide-screen monitor. With this book, you'll learn how to use the Tailwind for its flexibility and its consistency, from the smallest detail of your typography to the entire design of your site.

Noel Rappin
(90 pages) ISBN: 9781680508185. $26.95
https://pragprog.com/book/tailwind

Essential 555 IC

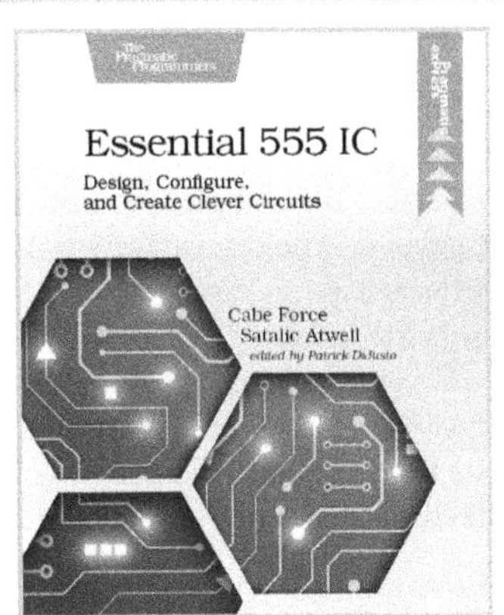

Learn how to create functional gadgets using simple but clever circuits based on the venerable "555." These projects will give you hands-on experience with useful, basic circuits that will aid you across other projects. These inspiring designs might even lead you to develop the next big thing. The 555 Timer Oscillator Integrated Circuit chip is one of the most popular chips in the world. Through clever projects, you will gain permanent knowledge of how to use the 555 timer will carry with you for life.

Cabe Force Satalic Atwell
(104 pages) ISBN: 9781680507836. $19.95
https://pragprog.com/book/catimers

Resourceful Code Reuse

Reusing well-written, well-debugged, and well-tested code improves productivity, code quality, and software configurability and relieves pressure on software developers. When you organize your code into self-contained modular units, you can use them as building blocks for your future projects and share them with other programmers, if needed. Understand the benefits and downsides of seven code reuse models so you can confidently reuse code at any development stage. Create static and dynamic libraries in C and Python, two of the most popular modern programming languages. Adapt your code for the real world: deploy shared functions remotely and build software that accesses them using remote procedure calls.

Dmitry Zinoviev
(64 pages) ISBN: 9781680508208. $14.99
https://pragprog.com/book/dzreuse

Apple Game Frameworks and Technologies

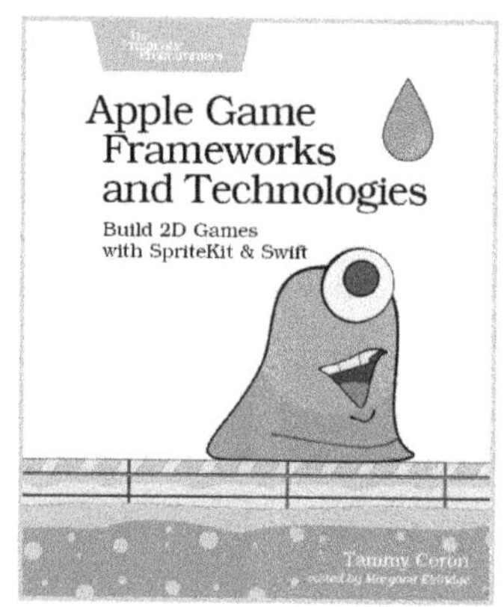

Design and develop sophisticated 2D games that are as much fun to make as they are to play. From particle effects and pathfinding to social integration and monetization, this complete tour of Apple's powerful suite of game technologies covers it all. Familiar with Swift but new to game development? No problem. Start with the basics and then layer in the complexity as you work your way through three exciting—and fully playable—games. In the end, you'll know everything you need to go off and create your own video game masterpiece for any Apple platform.

Tammy Coron
(504 pages) ISBN: 9781680507843. $51.95
https://pragprog.com/book/tcswift

Design and Build Great Web APIs

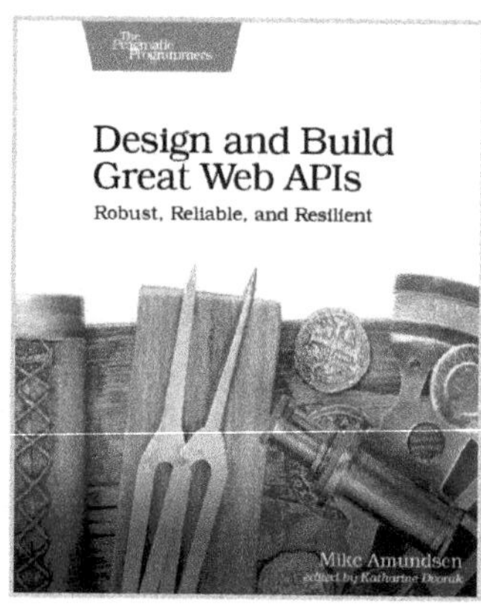

APIs are transforming the business world at an increasing pace. Gain the essential skills needed to quickly design, build, and deploy quality web APIs that are robust, reliable, and resilient. Go from initial design through prototyping and implementation to deployment of mission-critical APIs for your organization. Test, secure, and deploy your API with confidence and avoid the "release into production" panic. Tackle just about any API challenge with more than a dozen open-source utilities and common programming patterns you can apply right away.

Mike Amundsen
(330 pages) ISBN: 9781680506808. $45.95
https://pragprog.com/book/maapis

Distributed Services with Go

This is the book for Gophers who want to learn how to build distributed systems. You know the basics of Go and are eager to put your knowledge to work. Build distributed services that are highly available, resilient, and scalable. This book is just what you need to apply Go to real-world situations. Level up your engineering skills today.

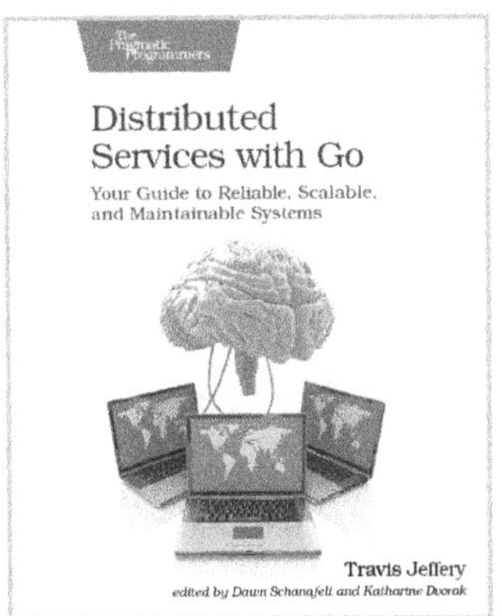

Travis Jeffery
(258 pages) ISBN: 9781680507607. $45.95
https://pragprog.com/book/tjgo

Genetic Algorithms in Elixir

From finance to artificial intelligence, genetic algorithms are a powerful tool with a wide array of applications. But you don't need an exotic new language or framework to get started; you can learn about genetic algorithms in a language you're already familiar with. Join us for an in-depth look at the algorithms, techniques, and methods that go into writing a genetic algorithm. From introductory problems to real-world applications, you'll learn the underlying principles of problem solving using genetic algorithms.

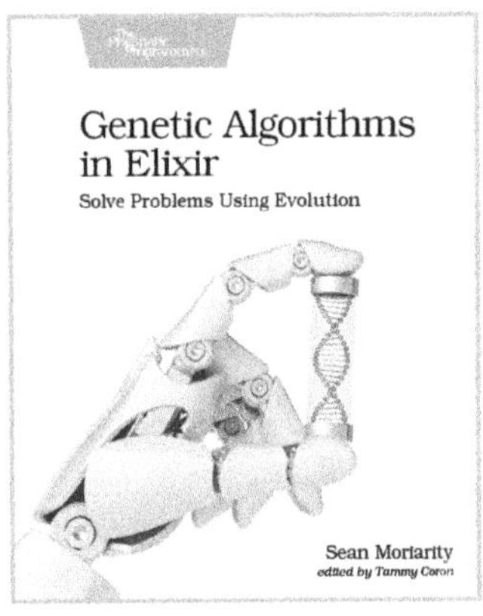

Sean Moriarity
(242 pages) ISBN: 9781680507942. $39.95
https://pragprog.com/book/smgaelixir

The Pragmatic Bookshelf

The Pragmatic Bookshelf features books written by professional developers for professional developers. The titles continue the well-known Pragmatic Programmer style and continue to garner awards and rave reviews. As development gets more and more difficult, the Pragmatic Programmers will be there with more titles and products to help you stay on top of your game.

Visit Us Online

This Book's Home Page
https://pragprog.com/book/mfjetpack
Source code from this book, errata, and other resources. Come give us feedback, too!

Keep Up to Date
https://pragprog.com
Join our announcement mailing list (low volume) or follow us on twitter @pragprog for new titles, sales, coupons, hot tips, and more.

New and Noteworthy
https://pragprog.com/news
Check out the latest pragmatic developments, new titles and other offerings.

Save on the ebook

Save on the ebook versions of this title. Owning the paper version of this book entitles you to purchase the electronic versions at a terrific discount.

PDFs are great for carrying around on your laptop—they are hyperlinked, have color, and are fully searchable. Most titles are also available for the iPhone and iPod touch, Amazon Kindle, and other popular e-book readers.

Send a copy of your receipt to support@pragprog.com and we'll provide you with a discount coupon.

Contact Us

Online Orders:	*https://pragprog.com/catalog*
Customer Service:	*support@pragprog.com*
International Rights:	*translations@pragprog.com*
Academic Use:	*academic@pragprog.com*
Write for Us:	*http://write-for-us.pragprog.com*
Or Call:	+1 800-699-7764

Distributed Services with Go

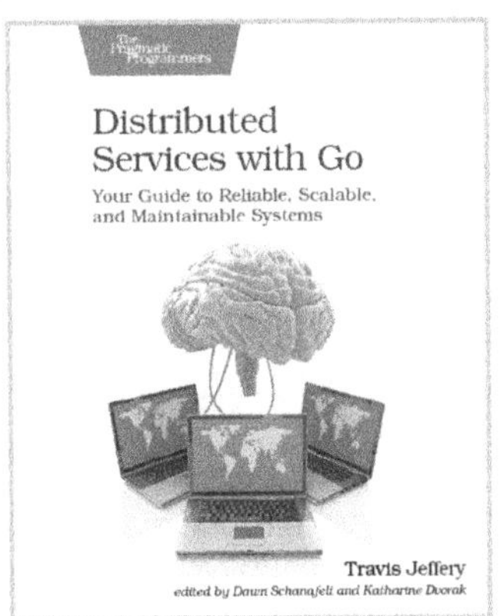

This is the book for Gophers who want to learn how to build distributed systems. You know the basics of Go and are eager to put your knowledge to work. Build distributed services that are highly available, resilient, and scalable. This book is just what you need to apply Go to real-world situations. Level up your engineering skills today.

Travis Jeffery
(258 pages) ISBN: 9781680507607. $45.95
https://pragprog.com/book/tjgo

Genetic Algorithms in Elixir

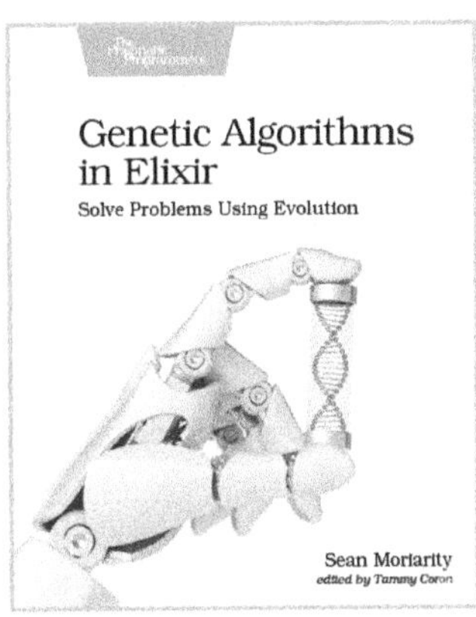

From finance to artificial intelligence, genetic algorithms are a powerful tool with a wide array of applications. But you don't need an exotic new language or framework to get started; you can learn about genetic algorithms in a language you're already familiar with. Join us for an in-depth look at the algorithms, techniques, and methods that go into writing a genetic algorithm. From introductory problems to real-world applications, you'll learn the underlying principles of problem solving using genetic algorithms.

Sean Moriarity
(242 pages) ISBN: 9781680507942. $39.95
https://pragprog.com/book/smgaelixir

The Pragmatic Bookshelf

The Pragmatic Bookshelf features books written by professional developers for professional developers. The titles continue the well-known Pragmatic Programmer style and continue to garner awards and rave reviews. As development gets more and more difficult, the Pragmatic Programmers will be there with more titles and products to help you stay on top of your game.

Visit Us Online

This Book's Home Page

https://pragprog.com/book/mfjetpack

Source code from this book, errata, and other resources. Come give us feedback, too!

Keep Up to Date

https://pragprog.com

Join our announcement mailing list (low volume) or follow us on twitter @pragprog for new titles, sales, coupons, hot tips, and more.

New and Noteworthy

https://pragprog.com/news

Check out the latest pragmatic developments, new titles and other offerings.

Save on the ebook

Save on the ebook versions of this title. Owning the paper version of this book entitles you to purchase the electronic versions at a terrific discount.

PDFs are great for carrying around on your laptop—they are hyperlinked, have color, and are fully searchable. Most titles are also available for the iPhone and iPod touch, Amazon Kindle, and other popular e-book readers.

Send a copy of your receipt to support@pragprog.com and we'll provide you with a discount coupon.

Contact Us

Online Orders:	*https://pragprog.com/catalog*
Customer Service:	*support@pragprog.com*
International Rights:	*translations@pragprog.com*
Academic Use:	*academic@pragprog.com*
Write for Us:	*http://write-for-us.pragprog.com*
Or Call:	+1 800-699-7764

Lightning Source UK Ltd.
Milton Keynes UK
UKHW031259210122
397519UK00003B/6